London and the Making
of Provincial Literature

MATERIAL TEXTS

Series Editors

Roger Chartier	Leah Price
Joseph Farrell	Peter Stallybrass
Anthony Grafton	Michael F. Suarez, S.J.

London

and the Making
of Provincial Literature

Aesthetics and
the Transatlantic Book Trade,
1800–1850

Joseph Rezek

PENN

UNIVERSITY OF PENNSYLVANIA PRESS

PHILADELPHIA

Published by
University of Pennsylvania Press
Philadelphia, Pennsylvania 19104-4112
www.upenn.edu/pennpress

Printed in the United States of America on acid-free paper
1   3   5   7   9   10   8   6   4   2

Library of Congress Cataloging-in-Publication Data
Rezek, Joseph, author.
London and the making of provincial literature : aesthetics and the transatlantic book trade, 1800–1850 / Joseph Rezek.
    pages cm.——(Material texts)
Includes bibliographical references and index.
ISBN 978-0-8122-4734-3 (alk. paper)
    1. English fiction—19th century—History and criticism. 2. Book industries and trade—England—London—History—19th century. 3. Book industries and trade—United States—History—19th century. 4. American fiction—19th century—History and criticism. 5. Irish fiction—19th century—History and criticism. 6. Scottish fiction—19th century—History and criticism. 5. Irish fiction—19th century—History and criticism. 6. Scottish fiction—19th century—History and criticism. 7. English fiction—Irish authors—19th century—History and criticism. 8. English fiction—Scottish authors—19th century—History and criticism. 9. National characteristics in literature. 10. Nationalism in literature. 11. Literature—Aesthetics. I. Title. II. Series: Material texts.
PR861.R482015
820.9'007—dc23   2015005986

To my enthusiastic parents,
Geoff and Jackie Rezek

Contents

Introduction

In 1800, a new kind of Irish literature arrived in London. Maria Edgeworth's *Castle Rackrent, A Hibernian Tale* was published by the storied firm of Joseph Johnson, a "formidable figure" in the late eighteenth-century book trade and publisher of famous radicals like Joseph Priestly, William Cowper, and Mary Wollstonecraft.[1] *Castle Rackrent* relates the decline of the landed Irish gentry through the fictionalized edited narrative of an Irish family's loyal servant, Thady Quirk. The text provides some help for its intended audience; "for the information of the *ignorant* English reader," its "Preface" remarks, "a few notes have been subjoined by the editor."[2] Late in 1798, Edgeworth sent the completed manuscript to Johnson, but he thought Thady's dialect narrative could benefit from even further explanation than the footnotes provided. At his instigation, she composed a copious "Glossary" defining "terms, and idiomatic phrases," as a new "Advertisement" explains.[3] The text's transnational address established a template that shaped the genre of the Irish national tale, a term coined by Sydney Owenson's *The Wild Irish Girl* (1806), which stages the marriage of an English traveler and a dispossessed Irish princess. The genre's wide-ranging influence—it "set a tone" for a century of Irish fiction and was of "formative importance for nineteenth-century realism"[4]—depended on its publication in London, where, ironically, all Irish "national" tales received their first editions.

In 1814, Scottish literature arrived in London like never before. That summer, Longman & Co., at the time publisher of more new books than any other firm in the city,[5] issued a novel that told the story of the 1745 Jacobite rebellion from the perspective of an ordinary English gentleman, Edward Waverley. Walter Scott's first foray into fiction, *Waverley; or, 'Tis Sixty Years Since*, was jointly published by Longman and Archibald Constable, in Edinburgh, where it was printed and from where 70 percent of its first edition were sent to London for distribution.[6] Inspired partly by the Irish national tale, Scott used his eponymous hero as a literary device to guide English readers through the unfamiliar territory of Scotland and Scottish history. Scott aimed "to emulate the admirable Irish portraits drawn by Miss Edgeworth," as he wrote, whose characters "have gone so far to make the English familiar with the character of their gay and kind-hearted neighbors of Ireland."[7] In so doing, he encapsulated the spirit of modern historical consciousness, offering to "world literature" a new genre, according to Georg Lukács, in which "extreme, opposing social forces can be brought into a human relationship with one another."[8] As a best-selling poet, an editor, and the business partner of his Edinburgh printer, the "great Scotch novelist," as he was known at the time, approached London as the principal arena of his success.[9]

In 1820, American literature finally arrived in London. That July, John Murray introduced a new title to his readers: Washington Irving's *The Sketch Book of Geoffrey Crayon*, a two-volume collection of literary pieces containing essays by an American traveling in England, sketches about Native Americans, and two romantic tales set in the Hudson River Valley, "Rip Van Winkle" and "The Legend of Sleepy Hollow." By this time, *The Sketch Book* had for over a year been appearing as a part publication in New York; Irving, then residing in England, was eager to find a British publisher. Murray himself initially demurred, and so Irving arranged for the first half of *The Sketch Book* to be issued at his own expense. As Irving continued to write sketches, the work's future remained uncertain, but luckily he had some powerful friends. Walter Scott persuaded Murray to take a second look, and by spring of 1820, plans were in place for the publication of a handsome two-volume edition, the text of which Irving heavily revised and rearranged with the new format in mind.[10] Buoyed by the prestige of Murray's firm—publisher of Lord Byron, the *Quarterly Review*, the works of Thomas Moore, and some of Scott's poems and novels—*The Sketch Book* launched Irving as "the first ambassador whom the New World of Letters sent to the Old."[11] The novels of James Fenimore Cooper appeared soon thereafter; in 1823, with the same publisher. This is what it meant for American literature to arrive in London; with John Murray, it arrived in style.

The most influential Irish, Scottish, and American fictions of the early nineteenth century were routed through the great metropolis of the English-speaking world. This book argues that the centripetal pull of London created a provincial literary formation that shaped the history of modern aesthetics. In seeking success in London, authors like Edgeworth, Owenson, Scott, Irving, and Cooper developed a range of literary strategies. To guide English readers through the unfamiliar territory of their fiction, they wrote authenticating prefaces, footnotes, and glossaries; to shore up their authority in the London-centered marketplace, they claimed exclusive local knowledge grounded in personal experience; to promote literary fellowship, they invested transnational marriage plots with allegories of cross-cultural communion; and to purify and exalt literary exchange, they revised texts for London republication and appealed to the special power of "literature" itself. These strategies coalesce around a paradox about artistic production: that literature both transcends nationality and indelibly expresses it. This seeming contradiction preoccupied many writers of the Romantic period who offered competing ideological claims for literature's universality and its embodiment of a particular nation's spirit. In this book, I trace a new genealogy of this paradox to the fiction of provincial authors who navigated a subordinate position within the London-centered marketplace for books. I argue, moreover, that the effects of such navigation helped define the distinctly modern idea that literature inhabits an autonomous sphere in society.

It was through success in London that Irish, Scottish, and American fiction were consecrated according to the logic of what scholars after Pierre Bourdieu have called the "literary field."[12] The city reigned as the cultural capital of the Anglophone Atlantic. Similarly to the way Paris operates in Pascale Casanova's "world republic of letters," but with significant differences, London in the early nineteenth century nurtured a highly concentrated literary scene no English-language author could ignore.[13] Publication in the metropolis was compulsory for provincials seeking profit and legitimacy—at home and abroad—and some of them met that condition strategically, uneasily, and with great success. If, as Eric Hobsbawm has famously claimed, "the national phenomenon cannot be adequately investigated without careful attention to the 'invention of tradition,'" then the "invention" of Irish, Scottish, and American literatures must be located within the cross-cultural procedure of distinction only London could perform.[14] These literatures were not born within the nation through an insular process of organic unfolding, nor did they develop as symptoms of nationally delimited historical contexts. They were made in the transatlantic marketplace through an uneven process of struggle and triumph. Many authors from Ireland, Scotland, and North America published in London before 1800, but Edgeworth, Owenson, Scott, Irving, and Cooper hailed from cultures newly understood as "national" and as such were the first to be understood as producing, through literary expression, specimens of national culture. Their success became synonymous with national literary emergence itself. Long understood as separate traditions with discrete histories of their own, Irish, Scottish, and American literatures in fact constituted a single, interconnected *provincial literature* tethered to London.

Provinciality was a relational status acquired through engaging with metropolitan culture or petitioning it for approval. Derived from *provincia*, Latin for a distant territory under Roman rule (*provincia Britannia*, for example), and entering Middle English as the term for a bishop's diocese, the modern noun *province* indicates a region's subordination to centralized power and authority, secular or ecclesiastical. The adjective *provincial* has always carried such connotations, but only by the turn of the eighteenth century did it become derogatory, a slur—and then specifically with regard to expressive behavior: manners, attire, and, above all, speech (*OED*).[15] The word *provincial*, then, acquired negative connotations only as it came to describe modes of expression; it has always been an insult with particularly aesthetic implications. Feeling the sting of this, James Boswell tried to "improve" his Scottish accent while trolling around London. Assured by Samuel Johnson, however, that his "pronunciation was not offensive," Boswell rather unconvincingly advised his "countrymen" that "a small intermixture of provincial peculiarities, may, perhaps, have an agreeable effect."[16] Such linguistic differences shaped the reception of provincials well into the nineteenth century. Francis Jeffrey remarked in a review of *Waverley* that the novel's Scottish dialect would be "unintelligible to four-fifths of the reading population of the country,"[17] and in new footnotes Cooper wrote for the revised London edition of *The Last of the Mohicans* (1831), he distanced himself from "provincial terms" voiced by his American characters.[18] Irish, Scottish, and American authors carried the burden of provinciality as they hawked their wares in an imperial capital that fancied itself the new Rome.[19]

The making of provincial literature is best understood through attending to the production of books and the circulation of material texts between London and the provincial literary centers of Dublin, Edinburgh, and Philadelphia. These circuits of dissemination were improvised, frustrating, and unreliable, but they formed the condition of possibility for provincial literature to emerge. London's dominance was felt as much by provincial readers and book trades professionals as it was by the authors whose metropolitan successes established them as national heroes. Booksellers reacted to and harnessed London's economic power by making inroads into its marketplace, devising ways to circumvent that marketplace, and developing innovative techniques to reach provincial readers. Readers were beholden to a London book trade that supplied the vast majority of texts, imported or reprinted; some embraced metropolitan culture as a badge of sophistication, while others resented that culture's influence and authority. Situated in the fraught position between local literary scenes and a distant cultural capital, provincial authors, publishers, and readers responded with anger, excitement, resignation, ingenuity, and a fascinating array of economic and aesthetic practices that defined an era in literary history.

Such practices have remained unnoticed despite the surge of scholarly interest in transatlantic literary studies over the last quarter century. Dozens of important books have appeared since Robert Weisbuch's *Atlantic Double-Cross* (1986) and Paul Gilory's *The Black Atlantic* (1993), two foundational texts. Most transatlantic scholarship of the eighteenth and nineteenth centuries has either opened up one side of the Atlantic to a myriad of crossings or influences—in Americanist scholarship, usually with England as a single point of reference—or traced parallel stories in Britain and the United States while conceiving of the two nations in a binary relationship. This binary model of competition, however, does not recognize London as the force that put Irish, Scottish, and American literature on common ground. Comparative scholarship on Scotland and America (a venerable subfield its own), moreover, has not reckoned with the book trade's concrete effects in forming what John Clive and Bernard Bailyn called "England's cultural provinces," nor has it found an appropriate place for Ireland as a provincial analog.[20] The field of transatlantic studies has proliferated to such an extent that it has become difficult to generalize about its methodological commitments, encompassing as it does traditional studies of literary influence, theoretical meditations on Atlantic modernity, and historicized accounts of discrete locales embedded in transatlantic contexts and circuits of exchange. This book takes "literature" as a category of Atlantic modernity to be investigated through the local sites, transatlantic circuits, and cultural pressures of its emergence. It provides further evidence that the burden of proof now lies with those scholars who still wish to treat literary history in strictly national terms. "The nation," as Thomas Bender explains, "cannot be its own context."[21]

The term *transatlantic* was used often in the period to characterize objects, ideas, and persons that crossed the Atlantic Ocean or phenomena defined by such crossing; it is in this general sense that I adopt it here. Scott, for example, upon reading a parody of his *Lay of the Last Minstrel* published in Philadelphia, called it a "a tolerable piece of dull Trans-Atlantic wit"; Irving, discussing the importance of "english reviewers," declared that "if these transatlantic censors praise [a book], I have no fear of its success in this country"; and the *Quarterly Review*, reviewing *The Sketch Book*, referred to "the publications of our transatlantic brethren."[22] Edgeworth also conceived of the ocean as a conduit for traveling texts. She sustained a number of correspondences with friends "across the Atlantic," as she put it in a letter to the wife of Boston bookseller George Ticknor.[23] These included one Mrs. Griffith, who sent her the latest American novels. "I am very much afraid that I shall never be able to satisfy you about the Last of the Mohicans," Edgeworth wrote on April 20, 1826, "but it is early times with us yet—as we began it only last night." The next day, she wrote an extra line between paragraphs before sending the letter: "April 21—Last night we got into the cavern that is a sublime scene—we begun to be much interested."[24] Edgeworth later made sure the novelist learned of her approval. "If Mr. Cooper, the author, is in London and is known to you," she wrote to Albert Gallatin, "I beg you to make known to him my admiration of his Novels—The Last of the Mohicans especially is a most interesting and original work. I wish he would come to Ireland."[25] Provincial authors were deeply connected to each other through the transatlantic circulation of books, reading, literary influence, claims of artistic affinity, professional relationships, and friendship.

Scholars of American literature have often dismissed the first three decades of the nineteenth century either as a fall from the republicanism of the Revolutionary era into an insular and liberal nationalism or as a prelude to the more interesting productions of the antebellum period, when the rise of abolitionism, Jacksonian democracy, and the "American Renaissance" finally produced a literary culture worth our careful attention. In fact, this was a period in which a complex and influential provincial aesthetics emerged in concert with the wildly popular literatures of Ireland and Scotland. Irish and Scottish literary texts, especially those by Edgeworth and Scott, were among the most widely reprinted and highly respected works of the time. Nineteenth-century American literature begins with the thorough absorption of these provincial literatures. Everyone knows about Scott's importance—if not Edgeworth's—but few Americanists read their novels with the attention they initially received and still deserve, George Dekker's *The American Historical Romance* (1987) notwithstanding.[26] In attending to this, by way of the book trade, this study fills a chronological gap between two books that have done much to shape the debate about early American literature and print, Michael Warner's *The Letters of the Republic* (1990) and Meredith McGill's *American Literature and the Culture of Reprinting* (2003).[27] I offer the notion of provinciality as a way to comprehend American literature's constitutive entanglement with the print culture of the early nineteenth century and to highlight just how fundamentally transatlantic provinciality was.

Scholars of British literature have recently devoted their attention to the same Irish and Scottish authors whom Americanists have ignored. Romanticism itself—traditionally understood through the work of the six "great" English poets and now conceived more expansively to include all writing of the period (poetry and prose, by men and by women)—has been redefined to include specifically Irish and Scottish contributions to the history of the novel, the rise of cultural nationalism, and the aesthetics of empire.[28] But the literary history of Britain makes little sense without also addressing the material presence and popularity of American literature, which flooded the British marketplace especially in the 1820s. It is time for British literary historians to follow the lead of Americanists and acknowledge the importance of transatlantic reprinting. At least six hundred American titles were reprinted in London between 1800 and 1840, long before the well-known successes of *The Scarlet Letter* (1850) and *Uncle Tom's Cabin* (1852), including the works of Irving and Cooper and many texts by Charles Brockden Brown, Royall Tyler, Catherine Maria Sedgwick, John Neal, George Tucker, and Sarah Hale (see the Appendix)—and American literature was consistently reviewed in major British literary journals.[29] This book's focus on the importance of Irving's and Cooper's London editions begins a longer process of reconsidering other American writers whose works were published abroad. Irving's and Cooper's fraught provincial aesthetics contributed as much to Romantic-era notions of literary production as the literatures of the Celtic fringe.

More generally, *London and the Making of Provincial Literature* joins a growing scholarship devoted to connecting the history of material texts with a concern for aesthetics and literary form.[30] An unprecedented number of literary scholars have embraced book history, a field inspired by the rise of digital media and the sense that we are currently experiencing a sea change in the history of communication akin to the invention of the printing press.[31] Meanwhile, many literary critics, impatient with long-standing aversions to questions of aesthetic value, have proposed "a return to aesthetics" that has taken as many forms as there are meanings for the term *aesthetics* itself: a field of philosophical inquiry into a subject's experience of nature and of the object of art, a rubric for discussing an artwork's formal qualities, and a term for our politicized experience of the material world through our senses.[32] Very few scholars interested in aesthetics use the empirical evidence that grounds book history (although only some have abandoned historicism altogether), while most literary scholars who have embraced book history shy away from questions of aesthetics.[33] Yet provincial literature's necessary struggle with the London book trade helped shape one of the period's most pressing aesthetic questions: the place of "literature" in modernity. A new term, the *aesthetics of provinciality*, elaborated below, names the representational modes of Irish, Scottish, and American fiction that devised new theories of literature's distinctiveness from the tense crucible of cultural subordination. It is ironic that one result of success in London was the creation of three myths about the rise of Irish, Scottish, and American literatures as independent national traditions. Provincial literature, in contrast, was radically dependent. A different irony follows from this: out of such dependence, such embroilment in the materiality of the marketplace, provincial authors fashioned a powerful vision of the independence of literary experience. In establishing a direct connection between the London-centered book trade and the development of modern aesthetic theory, I argue that the history of books and the history of aesthetics are interdependent and mutually illuminating.

*   *   *

The remainder of this introduction provides (1) the material and theoretical ground for using the Anglophone literary field as a rubric for analysis and (2) the necessary philosophical context for the aesthetics of provinciality (which takes center stage in Chapters 3, 4, and 5). But first, a few words about evidence. This book uses a wide range of textual and material evidence gleaned from rare books archives, manuscript collections, digital archives, and primary and secondary sources. These include data about the distribution of books around the Anglophone Atlantic; the business correspondence of provincial publishers, including Mathew Carey in Philadelphia and Archibald Constable in Edinburgh; formal analyses of novels like Owenson's *The Wild Irish Girl*, Edgeworth's *The Absentee* (1812), and Scott's *The Heart of Mid-Lothian* (1818); manual textual collations of American texts revised for London republication, including Irving's *The Sketch Book* and Cooper's *The Pioneers*; Irving's editorial work at the reprint journal *The Analectic Magazine* (1813–1815); angry marginalia American readers scribbled in London-printed travel narratives; and numerous trans-provincial borrowings and appropriations, including the celebration of the idea of "America" in radical Irish magazines and the American adoption of Walter Scott's song "Hail to the Chief" as a nationalistic anthem during the War of 1812. The book concludes with an extended close reading of *The Scarlet Letter* (1850) as an allegory for changes in the structure of the transatlantic book trade at mid-century. I approach such evidence with various disciplinary tools and with different degrees of focus and attention, analytical decisions that vary from case to case. The language of booksellers' correspondence is examined closely because rhetorical analysis reveals the dynamics of provincial publishing far better than an approach that considers such correspondence a mere repository of information. Irving's and Cooper's entirely forgotten process of what I will be calling *transatlantic revision* is meticulously recorded and analyzed not only because it profoundly suggests their provinciality but also because they incorporated thousands of substantive changes they made for London into subsequent editions—authorial decisions all but lost to history but which inform the scholarly texts and reprints we read today. Edgeworth, Owenson, Scott, Irving, and Cooper are my principal focus simply because in their time, they were the most influential literary figures from their respective nations, although their reputations have fared unequally since then. Scott looms particularly large, as he did in the nineteenth century, partly because after immersing myself in the print culture of the period, such an emphasis seemed unavoidable and partly because we need to view his works in a new light as the provincial literary experiments they were. And finally, in an era defined by epochal events like the French, American, and Haitian Revolutions, the expansion of slavery and the British Empire, and the Napoleonic Wars, lesser happenings like the War of 1812 and the 1801 Act of Union of Great Britain and Ireland take center stage. Provincial literature arose from the edges of the literary field; minor historical events were its fuel and its fodder.

The Anglophone Literary Field

Irish, Scottish, and American literatures were "made" as material products of the book trade and cultural artifacts of the literary field.[34] Consider Irving, whose transatlantic triumph is as familiar as any story in American literary history. Yet the publication history that established it—his initial difficulties with *The Sketch Book*, followed by his success with John Murray—was guided by the economic, material, and cultural conditions of a London-centered book trade that alone could establish his arrival on the literary stage. *The Sketch Book* has stood for two hundred years as a rejoinder to Sydney Smith's contemporaneous jab in the *Edinburgh Review*: "In the four corners of the globe, who reads an American book?"[35] But the book, as an object, was not American at all. Printed in England and distributed in London with the financial backing and cultural sanction of Murray's firm, the edition of *The Sketch Book* that reached the four corners of the globe may have been written by an American but it was a product of the London trade. The seven-part periodical printed in New York was never easily available in Britain, even though the texts of a few sketches were reprinted in journals there. In Britain, Murray's heavily revised and transformed two-volume edition was sold. At this time of his career, Irving was ecstatic to find his works all dressed up as London imprints. "Murray is going to make me so fine in print I shall hardly know myself,"[36] he wrote to a friend as plans were made after *The Sketch Book* for a new edition of *The History of New York*. Aware of the signals that "fine" craftsmanship emanates, Irving reveled in the increased prestige acquired through his association with Murray. The uneven dynamics of the book trade seeped into the deepest level of his authorial identity as print and its materiality became a metaphor for that identity. Through success in London, Irving experienced a bewildering transformation.

Bourdieu's sociological account of literary production can be productively extended beyond the nation to incorporate struggles involving the uneven distribution of cultural capital across an entire linguistic field. The literary field in early nineteenth-century Britain did not put economic success in inverse relation to artistic success, as was the case in Bourdieu's nineteenth-century France.[37] This was true throughout the Anglophone world, where wide popularity reinforced an author's rise to prominence. Bourdieu famously argued that literary and artistic value are produced through a series of relations in society, including economic relations, that determine the definition of literature and art among writers, artists, and those involved in production and reception. Bourdieu considers "not only the direct producers of the work in its materiality (artist, writer, etc.) but also the producers of the meaning and value of the work—critics, publishers, gallery directors and the whole set of agents whose combined efforts produce consumers capable of knowing and recognizing the work of art as such."[38] In the early nineteenth century, provincial authors appealed to metropolitan publishers and readers for the recognition and prestige that they, as producers of the meaning and value of literature, could bestow.

London was the center of the Anglophone literary field because it was the capital of the British Empire, but the literary field's internal divisions cannot be easily mapped according to imperial politics. Those divisions were influenced both by the unstable Irish and Scottish unions of what Michael Hechter has called "internal colonialism" and by the culturally indeterminate disunion

of U.S. independence.[39] The United States had of course been politically autonomous since the Revolution, but deep and lasting material, economic, and
linguistic ties ensured American cultural dependence for decades to come.
In contrast, Scotland was more politically and institutionally embroiled with
England than ever before—amalgamated into Great Britain since 1707, cen-
tral to British nationalism since 1745, and throughout the nineteenth century
an integral partner in imperial expansion. Yet in the early nineteenth century,
Scotland retained a distinct cultural identity dating back to the Enlighten-
ment and grounded in the provincial capitals of Edinburgh and Glasgow.
Meanwhile, Ireland, a predominantly Catholic colony long excluded from
Protestant Britain and the benefits of empire, was newly absorbed into the
United Kingdom by the Act of Union in 1801, which dissolved Dublin's inde-
pendent Parliament and ended any hope of home rule.

   In the literary field, these relationships were not isolated from one
another—and not only because texts traveled across national boundaries. The
Act of Union, often considered a limited affair of the British Isles, in fact had
far-reaching consequences. The Union extended British copyright across the
Irish Sea and shut down a Dublin book trade that, during the eighteenth century, had supplied much of North America with cheap unauthorized reprints.
As the Dublin trade declined, booksellers in the United States fulfilled local
demand by manufacturing their own reprints and in the process built a provincial publishing industry that confirmed the cultural dominance of London
even as it grew significantly on its own.[40] The controversy leading up to and
following the Union also created an appetite in England for discourse about
Ireland that paved the way for the Irish national tale to emerge.[41] The result of
this, I will argue, was that Edgeworth and Owenson theorized an ideal relationship to English readers that banished contentious political debates in favor
of the purity of literary exchange. Such idealizations proved highly influential
as provincial strategies for success; Walter Scott adapted them in the cross-cultural address of the Waverley novels, and Irving and Cooper, avid readers not
only of Scott but also of Irish fiction, adapted them with an American twist.

   The advantages of the London book trade were demographic, economic,
and material. Its dominance, however, was inflected by the remarkably divergent histories of Irish, Scottish, and American bookselling, as Chapter 1
will demonstrate in detail. At the turn of the century, England's population
dwarfed Scotland's by a factor of five, and low English-language literacy rates
in Ireland, whose population in 1800 was over half that of England's, kept
its reading population comparatively small.[42] The population of the United

States almost equaled England's by 1830, but the persistent preference for Brit-ish reprints and a radical trade deficit in the importation of books—a ratio of twenty to one in the late 1820s—neutralized whatever effect the nation's growing readership may have had on the balance of cultural power.[43] London publishers also held long-standing trade monopolies that consolidated eco-nomic resources, shut out competition, and fostered the commodification and specialization of literary publishing. The London-printed book was often an imposing material object. Elegantly bound, composed of gathering after gather-ing of high-quality paper, marked clearly and precisely in fashionable type, and stamped with the imprimatur of an eminent publisher, such a book carried the London trade's authority out to provincial markets, where readers could easily compare it with their own smaller and scrubby reprints. This produced a hierar-chy of printed texts that reinforced geographically inflected cultural hierarchies: the materiality of the London edition powerfully reflected the authority of Eng-land itself, built up over centuries and extending far back in time.

The most significant challenge came from Scotland. In the eighteenth cen-tury, bookmakers at the height of the Scottish Enlightenment produced edi-tions of equal elegance and importance to their peers in London. In the early nineteenth century, the Scottish trade exploded, as Archibald Constable and William Blackwood launched a series of enterprising publishing ventures, in-cluding Constable's *Edinburgh Review*, founded in 1802; *Blackwood's Edinburgh Magazine*, founded in 1817; and the careers of Walter Scott and a constellation of other Scottish authors, all of which, as Ian Duncan has written, "made Ed-inburgh a literary metropolis to rival London."[44] Dublin, whose book trade was severely curtailed by the Act of Union, and Philadelphia, Boston, and New York, whose bourgeoning trades depended mostly on reprints, did not mount the kind of opposition Edinburgh mustered. Despite this, however, there persisted in Scotland what Jane Millgate has aptly called "the problem of London."[45] Lon-don capitalization and partnership enabled the most ambitious Scottish pub-lishing ventures, including Constable's and Blackwood's, and the great majority of Edinburgh-printed books were sent to London for sale and distribution. The *Edinburgh Review* only mattered, after all, because it left Edinburgh. In the 1820s, moreover, London publishers still issued over 80 percent of new titles within Britain as a whole.[46] The state of the book trade varied from place to place and changed significantly over time; London's dominance was not uniform or monolithic. However, Irish, Scottish, and American authors, readers, and book-sellers saw themselves as allies in the literary field and experienced and expressed their subordination in strikingly similar ways. By the 1820s, these similarities were increasingly apparent as provincial literature formed an intertwined and recognizable sector of the market.

The effects of provinciality in many ways confirm Pascale Casanova's provocative extension of Bourdieu in *The World Republic of Letters* (2004) to describe the cultural geography of "world literary space."[47] Casanova organizes such space along a continuum of dominant and dominated areas, where literary resources are unevenly distributed between the cultural capitals at the centers of the oldest, most established literary nations and impoverished peripheral nations defined by their "aesthetic distance" from such capitals.[48] Authors from dominated nations seek out publication and recognition in the major centers of literary production, "where literary prestige and belief converge in the highest degree."[49] Literary resources are concentrated in those cities whose economies sustain both the production of books and the social world of practitioners who foster debate about the meaning of "literature" itself. Casanova's paradigmatic literary center is modernist Paris, a city whose consecrating authority organized world literary space into rivalries and divisions remarkably non-coincident with the uneven power relations that define the international socioeconomic order.[50] In the early nineteenth century, London dominated its linguistic field with the kind of centralized authority Paris claimed, globally, a century later, but of course no two literary capitals are exactly alike. The importance of translation in modernist Paris did not obtain in a monolingual context, even though Irish, Scottish, and American authors presented their cultures to England in a process James Buzard, referring to *Waverley*, has called "translation without original."[51] More significantly, London's authority in the nineteenth century, unlike Paris's in the twentieth, did indeed overlap with its political and economic dominance as the capital of empire; London, unlike Paris, incorporated marketplace triumphs into its vision of literary excellence (as I have already mentioned), and London, unlike Paris, did not require peripheral authors to reject local literary taste for the sake of a universal standard. Despite these differences, conceiving of an author's distance from London as "aesthetic distance" has many advantages. It moves beyond the political determinism that has governed the study of Irish, Scottish, and American literature at least since Katie Trumpener's *Bardic Nationalism* (1997) expanded the Romantic canon under the rubric of empire and the rise of ideology critique made complicity or resistance to the hegemonic U.S. nation-state the most pressing question in American literary studies. The specific Bourdieuian agenda of Casanova's model also offers a concrete vision of literary competition that encourages us to eschew easy myths of cosmopolitanism to mark the tightly wound rivalries that inspired the undeniably Anglo-centric authors, booksellers, and readers in this study. Provincial literature was not circumscribed by national boundaries, nor did it transcend them; it flourished through the specific kind of cross-cultural struggle the literary field required.

How did Anglophone provincials fit into world literature, writ large (if we assume, with Casanova, that it exists)? On the most basic level, they were participants and contributors. Edgeworth, Owenson, Scott, Irving, and Cooper all engaged with a multilingual European culture made available to them through the importation of books, translation, and reprinting, as well as their own travels. Their works were translated into multiple foreign languages and often published abroad. Edgeworth was particularly admired in Russia, Irving in Spain, Cooper in Germany, and all of these authors in neighboring France. Scott's unparalleled impact on world literature can be seen in the spread of the historical novel as a global genre, from Japan to Brazil. Goethe coined the term *Weltliteratur* in the 1820s to describe an international literary marketplace that Marx and Engels later traced to the rise of the bourgeoisie.[52] As market-savvy professionals with thoroughly bourgeois values, the authors of this study fared so well in that marketplace, it may even seem like they weren't provincial at all. Yet the Romantic dream (or nightmare) of *Weltliteratur*, evidenced broadly in dissemination and influence, did not affect their formative struggle within the predominantly Anglophone marketplace that was the arena of their initial consecration. This book is concerned with that initial stage, the material conditions of its possibility, and the influential provincial aesthetics it inspired.

The Aesthetics of Provinciality

A paradox recurs throughout modernity: that a great work of literature is both particular and universal, that it arises from a distinct context defined by a unique worldview with its own internal values, and also that it transcends that context, that worldview, and those values. This is a cliché in our own multicultural times, one repeated in cultural contexts high and low, in countless book reviews and citations for literary awards. It is a paradox and not a simple contradiction because the opposed concepts mutually inform each other in a profoundly circular logic: the representation of particularity provides access to universal truth while universality accrues meaning and importance to the particular. Early nineteenth-century provincials wrote in an era during which the "nation" occupied a privileged relationship to both sides of this paradoxical coin. Literature was newly understood to be particularly national in its essence and, as such, an expression of what makes all nations part of universal human nature. This conception of literature was both attractive to Irish, Scottish, and American authors and deeply problematic. It was attractive because they could fashion themselves in the London marketplace as national spokespersons and their work as nationally distinctive. It was problematic because metropolitan readers were skeptical that representations of Irish, Scottish, or American national particularity had any purchase whatsoever on universality, partly because of English chauvinism but more profoundly because as sociopolitical entities, Ireland, Scotland, and the United States did not fit seamlessly into the category of the nation as the ideology of cultural nationalism defined it. Dependence on London ensured that these inescapable difficulties persisted, and it was out of such difficulties that the aesthetics of provinciality emerged.

Caught in an impossible wish that their works be accepted as both national and universal, provincial authors offered powerful claims for the unique place of literature in society. These claims developed out of the extreme pressure they put on cross-cultural literary exchange as the unavoidable strategy for approaching London. To ease such crossing, they retreated into what Richard Poirier long ago called "a world elsewhere," the belief that "through literature it is possible to create environments radically different from those supported by economic, political, and social systems."[53] Such a retreat was always ideological, as the Marxist critique of bourgeois aesthetics insists. According to that critique, the commodification of literature and the expansion of the reading public in the eighteenth and early nineteenth centuries led to idealizations of aesthetic experience that reject the marketplace and claim independence for the work of art.[54] Irish, Scottish, and American authors insisted, too, that literary production and exchange is a relatively autonomous endeavor. In turning to London, however, they derived this idea from an embrace of the marketplace, rather than its denial. Their literary sphere is "autonomous" not because of a pure Kantian commitment to nonpurposive aesthetic judgment, nor because they denied the messy world of commodification, but more generally because of an insistence that literature operates according to its own laws. *The aesthetics of provinciality consists of a range of representational modes, derived from geographically inflected cultural subordination, that vacillate between national and universal conceptions of art; it takes refuge in the belief that literature enjoys an exalted role in human affairs.* Such a belief had roots in Enlightenment theories of taste and received new force with the rise of Romanticism.

In many ways, Enlightenment thinkers provided hostile philosophical conditions for the provincial author who wished to represent his or her culture to English readers. A high premium was placed on resemblance. "[W]e are more pleased, in the course of our reading," writes David Hume in "Of the Standard of Taste" (1757), "with pictures and characters, that resemble objects which are found in our own age or country, than with those which describe a different set of customs."[55] For Hume and others, aesthetic pleasure derives partly from finding correspondences between one's own experience (derived from the senses) and artistic representation.[56] For Joseph Addison, the secondary pleasures of the imagination—those reserved for the experience of art rather than nature—"originate from comparing ideas of an original object with those from some representation of it."[57] Edmund Burke emphasized that for the imagination, "a pleasure is perceived from the resemblance, which the imitation has to the original."[58] The classic works of antiquity achieved this because they were understood to imitate a universal human nature that transcended time and place. The scant praise eighteenth-century writers reserved for novelty did not override their general prejudice against particularity.

Provincial authors found some solace in cultural nationalism, the view of Johann Gottfried Herder, as John Hutchinson describes it, that insists "the essence of a nation is its distinctive civilization, which is the product of its unique history, culture, and geographical profile."[59] Germaine de Staël espoused this view in works that were widely disseminated throughout the Anglophone world, including *Corinne; or, Italy* (1807), a novel delineating Italian manners and customs, and *De l'Allemagne* (1810), a study of German culture and philosophy. Staël praised "indigenous" works of literature with deep connections to "national feeling."[60] Buoyed by the increasing authority of vernacular works over the classics, cultural nationalism flourished through the logic of comparison. "Civilization continually tends to make all men look alike and almost really be alike," Staël writes in *Corinne*, "but one's mind and imagination delight in the differences which characterize nations."[61] Difference, in this view, rather than resemblance, accrues value to the literary. Such ideas were incorporated into provincial literature because of the exogenous address embedded even within the most insular expressions of national culture.

Not everyone shared Staël's delight in transnational comparison, however. Unfortunately for provincial authors, many English readers, critics, and booksellers continued to exult in their assumed superiority. A more fundamental problem was the association of nation with language. "In learning the prosody of a language," writes Staël, in a very Herderian passage, "we enter more intimately into the spirit of the nation by which it is spoken than by any other possible manner of study."[62] It follows that nations without a language lack their own "spirit," a problem elite Americans keenly felt after independence as they tried to found a national literature in the language of England. Irish and Scottish authors often enlisted dialect in the service of national distinctiveness, but dependence on London meant they could never fully leave English behind. English culture, meanwhile, silently absorbed cultural nationalism's valuation of the vernacular through the familiar alchemy of making English seem universal. In his preface to *Lyrical Ballads* (1802), for example, Wordsworth's "language really used by men" paradoxically invests an inherently local variant, English, with the general significance of "truth, not individual and local, but general, and operative."[63] The provincial author could never make such silent and seamless claims about her chosen language of representation.

The same Enlightenment thinkers invested in resemblance, however, also provided philosophical ground for the cross-cultural literary transaction. In "Of the Standard of Taste," Hume articulated the values of the unbiased critic, who "must preserve his mind free from all *prejudice*." "When any work is addressed to the public," Hume writes, "though I should have a friendship or enmity with the author, I must depart from this situation; and considering myself as a man in general, forget, if possible, my individual being and my personal circumstances."[64] Through transcending the contingences of the "personal," Humean disinterest grants universality to the observer ("man in general"); this locates value not in representation but in the integrity of judgment.[65] Adam Smith's *Theory of Moral Sentiments* (1759) provided a model of sympathy that complemented the selflessness of Hume's ideal critic. Smith's model, almost immediately absorbed as a theory of literature, not only encouraged the spectator or reader to forget his or her own personal interests through identifying with the other but endowed such identification with the highest moral value. "And hence it is," Smith writes, "that to feel much for others and little for ourselves, that to restrain our selfish, and to indulge our benevolent affections, constitutes the perfection of human nature."[66] Provincial authors appealed to the "benevolent affections" of metropolitan readers in heavily aestheticized Smithian gestures. These appeals shaped the kind of cross-cultural communion they imagined could overcome distance and national difference.[67]

Cross-cultural communion occurred in the very limited sphere of the literary. As John Guillory and Clifford Siskin have argued, by the Romantic period, the category of "literature" had disaggregated from other realms of culture.[68] The aesthetics of provinciality helped define the terms of this disaggregation by claiming for literature its own values and rules. Provincial authors banished politics and prejudice to promote literary exchange as a peaceful elite activity—what Siskin calls the "pleasurable familiarity of Literature."[69] That activity mingled Enlightenment ideals of disinterest and sympathy with a more quintessentially Romantic ideology that insists products of the imagination exist entirely for their own sakes. Literary exchange was imagined to be isolated, protected, and supervised according to rules only specialized practitioners could determine and fulfill. "Exchange" was, indeed, paramount, given the importance of cross-cultural communion, and its necessity marks an obvious difference between the aesthetics of provinciality and a Kantian or Coleridgean notion of aesthetic form as organic or nonpurposive. But even Kant, in the *Critique of Judgment* (1790), grants aesthetic pleasure a purpose once it is joined with the idea of communication. Regarding "the judgment of taste," Kant writes that "it does not follow that after it has been given as a pure aesthetic judgment no interest can be combined with it."[70] The highest form of interest that can be added to such a judgment is appreciation of its "universal communicability," which "almost infinitely increases its value" through demonstrating an "inclination to society."[71] The value of a judgment's universal communicability—tied to Kant's "common sense"—gives a social function to aesthetics that admits into its compass relations among persons. "In the sphere of aesthetic culture," Terry Eagleton writes, with regard to the Kantian imaginary, "we can experience our shared humanity."[72] Kant never describes pure aesthetic judgment as anything other than a priori determined, but the added indirect value of universal communicability provides a powerful model for a literary sphere defined through its own ideals.

The aesthetics of provinciality comprised a heterogeneous number of strategies and commitments—appeals to readers' sympathy, aestheticized displays of national character, figurations of cross-cultural communion—and different texts exhibit it in widely different ways. Owenson, Scott, and Cooper, for example, were more comfortable with relying on nationally defined conceptions of art than Edgeworth and Irving, for whom such conceptions were especially difficult to swallow, and Edgeworth never fully abandoned literature's didactic function for the more fully escapist fantasies of Irving and Cooper. London was at the center of all this, as subsequent chapters will show. For now, a famous set piece from *Waverley* can suggest the intertwined relationship between the history of books and the history of aesthetics that this project as a whole attempts to trace. At the end of that novel, Scott unveils a portrait of Waverley and Fergus Mac-Ivor, the Jacobite rebel and Highland chief who guides Waverley through the romanticized political landscape of Scotland. The portrait hangs in the hall of the newly dispossessed Baron of Bradwardine, whose lowland Scottish manor has been artificially restored by the English gentleman who purchased it after the war. By this time, Waverley has married the daughter of Bradwardine, and Mac-Ivor has been executed for treason. Scott's description densely crystallizes the implications of his fictional project:

> It was a large and animated painting, representing Fergus Mac-Ivor and Waverley in their Highland dress; the scene a wild, rocky, and mountainous pass, down which the clan were descending in the background. It was taken from a spirited sketch, drawn while they were in Edinburgh by a young man of high genius, and had been painted on a full length scale by an eminent London artist. Raeburn himself (whose Highland chiefs do all but walk out of the canvas) could not have done more justice to the subject.[73]

As many have noted, this portrait encapsulates the aestheticization of history the novel as a whole enacts.[74] Few have asked, how was the portrait made? Scott carefully divides labor between Edinburgh, the location of "high genius," and London, where "eminen[ce]" resides. In Edinburgh, a "young man" makes an unpolished and spontaneous drawing, an ephemeral "sketch" originating, Scott suggests, from deep within the "spirit" of the man himself. This is a Romantic description of the creative process, one that deploys the term *genius* in its emergent sense to indicate the "exalted ability," as Raymond Williams has written, of a "special kind of person."[75] Scott's location of such genius in Edinburgh—and the use he makes of it, to depict Highland dress and Scotland's sublime scenery—ties it indelibly to national culture.

Yet the drawing transforms significantly as it travels. In London, the once materially insignificant "sketch" expands into "full length scale" under the auspices of a culturally sanctioned figure, the "eminent London artist," who has distinguished it with his attention and with an elevated medium. Now a painting of magnificent size, it emanates an aura of permanence and authority that defines its artistic power. "The whole piece was generally admired," Scott writes.[76] The return of the sketch from London in its new material form involves the spectacle of its transformation into a serious art object. In mapping the portrait's production onto the geography of his own novel's production

and distribution—written and printed in Edinburgh, consecrated and sold
mostly in the full-scale London marketplace, received as a triumphant success back home—Scott provides a figure both for the plot of his novel and
for its making as a material and literary artifact. The tension in the passage
between the organic creativity of "genius" and the deliberate yet authoritative
skill of the "artist" reflects the tension within the aesthetics of provinciality between the nationally defined essence of the provincial writer and the aesthetic
value he claims while seeking acceptance in the metropolis. It also depends
on a retreat from the violent political conflict Scott's novel relegates firmly to
the past. This highly self-reflexive moment in *Waverley* exudes a theory of the
"literary" tied ineluctably to the geographically inflected hierarchies of the book
trade.

Limits and Structure

The activity of a small group of provincial authors, publishers, and readers
could never represent fully the relationship between print culture and literary
expression in the early nineteenth century, and I do not claim that it does. I
have necessarily left out an enormous amount of material, including poetry.
Fiction's evolving position as a newly legitimated genre makes it an ideal site
for tracing the struggles of writers who devised representational modes to fit
the contours of the marketplace, although this does not preclude my argument's relevance for Irish, Scottish, and American poetry of the same period.[77]
Most important, for me, however, this book does not directly address the print
culture of the early black Atlantic, which I have written about elsewhere and
continue to explore.[78] My research on Edgeworth, Owenson, Scott, Irving,
and Cooper has developed concurrently and in relation to research on Phillis
Wheatley, Ignatius Sancho, John Marrant, Olaudah Equiano, and William
Hamilton. I cannot proceed without drawing some points of comparison and
contrast within this interconnected Anglophone archive. London remained
the locus of ambitious book publication for all of these writers; Wheatley's
Poems (1773), Sancho's *Letters* (1782), and Equaino's *Interesting Narrative*
(1789)—like *Castle Rackrent* and *The Sketch Book*—were London titles shaped
by metropolitan ambitions. Wheatley's transatlantic pilgrimage from Boston
to London to oversee the publication of her poetry resonates with the centripetal journeys of elite provincials, and Sancho called Wheatley a "genius
in bondage" in an act of judgment deeply evocative of the aesthetic theories

explored in this book.[79] Yet early black writing entered the realm of print through processes quite different from those under investigation here. Authors like Edgeworth and Irving may have struggled with an uneven literary field, but early black writers faced a book trade that privileged whiteness and granted them access most often through patrons, editors, and amanuenses. Such differences were compounded and reinforced, of course, by wide differences in class and social status.[80] In *The Black Atlantic*, Paul Gilroy begins his critique of "the fatal junction of the concept of nationality with the concept of culture" with a powerful indictment of English cultural nationalism, an "aesthetic and cultural tradition" that "reproduced its nationalism and its ethnocentrism by denying imaginary, invented Englishness any external referents whatsoever."[81] In many ways, elite provincials were among those who most fully benefited from such a "fatal junction," however distanced they were from Englishness itself. Gilroy's assessment of black authors' resistance to and exclusion from dominant aesthetic ideologies has heavily influenced my account of the instantiation of those ideologies as an aesthetics of provinciality.

As we shall see, the social and economic inequalities of the Atlantic world provided provincial authors a litany of usable and marketable stereotypes rather than any serious impediment to success. Their fiction depends on a number of essentialized stock figures—dying Indians, dispossessed Irish Catholics, savage and noble Highlanders, enslaved Africans—as signs of national difference and authenticity. These were stereotypes to which their elite and popular readerships responded with eagerness and desire; with roots in stadial theories of history and racial difference, they were part of cultural nationalism's arsenal of ideological weapons. They were also mutually reinforcing as Irish, Scottish, and American authors analogized the manners and customs of their societies' marginalized populations.[82] These authors are not, perhaps, to be congratulated for overcoming the rather mild cultural differences and inequalities they faced in the literary field. Their careers are fascinating, however, precisely for the way provinciality transformed relatively minor rivalries into powerful literary fantasies. Irving writes, in a passage I discuss in Chapter 4, that "it should be the exalted ministry of literature to keep together the family of human nature."[83] Literature has surely done its share of pushing the "family" apart—the category "literature" (as Irving understands it) gained potency partly because it served the interests of a particular class; one of its social functions was to provide an instrument for elite Anglo-American solidarity. As Frederic Jameson reminds us, "All class consciousness of whatever type is Utopian insofar as it expresses the unity of a collectivity."[84] Writers like

Irving thought literature provided a precious and glorious collective escape. I am interested in tracing how this idea emerged from the utopian fantasies of provincial writers—both hidden within literary texts and on their surface.[85]

*   *   *

Six chapters progress from booksellers to authors to readers, from the material production and sale of literary texts (Chapters 1 and 2); to the London-centric careers of provincial authors (Chapters 3, 4, and 5); to the vehement reactions of those who rejected England's cultural authority (Chapter 6). The book ends with an epilogue that takes stock of the literary field from the mid-nineteenth century, by which time the balance of cultural power in the Anglophone world had begun to change. The project's chronology derives from the publication dates of two texts that mark its outer limits: Edgeworth's *Castle Rackrent* (1800) and Nathaniel Hawthorne's *The Scarlet Letter* (1850).

Chapter 1 analyzes economic data, patterns of distribution, publication statistics, copyright law, customary trade practices, and discourse about the book trade to establish London's centrality and mark significant changes in provincial publishing in the first three decades of the nineteenth century. It argues that the book trade can benefit from a perspective more radically at-tuned to transatlantic circulation than historians of the book have hitherto employed. Chapter 2 offers a case study on the publication of Walter Scott's fiction to illustrate one benefit of such a perspective. Scott's wildly popular Waverley novels were printed in Edinburgh but distributed mostly in London, where his Philadelphia publishers, Mathew and Henry Carey, acquired them for reprinting and sale in the United States. The Careys established an unprec-edented agreement with Scott's publisher, Archibald Constable, to purchase advance sheets of the novels before official publication. Using booksellers' cor-respondence and printed texts, I tell a new story about this transatlantic ar-rangement to argue that the London marketplace affected the transmission of what came to be called the "American Copy" of the Waverley novels.

Chapter 3 reassesses the effect of the 1801 Act of Union on the major fiction of Maria Edgeworth and Sydney Owenson, whose novels were the first to establish the representational modes of the aesthetics of provinciality. Edgeworth's *Castle Rackrent*, *The Absentee* (1812), and *Ormond* (1817), as well as Owenson's *The Wild Irish Girl* (1806), use formal devices like the marriage plot and travel narrative to project an ideal relation with English readers meant to ameliorate the political tensions that defined the relationship between Ireland

and England. While Edgeworth defines cross-cultural literary exchange within the universalized moral codes of Smith's *Theory of Moral Sentiments*, Owenson embraces the more Romantic fantasy that literature inhabits its own sphere in society. The discourse of national character to which these authors turn both supports and undermines the ideal author-reader relationships their novels enact through narrative form. I argue that politically reductive readings tied to the Act of Union cannot explain aesthetic practices that became hugely influential for Scottish and American authors who also sought out English audiences but for whom the Union itself was not a pressing concern.

Chapter 4 has two major goals: to establish the material presence of American fiction in London and to assess the effects of provinciality on the career of Washington Irving, the first American author to succeed abroad. Most British reprints of American texts were unauthorized ventures pursued by London publishers without the consent of American authors. But Britain, unlike the United States, allowed Americans with the right connections to negotiate copyright protection, a fact that made possible Irving's and Cooper's process of transatlantic revision. I argue that Irving's strategies of revision were shaped by his provinciality, formed initially by his work as an editor of *The Analectic Magazine* during the War of 1812 and compounded anew as he acquired John Murray as *The Sketch Book*'s London publisher. Irving's work as editor during a time of war inspired an ideological conception of the purity of literary exchange, a commitment that entirely governs the aesthetics of *The Sketch Book* itself. As a provincial, Irving evacuates his authorial persona of nationalized political commitments even as he offers a number of "American" tales to the marketplace for consumption.

Cooper and Scott, so often paired together, are rarely paired as provincials, and yet as I argue in Chapter 5, an attention to the importance of London has the potential to revise our understanding of the cultural work of their fiction. Many readers of Cooper and Scott have argued that their historical novels embody the needs of their expanding imperial societies. This chapter posits the Anglophone literary field as an equally appropriate arena for these ostensibly nationalist writers and argues that the cross-cultural address embedded in their fiction, and particularly in *The Pioneers* and *The Heart of Mid-Lothian*, produces the fantasy of an autonomous literary sphere that minimizes national politics for the sake of unadulterated literary exchange. While Scott's early Waverley novels take their cue from the Irish national tale and embed English readers with broad narrative allegories, Cooper's early Leatherstocking Tales take their cue from Irving and betray an address to such readers through transatlantic revision. Cooper's revisions to *The Pioneers* for Colburn and Bentley's "Standard Novels" series transformed that novel's marriage plot and its archetypical American hero, Natty Bummpo, into devices for Anglo-American camaraderie, and Scott's *The Heart of Mid-Lothian* allegorizes its relation to the London marketplace through Jeanie Deans's pilgrimage from Edinburgh to London, climaxing as she arrives in London to appeal to the sympathies of Queen Caroline—a striking figure for the English reader.

Chapter 6 considers provinciality from the perspective of readers in Ireland, Scotland, and the United States who rejected London's authority and channeled their resentment wholeheartedly into the service of a reactionary, anti-English nationalism. It begins with the volatile genre of metropolitan travel writing, in which English writers journey around the Atlantic world and publish their accounts back in London. These narratives infuriated many provincial readers who issued vehement objections in print and in marginalia they scribbled onto the offending books themselves. The chapter then considers two examples of the trans-provincial currents underpinning the nationalisms of Ireland and the United States. In Ireland, many harnessed the memory of America's struggle for independence to define an Irish nationalism that vehemently rejected England. In the United States, meanwhile, nationalists adopted the anti-English rhetoric of Walter Scott's poems to fuel their own defiance of England during the War of 1812. It was during the war that Americans adopted a song from Walter Scott's *The Lady of the Lake* (1810) as the official anthem of American presidents. Now referred to by its first words, "Hail to the Chief"—but never sung with its original words—this song was originally written as the imagined battle cry of a Highland chief who died fighting England.

The Epilogue assesses changes in the transatlantic book trade that resulted in the redistribution of cultural capital around the Anglophone Atlantic and the decline of London as the obvious point of reference for American writers. It does so through the career of Nathaniel Hawthorne, who wrote his earliest stories in the age of Edgeworth, Owenson, Irving, Scott, and Cooper. I argue that *The Scarlet Letter* is a profound reflection on the obsolescence of those authors' representational modes, one made possible by epochal changes in the conditions that originally produced them. At the end of the novel, Hester Prynne stays in New England to signal the legitimacy of a newly nationalized American marketplace that can accommodate its own ambitious fiction writers. The plot of *The Scarlet Letter*, as well as the relationship between "The Custom House" and the romance itself, reflects a newly organized literary field that no longer had a clearly authoritative audience to which writers turned for recognition.

Chapter 1

London and the Transatlantic Book Trade

British and American publishing were not separate affairs in the early nineteenth century. But how did they cohere? Recently completed multivolume histories of the book in Great Britain, Scotland, Ireland, and the United States, as well as a constellation of individual studies, have highlighted transatlantic connections by pointing to how printed texts circulated.[1] Readerly interest around the Atlantic fueled the importation of books and encouraged many publishers, in the absence of international copyright law, to issue unauthorized reprints of promising transatlantic titles.[2] Scholars interested in such circulation have for the most part considered it from one side of the Atlantic or the other, telling national stories with attention to their transatlantic valences. Borrowing from David Armitage, we might describe such an approach as "cis-Atlantic," in which the historian "studies particular places as unique locations within an Atlantic world."[3] The organizational principle of the multivolume histories can fairly stand as representative of this practice. If historians are "all Atlanticists now," as Armitage puts it,[4] then those who study books are of the "cis-Atlantic" variety. There is a fundamental tension at the heart of the field: most studies present extended diachronic accounts of the development of the book trade within a national space, even as they emphasize the movement of individuals, objects, and practices that undermine the nation as a heuristic category. Instead of privileging one local context and attending to transatlantic circulation, this chapter begins with circulation itself and asks how it brings different contexts into dynamic interrelation. To do this, it is necessary to abandon the common nationalistic thrust of most book history narratives in favor of a consideration of the book trade as an interconnected system.

I offer here a perspective on the late eighteenth and early nineteenth centuries attuned to the transnational movement of texts and to the geographically inflected cultural hierarchies that affected the meaning of such movement. Economic data, patterns of distribution, publication statistics, copyright law, and customary trade practices demonstrate London's centrality. We move from the London marketplace out to the late eighteenth-century book trades in Ireland, Scotland, and North America and forward to significant changes that shaped provincial publishing after the turn of the nineteenth century. The 1801 Act of Union between Great Britain and Ireland and the copyright law that immediately followed emerge as central events in the history of the transatlantic book trade. Throughout the period, and especially in the three decades after the Union, there was a tension between new, authorized, and copyrighted texts and an extremely active reprint industry that refracted London's cultural authority without overcoming it. After a detailed look at the rise of provincial publishing in the early nineteenth century, the chapter telescopes briefly out to the mid-nineteenth century, when the growth and nationalization of the U.S. book trade and the increasing consolidation of Edinburgh-London partnerships led to a British-versus-American model of competition in transatlantic literary publishing.

The subsequent chapter, a companion to this one, turns to the 1820s and offers an extended case study on Walter Scott to demonstrate the dynamism of the activity London catalyzed among booksellers in Edinburgh and Philadelphia. Scott's Waverley novels were printed in Edinburgh but distributed mostly in London, where publishers from Philadelphia initially acquired them for reprinting. Mathew and Henry Carey became Scott's most important American publishers by establishing a direct agreement with his Edinburgh publisher, Archibald Constable, for purchasing advance sheets. The transmission of what came to be called the "American Copy" of the Waverley novels was shaped by the power and pressures of the London marketplace for books. Understanding this requires close attention to the language of the book trade—in private correspondence, in periodicals, newspapers, advertisements, and (it turns out) in the Waverley novels themselves—acts of representation that are as much a part of book history as the more empirical evidence on which the discipline usually focuses.

The Provincial Trade Before 1801

London's advantages were partly demographic. By 1800, the population of England was 8.6 million compared to 1.6 million in Scotland, a stark advantage despite higher literacy rates north of the border. In 1800, Ireland's population stood at 5 million, but "the culture of the majority [was] still predominantly oral," and comparatively few read English.[5] The London trade also benefited from its proximity to the highest concentration of wealth and resources in the English-speaking world, which supported a marketplace of elite consumers who could afford the trade's latest productions. In the second half of the eighteenth century, there was only a slight decline in the total proportion of English-language books printed in London, from 90 percent in 1750 to 77 percent in 1790, and England supported far more circulating libraries than other areas, roughly ten times more than Scotland in 1800.[6] Trade monopolies and patterns of centralization worked to the advantage of London as well. Formal legal restrictions began in 1662 with a licensing act that restricted publication to members of the Stationer's Company, and the Statute of Queen Anne (1710) strengthened London's control over production by formalizing the rights of publishers even as it sought to limit them to a fourteen-year period (with the possibility of a fourteen-year extension). London booksellers embraced copyrights but pursued monopolistic trade practices to undermine limits to their duration, securing de facto perpetual copyright until the 1774 case *Donaldson v. Becket*. In that case, the House of Lords enforced legal limits and opened the market for the reprinting of old texts, as William St. Clair has emphasized, but this did not change the customary role of established London firms as originators of new and copyrighted books.[7] Such commodities were distinguished from cheaper reprints and remained luxury items compared to more commonly printed material, including newspapers, broadsides, chapbooks, prayer books, grammars, school books, anthologies, and abridged editions of steady sellers.

The commodification and specialization of the book trade compounded such distinctions as the rise of modern publishing increasingly shaped the market for new literary texts.[8] Enterprising booksellers abandoned printing to focus on publishing itself as a "specialist, capital-intensive commercial endeavor,"[9] investing in new authors and capturing certain sectors of the market through advertising campaigns in newspapers, circulars, and printed publication lists. Established London firms spent money on luxuries they highlighted in such advertisements, including new typefaces, high-quality paper, and expensive bindings. Publishers built and protected reputations through maintaining the high and showy material quality of their books. "The name of the publisher, like that of the author," writes Richard Sher, "[took] on the role of a brand name, influencing perceptions of the 'product' and patterns of consumption in profound ways."[10] This reinforced a hierarchy of printed texts, from the hefty quarto volumes of new poetry associated with high-class metropolitan publishing to the cheaply printed ephemeral texts associated with less capitalized firms.

Such dynamics were evident far from London because most readers in eighteenth-century Scotland, Ireland, and North America encountered literary texts as either London imports or reprints produced in cities like Edinburgh, Dublin, or Philadelphia. A 1793 catalogue from Edinburgh publisher William Creech suggests London's overwhelming importance in Scotland, especially as the origin for new, expensive, and large-format books.[11] A discussion of "New Books" in *The Scots Magazine* in 1778 devoted eight pages to books published in London compared to only two pages for Edinburgh.[12] Most books published locally in Scotland were at this time produced with London partnerships that were necessary to finance some projects and to reach the marketplace in the south. "I could wish a London Bookseller engaged in the publication," wrote James Beattie regarding his *Essay on Truth* in 1769, "because otherwise it would be impossible to make it circulate in England."[13] At times, the Edinburgh trade manufactured new editions that rivaled the format of expensive London books, but even so, that city's share in total production was relatively low. Only about 12 percent of the works of the Scottish Enlightenment—by authors like Beattie, Adam Ferguson, William Robertson, and David Hume—were published solely in Edinburgh without a London partner.[14] A customer perusing William Creech's 1793 catalogue would also have noticed a large number of cheap Scottish reprints of texts that originated in London. Printers in Scotland had long side-stepped London monopolies by trading heavily in such reprints, some of which were officially out of copyright but still claimed as protected.[15] Largely permitted to sell and distribute books in local and North American markets, the Scottish reprint industry eventually got in trouble when it encroached upon England, as was the case with Alexander Donaldson, whose reprint of James Thompson's *The Seasons* was at issue in the 1774 case that bears his name and that of the poem's London printer, Thomas Becket.

Ireland's book trade operated similarly to Scotland's even though in the eighteenth century, it remained outside of British copyright and avoided the legal battles of the Scottish trade. In Dublin, book buyers chose between new London editions and cheaper, perfectly legal reprints, sometimes sold side by side. "In Dublin—as elsewhere [in Ireland]," Mary Pollard writes, "the wealthy customer usually preferred the London edition to any other," while reprints satisfied the lower end of the market and, like reprints from Scotland, were also heavily exported to North America.[16] As in Scotland, authors from Ireland—including Jonathan Swift, Oliver Goldsmith, and Edmund Burke—sought London publishers for prestige, profit, and convenience (if they lived there) and also because Dublin editions, unlike new editions published in Edinburgh, were not copyright protected in Britain.[17] Some Dublin publishers established informal partnerships with London firms; George Faulkner, for example, published editions of Samuel Richardson by purchasing advance sheets of London texts so he could be the first to reprint them in Ireland.[18] For the most part, however, elegant and expensive London imports competed for a reader's attention with "reprints of London originals."[19] New literary works retained an especially strong association with London, since fiction and poetry were far less often reprinted than other kinds of texts.[20]

In North America before and after the Revolution, the book trade was also defined by the sale of London imports and cheap reprints, although many of the latter were also imported from Ireland and Scotland. Benjamin Franklin and James Rivington were supplied with books by business associates in London, and the latter bragged in the 1760s that he was "the only London book-seller in America."[21] The materiality of London-printed books sent clear signals: "Large paper, large format, and large type all enjoyed a high social status," Hugh Amory writes about the colonial period, "generated not only by the 'louder,' attention-grabbing volume of the text but also by the conspicuous waste of paper."[22] Such volumes contrasted to the cheap reprints from Ireland and Scotland and also to local reprints by colonials, including some who had been book trades professionals in Ireland, like Mathew Carey, or in Scotland, like Robert Bell. In the last decades of the century, the market for reprints in America was met mostly by imports from Ireland. The transatlantic dynamics of the American book trade changed little up through the 1790s; before and after the Revolution, for example, Thomas Jefferson preferred to read London texts in their Dublin editions because of their price and more manageable size.[23] Toward the end of the century, some important changes occurred, such as an increase in domestic reprinting, led by Carey; attempts to coordinate bookselling through trade sales; and an interest in new books of specifically American manufacture.[24] But a new federal copyright law in 1790 that granted U.S. residents and citizens rights to their texts did not much affect the general pattern of American bookselling.[25] *The Gentleman's Magazine* corroborates this in a 1796 article about the U.S. trade; "serious books would only do as imported," it writes, "as the people esteemed English-printed books much better than the productions of their own presses."[26] Charles Brockden Brown felt this keenly, as he admitted in a letter to his brother about arranging transatlantic editions of his novels. "The salelibility [*sic*] of my works will much depend on their popularity in England, whither Caritat has carried a considerable number of Wieland, Ormond, and Mervyn."[27] Up through the turn of the century, bookselling in North America was still characterized by the authority of the London trade, London imports, and the dissemination of London texts via cheap reprints.

The robust trade in reprints around the Anglophone Atlantic demonstrates the vibrancy of provincial publishing. But there was an important difference between two kinds of reprinting: the reprinting of old texts whose copyrights had expired and the reprinting of new texts (legally or illegally) from copyrighted London editions. The former practice was common everywhere following *Donaldson v. Becket*, including in London and England. Reprinting copyrighted texts, however, was largely the prerogative of provincial publishers. Before and after *Donaldson*, publishers in Scotland produced illegal reprints of in-copyright titles that undersold London editions, while Irish and American reprinters were not beholden to copyrights at all.[28] In all of these areas, original London editions were sometimes sold alongside unauthorized provincial reprints that echoed their originals. This produced a kind of double vision in Scotland, Ireland, and North America that did not characterize the marketplace in England. This double vision emphasized the provincial book trade's distance from London as it reinforced that city's traditional importance as the origin for new literary texts. In the provincial marketplace, a new and imported London edition signaled its high cultural status directly through its own materiality, while a local reprint alluded to such status through its text's known metropolitan origin. Distance from London was reflected in a reprint not in the book's physical journey to the hands of readers, as was the case with an import, but rather through the reprint's invocation of such distance as an immanent feature of the object itself. While readers of a London import were aware of its distant material origins, readers of a reprint felt the absence of a book's original London edition as a ghostly presence within it.

The Provincial Book Trade After 1801

Events surrounding the turn of the nineteenth century led to significant changes even as London's overall dominance persisted. Scholarship has typically marked the *Donaldson* decision as the most significant turning point in this period because the explosion of reprinting after 1774 expanded the availability of old texts. From the perspective of the provincial book trade, however, which had always trafficked in such texts, a later date emerges as more significant: 1801, the year of the Act of Union, which absorbed Ireland into Great Britain to create the "United Kingdom" and was accompanied with a Copyright Act that for the first time extended British copyright across the Irish Sea. The effects of this new law reverberated around the Atlantic: it led to the collapse of the reprint trade in Ireland and drove Irish book trades professionals to London or to the United States to find work. It also led to the rise of reprinting in the United States, which fueled the growth of that nation's book trade. Copyright in Ireland can be seen as the latest of three events in the history of intellectual property that attempted to regulate the relationships between the London trade and provincial publishers engaged mostly in reprinting. *Donaldson* was decided in favor of a Scottish reprinter who ignored customary London monopolies, and the 1790 U.S. law denied foreign authors copyright protection and sanctioned the wide reprinting of British texts. The U.S. federal copyright law has been described as "negligible" in its first decades, and the post-Union law has been cast mainly in a limited role for its impact on the Irish trade.[29] The reverberations of the events in Ireland and the United States—with one reprint trade shut down and the other sanctioned and on the rise—had more of an impact on the provincial book trade than did *Donaldson*, especially in the long term. By the 1820s, the U.S. reprint industry was able to invest capital in forging relationships with booksellers in Britain and also to produce their own books for the transatlantic marketplace. Meanwhile, the controversy over the Act of Union inspired a wave of Irish fiction that paved the way in London for the success of subsequent writers from Scotland and the United States who took such fiction as their model. By the 1820s and 1830s, provincial literature flooded the London marketplace and formed a recognizable sector of the market. The trajectories of the Irish, American, and Scottish trades diverged widely in the early nineteenth century, especially in regards to reprinting and the double vision it created, but they remained indelibly connected to London and, increasingly, to each other.

After the extension of British copyright, Irish reprinting and publishing was "almost annihilated," as one observer put it, and in the ensuing decades, imports soared.[30] "There is no encouragement for literary exertion in the Irish metropolis," wrote Robert Walsh in 1816, "the cautious Dublin bookseller will run no risk publishing an original work, however great its merit. It must appear in London, or not at all."[31] As in the eighteenth century, all major Irish authors published first or only in London. William Carleton wrote in 1842 that "until within the last ten or twelve years an Irish author never thought of publishing in his own country, and the consequence was that our literary men followed the example of our great landlords; they became absentees, and drained the country of its intellectual wealth precisely as the others exhausted it of its rents."[32] Even authors like Maria Edgeworth, who lived in Ireland and decried absenteeism, published in London, where Archibald Constable purchased her work, as he informed her in 1823.[33] "[T]he numbers of novels actually published in Ireland were tiny," writes Claire Connolly, and of the latter, most were co-published with London firms.[34] In the cases of James Gordon's *A New History of Ireland* (1804) and William Parnell's *Maurice and Berghetta* (1819), authorized Dublin editions were printed smaller than their London editions and resembled the cheap reprints of old.[35]

But the Act of Union and its Copyright Act should not be seen only in negative terms. The controversy over the Union served as what Ina Ferris has called an "incitement to intervention and discourse" about the question of Ireland that created a huge market for the kinds of answers published books could provide, including fiction.[36] This began with Edgeworth's *Castle Rackrent*, published in 1800 amid the debate over Union, continued with her other works and the spectacular success of Sydney Owenson, and also included novels by John Banim, Charles Maturin, and the poetry and fiction of Thomas Moore. Back in Dublin, they kept track of this. In an 1807 article about Owenson, the *Cyclopaedian Magazine* described her ascent: "The first publication from the pen of this lady was a small volume of poems printed in Dublin," and now "[h]er novels are eagerly purchased by the London booksellers, at the same price given to the most established writers of the age."[37] In 1825, the *Dublin and London Magazine* facetiously announced the success of an author by referencing the reprinting of his work. "The author of '*Tales of Irish Life*' has contributed two articles. They must be good; for nearly all the English papers, even the lofty *Times*, copied them."[38] Between 1800 and 1830, over one hundred novels on Irish subjects or by Irish authors were published in London, a genre that "emerged as a recognizable commodity on the literary market," and by the 1820s, an "Irish *line* of fiction begins to be defined" in the British periodical reviews.[39] In the decades that followed the Union, Irish writers took London by storm.

Across the Atlantic, meanwhile, the end of Irish reprinting left a gap in the market that American booksellers and publishers were happy to fill. This was increasingly apparent as the American reprint industry grew in the 1810s and 1820s. William Wakeman remarked in 1821 that previously to the Union, publishers in Dublin were "on the same footing as America . . . and every new book was reprinted here; but since the Copyright Act has been extended, that cannot now be done openly."[40] Mathew Carey's experiences as a printer in Ireland served him well as he became the leader in an industry whose wares included a hefty dose of new Irish literary texts published first in London. Edgeworth followed the American reprinting of her work, as one of her stories, "To-Morrow," demonstrates. Published in *Popular Tales* (1805), the story illustrates the perils of procrastination through narrating the downfall of Basil Lowe, who puts "things off till to-morrow."[41] Having driven into the ground his father's London bookshop, Basil travels to Philadelphia to try his hand at bookselling in the "new world."[42] Through the advice one character offers about Basil's former profession, Edgeworth announces London's centrality to the book trade through the refracted lens of the American scene:

> [B]ookmaking or bookselling, brings in but poor profit in this country. The sale for imported books is extensive; and our printers are doing something by subscription here, in Philadelphia, and in New York, they tell me. But London is the place for a good bookseller to thrive; and you come from London, where you tell me you were a bankrupt. I would not advise you to have any thing more to do with bookselling or bookmaking.[43]

Edgeworth's mention of subscription alludes to the New York reprinting of *Practical Education* in 1801, an edition supported by many eminent subscribers, including John Adams, Joseph Dennie, Charles Willson Peale, Benjamin Rush, and Noah Webster.[44] Her description of the "poor profit" bookselling brings in Philadelphia describes more accurately the Dublin trade in the wake of the Union, but her character's blunt and suggestive comment applies to the trade as a whole: "London is the place for a good bookseller to thrive." This did not stop a number of Irish tradesmen from following her character's trajectory across the Atlantic. Patrick Byrne, a radical Irish bookseller, fared well after he moved to Philadelphia in 1800, publishing hundreds of books, including treatises on the law and literary texts by George Colman, Hugh Blair, William Godwin, and Monk Lewis.[45] Frank Ferguson writes of emigrations like Byrne's that they "bolster[ed] American publishing . . . to the detriment of the Irish trade."[46] But if we consider Ireland and the United States as participating in a single, transatlantic book trade, the migratory effects of the Act of Union appear as a net gain.

In the early nineteenth century, as Rosalind Remer has argued, book trades professionals in the United States transformed themselves from a group of unorganized printers and retail booksellers into leaders of a burgeoning, market-savvy publishing industry. Mathew Carey epitomized this shift as he abandoned his craft as a printer to focus exclusively on publishing and all the risks and strategy it required. This included selling a large stock of imported books and also issuing his own reprints of new London titles. The latter practice dominated publishing as a whole, since in the absence of copyright protection for British authors, reprinting was more profitable than financing new works by Americans. The busy and profitable reprint trade fostered cooperation between booksellers, laid the groundwork for distribution routes between regional markets, and transformed the book production into a "capitalistic and venture-oriented profession."[47] Reprinting made sense not only because Americans wanted cheap editions of British texts but also because patriotically minded consumers were satisfied with books of American manufacture, regardless of the nationality of authors.[48] An 1818 *Catalogue of Novels and Romances* issued by Carey's firm provides an image of the market in literary texts, featuring well over three hundred imprints from a diverse range of authors, including Edgeworth, Scott, Godwin, Jane Porter, Henry Fielding, Fanny Burney, Samuel Johnson, Charles Maturin, Amelia Opie, Tobias Smollett, Henry Mackenzie, Daniel Defoe, Anne Radcliffe, and Jane Austen.[49] While a few American authors are listed, including Hannah Webster Foster and Hugh Henry Brackenridge, the vast majority are British reprints, some of which are advertised alongside the same text in its more expensive, imported London edition. The catalogue demonstrates the vibrancy of the book trade and its offerings, richly confirming James N. Green's assessment of the period: "The rise of American publishing was one of the fruits of independence, but paradoxically the trade was built on a foundation of British books."[50]

That foundation eventually enabled reprinters to invest in publishing American authors like Washington Irving and James Fenimore Cooper, as William Charvat argued long ago, but it would be wrong to assess early U.S. publishing only in relation to a narrative of national development.[51] Scholars like Green have helpfully treated the period on its own terms, with a focus on the dynamics of transatlantic exchange and without shame about the book trade's persistent provinciality, which was ensured by the demand for British reprints, the continuing authority of the London trade, and a huge trade deficit in the exchange of books between Britain and the United States—a ratio of twenty to one in 1828.[52] In contrast to London's centralized publishing industry, early

U.S. book publishing was fractured and decentralized, and while there was trade across regional boundaries, there was no nationalized market for books that could act as a counterweight to London.[53] Nor could the apparent demographic advantages much affect this, even though the United States' highly literate population increased rapidly, from 60 percent of England's population in 1800 to almost equaling it by 1830.[54] In 1820, Boston publisher Samuel Goodrich estimated that about three-quarters of the books this growing population bought were of English origin.[55] The London-printed book retained its customary authority throughout the period, as Carey himself suggested in his 1834 autobiography. In seeking to defend himself from his old political enemy William Cobbett, Carey framed his disadvantage in a frustrated language of posterity: "All the abuse ever leveled at me by Cobbett is embalmed in 'Cobbett's works,' published in London in the year 1801, in twelve volumes, and will be read when I am dead and gone."[56]

The book trade in early nineteenth-century Scotland might be less easily described as provincial. The unparalleled influence of the *Edinburgh Review*, founded in 1802, which the *Quarterly Review* took as its model (founded in 1809, with an opposite political agenda); the success of *Blackwood's Edinburgh Magazine*, founded in 1817; and the rise of Walter Scott as "by far the most popular author of the romantic period" are all signs of the preeminence of the Scottish book trade.[57] Sizing up these developments, Ian Duncan writes that "Scottish publications and genres dominated a globalizing English-language market and made Edinburgh a literary metropolis to rival London."[58] At the heart of this were the publishers of the two major journals, Archibald Constable of the *Edinburgh* and William Blackwood of *Blackwood's*. The former's transformative role in the Edinburgh trade can be compared to Mathew Carey's in Philadelphia. Constable's innovations began with the *Edinburgh*, the first literary journal to pay authors handsomely for content; continued with new commitments to Scottish literature unseen in the eighteenth century, with Scott as his crowning achievement; and included strategies to reach a mass market for copyrighted books, including issuing Waverley novels in multiple formats at different prices.[59] The growth of the Scottish trade was grounded in its increased focus on local book production, the rise of its influential literary journals, and the development of an astonishing array of popular and respectable fiction, including works by Scott, Jane Porter, John Galt, James Hogg, Christian Johnstone, John Gibson Lockhart, Mary Brunton, Elizabeth Hamilton, and Susan Ferrier.

Yet inevitably, the Scottish book trade depended on its ties to England.

"For while London had to be resisted, it could not be ignored," writes Jane Millgate about the early nineteenth century. "Whatever the literary talents of Scottish authors or the energy and skill of Edinburgh booksellers, demographic realities dictated that the bulk of the market for British books was in England, accessible only through some form of alliance with the London trade."[60] While the market share of Scottish booksellers increasingly included northern England, the London trade still dominated book production, by one estimate issuing about 85 percent of new titles a year in the mid-1820s.[61] *Blackwood's* organized its list of new publications according to city and, in the magazine's first year, listed 870 titles from London compared with 151 from Edinburgh. Copublishing practices between Edinburgh and London firms were increasingly common, but while many publications listed Edinburgh and London publishers on title pages, including nearly all of Scott's work, the *Edinburgh*, and even the London-based *Quarterly*, London firms retained financial superiority over their northern partners. Furthermore, it was Scottish publishers who aggressively sought the cooperation of well-known London firms, not the reverse.[62] Longman's financial stake in the *Edinburgh* enabled the journal to pay its contributors, and at the end of 1807, Constable sent 5,000 of 7,000 total copies of a single issue to London for distribution.[63] Scottish authors and publishers watched the London market closely, as William Blackwood informed his London publishing partner, Thomas Cadell, in a letter about Lockhart's *Adam Blair* (1822). "Be so good as to write me every thing you hear as you have no idea how much an Author is interested in any London news with regard to his book."[64] And finally, while Walter Scott was among the most valued authors of his London publishers—a list that included at times Longman, John Murray, and Hurst, Robinson—it was also true that he benefited enormously from his association with them.

In the post-1801 period, London's importance registered differently around the Atlantic: in Ireland as the almost exclusive location for publishing, in the United States as the origin of texts for reprinting, in Scotland as the distribution center for books. But there it was, as readers of the Philadelphia-based *Analectic Magazine* would have been reminded in October 1813. "Miss Edgeworth had been in London," reported the magazine, "enjoying a round of gratifying attentions from the polite and literary society of that metropolis. She had returned to Ireland, leaving a new work in the hands of the booksellers."[65] In London, the publishing industry continued on its track of specialization and commodification as high prices remained the norm for new books, 31½ shillings for a triple-decker novel by 1821, more than two weeks' salary for a law clerk or skilled craftsman.[66] By the end of the 1830s, all of the most prominent houses claimed Irish, Scottish, or American authors on their lists of texts as publisher or co-publisher, including Longman, Murray, Cadell, Henry Colburn and Richard Bentley, Richard Phillips, Simpkin and Marshall, and Joseph Johnson's successors.[67] Once an author's reputation was established, these publishers paid quite well for provincial fiction. Henry Colburn gave Owenson £550 for the copyright to *O'Donnel* (1814) and £1,300 for *The O'Brien's and the O'Flaherty's* (1827);[68] Joseph Johnson's firm paid Edgeworth £1,050 for *Tales of Fashionable Life* (1812), £2,100 for *Patronage* (1814), and £1,150 for *Harrington* and *Ormond* (1817);[69] John Murray paid Irving 1,000 and 1,500 guineas, respectively, for *Bracebridge Hall* (1822) and *Tales of a Traveller* (1824);[70] John Murray offered to split the profits of *The Pioneers* (1823) with Cooper, who also received from Henry Colburn a modest but respectable £200 to £300 per novel in the late 1820s, £1,300 for two novels in 1830, and £50 each when he revised many of them in the 1830s.[71] While it remains difficult to gauge the financial impact of London partnership on fees paid by Edinburgh publishers, such fees were indeed comparable, including Susan Ferrier's £1,000 for *The Inheritance* (1824) and John Gibson Lockhart's 1,000 guineas for *Renigald Dalton* (1823), both delivered by Blackwood.[72] Walter Scott received the highest sums of all, mostly from Constable: £1,700 for *Rob Roy* (1817), £4,000 for *Tales of My Landlord, Second Series* (1818), £4,000 for *Ivanhoe* (1819), and £5,000, delivered directly from Longman in London, for both *The Monastery* (1820) and *The Abbott* (1820)[73]

The success of provincial literature came in waves, first the Irish national tale, then the Waverley novels and other Scottish texts in the 1810s, then Irving's and Cooper's works and a barrage of Irish, Scottish, and American texts throughout the 1820s. By the early 1830s, collected editions of provincial literature appeared in quick succession. Robert Cadell led the way by reissuing the Waverley novels at monthly intervals for six shillings per volume. This edition, revised and newly annotated by Scott and known as the *Magnum Opus*, inspired other multivolume editions that were marketed as its companions. Colburn confidently reissued a number of his old titles, including Banim's and Owenson's, under the banner heading "Irish National Tales," which promised to complement "the uniform collection of Sir Walter Scott's admirable Tales."[74] Baldwin and Cradock, by the 1830s proprietor of Edgeworth's work, issued a collected and revised edition of "Miss Edgeworth's Tales and Novels" "[t]o be published," as they advertised, "in Monthly Volumes, of the Size and Price of the Waverley Novels."[75] In 1831,

Colburn and his partner and successor, Richard Bentley, announced their "Standard Novels" with the same strategy—"printed uniformly with the Waverley Novels"[76]—and led the series with Cooper, by far its most frequently occurring author. In 1834, Bentley marketed Cooper's novels on their own as a special subset; one advertisement listed *The Bravo* with the rest of his works, all revised and corrected especially for the Standard Novels, and included this blurb from the *Quarterly*: "The Spy, Pilot, Pioneers, &c. may be classed with Waverley."[77] Provincial fiction was no longer breaking news; it was a staple of the book trade, and its success and viability was confirmed by this kind of repackaging in the 1830s.

*   *   *

By the 1850s, a parallel trend toward nationalization occurred in the United States and Great Britain that caused a binational model of literary competition to replace the center/periphery model that dominated earlier. There is broad scholarly consensus about the emergence roughly at mid-century of what Scott E. Casper has called the "national book trade system" in the United States, one enabled by improvements in transportation, communication, financial structures, and distribution.[78] This is partly reflected in the founding of a number of long-lasting periodicals that touted their national readership, including the *Tribune* (founded 1841), *Godey's Lady's Book* (a bit earlier, 1837), *Harper's New Monthly Magazine* (1850), *Harper's Weekly* (1856), and the *Atlantic Monthly* (1857)—some of which began paying for content in the 1840s.[79] It is also reflected in the unprecedented reception of two American novels in Britain, both published in unauthorized editions: *Uncle Tom's Cabin* (1852), which sold an astonishing 1.5 million copies in Britain in its first year, making it "probably the greatest short-term sale of any book published in nineteenth-century England,"[80] and *The Scarlet Letter* (1850), an instant success, the publication of which Henry James called "a literary event of the first importance."[81] It was in the late 1840s, too, when Putnam issued Irving's and Cooper's works in elaborate revised, illustrated, and collected editions for national readerships. Although an equal relationship between Britain and the United States was still far into the future, it could at this point be perceived on the horizon.

In these decades, the Edinburgh and London trades integrated more fully than ever before, thus approaching what we could call a thoroughly British publishing industry. As Bill Bell argues, this occurred at the level of manufacturing:

By the middle of the nineteenth century, it had become increasingly difficult to speak in terms of a separate Scottish book trade, not only because of the permeation of the London trade by Scots, but because printers and publishers throughout Britain were coming to compete for the same expanding market. Scottish firms would soon dominate large-scale printing in particular, providing vast quantities of sheets for Britain's publishers until the middle of the twentieth century.[82]

Bell notes that British-ization can also be located at the level of author-publisher relations: "[T]his was a period in which English authors just as often found themselves at the behest of Scottish publishers."[83] The most significant example of this was Blackwood's, which opened a London satellite office in 1840 and became the publisher of English authors like Edward Bulwer-Lytton, George Eliot, and Anthony Trollope.[84] The same period witnessed the growth of an "indigenous Irish publishing industry" that further balanced the literary field in the British Isles.[85]

In the early nineteenth century, provincial booksellers navigated a dynamic transatlantic trade while enduring material and economic subservience to London. A few decades later, American and British publishers competed with each other in an increasingly binarized marketplace. When, precisely, full equalization between American and British publishing was achieved is beyond the scope of this study, but the establishment of an international copyright law in 1891 gestured toward an era of balance. In the twentieth century, New York City—buoyed by the kind of demographic and economic advantages London claimed two centuries earlier—eventually came to dominate the global English-language book trade, although to this day British and American publishers depend on each other for joint ventures. The twentieth-century shift from London to New York coincided with the rise of American global hegemony after World War II, when the British Empire began finally to wane. The interesting question remains, of course, of what status traditional publishing centers like London and New York will have as digital media continue to challenge and destabilize the geographies of literary production.[86]

Chapter 2

Furious Booksellers and the
"American Copy" of the Waverley Novels

The London book trade appears most interesting from the perspective of provincial publishers who tried to reach its marketplace, both to acquire books and eventually to sell their own. London was the teeming hub of their trade, an intense stage of fierce competition, and a high-stakes arena for professional maneuvering, especially for the trade in new, copyrighted literary texts. Nowhere was this more evident than with Scott's wildly popular novels, which tested the ingenuity of book trades professionals around the Anglophone Atlantic. The centripetal pull of the London marketplace catalyzed an important relationship in the early 1820s between Archibald Constable, Scott's Edinburgh publisher, and Mathew Carey of Philadelphia, his most important publisher in the United States. As noted in the previous chapter, the Waverley novels were printed in Edinburgh, but the majority of them were sold in London, where they reached their largest and most lucrative audience. For Mathew Carey and his son and partner, Henry, the city remained the distribution center of most books American publishers wanted to reprint—even those, like Scott's, that were issued first in Edinburgh.[1] The strategies Constable and his junior partner, Robert Cadell, pursued in dealing with London directly affected Carey's ability to reprint Scott during the hectic years when the demand for the Waverley novels overwhelmed literary publishers in the United States.[2] Meanwhile, the Careys' strategies as reprinters of Scott proved of concrete importance in Edinburgh as Constable and Cadell used them to their own advantage. The frenzy over Scott's novels put Carey's and Constable's firms into a direct relationship that circumvented London and proved mutually beneficial; it was forged through an intense conflict over transatlantic circulation.

Though marked by definite inequality—Scott belonged to Constable, after all, not Carey—the two provincial publishers became allies in the literary field. This alliance was in many ways exceptional, given Scott's unmatched popularity, but it remains instructive for the way it highlights London's importance in the book trade as a whole. "I am highly pleased with the communication respecting the Author of Waverley," one of Scott's London publishers, Joseph Robinson, wrote to Constable in 1825, about the latest novel, "and no doubt the work must be highly interesting to every individual in every corner of the Globe. However England is the great place for the sale of the Work to produce Profit for the Proprietors and therefore the mode of publication requires great Consideration."[3] In what follows, I provide a new story about such "mode[s] of publication," both from the perspective of this conceited metropolitan and the provincial booksellers who worked so hard to get around him.

Bringing Scott to market was a heated emotional drama with many acts: Constable's attempts to reach English readers, the difficulties Mathew and Henry Carey faced in cornering the American market, the epistolary exchange that brought the younger partners Henry Carey and Robert Cadell together as associates, angry disputes in American newspapers over errors in Carey's hastily produced Scott editions, and furious debates in Edinburgh and London over the transmission of the "American Copy" of the Waverley novels. The story concludes in 1831 when an anomalous episode involving the "American Copy" led Scott to represent the process of transatlantic reprinting in the extraordinary preface he wrote for his last novels, the fourth series of *Tales of My Landlord*.[4] The actors in this drama were a writerly and bookish crew, and I argue throughout that the language of the book trade is as interesting as it was important—as an expressive form, a means of establishing credit in business negotiations, a performative rhetoric of the marketplace, and, for Scott, an inspiring discourse for fiction. Michael Everton has recently argued that the business of publishing in the nineteenth century involved intense negotiations over morality, character, and ethics.[5] The negotiations over Scott's "American Copy" confirm this view and suggest that the book trade can only be understood by analyzing the language used to constitute it. My account also demonstrates the importance of the extralegal arrangements that governed the trade and to which scholars like Everton, Robert Spoo, and Melissa Homestead have recently turned.[6] Such informal codes, known as "courtesy of the trade," were especially important in the transatlantic marketplace for books because there were no accepted legal frameworks to guide production. The story of Carey, Constable, and Scott epitomizes the way that improvisation and custom affected transatlantic publishing. It also suggests that the American demand for Scott was far more important to his publishers than scholars have ever realized.

Early Trouble with the "American Copy"

Throughout Walter Scott's career, reckless capital investments soaked up the profits from his busy pen, as he underwrote his Edinburgh printer, James Ballantyne; encouraged costly publishing ventures; and built his vast medieval castle at Abbotsford. Such investments and entanglements made Scott, Constable, and Ballantyne vulnerable to the fluctuations of the market, factors that led to bankruptcy of the Waverley machine in 1826. Even at the height of his popularity, Scott could be short on cash, as was the case in the summer of 1819, when unforeseen delays in the publication of *Ivanhoe* (1819) and the receipt of its profits led Scott to go behind Constable's back and seek revenue elsewhere. The delay with *Ivanhoe* had to do with various complications, including difficulties with paper supply and arrangements with its London publisher. It was eventually published in late December 1819 by Constable and his joint partners Hurst, Robinson, a new firm that Constable helped establish in London in an effort to control the distribution of his books in England. Such efforts included a huge trade sale Constable orchestrated in London in November 1819, which featured the advance sale of *Ivanhoe* and the launch of the collected series *The Novels and Tales of the Author of Waverley*. Too impatient to wait for this, however, in August, Scott promised and sold the next two Waverley novels directly to Longman, who had been the partner in some of Scott's previous productions but with whom Constable had considerable difficulties. Constable was still to be the Edinburgh publisher of these next novels, *The Monastery* and *The Abbot*, but the London firm got top billing on their title pages as Scott pulled in "£5000 in Longmans beautiful and dutiful bills," as he wrote with apparent relief to Ballantyne.[7] This paid his debts in 1819, even though similar measures could not stave off the bigger crisis years later.[8]

Longman could provide money for Scott; for Mathew Carey, in Philadelphia, the firm could provide books. Carey's pioneering work in reprinting grew in the late 1810s with the increased involvement of Henry, who became his father's official partner in 1817. The Careys sought out pecuniary relationships with London publishers to ensure the speedy delivery of new books by familiar authors who were already market tested in the United States. The direct shipment of new books helped them preempt the publication of the same books by rival printers in New York and Philadelphia. About a year before Carey published his extensive catalogue of "Novels and Romances" (discussed in the previous chapter), Henry wrote to Longman with this proposal:

> We are very desirous to make some arrangement by which we
> should receive such new works that come out as may be likely to
> bear publication in this country. If you can make any such arrange-
> ments for us we will allow Two hundred fifty dollars per annum. . . .
> Our booksellers are so very active that it would require very
> considerable attention to forward them by first and fastest sailing
> vessels. We should wish to receive every new work of popularity and
> particularly those of Miss Porter, Lord Byron, Miss Edgeworth, W.
> Scott, Leigh Hunt, Author of Waverley, Moore, Miss Burney, Mrs.
> Taylor, Lady Morgan, Dugald Stuart, etc. etc.[9]

This list of desirable authors reveals much about American literary taste, not least through the irony of listing Scott twice, as himself and the anonymous "Author of Waverley." In response to this request, Longman recommended they employ John Miller to acquire and deliver books. Miller became the London agent to Carey's house, a role he sustained through the 1820s, even as he shepherded many American texts into transatlantic editions, including the first, self-financed volume of *The Sketch Book* as well as fiction by Catherine Maria Sedgwick and James Fenimore Cooper. Miller shipped Carey new works as soon as they were available in the metropolis. The scene in London could be especially hectic as the latest Waverley novel arrived from Edinburgh. "The Smack Ocean, by which the new work was shipped, arrived at the wharf on Sunday," Constable wrote to Scott about the delivery of *The Fortunes of Nigel* in 1822; "the bales were got out by *one* Monday morning, and before halfpast ten o'clock 7000 copies had been dispersed."[10]

In the United States, the demand for Scott was just as intense, and even a twenty-four-hour advantage could result in enormous profits for the reprinter who published first. This led the Careys to pursue more innovative measures than their arrangement with Miller: the purchase of advance sheets of Waverley novels, sometimes in proofs, before official publication. The first Scott novel to be received in Philadelphia early was *Rob Roy* (1817), dispatched in December 1817, eight months after Carey wrote to Longman with his initial proposal. The exact circumstances of the transatlantic sale of *Rob Roy* are unknown, but the dynamics of the London book trade made it possible. The advance copy of *Rob Roy* became available for transatlantic purchase as part of a deal Constable made with Hurst, Robinson to purchase his overstocked books and distribute them in London and overseas, including America. Such stock included the *Edinburgh Annual Register*, which Constable suggested they print "for the American market and say edited by Walter Scott, Esq—which is actually the fact."[11] The American demand for imported books clearly helped Constable: the potential profits from their sale provided him with leverage when he was making the distribution deal with Hurst, Robinson. This was the case with *Rob Roy*, which Constable offered them as an incentive for purchasing more than 1,200 copies of the *Encyclopaedia Britannica* meant for the London market. Hurst, Robinson found a buyer in Thomas Wardle, an American living in London, who, like John Miller, acted as an agent for American publishers; Wardle then sold *Rob Roy* to a bookseller in Philadelphia, probably Mathew Carey.[12]

Hurst, Robinson's claim on these advance sheets was not, however, secure, and neither was Carey's. In 1819, Constable received multiple offers from American publishers for *Tales of My Landlord, Third Series* (1819), and he leveraged such offers while dealing with Hurst, Robinson. In February 1819, Constable wrote to them, "We have had a good offer from Philadelphia for an early copy of this work—& you have not said what you will give for it."[13] In March he declared, "We have offers of £50 for an early copy from 3 different quarters, and having so many expenses attending business we really cannot afford to make your American agent a present of this work as we did the last."[14] It is not clear if Hurst, Robinson ended up purchasing these sheets, but it is clear Carey did not obtain them. *Tales of My Landlord, Third Series* was published first by Moses Thomas of Philadelphia and J. Haly & C. Thomas of New York, who declared in an advertisement that "the copy from which the present edition is printed, was sent from Edinburgh previous to the publication of the work there."[15] Advance sheets were apparently up for grabs.

Hurst, Robinson hurried and soon acquired *Ivanhoe* for their agent, Wardle, who sold it to Mathew Carey. By then, the Edinburgh publishers had a new term for advance sheets—the "American Copy," as Cadell put it in numerous letters to Constable.[16] The practice of transmitting sheets via Hurst, Robinson and Wardle continued with *The Monastery, The Abbot, Kenilworth* (1821), *The Pirate* (1821), and *The Fortunes of Nigel* (1822). Each volume was shipped as soon as it was printed. Carey could therefore expect the three volumes of a single work to arrive on separate ships, sometimes over the course of a few weeks or months, and he printed each volume as it arrived. Beginning

with *Kenilworth*, Carey previewed each new Waverley novel in the Philadelphia paper *The National Gazette* by printing excerpts when he received the
first shipment. As insurance while dealing with Wardle, Carey continued to
instruct John Miller to send complete copies of the novels from London when
they were published. In a few cases, the arrival of Miller's copy proved crucial,
since the arrangement with Wardle was tenuous and sometimes unreliable.[17]

A direct agreement between Carey's and Constable's firms emerged out of
a heated dispute in 1822 between the two junior partners, Henry Carey and
Robert Cadell, over this indirect process of acquisition. These junior partners
were far more interested in exploring the transatlantic arrangements than their
seniors. In 1817, Cadell wrote with great optimism to Constable about selling
books in America, and in 1822, he declared that "with good management we
may get a good thing from America—the Pirate has set them all at us."[18] The
epistolary exchange that established the agreement is more significant than
David Kaser, its only other commentator, suggested when he considered it
half a century ago.[19] Not only did it bring the firms together, as Kaser notes,
but it also reveals dynamics and frustrations endemic to provincial publishing,
as London remained a problem and professional alliances proved both allur-
ing and troublesome. In the letters, the younger Carey and Cadell exhibited a
fascinating combination of hostility and desire. The demand for Scott's novels
lent urgency to the matter, while the lack of copyright regulations meant that
honor, courtesy, and pride provided the rules of conduct.

In the spring of 1822, Constable and Cadell heard a rumor, eventually
proved false, that a reprinter in Philadelphia was purchasing advance sheets of
the Waverley novels from a thief in the Ballantyne printing house. On April
27, Cadell wrote to Carey & Sons accusing them of this illegitimate method of
acquisition, suggesting it had not occurred to him that they could have been
the beneficiaries of Hurst, Robinson's connections with Wardle. Cadell's letter
is remarkably harsh in its tone and presumption of guilt:

> We now address you in consequence of being put in possession of
> information, that you have for some years, and are now, in the way
> of procuring the sheets of the new works published by us from the
> pen of the Author of Waverly [*sic*], through the means of some one
> of the workmen in the Printing Office where the productions of
> that Author are printed.
>
> It may at present be sufficient to state, that we have taken
> means to put a stop to so irregular a proceeding, and if you suffer

any disappointment in the matter, it will mainly arise from the
course you have pursued being one of great uncertainty, to say
nothing of the gross want of honesty in the person so transmitting
early copies of the sheets to you.[20]

Although it was the thief in the shop whom Cadell accused of "gross" dishonesty, the insult overflowed onto Carey himself, embroiled as he allegedly was in
such an "irregular" proceeding. Cadell's arrogance is manifest in his certainty
of Carey's guilt, his own ability to "put a stop" to the crime, and the implicit
lesson he wished to teach the American about how to behave like a gentleman
bookseller. His anger derived not only from the apparent violation of Ballantyne's printing office—still closely guarded to protect Scott's anonymity—but,
as quickly becomes clear, from the injustice of missing out on the transaction.
He questioned not the propriety of Carey's procuring advance sheets, just his
supposed method of acquisition. Cadell wanted the money himself: "[We]
have no objections to treat with you or any respectable house for the privilege
of any early dispatch we make of the sheets of any work of this author; there
will be many more productions from the same pen, and if it is any object to
you to have the early possession of such works surely it is to you greatly more
certain to transact direct with the proprietors than through any disrespectable
channel, but perhaps you are not aware of the source from which you procure
the sheets being irregular."[21] The concession he made at the end of this passage
merely trades the presumption of dishonesty for one of ignorance and does
little to mitigate the accusation that Carey was flouting common courtesies of
the trade. In the absence of an actionable legal offence, Cadell reasserted his
firm's ownership of the Waverley novels and resorted to shame as a disciplinary tactic.

In the rest of the letter, he suggested that Carey purchase the sheets from
him, an ironic move given his disdain for Carey's supposed methods. Cadell
reported that he initially heard about the stolen sheets from a publisher in
Baltimore who had written to him about the rumor and offered to purchase
subsequent sheets himself. Cadell passed over the request from Baltimore and
offered the deal instead to the offensive Philadelphians, whose enterprising negotiation of the marketplace Cadell seemed, despite himself, to admire. "[I]f as
that letter [from Baltimore] states you have successfully brought out many of
these books in succession," he wrote, "we think there is a better chance of your
understanding the matter than any person in a great degree unacquainted
with it"; should they come to terms, he could "forward any portion of any new

work."[22] It was precisely within the apparent irregularity of Carey's practices that Cadell found evidence of his competency. In showing his own preference for the experienced Philadelphia firm, furthermore, Cadell betrayed his firm's own preference—quite outside economic motivations—that the Waverley novels receive a "respectable" edition in the United States.

Upon receipt of this letter, Henry Carey was immediately concerned with defending his firm (now H. Carey & Lea), a simple task given the facts of the case but also an urgent one given the great potential of establishing a new relationship with Edinburgh. The letter he wrote in response, addressed to Archibald Constable, gave a full explanation of his actual practice, including the amount he paid Wardle for each novel, though he did not name Hurst, Robinson in order to avoid "any difficulty between you and them." The letter is notable for both offended pride and solicitation. The backhanded preference Constable & Company showed for Carey over the gossipy Baltimore firm may have been an additional provocation over and above his actual innocence:

> Had you known us at the time you wrote that letter we presume
> you would not have thrown out the ideas it contains with regard to
> our obtaining the books in the manner you speak of. Where we are
> known we do not imagine any such charge could be thought of as
> we have endeavored to conduct our business with as much regard
> to correctness as any house in this Country. Messr Longman &
> Co—Mr Miller . . . are our correspondents in London, to them you
> may refer for any information that you may desire respecting us. We
> mention these names from a desire that the impression you have
> received may be effaced. Had such a charge come from any person
> who had an opportunity of knowing us, we should hardly have
> considered it entitled to refutation.[23]

Carey's frustration is palpable in the repeated invocation of his firm's obscurity ("Had you known us," and so on). As Everton has written, "The rank of a printer or publisher depended on his character and reputation in trade."[24] Such a reputation was not easily acquired across the Atlantic. Of course, Carey was disingenuous to claim that Constable's ignorance was the only reason he deigned to refute this charge. The stakes were quite high, as a direct arrangement with Constable & Company could finally give him the real advantage he wanted in the reprint market and also solve continuing difficulties with his indirect London connection.

However disguised, the high stakes are revealed in the measures Carey took to vindicate his honor, including the invocation of his London agents, the detailed account of his dealings with Wardle, and his defense of the anonymous party Hurst, Robinson, who Carey well knew were Constable's London partners: "Were we to mention the name of the house by which [the sheets] have been furnished you would be astounded to hear that such a house would be guilty of such conduct." "For ourselves," Carey continued, "we feel perfectly free from the slightest impropriety in the transaction & we presume you will be convinced of the same & regret having charged us as you have done." He was confident enough to call a witness on his own behalf to turn the tables on the Edinburgh publisher, who now played the fool: "Since the receipt of your letter this morning we have seen the agent [Wardle] & he informs us that when he was last in London, one Vol of one of the works was rec'd & the head of the house assured him that it had that morning been put into his hands by *Mr Constable himself*."[25] The arch tone was clearly a method, in itself, of earning credit in the eyes of his opponent; Carey's honor was defined through its capacity to be thoroughly offended.

Carey also proved as capable as Robert Cadell in making a proposal couched in condescension and negativity. He aimed low in his offer for future novels, as anyone might while negotiating a price, but he emphasized over and over again that advance sheets might be less valuable than Constable & Company would wish. For most of the novels, he paid either $100 or $200, Carey wrote, and he added that "from these prices you may judge the value of the copies here," even, as he said, "where the agent has the opportunity of making arrangements with any or all the Booksellers in the country." Without a middleman, they might command an even lower sum, since in the current arrangement, agent and supplier split the profits. As Carey pointedly phrased it, "We could not believe that a house engaged in so large a business as they [Hurst, Robinson] would be guilty of so much rascality for the thrifty compensation they receive." The implication was that such a cheap bundle wouldn't even be worth stealing. In this context, his actual offer appears generous: "We are willing to pay fifty five pounds (about $250) for the first Copy of his future works." Although this is more than twice what they paid for *Ivanhoe*, Carey felt it necessary to explain his low bid even further by mentioning that the swift arrival of the published books would erase the advantage of advance sheets, since in such cases, any bookseller "is sure of having the opportunity of taking part of an edition at cost of paper & print in less than 5 days after us."[26] Throughout the letter, Carey seemed as interested in explaining the demand structure of the American book trade as he was in introducing himself as an honorable tradesman. In doing so, he allowed a hint of condescension, as if to assure the Edinburgh publisher that if he wanted to profit from content that would otherwise be free, he must know whereof he spoke.

The establishment of this relationship was more urgent in Philadelphia than in Edinburgh because Carey depended much more on profits from Scott's novels than Constable did on fees from America. But in Edinburgh, Cadell was determined to take as much advantage of the American demand for Scott as he could. In investigating the supposed breach of Ballantyne's printing office, he sent an inquiry to Hurst, Robinson, in a move that suggests he had not quite forgotten their claim on advance sheets. He soon received a satisfying reply, and the day after he wrote to Philadelphia, he wrote to Constable with an update on the matter. In this letter, Cadell gloated about the international demand for Scott's novels, declared his own optimism about profit, and indicated his desire to circumvent the London trade:

> I have today a letter from [Joseph] Robinson, very reasonable, about the American Copies—the fact is he must be so, as we are at this moment in correspondence with Baltimore, Philadelphia, and New York on the same subject—R. alludes to arrangements for the Continent—I already stated to you that I have made a German arrangement—and I would suggest that whoever calls on R. should be referred to this, as we may get into confusion, and there is no occasion for any London commission on such matters—we are the managers and patrons of the books, have all the risks of Author and his connections and must make hay while the sun shines—I have no hesitation in saying if we manage these works with attention we will make £1000 extra on each.[27]

It is unclear how Cadell could imagine making £1,000 on the kind of novel he had hitherto sold for only about £75, even with the Continent as a potential foreign market. What is clear is both his commitment to selling Scott's books in unprotected markets and his palpable desire to take London out of the equation. As for Constable, he was more concerned with problems closer to home, namely, at Ballantyne's. "The waste, thieving, and destruction during the last 18 years has been enormous," he wrote to Cadell, in an immediate reply that presumed the printer's guilt. "It would almost be worth our while to pay a warehouseman to superintend our property in the printing office. A

severe example ought to be made of some of them."[28] The transmission of the
"American Copies" had always been handled with care, for fear they would
be leaked to the press during a long, circuitous, and secret journey through
the hands of various agents in Edinburgh, London, and Philadelphia. Writing
to Hurst, Robinson regarding *The Monastery*, for example, Cadell cautioned,
"We send you with this under a sealed cover Vol 1st of the M[onastery], which
you may wish to send across the Atlantic but the parcel must on no account be
opened."[29] Transmitting sheets this way was a confidential business, containing equal parts profit and paranoia.

Furious Booksellers

Back in Philadelphia, as Carey waited for Constable to reply to his self-
vindication, problems resulting from his arrangement with Wardle and Hurst,
Robinson caused glaring errors in editions of the two latest novels, *The Pirate*
and *The Fortunes of Nigel*, which Carey issued, respectively, in February and
July 1822. Because of changes made in Edinburgh after the shipment of the
"American Copy," *The Pirate* was missing a chapter and *Nigel* a preface—
discrepancies that infuriated booksellers all over the Eastern Seaboard. Carey
distributed the missing chapter of *The Pirate* on its own, and he belatedly
printed the preface to *Nigel* in the second volume.[30] The ensuing outcry meant
that Carey had to publicly explain embarrassing errors while he was appealing
to the firm that had it in its power to prevent them. In late July, a sarcastic
screed in the *Boston Daily Advertiser* complained about Carey's editions, setting off a short dispute that illustrates just how *un*courteous the reprint trade
could be. The dispute brought the language of the book trade to the fore-
ground, as the different parties argued about transatlantic reprinting and its
effect on the integrity of texts.

The Boston complaint illustrates that, like Constable, its writer had heard
his own rumors about Carey's London connection:

> [We] have had the misfortune to see a copy of the Philadelphia
> edition [of *The Fortunes of Nigel*], in which *the whole introductory
> chapter is omitted*. This Philadelphia edition is from the same press
> that also gave us the *Pirate* without a chapter. . . . These enterprising
> publishers are said to have an agent in England, who forwards them
> the new productions, in sheets, as they come from the press. When

it is about time for the whole work to reach the hands of other
American booksellers, the publishers of these Philadelphia editions,
it seems, reprint what sheets they have received, more or less, and
if a very characteristic introduction has not yet come to hand, or a
chapter is wanting in the middle, why it only increases the interest of the story, and, in the course of the season, the missing sheets
will arrive—be reprinted—and sent (wonderfully liberally) *gratis*, to
those who have bought the book. . . . We should not be surprised if
these Philadelphia editions should rival the renowned *Irish* pirated
editions abroad.[31]

The Boston paper ridiculed Carey for unacceptable results and for his pre-
tentious attempt to achieve insider status among English booksellers—just
the kind of fool's errand an "Irish" printer might pursue. In thus insulting
Irish editions, the Boston paper invoked Mathew Carey's well-known national
origins and belittled reprinting as a practice despite the writer's obvious desire that it prove effective. In this notice, authority resides in Britain, where
the "whole work" was issued in complete and unadulterated form. Through
fashioning excuses for the error in an ironic language of aesthetic pleasure ("it
only increases the interest of the story"), the complaint located Carey's highest offense in the destruction of the work's unity. The "missing sheets" were
the sign for the breakdown of the text as well as Carey's commitment to its
cultural value.

Henry Carey's use of advance sheets proved more difficult to defend than
the means he used to acquire them. His reply, printed in the *National Gazette*
and reprinted in the Boston paper, included a defense of his father's native
land—"the same as Montgomery and Emmet," but his excuses only confirmed the unreliability of his practice and, worse, tried to fashion his blatant
commercial strategy as a public service. Volume 1 of *The Pirate*, he explained,
"had the appearance of being complete," but after examining "another English copy," it was revealed "the author had *added* a chapter." Regarding *The
Fortunes of Nigel*, he said that they rushed to distribute its first volume "to
guard against the edition, which . . . would be published in New York, immediately upon the receipt of the London copy," but then he "found, upon receiving the remainder of the work, that there was an introduction," and so he
inserted it in volume 2. He attributed all this to "a desire to benefit the public," to "enable us *early* to lay before them the most interesting of the English
publications," and he trumpeted "the pains we have taken and the expense

we have incurred" to make this possible. Against all evidence to the contrary, but perhaps because of the Boston writer's sarcasm, Carey implied the attack derived from envy about a London connection—as if it had done any good. "We trust it is not necessary to contend with an enemy who thus, without a name, shoots his poisoned arrows from his ambush, and would wound us even unto death for no other avowed reason than because we 'have an Agent in England' who forwards us 'the new publications, in sheets, as they come from the press,' to the end that we may as early as possible, gratify and inform our fellow countrymen."[32] Carey presumed his customers wanted to be up to speed with the literary scene in England. He tried to deflect the controversy by trading one temporality for another: the time pressure of the fierce reprint trade—where one day can make the difference—for a broader temporal context that bridged the Atlantic. The *National Gazette* reinforced this broader temporality in a note appended to Carey's defense that also avoided the issue of the edition's actual integrity: "What could be more absurd and unjust, than to arraign them for their exertions to supply the American public with the new productions of the British literati, as early almost as the readers of London are supplied."[33] The provinciality of the American literary field is reflected in this entire exchange not merely through the evident demand for British literature but more profoundly by the continual invocation of London and England as the center of literary commerce and the location that governed literary time.

Not long after this domestic controversy, Carey received a letter from Constable's firm that must have been extremely welcome. His self-defense was a resounding success, at least in establishing the facts about the "stolen" sheets. Indeed, the idea of a thief in Ballantyne's print shop was pure fiction, and all parties were soon exonerated. "[W]e have no doubt the fault is on this side of the water," Robert Cadell conceded, on behalf of Constable, suggesting too that Carey's reply was successful because of its combative style: "[We] assure you, after such a letter it would ill become us to testify any other feeling than respect for the writers of it. The tone of candour throughout cannot fail to draw forth these feelings—and we hope we may have from time to time the pleasure of your correspondence."[34] Even though flattery is standard on the occasion of an apology, in calling this "pleasure," Cadell was clearly working hard to control the damage incurred by thus annoying his new associate. He may also have been motivated by a desire to vindicate his employer, Constable, whose authority Carey invoked in his earlier letter. "[O]ur Mr. Constable has been, from bad health unable to attend to business for 18 months past," Cadell informed Carey, in perhaps a slight admission of his own guilt in mismanaging the situation.[35] Indeed, only a few days earlier, Constable had written to Cadell with some bewilderment about their American connections: "I have many applications for copies to send abroad, of Peveril of the Peak, but being ignorant of the arrangements that have been made, am prevented from giving even a satisfactory answer."[36] America was clearly Cadell's territory, not Constable's, and he further sought to smooth things over by providing a document certifying Wardle's purchase of the novels since *Ivanhoe*. Wardle traveled all the way to London to secure this confirmation, even though his services as a middleman were no longer required.[37]

Though it was relatively straightforward to resolve the dispute over courtesy and honor, the negotiation over pricing proved more difficult, since Cadell lost no time in claiming his firm's advantage as proprietor. In this perhaps he was encouraged by two new offers from America to pay for advance sheets, which he received from Thomas Dobson and W. G. Gilley at the height of Carey's problems with *The Pirate* and *Nigel*.[38] In his defensive reply, Carey had labored to demonstrate the generosity of offering £55 per volume, but in London, John Miller was unable to secure less than £75, or £25 per volume, for the next novel, *Peveril of the Peak* (1823). "I could not make a better bargain with Constable & Co.," Miller wrote; "they would not give way in the slightest degree."[39] Carey agreed to this, but *Peveril*, like the last novels, also proved difficult: Scott wrote an extra volume and Constable insisted on the increased price of £100. This made Carey furious but to no avail. "We think the demands of Messrs. Constable as improper as any we have known," he wrote to Miller, but still had little choice: "we hope," he continued, "that you have made some arrangements with them; as it would be in the highest degree vexatious to us to be delayed."[40] Though Carey desired that the novels be sent through Liverpool, subsequent novels were still sent through London, a task managed most often by Miller, acting as the Careys' agent.[41]

The distribution of the next novel, *Quentin Durward* (1823), caused trouble on both sides of the Atlantic. Scott's eleventh-hour addition of a postscript gave Carey the unwelcome task of defending himself yet again in the *National Gazette*, where he printed the extra text. On this occasion, Carey revealed his new, direct, and costly arrangement with Constable; confidently attributed any faults of his edition to its source, which, now identifiable, was beyond reproach; and emphasized, once again, that his service to the public resided not in shutting out his own competition but in narrowing the transatlantic time delay:

The American publishers of Quentin Durward have this day received advice from Edinburgh, that a small addition . . . has been
made to the work subsequently to the dispatch of their copy. Having paid Messrs. Constable & Co. a large sum to have the volumes
forwarded several days previous to their appearance in London,
those gentlemen were pledged to furnish them complete; and their
high standing in society warrants the belief that they had no idea of
an addition. . . . Under their present arrangement with the publishers, nothing but so extraordinary a circumstance as the present,
could have caused such an error. They hope it will be received as
an apology for the omission, that the work was published here in
twenty-two days after the day fixed for publication in England, and
that no copy except their's [*sic*] has yet been received in this country,
nor will probably be received for eight or ten days, although published in this city a week since.[42]

In trumpeting their "present arrangement," Carey insisted that his circumstances were more reliable than before, even though they still resulted in an
incomplete edition. Once again, he trusted that ample compensation for the
error lay in his publication of the novel more than a week earlier than would
have been possible without the "large sum" he sacrificed for the occasion.

Back in Edinburgh, an episode also involving *Quentin Durward* demonstrated that great anxiety surrounded the "American Copy" and its transmission. In London, a magazine got its hands on an early copy of the novel and
printed copious extracts before it was officially published. Constable and Cadell, furious at the scoop, assumed—wrongly, it turned out—that the "American Copy" was the source of the extracts and shot off a number of accusatory
letters. Constable immediately blamed the Careys' agent for the leak: "Miller's
conduct is most disgraceful," he wrote to Cadell, "and I now say must be pun-
ished."[43] Meanwhile, in a tense correspondence with Cadell, Joseph Robinson,
whose firm was formerly the trustee of the "American Copy," saw fit to vent
his feelings about the new arrangement between Constable and the Careys
and cast a number of aspersions on Miller, now his rival, who was often in financial trouble and, according to Robinson, was not to be trusted. This clearly
wasn't just about the money. Robinson was indignant:

I think you might in great fairness have *continued* to give us the
[copy] for America at all events it should not have been sent to

a London Booksr (*3 times a Bankrupt*). I confess I felt hurt some
weeks ago when told in confidence by a particular friend that he
had seen part of Q. D. in the hands of your *Confidential Booksellers
& Foreign agents*. . . . I will not say all I feel on this head but I think
if any Bookseller in London was to be trusted with these sheets it
might have been the individual who *has been trusted* and confided in
on *many* important matters both of business and personal interest.[44]

The "American Copy" had become a sign of intimacy between booksellers.
This was because of the risk of sending the sheets, in vulnerable packages,
through London—a metropolis teeming with eager printers and thousands
of readers desperate for Scott's novels. Perhaps Robinson, at that time an established London bookseller, can't be blamed for reproaching Cadell's trust in
a bunch of Americans. Such scolding apparently was not enough, however.
Robinson added a postscript to this letter threatening to complain to Scott
himself, by way of Ballantyne. The comments were added quickly, later that
night, and written crosswise on the page: "I feel so much hurt about the confidence you have given to Miller & refused to me that I return home this evening not fully decided as to the propriety of my writing or not to the authors
agent [Ballantyne] to refer him to you to be informed who it is that violated
his engagement. We are the sufferers but you are the sinners."[45] (See figure
1.) As was true of the earlier dispute between Carey and Cadell, a number of
nonquantifiable values were at stake, including trust, confidence, and honor.

Robinson's accusation predictably failed to defuse any tension among this
emotional bunch. "Robinson has no right to assume the tone he does," Cadell
wrote to Constable: "what right has he to sulk."[46] Soon Robinson made good
on his threat of writing to Ballantyne, and Cadell, writing to Constable, basi-
cally lost it:

I cannot but feel much incensed at Robinson's conduct . . . now, I
do say, that Robinson, *our agent*—without any share in the book—
without having concern with the contracts—or the author, or
the risk—or the advance—to have the impertinence to write to
Ballantyne *accusing us* is not to be borne—I say it is a piece of high
impudence & effrontery. . . . I cannot get over Robinson . . . all I
can say is this[:] that I will not be able to submit to it. That we who
have large advances—insurances—risks &c to make for the greatest
living author are to be brow beaten by one London Commission

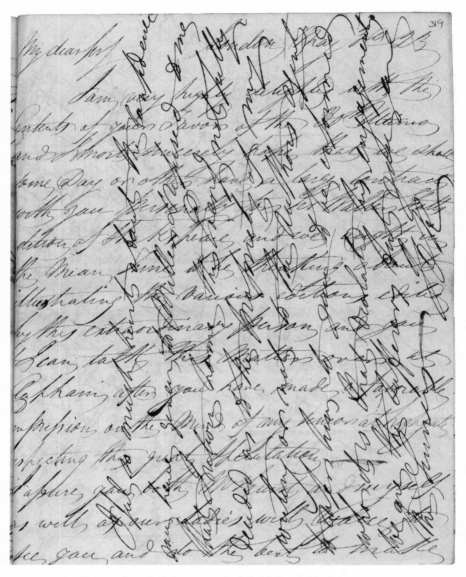

Figure 1. Joseph Robinson to Archibald Constable, May 3, 1823.

agent—who only this week before had any right to the book at all—you will be assailed with noise and uproars.[47]

Cadell's fury was directed straight toward London, where Scott's books were mostly sold, and where, as Robinson well knew, most of the money was. The fault with *Quentin Durward* lay, in the end, in an unexpected quarter—with a dramatist who had been given a copy to write a theatrical adaptation.[48] As his booksellers raged and tattled, Scott himself kept his cool. "I think you are right to be satisfied with an apology," he wrote to Constable, and—no doubt pleased with the offenders—he later added, "Do not be hard on them."[49]

Scott and the Romance of Transatlantic Reprinting

Toward the end of Scott's life, another scoop in the London press—this time actually traceable to the "American Copy"—brought the transatlantic book trade straight into the realm of fiction, in Scott's last work, the fourth series of the *Tales of My Landlord* (1831), which contained both *Count Robert of Paris* and *Castle Dangerous*. In a fascinating reversal of usual practice, the American reprint of this text appeared before the original. Delays in Edinburgh meant that Carey excerpted the first volume of *Count Robert* in his Philadelphia newspaper a full five months before the entire work was published in Britain. This gave the paper plenty of time to get across the Atlantic, and the excerpt, published in Philadelphia in July, was reprinted in a few London newspapers in August.[50] In a headnote to the excerpt, the editors of the *Athenaeum* explained to readers the origins of the traveling text. Scott's novels, they wrote, "are regularly transmitted across the Atlantic, and the American bookseller, less cautious or less particular than Mr. Cadell, has given the following very copious extract to the National Gazette, a literary Philadelphia paper, for a copy of which we are indebted to [a] friend."[51] Scott found humor in the situation, and when he wrote his preface to *Count Robert* a few months later, he made the transatlantic publication of his work its subject and subtext.

The novel's fictionalization of the episode considers transatlantic reprinting in a number of registers. First, Scott openly ridicules American printers who went to press with early versions of novels that did not include his final corrections and additions. The "Introductory Address" is narrated by Jedediah Cleishbotham, of Gandercleuch, the fictional character who has edited and prepared the previous *Tales of My Landlord*—including *Old Mortality* (1816), *The Heart of Mid-Lothian* (1818), and *The Bride of Lammermoor* (1819), all of which derive from manuscripts written by Jedediah's late antiquarian associate Peter Pattieson. Jedediah has recently found two additional manuscripts, *Count Robert* and *Castle Dangerous*, but leaves them aside until Peter's surviving brother, Paul, shows up in Gandercleuch demanding them for his own use. Paul is a schemer and a rascal, and the manuscripts are in terrible shape, but Jedediah nevertheless employs him to prepare the texts and agrees to split the profits. At one point, Jedediah approaches Paul to complain about his progress, and the latter bursts out with this revelation: "Our hopeful scheme is entirely blown up. The tales, on publishing which we reckoned with so much confidence, have already been printed; they are abroad, over all America, and the British papers are clamorous." Jedediah, astonished, asks "whether this American production embraces the alterations which you as well as I judged necessary, before the work could be fitted to meet the public eye," and, receiving a negative answer, declares he would have never "remit[ted] these manuscripts to the press" unless "they were rendered fit for public perusal."[52] This exchange about the "American production" emphasizes Scott's control over the texts as author. Jedediah's complaint echoes those Carey faced at home from customers frustrated with faulty editions and, like those complaints, reinforces the superiority of authorized British publication over piratical American reprints.

Paul is not just a bringer of bad news, however; he is also a suspect. Jedediah accuses him of selling the manuscripts during an argument that resembles the initial dispute between Cadell and Carey over this same issue. Jedediah here is Cadell, and Paul is the falsely accused agent for Carey and also his defender: "I must of necessity suspect you to be the person who have [*sic*] supplied the foreign press with the copy which the printers have thus made an unscrupulous use of, without respect to the rights of the undeniable proprietors of the manuscripts" (xxxix). Paul responds by saying, "In the first place, these manuscripts . . . were never given to any one by me, and must have been sent to America either by yourself, or some one of the various gentleman to whom, I am well aware, you have afforded opportunities of perusing [them]" (xxxix–xl). Paul's defense proves less effective than Carey's, however, and Jedediah walks away absolutely convinced that he was "directly at the bottom of the Transatlantic publication, and had in one way or another found his own interest in that nefarious transaction" (xli–xlii). In reality, of course, the "Transatlantic publication" was authorized by the "proprietors of the manuscripts" in an arrangement of many years' standing. This denial of the transatlantic arrangement, in addition to the repeated characterization of Paul in negative terms—"seedy," "rusty," "obstina[te]," "impuden[t]," "odious," and "destitute of . . . amiable qualities" (xviii, xix, xx, xxxvii, xlii, xix)—suggests that Scott is denigrating American publishers.

But Scott is a great ironist, and nowhere is this more evident than in the prefaces to the Waverley novels, where we meet editors, antiquarians, legal scholars, roaming storytellers, royal ancestors, and any number of characters like Jedediah Cleishbotham who serve as unreliable sources for the novels that follow. It is impossible, therefore, to take Jedediah entirely at his word, and at times the preface suggests a more complicated view of Paul Pattieson and a more generous take on reprinting. In employing Paul to edit the manuscripts, for example, Jedediah has angered the people of Gandercleuch, who consider it an inexcusable act of neglect; as his wife reports, the local gossips believe he "spends all his time in tippling strong drink with the keeper of the public house" and leaves "book-making, and a' the rest o't, to the care of his usher" (xxvii–xxviii). Indeed, when Jedediah first reveals he has discovered *Count Robert* and *Castle Dangerous*, he provides no good reason for ignoring them before he "threw the manuscripts into [his] drawer" (xvii). He is not careful in accounting for the texts, and after handing them over to Paul, he holds "a sincere confidence that all was going on well" (xxiii). Scott prepares us to observe him in the same mistake Cadell initially made with Carey and thus undermines his own apparent critique of transatlantic publication.

A suggestive passage offers an implicit reconsideration of the actual relationship between Carey's and Constable's firms that the preface misrepresents. Jedediah's internal thoughts invoke the circumstances of Cadell's negotiation with Carey:

> I began to perceive that it would be no light matter . . . to break up
> a joint-stock adventure . . . which, if profitable to him, had at least
> promised to be no less so to me, established in years and learning
> and reputation so much his superior. . . . I resolved to proceed with
> becoming caution on the occasion, and not, by stating my causes
> of complaint too hastily in the outset, exasperate into a positive
> breach what might only prove some small misunderstanding, easily
> explained or apologized for, and which, like a leak in a new vessel,
> being once discovered and carefully stopped, renders the vessel but
> more sea-worthy than it was before. (xxxiv–xxxv)

The "joint-stock adventure," in which Constable & Company provided sheets and Carey payment, was indeed "profitable" to Carey and "no less so" to

Constable; Cadell certainly considered himself and his senior partner "established in years and learning and reputation so much [the] superior" of their Philadelphia colleagues; his initial "complaint," with its combination of both reprimand and solicitation, labored to avoid a "positive breach"; the issue of the stolen sheets proved a "small misunderstanding, easily explained or apologized for"; and the "leak" Constable and Cadell supposedly discovered at their printers was indeed "carefully stopped" by the arrangement with Carey, which provided revenue that "render[ed]" his company "more sea-worthy than it was before." The passage implicitly issues a more balanced view of transatlantic publication than that contained in Jedediah's other remarks and casts his own confidence in Paul's guilt in terms just as faulty and presumptuous as Cadell's repeated and unfounded suspicions. The resonances suggest the preface as a whole is more generous with America than it seems.

The eventual fate of the manuscripts brings to an intriguing point Scott's consideration of his American publishers, which in the end amounts to something of an homage. For a moment, Jedediah considers amending the text with "adequate corrections of [its] various inconsistencies," but he decides, in an allusion to Scott's own declining condition, that "the state of [his] health" would make such an exertion "imprudent" (xlii–xliii). So he lets the American edition stand for itself, and we, as readers, turn the page and begin *Count Robert*. Scott has cast his own novel as a transatlantic reprint derived from the American edition. He has used the story of transatlantic publication as a literary device to apologize for faults in his composition, as elaborate a performance of authorial humility as any in the history of romance. In having Jedediah attribute to reprinters the lack of judgment his readers would inevitably trace only to himself, Scott allies himself with American publishers, gleaning benefits from them in the literary realm just as his late publisher, Constable, gathered profits from them as a bookseller.

*   *   *

Scott's last novel reached the London marketplace by way of Philadelphia, an unusual geography made possible by delays in its publication. The episode signals, more broadly, that change had come to the book trade. The relationship between Constable's and Carey's firms exemplifies the cooperative transatlantic practices that became more common as publishers on both sides of the Atlantic devised extralegal arrangements in order to profit from selling books not easily protected by copyright. The acquisition of advance sheets in the United

States was analogous to the processes that that led to authorized London editions of American texts—like Murray's edition of *The Sketch Book* and dozens of other books in the 1820s—all of which depended on courtesies of the trade and the careful timing of a work's transmission to the printer. These cooperative practices defined transatlantic publishing in subsequent decades as the nature of the book trade's connectedness changed from a system dominated by the dissemination of London texts out to provincial markets to a more mixed system in which dissemination occurred in multiple directions. The episode with Scott's last preface is one small example of this: the reprinting of Philadelphia's *National Gazette* in London suggests that American texts were traveling more than ever before as the U.S. book trade continued to grow. Throughout the early nineteenth century, London proved extremely persistent as the center of the transatlantic trade and of English-language culture more broadly, but between 1800 and the 1830s, a considerable amount of excitement animated the provincial book trades. The following three chapters show how these dynamics shaped the aesthetic practices of the most influential Irish, Scottish, and American authors of the period.

Chapter 3

The Irish National Tale and
the Aesthetics of Union

In *Pride and Prejudice* (1813), Elizabeth Bennet doesn't get to see the Lake District. "No scheme could have been more agreeable to Elizabeth," Jane Austen writes, and when Mrs. Gardiner initially proposes a trip north, she is ecstatic: "'My dear, dear aunt,' she rapturously cried, 'what delight! what felicity! You give me fresh life and vigour.'"[1] The proposal catches Elizabeth at a moment of disillusionment with the marriage market, which has produced only a series of disappointments. "What are men to rocks and mountains?" Elizabeth asks, when the Lakes are offered to her, and in anticipation, she banishes all "disappointment and spleen" (*P*, 190). When Mrs. Gardiner eventually shortens the trip to the much closer county of Derbyshire, this romanticism has vanished; while "excessively disappointed" at the change, Elizabeth is quickly "satisfied" and "all" is "right again" (*P*, 264). She later writes to Mrs. Gardiner of her engagement to Darcy and renounces her enthusiasm altogether: "I thank you, again and again, for not going to the Lakes. How could I be so silly as to wish it!" (*P*, 390). In the novel's concluding pages Austen thus cures an already quite transformed Elizabeth of a final prejudice as she approaches married life. Indeed, *Pride and Prejudice* as a whole joins Elizabeth in a renunciation of her initial raptures. But what is objectionable about them? The novel provides two intertwined answers, one internal to the marriage plot and one that gestures far outside it. The cancellation of the trip to the Lakes in favor of Derbyshire paves the way for Elizabeth's marriage with Darcy, since it makes for a different kind of tourism: of Pemberley itself, which teaches Elizabeth that some men are *not* worth sacrificing for "rocks and mountains." The novel's concluding sentence highlights the importance of the changed travel plans to the novel's principal action: "Darcy, as well as Elizabeth, really loved [the Gardiners]; and they were both ever sensible of the warmest gratitude towards the persons who, by bringing her into Derbyshire, had been the means of uniting them" (*P*, 396). Over the course of the novel, Elizabeth's initial "silly" visions of sublime nature deepen—as they should, Austen suggests—into visions of marriage.

Such contraction reinforces Austen's status as the novelist of what Franco Moretti has called "a small, homogeneous England."[2] Austen's rejection of Elizabeth's early desire for travel outside a "small" England epitomizes the narrow geography we find throughout her novels. The correction of Elizabeth's disposition is accompanied, in this view, by a contraction of space. While Austen marks out courtship as the appropriate subject for the novel as a genre, she simultaneously marks out the "midland counties" as its appropriate setting.[3] The linkage of Elizabeth's reformation to the generic and geographical scope of Austen's particular brand of realism suggests the predicament of Irish fiction writers, since they hailed from a more distant place than one to which Mrs. Gardiner or anyone else in Austen's novels would likely propose a tour. Although Maria Edgeworth and Sydney Owenson did not conceive of a homogeneous English space as belonging particularly to Jane Austen, as provincial writers, they felt their distance from it acutely. This chapter focuses on the effects of provinciality for Edgeworth's and Owenson's Irish novels, which display an extraordinary self-consciousness about the unfamiliarity of their subject matter to their principal reading public, which, like Austen's, was gathered around the London book trade.[4]

In Edgeworth's *Castle Rackrent* (1800), *The Absentee* (1812), and *Ormond* (1817) and Owenson's *The Wild Irish Girl* (1806), the two authors developed literary strategies to mitigate the effects of the distance between their subject and their audience, strategies that Austen, writing of her "small" England and exclusively addressing it, could do without. Such distance was compounded by long-held and virulent anti-Irish prejudice; to compensate for both, Edgeworth and Owenson use self-reflexive formal devises like the marriage plot, travel narrative, and paratexts to project an ideal relationship with English readers that downplays the otherwise vexed political intercourse between Ireland and England. For Edgeworth, this relationship takes shape in the realm of universalized moral codes grounded in the Scottish Enlightenment, while for Owenson, it forms within a more extreme fantasy that casts literary exchange as inhabiting an autonomous sphere of its own. Both of these projections—one harkening back to the eighteenth century, the other looking forward to the nineteenth—are developed through near-constant but inconsistent appeals to national character, which both sustain and trouble the ideal author-reader relationships their novels enact through narrative form. The complicated tensions and idealizations in Edgeworth and Owenson first shaped what this and the subsequent two chapters call *the aesthetics of provinciality*, a representational mode that ameliorates an author's subordinate position in the literary field by projecting literary exchange into an exalted realm. The works of Edgeworth and Owenson, like those of Walter Scott, Washington Irving, and James Fenimore Cooper after them, do not inhabit this realm in reality—but it is an ideal to which their various literary experiments aspired.

Reverence for England has earned Edgeworth and Owenson bad reputations among scholars who would have preferred defiant Irish nationalism.[5] Moving from a narrative of Edgeworth's career to a revisionist close reading of Owenson's *The Wild Irish Girl*, I consider these authors' dependence on London—"this great metropolis," as Edgeworth put it in an 1808 preface[6]—as a response to the uneven distribution of cultural capital rather than a lamentable symptom of colonialism. The increased attention that Edgeworth and Owenson have received in recent decades can indeed be attributed to the rise of empire as a concern for literary studies, which has inspired scholars to demonstrate the mutual constitution of literary and imperialist discourses within the Irish "national tale," a genre that was highly visible in its time but had long fallen from view.[7] But we miss something fundamental about Edgeworth and Owenson if we understand their novels exclusively through the lens of empire. Influential readers of the national tale have consistently linked it to the 1801 Act of Union of Great Britain and Ireland, which absorbed Irish Parliamentary autonomy and catalyzed a crisis in the political and cultural self-understanding of Britain.[8] According to such "Unionist" readings, each Irish novel of the period can be placed along a spectrum of political resistance or complicity. Ina Ferris's definitive account, *The Romantic National Tale and the Question of Ireland* (2002), works within a Unionist logic but considers such questions with remarkable subtlety.[9] Ferris shows that Irish fiction sought to shape a public discourse that operated as much within a "civic forum" as it did on "the imperial stage."[10] In focusing on the literary implications of the question of Ireland, Ferris resists the urge to reduce the writings of Edgeworth, Owenson, Charles Robert Maturin, and John Banim to political statements of one kind or another, arguing forcefully for the importance of the *belles lettres* genre of travel writing about Ireland (also always published in London) as well as

Romantic-era conceptions of history, historical consciousness, sympathy, and communication. The Irish national tale, written within the "awkward space of Union," was a subtle, fraught, and conflicted genre that "disorder[ed] the metropolitan discursive field" through deceptively "mundane frictions of discomfort and agitation."[11] This chapter turns to conditions related to but importantly distinguishable from Ferris's nationally based historicist method: the structure of the early nineteenth-century marketplace for books, as reflected in literary strategies rather than overtly political ones. This requires a shift from one set of contentious issues, exemplified by Unionist readings, to the literary tensions invoked by a reading of *Pride and Prejudice* that links genre, narrative, geography, and cultural authority.

Irish fiction of this period depended on the London marketplace for its very existence as "literary" discourse. This transcultural movement is embedded, ineluctably, within a generic blueprint that cannot be explained entirely through the Union as a heuristic touchstone. Nor can Unionist readings explain Irish fiction's influence on other provincial writers around the Anglophone Atlantic also motivated by the ambition to succeed in London. Almost immediately after the success of the national tale, Scottish and American writers absorbed the genre and adapted it to their own circumstances as outsiders with close cultural ties to England. Scott's acknowledgment of Edgeworth as an inspiration in the postscript to *Waverley* (1814) established a connection with Ireland upon which many scholars have elaborated (also in relation to Owenson, whose influence Scott elided), but the importance of Irish fiction to American literary history has gone almost completely unacknowledged.[12] Just as the paradigm of empire is partly responsible for the surge of interest in Irish fiction, so, too, is it responsible for the difficulty of seeing the genre's relevance for the newly independent United States. Yet Edgeworth and Owenson devised literary strategies that shaped the aesthetic practices of three decades of provincial literature on both sides of the Atlantic. This chapter identifies such strategies in order to demonstrate the salience of the national tale's theory of cross-cultural literary exchange. To do so, it traces a trajectory in Edgeworth's and Owenson's work (though not a strictly chronological one) from irony to sympathy to a radical vision of aesthetic communion. Subsequent chapters demonstrate the portability of that theory for other provincial writers who had their sights set on London.

Austen proceeds with the knowledge that her fiction needn't travel elsewhere for recognition. In *Pride and Prejudice*, she explicitly excludes an audience unfamiliar with her fictional landscape. When the novel takes Elizabeth and the Gardiners north toward Pemberley, Austen includes a rare remark about her intentions: "It is not the object of this work to give a description of Derbyshire," she writes, "nor any of the remarkable places through which their route thither lay; Oxford, Blenheim, Warwick, Kenelworth, Birmingham, &c. are sufficiently known" (*P*, 265). The claim to universality implicit in this statement is a function of Austen's secure place in the cultural capital of her time, wherein England and Englishness passed effortlessly as the standards against which writers measure themselves. Edgeworth and Owenson wrote about places that are unknown to the reader whom in this remark Austen does not even need to identify.

Maria Edgeworth and Universal Sympathy

A view of Edgeworth's career from her first Irish novel to her last demonstrates how her strategies of addressing England changed over time as she rose to the heights of literary respectability and renown. They begin with the complex ironies of *Castle Rackrent* and its elaborate paratextual apparatus devised for "the *ignorant* English reader,"[13] continue with meditations on Irish-English union through travel narrative and the marriage plot in *Ennui* (1809) and *The Absentee*, and culminate with *Ormond*, which self-consciously reckons with cross-cultural address through a depiction of Ireland as a discrete and independent space. In *Castle Rackrent*, Edgeworth accommodates her English readers through the camaraderie of humor and satire; in her later Irish novels, she turns to a model of sympathy best understood through Adam Smith's *Theory of Moral Sentiments* (1759).[14] Smith's emphasis on the imagination's role in engaging the sympathies of a spectator, perhaps the most influential aspect of his work on the history of fiction, shaped Edgeworth's negotiation of the transcultural literary relationship figured in *The Absentee* and *Ormond*. These two novels are Smithian experiments of very different kinds, but both of them are animated by the collision between Edgeworth's commitment to representing Irish scenes and characters and her project of bridging the Irish-English divide through an embrace of universalizing moral codes. Provinciality fuels the rhetoric of her fiction as she writes the Irish within the exalted and Enlightenment category of "human nature." The vehemence of this proposition characterizes Edgeworth's fiction even as her claims for universality betray at every turn their own limits. In *Ormond*, as we shall see, she connects her moral universalism to a meditation on the meaning of novel reading itself.

The humor and self-consciousness of *Castle Rackrent* derive partly from Edgeworth's uneasy position as an Irish writer making her way for the first time in London. The book's composition and material history bear traces of this: the "Glossary" Edgeworth wrote so terms and phrases would be "intelligible to the English reader" was printed at the eleventh hour and included as front matter in the book's first edition, rather than as an appendix (*C*, 123). This awkwardness immediately sets up the address to England as a problem *Castle Rackrent* never solves as it narrates the downfall of an Irish family over the course of many generations through the monologue of Thady Quirck, one of their servants. The last-minute Glossary added another voice to a book already animated by the radical juxtaposition of Thady's own voice and the quasi-ethnographic editorial discourse of the text's footnotes. In some cases, the Glossary elaborates upon material already treated by footnotes, such as the term *fairy-mount*, which one footnote ridicules and the Glossary explains more generously with historicizing sensitivity (*C*, 71, 129–131). The novel's competing discourses and the instability they foster make it almost impossible to determine Edgeworth's representational intentions or their precise effects.

While the presence of an implied metropolitan reader dominates the book's editorial matter, at times such a perspective also appears directly within the main narrative. In one episode, Thady and Sir Kit, a landlord, fail to communicate their local knowledge to a new arrival in a scene that sets them up in explicit contrast to the explanatory paratexts. While traveling in England, Sir Kit has married a wealthy Jewish heiress in an effort to allay his financial trouble. Upon the couple's return, Thady describes Lady Kit—one of Edgeworth's most vicious caricatures—as a "stranger in a foreign country" (*C*, 76). She asks Thady and Sir Kit a series of questions as Edgeworth presents her as a foil to the English readers addressed in the book's footnotes and glossary. In such moments, the two Irishmen, like their interlocutor, are also foils—to Edgeworth's authorial persona who endeavors to make such things intelligible. In the first of these moments, Lady Kit interrupts a conversation between Sir Kit and Thady:

> "Is the large room damp, Thady?" said his honour. "Oh, damp, your honour! how should it but be dry as a bone . . . it's the barrack-room your honour's talking on." "And what is a barrack-room, pray, my dear?" were the first words I ever heard out of my lady's lips. "No matter, my dear!" said he, and went on talking to me, ashamed like I should witness her ignorance. To be sure, to hear her talk one might have taken her for an innocent. (*C*, 77)

Neither Thady nor Sir Kit defines "barrack-room" for Lady Kit, a failure that repeats as she asks, "'What's this, Sir Kit?' and what's that, Sir Kit?' all the way we went" (*C*, 77). From the point of view of Thady, these questions mark her with an "ignorance" for which Edgeworth's actual readers could hardly blame her, thus reinforcing the ironic distance between Thady and the text's stance as a whole. At this moment, the novel's editor steps in where its characters fail and defines *barrack-room* in the Glossary: "Formerly it was customary, in gentleman's houses in Ireland, to fit up one large bedchamber with a number of beds for the reception of occasional visitors. These rooms were called Barrack-rooms" (*C*, 132). This frank answer condemns Sir Kit's anxious evasion and gestures toward the kind of literary exchange Edgeworth thinks is possible as she carves out an authoritative position. That position is thrown into relief through the comic triangulation of Sir Kit, Lady Kit, and Thady, whose interactions suggest precisely how *not* to proceed in reading or writing about Irish culture.

Edgeworth's rise to prominence coincided with a display of more positive modes as she turned from irony to sympathy as a strategy for enveloping her English readers. *Castle Rackrent* itself became quite popular—by 1804, it had gone through four London editions, three editions in Dublin, its first American edition, and translations into French and German—and it was reportedly enjoyed by both Prime Minister William Pitt and King George III.[15] Edgeworth's reputation peaked a decade later with *The Tales of Fashionable Life*, Series I and II, which included the novels *Ennui* and *The Absentee*. *The Absentee* follows the travels of the English-educated Lord Colambre from London to Ireland as he learns about things Irish, falls in love with an Irish heroine, and decides to settle there. *Ennui* contains a similar cross-cultural plot in which Lord Glenthorn, living in London and suffering from the book's eponymous mental condition, is banished to his family's Irish estate, where he receives a morally edifying education. Both novels follow the classic cross-cultural structure of the national tale, a pattern set in Owenson's *The Wild Irish Girl*, discussed below. The materiality of *The Absentee*'s first edition reinforced that text's educational agenda as well as the geographical separation of its two scenes of action. The opening chapters of *The Absentee* are set in London, the place of the book's publication, and they were printed at the end of the fifth volume of *Tales of Fashionable Life*. The volume's last page announces that "lord Colambre left London the next day,"[16] and the next volume opens as he enters the Bay of Dublin, where his journey—and the reader's—begins. The final volume of the series thus stands alone as a fictional travel narrative to Ireland wherein the Anglicized protagonist's sympathies are continually activated.

Colambre is the English-educated son of Irish landowners who have abandoned their estates to live in high London society. The novel illustrates the folly of such absenteeism, and at its end, Colambre saves his bankrupt father upon the condition that his family returns home. Colambre's disgust, early in the novel, at his Irish mother's failed attempts to "pass for English" in London provokes him to leave for Ireland to "judge of that country for himself" (*A*, 2, 79). For Colambre, this is a moral journey, and he comes eventually to embrace his responsibilities. Edgeworth uses sympathy in two ways to make sure her readers congratulate him for this: as an obvious surrogate for English readers, Colambre excites their sympathy with the Irish characters he encounters, and he also inspires their sympathy with him directly as he accepts his duty as a benevolent landlord. The first strategy hinges on a sympathetic reckoning with national difference while the second embraces a universalizing moral sensibility shared alike by authors, readers, and subjects in the literary realm. Colambre's Anglo-Irish identity allows for the doubleness of the text's sympathetic registers. All in all, *The Absentee* attempts a gentler and more earnest bridge across the English-Irish divide than we find in *Castle Rackrent*.

In *The Theory of Moral Sentiments*, Adam Smith powerfully links the imagination to a capacity to "bring home to our own breast" the experiences of others, a central goal of Edgeworth's as she represents the experiences of Irish characters.[17] Colambre's capacity to sympathize helps "bring home" to himself the situation of the Irish as he "obtain[s] a just idea of the state and manners in Ireland" (*A*, 81). The goal is to enact a union of sentiments between England and Ireland, although rigid social hierarchies in Edgeworth's work test the limits of a theory that depends so much on mutual recognition.[18] Smith emphasizes that sympathy does not easily traverse wide differences, such as those of class, race, or nationality—or even merely when the "happiness or misery of others . . . in no respect depends upon our conduct, [or] when our interests are altogether separated and detached from theirs" (*T*, 160). *The Absentee* activates the sympathy of English readers by teaching them that their own interests are, indeed, united with and attached to Ireland. Colambre's education is forwarded with the help of the English officer Sir James Brooke, who can distinguish between "representations and misrepresentations of Ireland," in contrast to one Lady Dashfort, a "worthless Englishwoman of rank" for whom the Irish are "Barbarians!" (*A*, 81, 92, 100). As Colambre proceeds judiciously through Dublin, Wicklow, and his family's county, he treats each "new scene [that] presented itself to his view" with unvarying attention and interest (*A*, 161). One episode with his father's agent models cross-cultural sympathy to its fullest. Traveling in disguise, Colambre surveys his family's estate and encounters Mr. Burke, whom a local innkeeper describes as a "right good agent" who "does best for all" and makes sure that "all [is] fair between landlord and tenant" (*A*, 131, 132). Mr. Burke soon explains how such fairness puts him at risk for losing his job, since he does not squeeze his tenants for as much rent as he could; "as an Englishman, sir," he tells Colambre, this "must be unintelligible to you" (*A*, 134). A letter of dismissal arrives the next night, and in an emotional scene, Mrs. Burke addresses their incognito guest, "[N]ow is it not difficult for me to bear patiently to see him ill treated?" (*A*, 137). Colambre declares that "even I, who am a stranger, cannot help feeling for both of you, as you must see I do" (*A*, 137). Colambre's disguise allows Edgeworth to present the scene as an exemplary cross-cultural case.[19] The moment of sympathy is more remarkable because a recent disappointment in love has made it difficult for Colambre to allow the experience of others to "come home to his feelings" (*A*, 129). But the experience of the Burkes overrides this insensibility, and he promises "justice—as far as it is in my power" (*A*, 138). Upon returning to London and his family, Colambre convinces his father to reinstate Mr. Burke, and he judges, appropriately and maturely, that it's best to return his family to Ireland.

Edgeworth also promotes sympathy between her readers and protagonists in scenes that downplay national distinctions. The reader of *The Absentee* is meant to sympathize with Colambre as a genteel Anglo-Irish subject who follows the dictates of his conscience. His resolution to live in Ireland only has to do with Ireland itself insofar as that is the arena of his responsibility. Right from the start, Edgeworth applies her didactic aim to a larger context, introducing the term *absentee* for the first time to condemn an *English* landlord whose wife's "passion for living in London" has removed them from the country. "The Irish channel," Edgeworth writes, "did not, indeed, flow between him and his estate . . . [but] the consequence, the negligence, the extravagance, were the same" (*A*, 54). For all its showcasing of national character, the novel works hard to minimize the importance of national difference. "Is this Ireland?" Colambre asks himself after viewing his father's neglected estate:

> No, it is not Ireland. Let me not, like most of those who forsake
> their native country, traduce it. . . . What I have just seen is the
> picture only of that to which an Irish estate and Irish tenantry may
> be degraded in the absence of those whose duty and interest it is to

reside in Ireland, to uphold justice by example and authority; but who, neglecting this duty, commit power to bad hands and bad hearts—abandon their tenantry to oppression, and their property to ruin. (*A*, 162)

Adam Smith personifies the conscience as "the man within the breast, the abstract and ideal spectator of our sentiments and conduct," the "impartial spectator" we consult as a guide to our actions (*T*, 177–178). Here we see this internalized spectator at work in a passage that highlights a tension between national particularity (Colambre claims Ireland as his "native country") and an appeal to universality, registered in the abstract terms "duty," "interest," "justice," and "authority." The implied spectator of his actions—or the "spectatorial reader," in James Chandler's recent phrase—cannot fail to approve of his conduct and, with such approval, to sympathize.[20]

Smith ranks benevolence and gratitude highest in his pantheon of virtues, and Colambre's situation vis-à-vis his Irish estate perfectly stages both of them—especially insofar as *benevolence* and *gratitude* in both Smith and Edgeworth are terms that mask uneven power relationships. "We have always," Smith writes, "the strongest disposition to sympathize with the benevolent affections," a notion he elaborates in relation to a spectator's approval of scenes of gratitude, which produce sympathy only if we "entirely go along with" the "motives" of the benefactor (*T*, 48, 88). "Our heart must adopt the principles of the agent [i.e., benefactor] . . . before it can entirely sympathize with, and beat time to, the gratitude of the person who has been benefited by his actions" (*T*, 88–89). Colambre inspires a reader's sympathy as he tries to convince his parents to restore the family to their positions as landowners. Late in the novel, he pleads with his mother, Lady Clonbrony:

[R]estore my father to himself! Should [his] feelings be wasted?—No; give them again to expand in benevolent, in kind, useful actions; give him again to his tenantry, his duties, his country, his home; return to that home yourself, my dear mother! . . . Return to an unsophisticated people—to poor but grateful hearts, still warm with the remembrance of your kindness, still blessing you for favours long since conferred, ever praying to see you once more. (*A*, 201)

Colambre desires benevolence like a passion, and the heart of the "spectatorial reader" beats time along with him. For Smith, our sympathy with the benefactor is direct and our sympathy with the recipient indirect, whose experience of the act is irrelevant to "our sentiments with regard to the merit of him who has bestowed it" (*T*, 94). This privileging of benefactors dovetails neatly with Edgeworth's focus on Colambre's point of view throughout the text at the expense of the tenants themselves.

Colambre's virtue elicits sympathy exclusive of its national valence, a commitment to universality reinforced by the novel's marriage plot. At one point, Lady Clonbrony demands an explanation for Colambre's reluctance to marrying an heiress: "What are you afraid of?" she asks. "Of doing what is wrong," he replies, "the only thing, I trust, of which I shall ever be afraid" (*A*, 70). After such assured moralism, Colambre cannot fail to be a good fit for Grace Nugent, an Irish ward of the family's, who comes recommended only for her virtue: "With plain, unsophisticated morality, in good faith and simple truth," Edgeworth's narrator tells us, Grace "acted as she professed, thought what she said, and was that which she seemed to be" (*A*, 43). Over the course of the novel, moreover, Colambre learns not to generalize on a national level: while before his travels he wishes to observe "the state of manners *in Ireland*," as quoted above, upon his return, he produces a "full and true account of all he had seen in his progress through *his Irish estates*" (*A*, 81, 182; emphasis added). Just as she separates somewhat her hero's positive qualities from nationality, Edgeworth also transforms her heroine: in order for it to become possible for Colambre to marry Grace Nugent, Edgeworth strips her of her Irish name.[21] The final chapters of the novel involve an elaborate crusade to establish Grace's legitimate birth, which reveals that her father was actually English. The novel thus conjoins two ambiguously situated protagonists: Lord Colambre and "that miss Nugent," as an Irish domestic puts it, "who is no more miss Nugent, they say, but miss Reynolds" (*A*, 266). Such ambiguity cloaks a particularly elite, protestant, Anglo-Irish identity with a universalism meant to resonate with a metropolitan readership, also elite, also protestant. Walter Scott thought Edgeworth succeeded admirably. In the General Preface to the Waverley novels, he commended her ability to "procure sympathy for [the] virtues" of Ireland's inhabitants, whom she "introduce[d] . . . to the sister kingdom" in a novelistic practice he acknowledged inspired his own.[22]

*   *   *

In 1813, Edgeworth traveled to London, where the "great popularity" of her latest *Tales*, including *The Absentee*, led to her reception among many notable metropolitans.[23] She met the Prince Regent, Lord and Lady Wellington, and Lord Byron (whom, predictably, she disliked).[24] She wrote to her Aunt Ruxton of the "the grant panorama" of the city, whose acceptance surprised her: "I have enjoyed more pleasure," she wrote, and "received a thousand times more attention, more *kindness* than I could have thought it possible would be shewn to me."[25] At this time, Edgeworth's reputation glided along at the highest level it would attain in her career. Many of her contemporaries appreciated the interplay in her novels between national character and moral universalism. Francis Jeffrey, editor of *Edinburgh Review* and Edgeworth's colleague and friend, credited her with a unique ability to bridge the general and the particular: "She not only makes us know and love the Irish nation far better than any other writer, but seems to us more qualified than most others to promote the knowledge and the love of mankind."[26] Increasingly, reviewers reserved their praise for her Irish scenes as they expressed frustration at her novels set in England, especially *Patronage* (1814).[27] "Whenever the scene lies in Ireland," wrote the *Monthly Review*, *The Absentee* "is delightful," and the *Critical Review* applauded moments when "Miss Edgeworth takes us back to her own country, and to the people whom she so well understands."[28] Edgeworth's reputation depended much on her national identity: "We do not know whether we envy the author most," Jeffrey wrote, about *The Absentee*, "for the rare talent that she has shown . . . or for the *experience* by which its materials have been supplied."[29] Edgeworth struggled with the common association of her authorship and particularity or, in the parlance of the reviews, the "national" or "characteristic" focus of her fiction.

Edgeworth's last Irish novel, *Ormond*, responds to this paradoxically by endowing an almost exclusive Irish scene with her strongest yet appeal to universality: this time through a self-confident depiction of Ireland and a self-conscious depiction of Smithian sympathy as process that governs novel reading. *Ormond* is Edgeworth's most overlooked Irish fiction, perhaps because it followed on the heels of Scott and Austen, novelists incalculably influenced by Edgeworth but who far eclipsed her in literary history. Like Scott, Austen read Edgeworth approvingly; "I have made up my mind to like no Novels really," she wrote to her niece, "but Miss Edgeworth's, Yours, and my own."[30] Edgeworth read *Pride and Prejudice* on her way to London in 1813, was "much entertained" with *Mansfield Park* (1814), and later enjoyed reading the copy of *Emma* (1816) Austen sent herself.[31] In 1814, Edgeworth wrote an affecting letter to Scott after she read *Waverley* in order to thank him for the "honour you have done us" in the tribute to her "authorship" on its "last page."[32] *Ormond* owes much to these two authors; published as her reputation waned, its belatedness may have inspired her to push past the patterns that shaped her earlier fiction.

Set in the 1760s, *Ormond* features a hero born and bred entirely in Ireland and a scene of action that highlights conflicts and contrasts internal to Ireland rather than those between Ireland and England. Thus dispensing with a Colambre-like surrogate for her readers or an abundance of explanatory paratexts, this London-published book asks its readers to make the imaginative leap to Ireland on their own. The novel follows the history and education of the orphaned Henry Ormond as he negotiates between two role models: his guardian Sir Ulick O'Shane, a worldly nobleman who entertains fashionable acquaintances in Castle Hermitage, the seat of his estate in western Ireland, and Sir Ulick's cousin Cornelius O'Shane, better known as King Corny, who rules the Black Islands—across a nearby lake—with all the romance and indulgence of a feudal lord. Edgeworth contrasts the self-interest and worldly affectations of the former with the sincere but intemperate behavior of the latter as Ormond develops from a naïve young man into a mature adult. Ormond eventually marries Florence Annaly, an Irish heroine who embodies domestic morality and with whom he works as a reformer on behalf of Catholic education. Besides a trip to Paris, where Ormond visits King Corny's daughter, the novel takes place entirely in Ireland, where Ormond eventually settles with Florence on the Black Islands, having used an inheritance to purchase the estate.

The first half of the novel transfers the main geographical trajectory of *The Absentee* from an England-Ireland axis to an axis between neighboring Irish estates. The novel opens, like *The Absentee*, with a scene from fashionable life, featuring Sir Ulick presiding over an elaborate dinner at Castle Hermitage. Sir Ulick soon sends Ormond "across the lake" to the Black Islands, which effects his removal from "the world" to "a remote island," where King Corny takes over his education.[33] This movement is analogous to Colambre's journey: a retreat from society through a journey to an "island"; but Edgeworth narrows her geography to an Irish fictional world that subsists on its own terms without England as an explicit point of reference. Through contrasting two Irish estates, she produces the atmosphere of an Irish neighborhood as complex, independent, and interactive, as the midland settings in Jane Austen. Edgeworth takes her Irish setting for granted, including only a minimal amount of footnotes and leaving Irish terms undefined. We are far from the heavily annotated *Castle Rackrent*: in this novel, King Corny mentions his estate's "barrack-room" without the explanatory contexts of footnotes or a glossary

(*O*, 35). Ormond's journey around Ireland functions not as his attempt to discover the "state of Ireland," Colambre's original goal, but rather as a testing ground for his character.

If in *Ormond* the contrast between Castle Hermitage and the Black Islands replaces the contrast between England and Ireland, the introduction of an entirely new geographical axis between Ireland and France circumvents the British metropolis. Paris, not London, is celebrated as the height of fashion and culture, principally through the charismatic Mlle. O'Faley, King Corny's sister-in-law, who comes to stay in the Black Islands after a life spent abroad. "Miss O'Faley was said to be a great acquisition in the neighborhood," Edgeworth reports, "she was so gay, so sociable, so communicative; and she certainly, above all, knew so much of the world; she was continually receiving letters, and news, and patterns, from Dublin, and the Black Rock, and Paris" (*O*, 77). Mlle. O'Faley is of Irish descent, but she is eminently European; her transnational connections notably exclude London. When Ormond visits Paris, he "admired" "the Louvre, the Place de Louis XV" and "the drives on the Boulevards," but "in his secret soul, preferred the bay of Dublin to all he then saw of the banks of the Seine" (*O*, 242). Ormond's capacity for judgments of this kind resemble Colambre's when he travels to Ireland: but while an English education prepares the hero of *The Absentee* for his journey, Ormond's education in "an obscure part of the country" (*O*, 111) prepares him well enough to consider the highest cultural markers of the *ancien régime*. And he easily leaves them behind, demonstrating a resistance to French society similar to that of Dora, King Corny's daughter, whom he has come to visit and who "did honour to Ireland by having preserved her reputation" even amid "dissipated French society" (*O*, 295). Ormond's sojourn in France also suggests the relative superficiality of any distinction between English and Irish, since Ormond is alternatively characterized as both by his French hosts. They discourage his moderation lest he appear too English and playfully ridicule the way he "dances like an Englishman" (*O*, 257). Dora refers to him as "*le bel Anglois*" but then "change[s] the term to '*mon bel Irlandois*,'" with no obvious motivation for the distinction (*O*, 254). Like Lord Colambre in *The Absentee*, Ormond becomes more and more recognizable to his English readers as part of a universal "human nature."

Edgeworth's only protagonist born and bred in Ireland, Ormond is also the only one who reads novels. In two extraordinary scenes of reading, Edgeworth brings universality to bear on a depiction of sympathy that she connects to the literary transaction. In the opening chapter of the novel, Edgeworth invokes Adam Smith's "cool or indifferent spectator" (*O*, 7) in relation to one character's unfounded jealousy, and the novel includes many Smithian moments of sentiment and sympathy. In one of these, we witness a young Ormond eagerly and dangerously devouring volume after volume of *Tom Jones* and in another steadily and properly making his way through *Sir Charles Grandison*. Here is Ormond with the former:

> [O]nce he had opened the book, he could not shut it: he turned over page after page, peeped at the end, the beginning, the middle, then back to the beginning; was diverted by the humour—every Irishman loves humour; delighted with the wit—what Irishman is not? and his curiosity was so much raised by the story, his interest and sympathy so excited for the hero, that he read on, standing for quarter an hour, fixed in the same position. . . . Closing the book, Harry Ormond resolved to be what he admired—and, if possible, to shine forth an Irish Tom Jones. (*O*, 61–62)

And here he is with the latter:

> Sensible as Ormond was of the power of humour and ridicule, he was still more susceptible, as all noble natures are, of sympathy with elevated sentiments and with generous character. The character of sir Charles Grandison . . . touched the nobler feelings of our young hero's mind, inspired him with virtuous emulation, and made him ambitious to be a *gentleman* in the best and highest sense of the word: in short, it completely counteracted in his mind the effects of his late study. (*O*, 69)

Like Samuel Johnson, Edgeworth prefers Richardson to Fielding, and Ormond's reading is mapped on a clear learning curve toward virtue. Yet the passages are more layered and interesting than they first appear. Ormond, both the character and the novel, are in fact modeled on *Tom Jones*, the book Edgeworth ostensibly rejects. And this isn't the only indication of the ironies at play: Ormond's reading of *Grandison* doesn't prevent him, one chapter later, from becoming, like Tom Jones, susceptible to "silly girls" and behaving like a "mere dancing, driving, country coxcomb" (*O*, 80). Moreover, an early scene of powerful sympathy with the tenant Moriarty Carroll is far more effective in turning Ormond away from Tom Jones–like dalliances than all the virtues portrayed in Richardson (*O*, 65–66), and later in the novel a scene of disgust with another character, White Connal, finally teaches Ormond the meaning of the word "coxcomb," a role he only then definitively rejects.[34] Ormond's real education in this *bildungsroman* comes not through his reading but through his interactions with actual people. In this, he is similar to other characters in the genre who read books in their youth, including Edward Waverley. What, exactly, is Edgeworth, the novelist, saying about the purpose of novels?

The answer is surprising for this most didactic of writers. In these scenes, novels provoke a diverse range of pleasures: "divers[ion]," "humour," "curiosity," and "interest"; they "touch" and "inspire" Ormond and foster "ambition" and "noble feelings." This happens because of his instinctual capacity for sympathy, a word that entirely structures both scenes of reading. Smith argues that sympathy gives us pleasure as an emotion in itself, no matter what feeling inspired it; this was the aspect of his theory that David Hume thought was particularly original.[35] As spectators, the act of sympathy both demonstrates and activates our approval of the agent's emotions; Smith calls this "the sentiment of approbation," and in a footnote to the second edition of the *Theory of Moral Sentiments*, he insists on the pleasure of sympathy for its own sake:

> In the sentiment of approbation, there are two things to be taken notice of; first, the sympathetic passion of the spectator; and, secondly, the emotion which arises from his observing the perfect coincidence between this sympathetic passion in himself, and the original passion in the person principally concerned. This last emotion, in which the sentiment of approbation properly consists, is always agreeable and delightful.[36]

Edgeworth uses the highly self-conscious scenes of *Ormond* to indicate that this kind of pleasure is proper to novel reading itself. The purpose of fiction, she suggests, is the pleasure it gives us as inherently sympathetic reading subjects exercising our faculty of sympathy. The fact that novel reading fails to form Ormond's character gestures toward a theory of fiction that assigns it a role outside and cordoned off from adulterated worldly experience. Note that even though Ormond reads *Tom Jones* quite carelessly—skipping around from beginning to middle to end—he also at times stands there rapt and frozen, "fixed in the same position." Despite his subsequent decision to imitate Tom Jones, this suspension of Ormond's bodily movements conceives of novel reading as a tangible aesthetic retreat. Novels and tales, it seems, are not as purposive as we might wish them to be, a thought that jars with the educational thrust of Edgeworth's oeuvre but nevertheless powerfully emerges in these scenes. As Ormond reads, moreover, Edgeworth traces an implicit genealogy of her work as a novelist in toward the metropolitan English tradition and back to the classic eighteenth-century Fielding-Richardson dialectic. It is a powerful argument for the universality and the specificity of her literary productions, which she forwards through positing the relative powerlessness of fiction, despite or because of the pleasure it brings. In the preface that accompanied *Ormond*, Richard Lovell Edgeworth wrote that "the moral of this tale does not immediately appear, for the author has taken particular care that it should not obtrude itself upon the reader."[37] Edgeworth's moral is not "moral" in a typical sense; in *Ormond*, she stages scenes of sympathetic reading to draw a boundary around fiction as a unique endeavor.

The Radical Aesthetics of Sydney Owenson's *The Wild Irish Girl*

Sydney Owenson—notorious, politically radical, half Catholic, and the daughter of an actor—was Edgeworth's great rival and antagonist in the literary field, yet the two shared many priorities as provincials. Owenson herself claimed that the idea of writing *The Wild Irish Girl* originated on a trip to London, during "the course of one of the many conversations which occurred on the subject of my (always termed) 'unhappy country.'"[38] The resulting novel is a wildly discursive performance that hangs an enormous amount of information, history, description, romance, song, and national feeling on an epistolary structure that mirrors the novel's material publication: it comprises letters written in Ireland meant for consumption in London—"the emporium of the world."[39] The fact that the letters are written by a traveling Englishman, Horatio M——, instead of an Irishwoman, like Owenson, enacts a compelling reversal of the gendered and national valences of the novel's authorship and indicates this novel, and the genre of which its remains paradigmatic, is more complicated and self-aware than it at first seems. That complexity resides in the tension between the novel's discursivity and its narrative form as a romance. The projected marriage between the letter-writing Horatio and the titular Irish "girl," the princess Glorvina, has been consistently read as an allegory of the 1801 Act of Union. This interpretation, however, is based on a significant blindness to the novel's marriage plot. Owenson grafted onto the novel a second, failed marriage trajectory that points to the text's promotion of an idealized author-reader intimacy at the direct expense of its ostensible political concerns. She uses the marriage between the Englishman Horatio M—— and the Irish princess Glorvina to theorize an idealized aesthetic relationship between an Irish writer and her English readership. The tendency to link this marriage to the Act of Union has sidelined Owenson's negotiation of her own cultural legitimacy, which she promotes in her novel by appealing to the ideological notion of an autonomous literary sphere. The Horatio-Glorvina marriage trajectory is resolved only after Horatio's father fails to marry Glorvina himself. Owenson associates Unionist politics with this failed marriage plot and the literary sphere with the one that succeeds. The formal structure of *The Wild Irish Girl* thus denies an exclusive causal relation between imperial politics and Owenson's literary strategies. The novel, which preceded *Ormond* by a decade, represents a more forceful theory of the "literary" than Edgeworth registers in her scenes of novel reading.

The marriage between Horatio, whose letters comprise the bulk of this epistolary novel, and Glorvina seems to enact a compelling reconciliation, since Horatio is a direct descendant of the English colonizers who conquered and possessed the Irish kingdom that Glorvina's father, the prince of Inismore, would otherwise have ruled by hereditary right. During the novel, Horatio conceals his ancestry, fabricates a new identity, gains admittance to the castle at Inismore, and, remaining in disguise, eventually wins the heart of Glorvina. The novel ends with a letter from Horatio's father, the Earl of M——, endorsing the union of the two warring families; "Let the names of Inismore and M—— be inseparably blended," he writes, "and the distinctions of English and Irish, of protestant and catholic, be for ever buried."[40] This language has been used as evidence for how the novel effects a "solution" to the problem of a political "union" between colonized and colonizing nations.[41] Owenson's elaborate dramatization of the novel's resolution, however, undermines this allegorical reading completely. We cannot take the Earl's Unionist rhetoric at face value, since the resolution of the plot occurs after Horatio's father attempts to marry Glorvina under false pretenses.[42] Like his son, the Earl conceals his identity in order to ingratiate himself with the prince and his daughter: we learn at the end of the novel that long ago, Glorvina had agreed under pressure to marry the Earl, known to her and her father merely as the "GENTLEMAN" (*W*, 208), in order to alleviate debt, thus (in the words of a nursemaid) "sacrificing herself for her father" (*W*, 229). Horatio and his father remain entirely unaware of each other's movements around Inismore even though they occur almost simultaneously during the novel's action. To the reader, who has access to the story only through Horatio's letters, the father's trajectory remains quite obscured. While Horatio mentions his father's intentions to marry an un-named Irish woman, and while the existence of a rival for Glorvina's heart haunts Horatio throughout the second half of the novel, he fails to connect the two circumstances.

Owenson weaves them together in a "Conclusion," the novel's penulti-mate chapter and its only section written in the third person. The new narra-tor tells us that Horatio's father has arrived in Ireland, summoned Horatio to meet him in Dublin, and traveled west to retrieve his unknown bride. Horatio follows and is improbably led back to the castle of Inismore just in time to interrupt the wedding, already under way, between his father and Glorvina. Horatio rushes to the altar, entirely unaware of the bridegroom's identity: "Stop, I charge you, stop!" he cries, "you know not what you do. . . . She is mine! mine in the eye of heaven!" (*W*, 231), and amid the ensuing confusion, an astonished father and son acknowledge each other. The elderly Irish prince indignantly demands, "What, and who are you? and to what purpose have you . . . thus combined to embitter my last hours, by threatening the destruc-tion of my child?" (*W*, 232), and then Horatio's father reveals his and his son's identities as the prince's hereditary enemies. The shocking emotional effect of this revelation literally kills the prince and leaves Glorvina "lifeless" "in the arms of the attendants" (*W*, 233). Glorvina eventually entrusts herself to her priest—"I have now no father but you," she tells him, "act for me as such!"— who recommends that she marry Horatio (*W*, 236). "It is my father they will destroy," Glorvina cries, when Horatio first rushes into the church (*W*, 232), and at her father's funeral, she addresses the two Englishmen "with a piercing shriek" and asks, "Which of you murdered my father?" (*W*, 234). The melo-dramatic violence of this novel's "Conclusion" cannot be subsumed or erased by the reconciliatory image of union the Earl expresses in his subsequent let-ter, not least because of his mendacious conduct toward the family he wishes to "inseparably blend[]" with his own.

In Owenson's separation of Horatio's and his father's motives, we can see how her engagement with the literary field differs from her negotiation of imperial politics. The conflation of the Earl's sentiments with Owenson's voice has abetted allegorical interpretations of the text, forwarded under the as-sumption that Horatio and his father have identical feelings toward Glorvina as well as identical motivations in marrying her. However, only the Earl, who fails to marry Glorvina, not Horatio, who does marry her, considers his mari-tal ambitions as symbolic of political reconciliation. The terms of Horatio's involvement with Glorvina, by contrast, reflect Owenson's conception of the literary transaction. While Katie Trumpener and others have suggested that Glorvina is Ireland's "allegorical embodiment"[43] and that Horatio's passion for her is synonymous with his passion for Ireland, this most accurately describes what the Earl thinks, and the novel rejects his ideas by excluding him from the marriage plot. The prominence of Horatio's point of view creates the illusion of a single narrative trajectory, but the competing trajectory of the Earl's relationship with the prince and Glorvina is just as important. *The Wild Irish Girl* can therefore be described as narrating the conflict between a transcendent aesthetic union and a national-political one.

It is the novel's failed marriage plot that is infused with overtly political rhetoric. When the Earl initially describes his unnamed fiancée to his son, he says that "the world will call the *union* disproportioned—disproportioned in every sense" (*W*, 221; my emphasis). After the sudden revelation of his identity, the Earl attempts to vindicate his motives to the dying prince. He uses a condescending tone while employing the familiar language of paternalism and benevolence; he had hoped "[t]o restore you to the blessings of independence; to raise your daughter to that rank in life, her birth, her virtues, and her talents merit; and to obtain your assistance in dissipating the ignorance, improving the state, and ameliorating the situation of those of your poor unhappy compatriots" (*W*, 232). The Earl's assumption of an incognito is actually quite charged. We learn that he first appears in Inismore during the 1798 rebellion and that he inspires the "trust" of the prince as a "refugee" who claims affinity with the rebels: "This mysterious visitant," an elderly domestic tells Horatio, "was some unfortunate [English] gentleman who had attached himself to the rebellious faction of the day, and . . . had thrown himself on the mercy of the prince" (*W*, 207–208). His disguise is therefore of the worst kind: it is the reverse image of his actual position as an apologist of English imperialism. It is no wonder, then, that Glorvina blames him instead of Horatio when the prince dies from shock. "'Which of you murdered my father?'" she asks; then, "looking tenderly on the younger M.," she "softly" adds, "'It was not you, my love!'" (*W*, 234). In the Earl's final letter endorsing the novel's successful marriage, he projects his own political motives onto his son, writing that he will "look forward with hope to this family alliance being prophetically typical of a national unity of interests and affections" (*W*, 241). But the Earl's attribution of huge political implications to his son's marriage more accurately characterizes the opinions of the older English suitor, who describes his Irish bride as "the most precious of all donations" and his own marriage as "retributing the parent through the medium of the child" (*W*, 233, 238) than a younger one whose raptures for his "love" do not carry the weight of political meaning.

Horatio disguises himself as an artist, not a rebel. This major difference allows Glorvina to excuse Horatio of any blame for her father's death and then to marry him. Throughout the novel, Owenson constructs Horatio as a surrogate for an English reader highly qualified to make aesthetic judgments. Painting is Horatio's "most cultivated talent," and in this capacity "as a man of genius," he becomes "distinguished . . . by the partiality and condescension of the Prince" (*W*, 53, 62, 61). Horatio's transformation of his experience into an artistic medium signifies his easy access to cultural capital, a notion that Owenson pursues as Horatio sketches a portrait of Glorvina. A view of her with the harp "interest[s]" Horatio enough for him to "take her likeness" (*W*, 94), and he peruses her with a keen eye. She has "a form full of character, and full of grace," whose "countenance breathed all the fervour of genius" and whose "costume" has "singular elegance" (*W*, 94–95). He also praises her expression: "her voice's full melodious powers . . . wind[] round the heart, while she enlightens the mind, and entrances the senses" (*W*, 97). His verbal portrait of her invests the painted sketch—"a most striking resemblance" (*W*, 97)—with an evaluative aura and demonstrates his appreciation of an art object as much as a skilled eye in thus judging it. Horatio's good taste also emerges at other moments, when he opines about the Ossian controversy (*W*, 103–116), embarks on "an impartial examination and unbiased inquiry" of old Irish ballads (*W*, 85), is ready to become a "*historiographer* to the prince of Inismore" (*W*, 89), and sketches that prince's castle (*W*, 94). Like a reviewer in a literary journal, Horatio only selects anecdotes worthy of reprinting; a "controversial dialogue" on religion, he writes to his London correspondent, "as it would stand a very poor chance of being read by you, will stand none at all of being transcribed by me" (*W*, 148). Owenson constructs Horatio as a discerning and knowledgeable reader and rewards him, not his father, with marriage.

Furthermore, *The Wild Irish Girl* connects Glorvina so thoroughly with Owenson the author that it becomes difficult to separate the two. Owenson herself promoted this association throughout her career, wearing traditional Irish dress, harp in tow, when she appeared in public and inscribing more direct references to authorship in later Irish novels, including the governess in *O'Donnel* (1814) and the eponymous heroine of *Florence Macarthy* (1818), who actually writes novels.[44] *The Wild Irish Girl* establishes the connection between Glorvina and Owenson through Horatio's comments on gender ("I listened," Horatio writes as Glorvina sings with her harp, "[it] was the voice of a *woman*!"), on her antiquarian expertise ("of nothing which concerns her country is she ignorant"), and through his shock at her talent ("Where can she have acquired this elegance of manner!—reared amidst rocks, and woods, and mountains!") (*W*, 50, 90, 66). Beyond this, some of Glorvina's avowals sound like possible descriptions of Owenson's own overdramatic style as a writer ("Our national music," she tells Horatio, "like our national character, admits of no medium in sentiment") and her digressive narrative technique ("I never could draw a perpendicular line in my life," she tells him, "so you must guide my hand, or I shall draw it all zig-zag") (*W*, 70, 94). Personal anecdotes in the footnotes that prove Owenson's local knowledge also reinforce the connection between her authorial persona and her heroine.[45]

The Wild Irish Girl, finally, establishes the homology between Glorvina and Owenson at the expense of another: that between Glorvina and Ireland itself. Owenson constructs Ireland as a differentiated society, no one part of which carries the weight of representativeness. This resistance to national identification is similar to Edgeworth's universalist appeals to sympathy. Ireland comprises Irish-speaking peasants (*W*, 19–22); hospitable "*independent country gentlemen*" (*W*, 188); "poor scholar[s]" who receive alms from their parish (*W*, 122); brutal agents for absentee landlords (*W*, 32–34); the people of northern Ireland, where "the Scotch character" is "engrafted" on the Irish (*W*, 168); and the urban spaces of Dublin and Belfast, the former a "miniature copy" of London and the latter the "*Athens* of Ireland" (*W*, 16, 193). The "superior and original" Glorvina cannot encapsulate this heterogeneity, not least because of her musical talent. Owenson connects her directly with Turloch Carolan, "the most celebrated of modern Irish bards," whose airs she fondly sings (*W*, 87).[46] Glorvina also has wide-ranging literary taste: "When my spirits are sunk and dreary," she declares, "I fly to my English Ossian," referring to the work of James Macpherson (*W*, 112). Most important, though, Owenson emphasizes Glorvina's distance from typical Irish ethnicity in her manner of speech. The Irish "brogue," Horatio tells his London friend, is "generally confined to the lower orders of society"; Glorvina's English, by contrast, is "grammatically correct, and elegantly pure . . . spoken with an accent that could never denote her country" (*W*, 127). Glorvina is as much the emblem of Owenson's artistic identity as Horatio is of an English reader capable of aesthetic judgment.

*   *   *

The importance of *The Wild Irish Girl* lies less in its negotiation of the politics of empire than its subsuming of national difference into an aesthetic register—one that privileges Englishness, just like the London-centered book trade that supported it. Owenson separates, rather than conflates, a cultural nationalism dependent on an artistic relation and a political nationalism reinforced by an imperial agenda. This novel's aesthetics *are* its politics: through the novel's double marriage plot, Owenson stubbornly suggests that aesthetic experience has less to do with a worldly agenda than the urgency of the post-Union historical moment seems to require. As with Edgeworth's appeals to universal sympathy, Owenson's attempts at separation participate in an emergent ideology that claims for the "literary" a unique place in modernity. The strategies and fantasies animating Edgeworth's and Owenson's aesthetics of provinciality reach for and retreat into a literary transaction as complex as the stridently political discourses that swirled, dizzyingly, through and around them. This was something of a defensive act. The "whole beauty and grandeur of art," writes Sir Joshua Reynolds in *Discourses on Art* (1797), "consists . . . in being able to get above all singular forms, local customs, particularities, and details of every kind." Works that "depend for their existence on particular customs and habits, a partial view of nature, or the fluctuation of fashion, can only be coeval with that which first raised them from obscurity."[47] Irish writers could never fully avoid the charge that their novels suffered from precisely this defect, that they only offered readers a "partial view of nature." The value of a nationally defined literature—one "rooted in our own soil," as Germaine de Staël puts it in *De l'Allemagne* (1810)—was helpful but ultimately not entirely sufficient.[48] The belief that literary exchange has its own its intrinsic worth aided and abetted the Irish writer's entrance into London. Countless provincial authors followed in her footsteps.

Chapter 4

Washington Irving's
Transatlantic Revisions

Who knows about Tarry Town? In the opening paragraph of "The Legend of Sleepy Hollow," Diedrich Knickerbocker brings us way up the Hudson River only to introduce a village that apparently doesn't need introduction. "In the bosom of one of those spacious coves which indent the eastern shore of the Hudson," Washington Irving writes, in his persona's voice, "there lies a small market town or rural port, which by some is called Greensburgh, but which is more universally and properly known by the name of Tarry Town." The nick name "Tarry Town" has become "universal," we subsequently learn, because of an old folk tale deriving from the complaints of "good housewives" grown tired of their husbands tarrying too long at the village tavern. Here, the knowledge that matters—"proper" knowledge—comes not from official records but from traditions that transmit knowledge down from "former days." Only such transmission makes a name "universally" known, an adverb that grants to the upper Hudson its own centrality as a community with customs rooted in place and in history. It is a truth universally acknowledged, Irving suggests, that Greensburgh is more properly known as Tarry Town. This seems like a grand proposition with which to begin a quaint Dutch tale, but Irving goes for it, at least in the version of "Sleepy Hollow" that was first published in New York in March 1820. When Irving revised the story for London publication, he hedged his bets: "There lies a small market town or rural port," he writes in that edition, "which is more *generally* and properly known by the name of Tarry Town."[1] Once a place "universally" known (at least in the opinion of Knickerbocker), this little corner of the Hudson is now "generally" known, a place whose inhabitants share knowledge common only to themselves. The fame of Tarry Town, it turns out, is not so impressive; its folk traditions, now rather circumscribed; its centrality, decentered. After all, the Hudson River is much closer to New York, the site of this tale's original publication, than to London, its new home—where few readers, even imagined ones, could plausibly have "universal" knowledge about any of its coves and shores.

This single word substitution is one of thousands of changes to *The Sketch Book* Irving made in the forgotten process I call *transatlantic revision*. The substitution of "generally" for "universally" encapsulates a shift in Irving's status from a writer addressing his local literary scene to one launching himself into a marketplace that effortlessly claimed the universality of its own perspective. As with the Irish fiction of Maria Edgeworth and Sydney Owenson discussed in the previous chapter, Irving's provinciality stands in contrast to the self-assured Englishness of a writer like Jane Austen. When he joined the lists of the eminent London publisher John Murray (also Austen's publisher, although at the time she was not a star author), Irving understandably became quite nervous. As he revised *The Sketch Book* for Murray's new edition, he wrote to his friend Henry Brevoort from London, "I shall not send any more manuscript to America, until I put it to press here. . . . The manner in which the work has been received here, instead of giving me spirit to write, has rather daunted me for the time."[2] The daunting task would have a major impact, since Murray's edition became the basis for all subsequent authorized versions of *The Sketch Book*, including new American editions printed in the mid-1820s, Irving's "Author's Revised Edition," and the scholarly and popular editions we currently read today. Despite the staying power of his revisions, literary scholars have never considered them worthy of independent study.

This chapter argues that Irving's revisions dynamically reflect his subordinate position in a literary field that privileged London. More specifically, I show that Irving's revisions to *The Sketch Book* swing between modes of representation that tie literary expression to the essence of national identity and to the kind of universality Irving, in London, can no longer grant the inhabitants of Tarry Town. Born from his provinciality, such modes combine to project literary exchange into a purified and idealized realm far removed from politics.[3] The roots of this idealization lie in a little-studied phase of Irving's early career that gave him a unique perspective on the uneven dynamics of the book trade. During the War of 1812, he edited *The Analectic Magazine*, a Philadelphia miscellany for which he selected British periodical texts for reprinting and also contributed a number of original pieces. This experience as editor of a British reprint magazine in one province of the literary field informed the representational modes of *The Sketch Book*, when, as an author, he arrived in its center. While most scholars have apologized for Irving's Anglophilia by relating his writing to American anxieties, crises, and politics, this chapter considers his focus on England as part of a fraught strategy for success.[4]

Irving's idealizations resonate with those found in Edgeworth and Owenson, who were both popular and beloved in the United States, as the wide reprinting of their work abundantly proves. Many prominent Americans subscribed to editions of Edgeworth's writings, including John Adams, Joseph Dennie, Timothy Dwight, Benjamin Rush, and Noah Webster, and Thomas Jefferson recommended her novels and tales, writing to a friend that "they are all good."[5] James Fenimore Cooper credited "Miss Edgeworth alone" for having "supplanted the sentimentalists, before Scott was known," and Catherine Maria Sedgwick dedicated her first novel, *A New-England Tale* (1822), to Edgeworth with great admiration.[6] In the first decades of the century, Sydney Owenson received boisterous tributes during St. Patrick's Day celebrations in Irving's home town of New York.[7] As with Edgeworth and Owenson, Irving was often received according to the logic of national culture. In a review of "Mr. Irving's comic pencil," *Blackwood's Edinburgh Magazine* linked him to the provincial literary formation this book as a whole describes. It called on Irving to "favour us with a series of novels, on the plan of those of Miss Edgeworth, or, if he likes that better, of the author of Waverley, illustrative of the present state of manners in the United States of America"; "if he will set boldly about *An American Tale, in three volumes duodecimo*, we think there is no rashness in promising him an easy, a speedy, and a glorious victory."[8] Irving's victories never included a novel, but they continued well after *The Sketch Book* and *The History of New York*, the first London edition of which was the occasion for this *Blackwood's* review. Irving's work on the *Analectic* and *The Sketch Book* announces his kinship with these Irish writers who also navigated the London book trade.

Irving's aesthetics of provinciality was shaped by his immersion in a print culture that was flooded with unstable material texts, unregulated by strict copyright laws, and unconcerned with proprietary authorship. Such texts were subject to a host of agents—editors, compositors, printers, reprinters— and contained within a variety of formats—books, periodicals, newspapers, anthologies, and adaptations. This dispersal of literary authority belied the imagined, intimate connection between author and reader that many works, including Irving's, so powerfully invoke. For decades, literary scholars responded to this textual instability by banishing it for the sake of that author-reader connection, which, although always a fantasy, seemed for a long while solid ground on which to build a discipline. This strategy is epitomized in postwar textual editing practice, known as the Greg-Bowers method, which sought to provide readers with composite texts that approached as nearly as possible an author's final intentions. The standard editions built on these principles, "MLA approved" and often reprinted, betray a desire to filter out the noise of the marketplace so we can listen more directly to our authors.[9] More recently, literary scholars have embraced textual instability; inspired by the interdisciplinary approach of book history, such an embrace acknowledges all the stages of a text's production as equally important, from composition to printing to distribution, reprinting, reading, and reception. "In reprint culture," writes Meredith McGill, "authorship is not the dominant mode of organizing literary culture."[10] This new perspective moves away from traditional literary history toward a history of reading and material texts and, in so doing, necessarily abandons the nation as the defining unit of analysis. In the absence of the author and of the nation, we have tuned in to another archive and are listening to materiality itself.[11]

My account of Irving revisits authorship as a phenomenon, not in the name of nostalgia but rather to uncover market effects not evident from focusing exclusively on the perspective of readers. As Bourdieu would insist, the authorial career—including an author's various "position-takings" in the literary field—remains a useful rubric for understanding literary production.[12] Indeed, this book as a whole turns to the career not to fetishize authorial intention but instead to denaturalize texts with reference to the contingencies that shaped them. Irving's idealization of the literary exchange participates in the same fantasy that grounds the Greg-Bowers model of textual scholarship: that there is an ideal literary text that can produce an ideal experience of reading. It is a fantasy that has erased the messy and uneven transatlantic process of the making of *The Sketch Book*.

This chapter begins by placing the London publication of *The Sketch Book* within the larger history of the transatlantic reprinting of American literature. Literary scholars have overlooked the London republication of American texts, which was common long before the success of mid-century novels like *The Scarlet Letter* (1850) and *Uncle Tom's Cabin* (1852). Like American reprints, most British reprints (including these two famous texts) were piracies, unauthorized ventures pursued by London publishers without the consent of American authors. However, British copyright law made it possible for American authors to control the publication of their own authorized editions.

Unlike the United States, which had residency and citizenship requirements for copyright, Great Britain allowed an author to secure de facto copyright as long as the British edition was unique, either printed before the book's American edition or revised heavily enough to claim the status of a new work.[13] In rare cases, transatlantic publication provided the possibility of the sort of revisions that defined *The Sketch Book*. As the subsequent chapter will show, transatlantic revision was also central to James Fenimore Cooper's early novels, including *The Spy* (1821), *The Pioneers* (1823), and *The Last of the Mohicans* (1826)—all of which Cooper revised for Colburn and Bentley's "Standard Novels" series in the 1830s. As with Irving, modern editors of Cooper have ensured the preservation of these revisions in scholarly editions and the trade reprints that incorporate them. After my discussion of the London republication of American fiction, the chapter turns to Irving's work at *The Analectic Magazine* and the remarkable transformation of *The Sketch Book* itself.

The London Republication of American Fiction

Clarence Gohdes estimates that "no less than six hundred" American titles were reprinted in London in the first four decades of the nineteenth century, and this includes all genres—religious writing, historical texts, philosophical works, poetry, and novels.[14] The possibility of authorial control over such reprints depended, as it did in the colonial period, in developing personal relationships with London publishers who could purchase the text and retain it as property, a feat that few American authors before Irving and Cooper managed to accomplish. Before 1820, notable editions and reprints appeared by Susanna Rowson, Royall Tyler, Charles Brockden Brown, and James Kirke Paulding. Brown's publisher traveled across the Atlantic to arrange for London editions on his own, with Brown's consent but without his direct supervision.[15] The Minerva Press ended up repackaging the American sheets of *Ormond* with a new title page, while *Arthur Mervyn* was reset for an entirely new edition (*Wieland*, though advertised by Minerva, probably did not receive its first London edition until after Brown's death in 1811).[16] After Irving's ordeal of revising and rearranging the authorized London edition of *The Sketch Book*, he dealt directly with Murray for his subsequent works. Irving's success, and Cooper's after him,[17] made it more tenable for London publishers to print American texts, resulting in a flood of reprints by authors like James MacHenry, John Neal, George Tucker, Sarah Hale, and Catharine

Maria Sedgwick. Sedgwick carefully supervised the London publication of her novels, as Melissa Homestead has recently established. Others, like John Neal, tirelessly complained about unauthorized reprinting.[18] This book's Appendix provides information for those American fictional works published between 1797 and 1832 that received London editions, indicating whether the London edition was authorized or unauthorized (so far as we know).

There were always textual and material differences between the original American editions and British reprints. It was customary for British reprinters to conform a foreign text to their own styles and formats, which often involved changing spelling and punctuation, modifying words according to local usage, and deleting material that would offend British censors and readers. Just as American reprints of British novels usually squeezed three volumes into two, British publishers expanded two-volume American novels to fit their customary three-volume format, as was the case with the early London editions of Cooper. Often, British reprints dropped an initial preface or advertisement to the American edition, as with the 1828 London edition of Sedgwick's *Hope Leslie*. British reprinters sometimes modified the title of an American text, perhaps to advertise its pseudo-ethnographic or historical content, as in the extended subtitle of Cooper's *The Spy*, which was pirated in London by W. B. Wittaker as *The Spy: A Tale of the Neutral Ground, Referring to Some Particular Occurrences During the American War; also Pourtraying American Scenery and Manners* (1822). In extreme cases, an American text was heavily annotated by a British editor, as with John Lambert's London edition of Irving's *Salmagundi Papers* (1811), which includes an elaborate introduction and many footnotes interpreting the text and explaining local references. For the most part, however, the point of British republication was easy money, as it was in the United States, and often the hand of a meddling editor cannot be found; in a remarkable irony, some British typesetters reprinted the American copyright page along with the rest of the text.[19]

Transatlantic revision was rare and entirely dependent on literary networks and personal relationships with publishers. In contrast to Irving and Cooper, for example, Sedgwick did not revise her authorized London editions for republication. As we shall see, Irving's revisions to *The Sketch Book* were catalyzed by an expansion of his professional acquaintance and connections that interrupted the serial publication of the work in New York and determined its future. For Cooper, transatlantic revision occurred in two stages: first when he made minor changes for initial London editions and second when he substantially altered his novels a decade later. Starting in the 1830s, the British publication of American literature escalated dramatically and included nearly all familiar authors of the nineteenth century. While the American reprinting of British fiction always exceeded in scale the British reprinting of American fiction, in the second half of the century, the busy traffic in texts in both directions "created a kind of Anglo-American public sphere," as Amanda Claybaugh has written, wherein "the people of Great Britain and the United States constituted a single reading public."[20] American titles filled the lists of respectable reprint series like Bentley's "Standard Novels" as well as less expensive runs like Routledge's "Railway Libraries," J. R. Smith's "Libraries of Old Authors," J. Cunningham's "Novel Newspaper," and Bohn's "Cheap Series," which were reprinted in two columns and small type. Some reprint series were devoted exclusively to American texts, including John Green's "Standard American Literature," begun in 1840, and Sampson Low's "American Copyright Series," begun in 1871.[21] Transatlantic revision remained uncommon, since later in the century, if American authors secured British copyright, they often published the same text simultaneously, perhaps only with a modified preface, as was sometimes the case with Nathaniel Hawthorne, Ralph Waldo Emerson, Mark Twain, William Dean Howells, and Henry James.

In the unpredictable world of transatlantic reprinting, however, exceptions are often the rule, and it remains difficult to generalize. While the impossibility of British authorial control over texts in the United States for the most part prevented transatlantic revision in the opposite direction, the 1794 Philadelphia edition of *Charlotte Temple*, previously thought a piracy, was actually pursued with the approval of Susanna Rowson, who may have had a hand in the more than four hundred variants from that novel's original London edition.[22] William Wells Brown's revisions to *Clotel* occurred in the other direction as well; Brown originally published that text in London in 1853 and modified it substantially for future American editions in 1864 and 1867.[23] The most famous case of transatlantic revision remains frustratingly elusive on the question of authority: *Moby-Dick*. As was increasingly the custom for an established author, Melville arranged for the simultaneous transatlantic publication of that novel, which was issued in London by Bentley as *The Whale* in October 1851 and in New York by Harper's as *Moby-Dick* one month later. But the New York text was stereotyped and in proofs long before the London text was set in type, and Melville made changes to the American proofs before he sent them to Bentley, whose firm in turn revised it according to house style and some of its own priorities. *The Whale* includes over seven hundred instances of substantive variation from *Moby-Dick*, including the omission of the Epilogue and Chapter 25; the

omission or modification of many words and passages, such as offensive religious language; and the addition of passages and footnotes. Melville's editors
have always struggled to characterize these revisions, but, again, in absence of
the corrected American proofs or knowledge of Melville's process of revision, the
authority of the changes is difficult to trace.[24]

In general, of course, authorial revision has occurred throughout literary
history, from Milton to Whitman. In the early nineteenth century, transatlantic revision in Irving and Cooper occurred in response to the specific circumstances of an Anglophone literary field with London at its center. Washington
Irving was the first author from the United States to navigate this landscape
successfully, and the story of his early career as a provincial editor and author
highlights its definitive features and lasting effects.

The Analectic Magazine and the "Exalted Ministry of Literature"

After the local success of satirical works like *Salmagundi* in 1807–1808 and *The
History of New York* in 1809, Irving turned to *The Analectic Magazine*, a publication that exemplifies American provinciality in a transatlantic literary field
unregulated by copyright law. In his role as editor, which he fulfilled from the
journal's founding in January 1813 until January 1815, Irving selected British
texts for reprinting and also published some original content by Americans,
including himself. Irving contributed a few biographical sketches and two
pieces he eventually revised for Murray's edition of *The Sketch Book*, "Traits of
Indian Character" and "Philip of Pokanoket." His editorship of the *Analectic*
coincided with the controversial War of 1812 and the huge outpouring of nationalist sentiment it produced. Irving's contradictory position as the steward
of British literature in America during a time of war led to his promotion of
Anglo-American literary sharing defined by a retreat from politics and a desire
for transcendence. The very few scholars who have mentioned the *Analectic*
dismiss his involvement as a minor episode between his earlier domestic success and the international phenomenon of *The Sketch Book*.[25] His editorship is
crucial, however, because it suggests the magazine had a role in turning him
toward elite literary fantasies. Irving thus participated in what Edward Cahill
has recently described as an early nineteenth-century shift, driven by Federalist criticism, toward a notion of aesthetics as "not only distinct from the realm
of politics but opposed to it."[26]

Irving's editorship has been understood as an instance when he succumbed to the patriotic fervor of the war, since he printed a number of American naval biographies and patriotic songs, most notably Francis Scott Key's "The Defence of Fort McHenry," known now of course as "The Star Spangled Banner."[27] Stanley Williams in his early biography set the usual tone; he highlights Irving's "patriotic passages in the Analectic Magazine," recording the "joy" Irving expresses as he sees "the flag of our country encircled with glory, and our nation elevated to a dignified rank among the nations of the earth."[28] In fact, this nationalistic rhetoric is not at all typical of Irving's contributions to the magazine. In the same sketch Williams cites, Irving admits that "[t]here is a point, however, beyond which exultation becomes insulting, and honest pride swells into vanity. . . . For our parts we truly declare that we revere the British nation. One of the dearest wishes of our hearts is to see a firm and well grounded friendship established between us" (December 1813, 495–496). Here and elsewhere in the *Analectic*, Irving's overtures toward Britain suggest an affection untainted by military hostility. In one instance, Irving hopes that, "[a]s the nations must inevitably, and at no very distant period, come once more together in the relations of amity and commerce, it is to be wished that . . . we may never cease to esteem and respect each other" (August 1813, 134). Most of Irving's writing during the war points toward earning the respect of the British by way of an appeal to "rank" and "esteem." In American literary history, the period during and after the War of 1812 is usually characterized by the spread of romantic historicism and Scottish associationist philosophy, which encouraged the use of local history and legend as sources for a literary culture that would by definition be national.[29] An account of the *Analectic* as a whole reveals how Irving's engagement with the British literary press helped him navigate his conflicted relationship with such literary nationalism.

The magazine's structure and content provide a unique window into Irving's artistic and intellectual life, because editing was itself a practice in criticism.[30] The table of contents for the November 1813 issue of the *Analectic*, pictured in Figure 2, can be used as a guide to its typical structure. Each issue began with two or three long "Reviews," attributed to their original sources and usually taken from major publications like the *Edinburgh Review*, the *Quarterly Review*, or the *Monthly Review*. This opening section always filled at least half of an issue but often comprised more. The next section of the magazine, which marked "Original" articles written for the *Analectic*, was more variable in length, at times reaching that of the "Reviews" section but sometimes not present at all. Each issue concluded with a section for gossip called "Literary Intelligence," and before this there was a short selection of "Poetry"

by British and American authors. The section called "Spirit of Magazines" usually comprised about a fifth of each issue but included, as the November table
of contents suggests, a wider variety of material than the other sections of the
magazine. Irving collected that material from British magazines usually without attributing them to particular sources, sometimes reprinting a review's extracts of primary texts without the opinions of reviewers or a combination of a
reviewer's comments along with extracts while eliding any difference between
them. The result is a series of extracts from published books that, but for the
section heading, looks like a series of passages selected from the direct perusal
of many primary sources. The "Spirit of Magazines" section encapsulates the
etymology of the title Irving chose for the magazine, which comes from the
Greek *analektos*, meaning "things gathered or picked up" (*OED*). The term
entered the English language in the seventeenth century as a meaning for frag-
ments of food left after a meal, and in the eighteenth century, it was applied
specifically to literary anthologies. We can think of Irving as an unwanted
guest at the banquet of the British cultural elite, watching as they taste the offerings of the day, approving of certain dishes, discarding others. Irving has his
eye on the food, not their verdicts, and grabs what's left in order to present the
dishes themselves, on their own. For the "Spirit" section, he cobbles together
a heterogeneous plate of leftovers, an improvised dish that lays claim to being
more delectable than the original meal. The true "Spirit" of the magazine
editors becomes their reading, not their opinions. The section highlights the
critical agency of Irving's readers; he wants you to know what they're eating,
across the Atlantic, but not what they think; he leaves the tasting up to you.

The contents of the *Analectic* during its two-year run under Irving—
reprinted British reviews, original reviews and sketches by American writers, and numerous excerpted texts and poems—reveal the struggle between
cultural nationalism and the contrasting idea that national difference has a
minor role to play in literary exchange. Many of the articles Irving reprinted,
along with his own writing, suggest that he came to embrace a notion of literary production that is particularly and explicitly Anglo-American, paradoxically both national and universal. The pull of cultural nationalism emerges
in the *Analectic* in a number of articles Irving chose to print. James Kirke
Paulding, for example, wrote biographical sketches about American military
heroes that highlighted "NATIONAL GLORY," as Paulding put it in a notice
of Captain Isaac Hull (March 1813, 275). An anonymous piece on the life
of John Aylwin, Captain Hull's sailing master, echoed Paulding's patriotism,
and Gulian Verplank contributed patriotic sketches of Oliver Ellsworth, third

ANALECTIC MAGAZINE.

FOR NOVEMBER, 1813.

CONTENTS.

Correspondance, Littéraire, Philosophique et Critique. Adressée à un Souverain d'Allemagne, depuis 1770, jusqu'à 1782. Par le Baron De Grimm, et par Diderot. 5 Tomes, 8vo. pp. 2250.

[From the Edinburgh Review, for July, 1813.]

THIS is certainly a very entertaining book—though a little too bulky—and the greater part of it not very important. We are glad to see it, however; not only because we are glad to see any thing entertaining, but also because it makes us acquainted with a person, of whom every one has heard a great deal, and most people hitherto known very little. There is no name which comes oftener across us, in the recent history of French literature, than

VOL. II. *New Series.* 45

Figure 2. *The Analectic Magazine*, Philadelphia, November 1813.

Courtesy of the Library Company of Philadelphia.

chief justice of the U.S. Supreme Court; Samuel Adams; and Fisher Ames, a political theorist and congressman whose writing features "images of native growth," as Verplank writes, "drawn from the peculiar scenery and manners of our country."[31] Irving's sampling of British critical discourse suggests that such nationalist commitments give literary expression legitimacy. The first issue of the *Analectic* featured the *Edinburgh Review*'s treatment of Edgeworth's *Tales of Fashionable Life* (1812), which singled out her Irish scenes and characterizations in *The Absentee* for its highest praise (January 1813, 22–47). Likewise, a review of the second volume of Thomas Moore's *Irish Melodies* (1811), reprinted from the *Monthly Review*, affectionately quotes Moore's own gratitude for the kind reception of his earlier work; "we feel so proud," Moore writes, "for our country's sake and our own, of the interest which this purely Irish work has excited" (October 1814, 282). A wide selection of the literary opinions of Germaine de Staël gives further authority to such ideas; the *Edinburgh Review*'s summary of Staël's *De la littérature considéré dans ses rapports avec les institutions sociales* (Paris, 1800), for example, informed Irving's readers that "all the peculiarities in the literature of different ages and countries, may be explained by a reference to the condition of society, and the political and religious institutions of each," a stance that informed Staël's description of the "national taste and genius" prevailing in several major European countries (September 1813, 180). This theory of literature is consistent with Scottish associationist theories of taste, represented in the *Analectic* in reviews of aesthetician William Greenfield's work, which argues that aesthetic experience depends on what Archibald Alison called "national associations" or the accumulated myths and legends of a particular nation as reproduced in works of the imagination.[32]

Such loyalty to and emphasis on nationalized aesthetics, however, contradicts the valorization of a presumptive universalism equally present in the reprinted articles of the *Analectic*. Unlike the *Monthly Review*, the *Quarterly Review* criticized Thomas Moore for considering "topics merely Irish" and encouraged him in the future to "exclud[e] all topics of a local or political nature" (February 1813, 143). Irving reprinted a short notice, from London's theater newspaper *The Globe*, that praised an American actor for concealing his nationality to ensure judgment according to a universal standard, exclusively "by the force and being of his professional talents" (October 1813, 343). The *Scottish Review* praised their compatriot James Hogg for finally abandoning an "imagination . . . shackled down by local habits" for one that "soar[ed]" beyond them (February 1814, 129). Anxiety about such limits had gender implications as well. Staël's championing of national particularity dovetailed

neatly with Madame de Genlis's praise of female writers, featured in a reprinted review of her book on the importance of women to French literature,[33]
and the *Quarterly Review* condescendingly linked particularity to the female
gender. The "minds [of women]," they wrote in a reprinted review of Lady
Mary Wortley Montagu's letters, "are of a less bold, original, and independent
cast" than the minds of men, insisting that women "partake much more strongly
and uniformly than ourselves of the character of the age in which they live, and
the society to which they belong" (March 1814, 217). If a feminine intellect so defined was considered a liability, as the *Quarterly* intends it to be, then an aesthetics that adheres to the particularities of a national culture suffers in the bargain.

Reprinted articles return again and again to the theme of privileging the
Anglophone world, a strategy that foregrounds Irving's advocacy of literary exchange among elite groups within it at the expense of any real commitment to
outsiders. Indeed, the *Analectic* covered a remarkably expansive range of topics
without embracing a cosmopolitan perspective. While travel narratives by European explorers appear in Irving's selections on Africa, China, India, the South
Pacific, and South America, and the magazine demonstrates a frequent interest
in European countries, particularly France, as well as the lands of antiquity and
the Middle East, British and American topics receive by far the most attention.
The world was refracted through a particular point of view, neatly epitomized
in a comment about the "Sandwich Islanders" recorded in reprinted excerpts
from John Turnbull's *Voyage Around the World* (1805). Turnbull congratulates the
Islanders for having "so eagerly availed themselves" of their "intercourse with the
Anglo-Americans" to learn English (November 1813, 418).

Irving capitalized on the close ethnic, racial, and cultural kinship between
Britain and the United States to downplay the national and political differences
that would otherwise divide the two nations. Early during the War of 1812,
the *Edinburgh Review* addressed one conflict that prompted open hostility—
the impressment of American sailors into the British navy—and argued that
the practice has "naturally arisen from the resemblance of the two nations in
language and manners" (March 1813, 241). An "Ode to the Sons of Britain
and America" reprinted from the *Monthly Review* warns that war would bring
a decline in "Commerce," and it encourages peace between "brother[]" nations who both value "Freedom" and "worship Heaven" "in one language"
(March 1813, 277–278). In Irving's own headnote to a *Quarterly Review* article,
he hopes that "national hostilities" won't prevent American readers from ap-
preciating the following "sirloin of real old English roast beef": an article that
counters Malthusian economics by predicting that current and former British

colonies will absorb England's excess population. "[T]he union of reverential attachment" and "common interests," the *Quarterly* writes, will ensure that the United States will remain a reliable repository for what is "civilized," "intellectual" and "ennobling" about the English (July 1813, 50–51).

Irving was capable, of course, of viewing the British literary press with some critical distance. This was especially evident with regard to rampant politicization, which Irving thought was distasteful. Exemplified in the rivalry between the Whig *Edinburgh Review* and the Tory *Quarterly Review*, partisanship often determined how a given book would be judged. Irving regularly put the two periodicals in implicit dialogue and even once directly juxtaposed their views on the same novel, Edgeworth's *Patronage* (1814). In an editorial note to this pairing, Irving noted, "It is often not less instructive than amusing to observe the very different lights in which the same object may appear to persons of dissimilar tastes and habits of mind" (July 1814, 14). All political bias is bad for Irving, and it is his duty to rescue literature from its clutches, as when he "transplant[s]" a poem from "a political paper" into his magazine—"a more congenial soil" (August 1814, 170). Throughout the two years of Irving's editorship, as he collected, read, judged, collated, and edited British articles for reprinting, we can observe a steady separation of literary discourse from a world otherwise politically defined—by party, by nationality, by war. This separation encourages a faculty of taste trained to judge the "spirit" of literature on its own terms.

Among the original articles that Irving printed in the *Analectic* was his own short biography of Scottish poet Thomas Campbell, first published as a preface to the New York edition of Campbell's work Irving edited in 1810. For the March 1815 issue, he revised this piece and wrote a striking footnote that describes his fraught position as an editor of British reprints during the war. It was added to an extremely reverent passage on British writers. In 1810, he had declared such writers "the adopted citizens of this country" to whom Americans turn "with such feelings as the Egyptian, when he looks towards the sacred fount of that stream, which, rising in a far distant country, flows down upon his own barren soil, diffusing riches, beauty, and fertility."[34] After the war, Irving clearly felt that such reverence needed some defense:

> Since this biographical notice was first published, the political relations between the two countries have been changed by a war with Great Britain. The above observations, therefore, may not be palatable to those who are eager for the hostility of the pen as well as the sword. The author, indeed, was for some time in doubt whether

to expunge them, as he could not prevail on himself to accommodate them to the embittered temper of the times. He determined, however, to let them remain. However the feelings he has expressed may be outraged or prostrated by the violence of warfare, they never can be totally eradicated. Besides, it should be the exalted ministry of literature to keep together the family of human nature; to calm with her "soul-subduing voice" the furious passions of warfare, and thus to bind up those ligaments which the sword would cleave asunder. The author may be remiss in the active exercise of this duty, but he will never have to reproach himself, that he has attempted to poison, with political virulence, the pure fountains of elegant literature. (March 1815, 246)

This passage constructs the literary as a balm for human nature, "pure," "elegant," and tied ineluctably to congregation and community. Irving has found a new purpose during the war: henceforth, he will embrace what he calls the "exalted ministry of literature." Driven by a powerful ideological fantasy, he attempts to carve out a particularly literary place in society, one free from the "embittered temper of the times." His practices as editor played a large role in forming his notion of what kind of administering the world of "literature" required for its "soul-subduing voice" to be heard above the "political virulence" that otherwise governed human affairs.

Transatlantic Revision in *The Sketch Book of Geoffrey Crayon*

The Sketch Book and its transatlantic publication demonstrate how this new commitment played out. Irving left New York for England in 1815, after the peace was declared, and in 1819, he began sending manuscripts from London to his friends in New York to arrange for their publication. The work appeared in seven numbers, comprising four or five sketches each, between June 1819 and September 1820. Early on, Irving learned of the unauthorized reprinting of some of the sketches in British magazines. In the effort to secure copyright, he proposed a London edition to John Murray, whom he had met a year previously through a letter of introduction from Thomas Campbell. Murray politely refused, and after Irving considered appealing to Archibald Constable, he secured a deal in London with the relatively unknown John Miller, who reprinted the first four American numbers as one volume that Irving financed at his own expense. Miller's edition contained minor revisions, some of which reflect Irving's cognizance of his new English audience. Soon thereafter, Miller's firm ran into financial trouble, and Walter Scott, an acquaintance for whom Irving could also thank Campbell, convinced Murray to purchase *The Sketch Book*. Murray replaced Miller's title page with his own on the unsold copies of the first volume and agreed to publish a second volume comprising the fifth and sixth American numbers as well as the content of what became the final American number, which was published in New York two months after Murray's edition appeared in London.[35] In his own retrospective account of this process, Irving calls Murray "The Prince of Booksellers," and one immediately notices the difference he made.[36] Irving added three pieces that did not appear in the American edition—

Table 1. The Transatlantic Publication of Washington Irving, *The Sketch Book of Geoffrey Crayon* (New York, 1819–1820; London, 1820)

Before the acquisition of John Murray, Irving made no significant changes.

First New York Edition, Van Winkle, 1819	*Part No.*	*First London Edition, John Miller, 1820*	*Vol. No.*
Prospectus	1	Advertisement	1
The Author's Account		The Author's Account	
The Voyage		The Voyage	
Roscoe		Roscoe	
The Wife		The Wife	
Rip Van Winkle		Rip Van Winkle	
English Writers on America	2	English Writers on America	
Rural Life in England		Rural Life in England	
The Broken Heart		The Broken Heart	
The Art of Book Making		The Art of Book Making	
A Royal Poet	3	A Royal Poet	
The Country Church		The Country Church	
The Widow and Her Son		The Widow and Her Son	
The Boar's Head, East Cheap		The Boar's Head, East Cheap	
The Mutability of Literature	4	The Mutability of Literature	
Rural Funerals		Rural Funerals	
The Inn Kitchen		The Inn Kitchen	
The Spectre Bridegroom		The Spectre Bridegroom	

the Indian sketches originally published in the *Analectic* and "L'Envoy," a post-script addressed to English readers; he rearranged the order of sketches; he added a dedication to Walter Scott; and he postponed the publication of the American edition until after Murray's had appeared. Murray's importance is reflected in the fact that when Irving published the first volume of *The Sketch Book* quietly and at his own expense, he made no significant changes to its structure. Table 1 highlights the impact of Murray's intervention.

Table 1. Continued

After the acquisition of John Murray, Irving made many significant changes.

First New York Edition, Van Winkle, 1819–1820	Part No.	First London Edition, John Murray, 1820	Vol. No.
	5	**Dedication to Walter Scott** **Westminster Abbey**	**2**
Christmas		**Christmas**	
The Stage Coach		**The Stage Coach**	
Christmas Eve		**Christmas Eve**	
Christmas Day		**Christmas Day**	
		The Christmas Dinner[a]	
		Little Britain	
		Stratford-on-Avon	
		Traits of Indian Character[a]	
		Philip of Pokanoket[a]	
John Bull	6	**John Bull**	
The Pride of the Village		**The Pride of the Village**	
		The Angler	
The Legend of Sleepy Hollow		**The Legend of Sleepy Hollow**	
Westminster Abbey	7		
The Angler			
Stratford-on-Avon			
Little Britain			
		L'Envoy[a]	

[a] Indicates sketch not in first New York editions. N.B.: The sketch "Christmas Dinner" first appeared in the second New York edition.

An account of Murray's edition suggests the lasting influence of the literary ideology Irving embraced while editing the *Analectic*. In a general sense, the transatlantic content of both the New York and the London editions of *The Sketch Book* promotes Anglo-American literary fellowship. Having traveled for a few years in England, Irving invents the fictional American persona Geoffrey Crayon to model good literary tourism and reporting. Crayon sketches with good faith, keeping the "fountains of elegant literature" pure as ever, and his affectionate melancholy combines with generous accounts of the various strata of life in the British Isles—in Dublin, Liverpool, northern England, all over London, in Wales, and out in the countryside. Even in the sketch that seems most to trade in national stereotypes works to expose their falsity. In the version of "John Bull" published in New York, Crayon blames the English for "giving ludicrous appellations . . . not merely [to] individuals, but nations." The stereotype John Bull is "absolutely present to the public mind," he writes, and argues that its prevalence is a self-fulfilling prophesy: "Perhaps the continual contemplation of the character thus drawn of them, has contributed to fix it upon the nation."[37] Irving divorces the idea of national character from anything essential about the people of a nation, arguing that its truth resides merely in the tendency to identify national character, not in character itself. *The Sketch Book* as a whole generously depicts English culture and gently defends Americans from prejudicial English views, as in the sketch "English Writers on America," which begins, in the New York edition, "It is with feelings of deep regret that I have noticed the literary animosity daily growing up between England and America."[38]

Irving's attachment to the purity of literary exchange received extra force when the possibility of reaching a vast English readership suddenly became real to him. As Ben McClary has written, "The name of John Murray on [Irving's] published works" was "the most valued status symbol to which an author could aspire."[39] Irving's transatlantic revisions came with a change in the project's order of magnitude. This ensured wide exposure, including a larger audience in the United States, as Irving himself implied when he wrote to his brother that he was "highly gratified with the success of my literary enterprise in this country. After all I value success here chiefly as tending to confirm my standing in my own country."[40] As I have mentioned, the acquisition of Murray had an immediate and lasting influence on the textual history of *The Sketch Book*. We are familiar with the content of Irving's transatlantic revisions, but we are unaware that they *are* transatlantic revisions. The first American editions remain highly valuable as collector's items, but few ever read them.[41]

Not every revision can be described as a response to London publication, and some of them overlay his vision of Anglo-American camaraderie with a tinge of self-consciousness and irony. But most revisions express Irving's provinciality and its attendant idealizations. (For the sake of discussion, I will refer to the first American numbers as the New York text and to Murray's edition as the London text.)

The London text opens with a homage to his fellow provincial, Walter Scott: "To Walter Scott, Bart., this work is dedicated, in testimony of the admiration and affection of the author."[42] After this comes "Westminster Abbey," a sketch composed first for the London text, since it was printed there first and only afterward in New York.[43] It begins with Geoffrey Crayon "pass[ing] several hours in rambling about Westminster Abbey" and describing the relics he finds there.[44] The sketch is notable for its description of "Poet's Corner," where "visitors to the abbey remain longest."[45] Crayon first wonders why this is the case and then argues for the unique status of literature in human experience:

> They linger about these [monuments to "literary men"] as about the tombs of friends and companions; for indeed there is something of companionship between the author and the reader. Other men are known to posterity only through the medium of history, which is continually growing faint and obscure; but the intercourse between the author and his fellow men is ever new, active and immediate. He has lived for them more than for himself; he has sacrificed surrounding enjoyments, and shut himself up from the delights of social life, that he might the more intimately commune with distant minds and distant ages. . . . Well may posterity be grateful to his memory; for he has left it an inheritance, not of empty names and sounding actions, but whole treasures of wisdom, bright gems of thought, and golden veins of language.[46]

We might take the distinction Irving allows here between "distant minds" and "distant ages" seriously, wrench this passage from its focus on the past, and consider it a meditation on Irving's own relation to "distant" readers of the present day—on the relation between "the author and his fellow men" in England, not so distant (for him) any more. "[I]ndeed there is something of companionship between the author and the reader," Irving writes, describing as fact what he in fact desires. The sacrifice of the apparent "enjoyments" and "delights of social life" protects the literary transaction from any interference,

including the "history" of "sounding actions" that "grow[s] faint and obscure."
Such isolation is amply rewarded by the "companionship," "treasures," "gems,"
and "gold[]" reading provides. For Irving, author and reader are enclosed in a
particularly literary intimacy.

Some of Irving's transatlantic revisions excise rare moments when an account of the English approaches a disrespectful tone. This occurs, predictably,
in changes Irving made to "John Bull." In that jocular sketch, the New York
text derisively describes John Bull as holding up his boots on "spindle shanks,"
whereas in the London text, he merely wears them on "once sturdy legs."[47] In
the New York text, John Bull "*crawls* about, whistling to himself," whereas in
the London text, he "*goes* about, whistling,"[48] and his dwelling is no longer
described as a "mouldering old mansion" but instead as an "old family mansion."[49] In the sketch "Christmas Day," Irving modifies a sarcastic comment
about the "old harper" who entertains the guests at Bracebridge Hall, thus
changing its national valence and perhaps unintentionally enhancing its rather
raunchy tone. In the London text, the harper "twang[s] his instrument with
a vast deal more power than melody." For American readers, the somewhat
masturbatory harper plays, too, "with a vast deal more power than melody,"
but also he sits there "twanging the roast beef of old England."[50]

More significant than these deletions and modifications, however, is the
addition of extensive new passages to "John Bull," the Christmas series, and
other sketches. Such additions represent some of Irving's most Anglophilic
moments. While Irving once described John Bull as crawling about on his
"spindle shanks," after transatlantic revision, he pictures him this way:

> His virtues are all his own; all plain, homebred and unaffected. His
> very faults smack of the raciness of his good qualities. His extrava-
> gance savours of his generosity. His quarrelsomeness of his cour-
> age; his credulity of his open faith; his vanity of his pride; and his
> bluntness of his sincerity. They are all redundancies of a rich and
> liberal character. He is like his own oak; rough without, but sound
> and solid within; whose bark abounds with excrescences in propor-
> tion to the growth and grandeur of the timber; and whose branches
> make a fearful groaning and murmuring in the least storm, from
> their very magnitude and luxuriance.[51]

This encomium manifests on the level of praise what more subtle accommo-
dations do on the level of narrative. The passage admittedly surrounds such

praise with a playful string of negatives; John Bull, filled with virtue, is also extravagant, quarrelsome, credulous, vain, and blunt.[52] Even so, Irving flatters his new readership through "redundancies" matched only by what this passage insists is their own "rich and liberal character." In "The Pride of the Village," to point to a smaller addition, a rural English farm girl is newly described "with all the dawning loveliness of the queen of May."[53] Furthermore, Irving added over one thousand words to his affectionate description of Christmas. A stage coach driver becomes in the London text a person of "great consequence and consideration along the road" as housewives "look upon him as a man of great trust and dependence," and "Old English famil[ies]" become "as well worth studying as a collection of Holbien's portraits or Albert Durer's prints."[54] We learn not only that "there is much antiquarian lore to be acquired" from the study of English faces[55] but also about several additional traditions. Irving wrote new passages describing "peacock pie," the "Wassail Bowl" and its ac-companying merriment, and the great Christmas masque featuring guests dressed as Robin Hood, Maid Marian, and the Lord of Misrule.[56] Geoffrey Crayon has more fun in the London text, and his pleasure is a fantastical mir-ror in which the English can view their most cherished customs.

This extended celebration of English customs involves a renewed em-phasis on history that works to transform *The Sketch Book* into a study in antiquarianism. Indeed, the well-known nostalgia of this text derives in large part from transatlantic revision. A handful of long footnotes introduced into the London text explain ancient English customs and make Bracebridge Hall not only a traditional English home but also the only place in England where some traditions survive. New notes explain "the old ceremony of serving up the boar's head," how "the peacock was anciently in great demand," that the Wassail bowl "is still prepared in some old families," and that "Masquings or mummeries were favourite sports at Christmas in old times."[57] In the London text, Geoffrey Crayon travels back in time to guide English readers through their history. "I felt also an interest in the scene," writes Irving in a new pas-sage, "from the consideration that these fleeing customs were posting fast into oblivion, and that this was, perhaps, the only family in England in which the whole of them was still punctiliously observed."[58] Similar discourse is newly present in "The Pride of the Village," which now includes descriptions of the May-pole as a relic of the past, rather than a contemporary practice; its use "had been promoted by its present pastor," Irving explains, "who was a lover of old customs."[59] *The Sketch Book*'s new antiquarian emphasis is thrown into relief by Irving's deletion of a footnote in the New York text that explained a *contemporary* English custom to American readers. In the note, which appears in the first of the Christmas sketches, he originally defined "the Waits" as "bands of music that go about the towns and villages of England, serenading for several nights preceding Christmas."[60] The deletion implies that Irving thought English readers would already know what he's talking about.[61]

Additional significant revisions shore up Irving's own authority on England, remove self-consciousness about his Anglophilia, and add self-deprecating and knowing remarks about literary taste. Besides the heavily footnoted traditions he added to the Christmas sketches, Irving also weaved in direct citations to explain references that were left undeclared in the New York text, as when he writes that Master Simon "could imitate Punch and Judy" and train the dogs "according to the directions of Jervaise Markham."[62] Irving deleted remarks in "The Stage Coach" that apologize to American readers for his love of the English, for "the rhapsody into which I have sometimes run" in describing Christmas. "The article was written on the approach of the festival," he explains in the deleted passage, and was therefore "set in motion by external circumstances."[63] In the London text, Irving need only excuse himself for bad form, as he does in an added passage to "The Pride of the Village." "I am conscious" that the particulars "have little to recommend them," he writes, and admits that they "left a deeper impression on my mind than many circumstances of a more striking nature."[64]

Some changes to "The Legend of Sleepy Hollow" reflect Irving's new preoccupation with English readers, including the substitution of "generally" for "universally" discussed at the beginning of this chapter. Such readers might have been ready to believe that Major André's tree, which forms a backdrop for the climactic chase scene, was "knarled, and fanstastic," but they might have been less convinced that it was also "vast," an adjective Irving deleted from the New York text.[65] Certainly, too, English readers were helped along by new footnotes that define the whippoorwill as "a bird heard only at night" and "the ancient city of the Manhattoes" as "New-York."[66] Other changes can be grouped with the many revisions to *The Sketch Book* that are interesting because they cannot be explained with reference to London republication. Irving modifies in a rather arbitrary way the list of belongings that a terrified Ichabod Crane leaves behind while fleeing town. In both editions, Ichabod's estate includes shirts, stockings, corduroy small-clothes, a book of psalm tunes, a rusty razor, and a pitch pipe, but only in the New York text does he own "a small pot of bear's grease for the hair, and a cast-iron comb."[67] London republication also fails to explain changes to Irving's characterization of what he calls the "visionary turn" of Sleepy Hollow's inhabitants. While in the New York text, they "have trances and visions, and see strange sights," in the London text, they "are *subject* to trances and visions, and *frequently* see strange sights."[68] The new words merely intensify a supernatural tendency already present in the story. The same can be said for the way Irving describes the contagiousness of such a "visionary turn." In the New York text, those who visit the town— including us readers, as imaginary visitors—"imperceptibly acquir[e]" a "visionary propensity"; in the London text, however, Irving writes that such a "propensity" is instead "unconsciously imbibed."[69] This makes visiting Sleepy Hollow more eerie, since we are no longer "conscious" of its effects. It is a revision that heightens the story's gothic and romantic aura but remains irreducible to the cultural significance of Murray's edition as I have described it. Irving obviously approached revision as an opportunity to explore a myriad of strategies and artistic choices.

At one point while preparing the London text, Irving wrote to Brevoort about writer's block. "I feel uneasy about the second volume, and cannot write any fresh matter for it."[70] This difficulty may have led him to capitalize on his identity as an American writer and include the Indian sketches that he had originally published in the *Analectic* in 1814. Readers in Britain loved few things more than stories about American Indians, especially from a native informant; this choice had obvious market advantages that proved too tempting to resist. "Traits of Indian Character" and "Philip of Pokanoket" appeared in heavily revised form and comprise some of the most distinctive material in the London text. Together, they promote Anglo-American camaraderie through exclusion. The contrast between the romanticization of Indian history offered in these sketches and the nostalgic portrait of English traditions throughout *The Sketch Book* further crystalizes what Irving called, in "English Writers on America," the "kindred tie!" between Britain and the United States.[71] Irving's revisions to these sketches work hard to banish contentious political concerns, including his earlier critique of Indian removal and violence on the frontier. This is implied in Irving's redefinition of "we" and "us" to mean "white men" and "Europeans," rather than "Americans," specifically, which it had earlier signified. In 1814, Irving's sympathy with the Indians reflect back on U.S. practices, as when he writes, in "Traits of Indian Character," "They cannot but be sensible that we are the usurpers of their ancient dominions" (February 1814, 149). In the London text, Irving changed "we" to "the white men," thus implicating the history of English colonials in the statement.[72] In an effort to diffuse blame for such usurpation, Irving deleted lengthy passages that directly

critiqued the U.S. government—of "enormities perpetrated, at which manhood blushes, and history drops the pen" (February 1814, 150)—and added a
footnote directly praising its "exertions to ameliorate the situation of the Indians."[73] In another passage Irving deleted, he described westward expansion
this way: "Before [encroaching settlement] went forth pestilence, famine, and
the sword; and in its train came the slow, but exterminating curse of trade.
What the former did not sweep away, the latter has gradually blighted" (February 1814, 146). Nothing so critical about settlement or so insightful about its
conditions survives in the London text.

Such deletions allow for a broadly Anglo-American lament at the disappearance of the Indians, which new passages frame as inevitable. With one
hand, Irving cuts politicized passages aimed at the U.S. government, and with
the other, he adds familiar stereotypes of noble savagery. His revisions transform the figure of the Indian from a victim of historically specific offenses to a
timeless adventurer of the natural world. "The eastern tribes have disappeared,"
Irving writes, "[a]nd such must sooner or later be the fate of those other tribes
which skirt the frontier. . . . [T]hey will go the way that their brethren have
gone before."[74] This new emphasis on inevitability and nostalgia comes hand
in hand with new self-consciously romantic passages. Such passages play into
familiar stereotypes, as when, in the London text of "Indian Character," Irving
uses elaborate similes to describe an Indian warrior: "As the ship . . . through
the solitudes of the ocean;—as the bird mingles among clouds . . . so the Indian holds his course, silent, solitary, but undaunted, through the boundless
bosom of the wilderness."[75] And in the London version of "Pokanoket," Irving
writes, "an Indian or two would be seen lurking about the skirts of the forest . . . as the lightening will sometimes be seen laying silently about the edge
of the cloud that is brewing up the tempest."[76] The new Indian sketches pacify
the deep conflicts and anxieties Irving showcased in their earlier incarnations;
they transform outrage into "elegance," and they promote the brotherhood
of Anglo-American cultural solidarity, born of shared aesthetic commitments
that repress guilt, violence, and responsibility.

There is no better example of such complacency than in the Christmas
sketches, which celebrate the jolly friendship between Geoffrey Crayon and
the antiquated squire of Bracebridge Hall. In those sketches, nostalgia works
exactly opposite to its function in Irving's treatment of the Indians: the squire's
homage to "customs . . . posting fast into oblivion" (as the London text newly
frames it) registers as a critique of modernity, whereas the ostensible lamenta-
tion of the "disappear[ance]" of the Indians (a word added to the London text)

is cover for a celebration of modernity.[77] This contrast is implicit in a new passage on the Wassail bowl that invokes the language of primitiveness:

> The old gentleman's whole countenance beamed with a serene look of indwelling delight, as he stirred this mighty bowl. Having raised it to his lips, with a hearty wish of a merry Christmas to all present, he sent it brimming round the board, for every one to follow his example, according to the primitive style; pronouncing it, "the ancient fountain of good feeling, where all hearts met together."[78]

The inclusion of the Indian sketches in the London text only highlights the implicit exclusions of this Christmas celebration, where "every one" includes only certain types of persons, and the great fun Geoffrey Crayon has is premised upon a tightening of the terms of affiliation—not, as the Squire might protest, an expansive appreciation of "all hearts" meeting together.

Irving closes the London text with "L'Envoy," a new postscript that addresses his English readers directly, thanking them for the "indulgence" with which his first volume has been received and acknowledging the "risk" of publishing a second. He knows he writes "in a strange land" and addresses "a public which he has been accustomed, from childhood, to regard with the highest feelings of awe and reverence." He then imagines how English cultural elites will judge his work. He takes some comfort in the book's heterogeneity, as a "miscellaneous" group of sketches, since readers of "different humours" can find something they like. In a playful passage that would remind an etymologist of the *Analectic Magazine*, Irving uses a gastronomical metaphor to describe the scene of reading:

> Few guests sit down to a varied table with an equal appetite for every dish. One has an elegant horror of a roasted pig; another holds a curry or a devil in utter abomination; a third cannot tolerate the ancient flavour of venison and wild fowl; and a forth, of truly masculine stomach, looks with sovereign contempt on those knick-knacks, here and there dished up for the ladies. Thus each article is condemned in its turn; and yet, amidst this variety of appetites, seldom does a dish go away from the table without being tasted and relished by some one or other of the guests.[79]

The superficiality of the conflict at this table indicates the low stakes at play in literary exchange when the invited guests are good friends. Indeed, despite his admission of awe and reverence, Irving exhibits some confidence about his ability to satisfy the appetite of the new English readership he is now inviting to dinner. The hyperbole of his guests' disapproval—"horror," "abomination," "contempt"—sneaks in a critique of their authority as judges even as it dramatizes how differences in taste can be reduced at the end of a meal to personal preference. Literature makes a good dinner party, where you only get political about the food. Underneath Irving's metaphor, we can hear the violence of social existence, including class conflict ("elegant horror of a roasted pig"), imperial expansion (hatred for "curry"), and misogyny ("knick-knacks" are "for the ladies"). But there is no place for these things in the world of taste, which, after the *Analectic*, Irving learns to construct as particularly literary and always Anglo-American. With this jolly image of his readers "relish[ing]" *The Sketch Book*, Irving concludes the London text, having newly arrived as a major player in the Anglophone literary field. As an editor, Irving was an unwanted guest. Now he's the cook.

*   *   *

Irving's retreat into the literary is not unlike Rip Van Winkle's famous flight from his Dutch village—as Leslie Fiedler describes it, "the flight of the dreamer from the drab duties of home and town toward good companions" who provide "an eternal playtime in the hills."[80] In John Murray's edition of *The Sketch Book*, Irving imagines an eternal playtime of the literary sphere, in which one desires, as a bewildered Rip does upon his return to town on Election Day, to avoid the "babylonish jargon" of the political world. Like the portrait of George III that the townspeople modify after the Revolution to depict "GENERAL WASHINGTON"—painting a red coat blue, adding a cocked hat—Irving's aesthetics of provinciality treats the national and political differences between Britain and the United States as fundamentally superficial, especially when there are stories to tell.[81] The transatlantic publication history of *The Sketch Book* suggests that Irving's conception of the transaction between author and reader—in which agency is distributed between them equally, as in a friendship—necessarily implicates his new English audience.

Early in *The Sketch Book*, Geoffrey Crayon gets booted from the British Library. In "The Art of Bookmaking," Crayon's wanderings around "this great metropolis"—an epithet Maria Edgeworth also used to describe London—bring him to a "scene" that reveals something about "the bookmaking craft."[82]

What he discovers in the British Library is a group of modern authors stealing mercilessly from their predecessors as they recycle old wisdom in bastardized and derivative forms. While dozing off, he has a dream-like vision of past authors yelling "Thieves! Thieves!" at the "unhappy culprits" who plunder their work—one of them with "all the appearance of an author on good terms with his bookseller."[83] Crayon's own laughter wakes him up, and the librarian asks him to leave. "I soon found that the library was a kind of literary 'preserve,'" Irving writes, "subject to game laws, and that no one must presume to hunt there without special licence [sic] and permission. In a word, I stood convicted of being an arrant [sic] poacher, and was glad to make a precipitate retreat."[84] It is a clever satire about the exclusiveness of the literary field, one that undermines its own critique of the "game" of authorship through the palpable sense that Irving wants to play along. "The Art of Bookmaking" was written for *The Sketch Book*'s second number, first published in New York in April 1819, well before he acquired his own London bookseller with whom to be on good terms. A year later, things have changed. "Since I have published with Murray," Irving wrote to Brevoort after *The Sketch Book* appeared, "I have had continual opportunities of seeing something of the literary world."[85]

Irving was now part of an exclusive club, and he soon benefited from its "game laws." This included puffery, the nepotistic practice of periodical reviewing. In 1821, Murray gleefully informed Irving that "[t]here is a review of the Sketch Book in the Quarterly, which you will like."[86] Usually harsh on American matters, the *Quarterly* was in this instance willing to make an exception, no doubt because Murray himself was its publisher. "This is one of the best samples which we have yet seen of American literature," the review begins in a glowing, if at times patronizing, account of the work of one of "our trans-Atlantic descendants."[87] "The author before us is the best writer of English, in our estimation of that term, that America has produced since the era of independence," the *Quarterly* declares, reserving its highest praise for "Sleepy Hollow" and "Rip Van Winkle."[88] In the latter of these, it writes, "there is a spirit, and an originality, that occasionally remind us of the Northern Enchanter."[89] We can see why Murray thought Irving would like this. One of the most eminent journals of the time has compared him to Scott, his patron and the dedicatee of his London debut. Never mind that many readers knew *The Sketch Book* and the *Quarterly* and the Author of Waverley shared a publisher.[90] Irving was now part of the "literary world," and no one would ask him to leave the room again. The *Quarterly*'s focus on "Rip" and "Sleepy

Hollow" began the process of making Irving into an "American" author. In my narrative of Irving's career, I have tried to present a different picture, one in which Irving is not "so nationalist a writer," as Michael Warner has described him,[91] but instead a provincial one, whose fantasies of literary exchange push the idea of "literature" far beyond the confines of national definitions. London and the uneven distribution of cultural capital are central to this story. As Irving's early career suggests, such uneven distribution is most visible when we investigate an author's struggle to overcome it.

Chapter 5

The Effects of Provinciality
in Cooper and Scott

Within a year of the transatlantic publication of Washington Irving's *The Sketch Book* (1819–1820), there appeared in London two other works also set in England written by provincials: James Fenimore Cooper's first novel, *Precaution* (1820), a domestic tale of the English countryside, and Walter Scott's *Ivanhoe* (1819), a romance of medieval England. In the winter of 1821, Henry Colburn issued an anonymous reprint of the New York edition of *Precaution* with material changes that disguised its American origins: it appeared as a triple-decker, the standard format for an English novel, instead of its original two volumes; its new epigraph was taken from a familiar English classic, Samuel Johnson's *Rasselas*; and it betrayed no indication of its transatlantic provenance, either on the title page or other paratextual matter. English reviews hardly questioned the national identity of the author, and, as William Cullen Bryant later wrote, it "passed from the first for an English novel."[1] An eager and ambitious Cooper worked quickly to publish his second work, *The Spy* (1821), set during the American Revolution, which immediately overshadowed his first and inaugurated his career as a novelist of his native land. *Precaution*, which hasn't been reprinted since 1912, has rarely found attentive readers—even Bryant "confess[ed]" that he "merely dipped into" it.[2] Cooper himself anticipated the novel's neglect when, in the preface to the 1831 revised edition of *The Spy*, he justifies the dismissal of *Precaution* with an apology for writing about England at all; his second novel was written in "atonement" for having ignored America in his first.[3] *Precaution* was "purely accidental," he writes, entirely owing to "precipitation and inexperience," even though his close involvement with the book's first edition clearly demonstrates his initial seriousness.[4]

The story of *Ivanhoe*'s publication, not to mention its legacy, couldn't differ more. In Edinburgh in December 1819, Ballantyne printed a first edition of eight thousand copies, six thousand of which were shipped to London; by late winter, many more had been printed, and three separate adaptations were staged in Drury Lane and Covent Garden.[5] So great was the American demand for the novel that Mathew Carey's early edition, printed from advance sheets, failed to saturate the market; nearly a dozen unauthorized editions of *Ivanhoe* appeared in Boston, Hartford, New York, and Philadelphia within three years.[6] The appearance of *Ivanhoe* marked the peak of the Author of Waverley's success, a fact reflected in the book's material features: it was printed on larger and finer paper than most novels (including Scott's previous work), and Constable timed its publication with the release of the first collected Scott edition, *The Novels and Tales of the Author of Waverley*, which helped confirm Scott's place as Britain's most prestigious living author.[7] Like most of his early novels, *Ivanhoe* remained popular throughout the nineteenth century, but unlike them, it never went out of fashion in the twentieth. While Cooper's attempt at an English novel has always been neglected, Scott's turn to England proved one of his most remarkable achievements. While Cooper's failure led him to a native subject, the success of *Ivanhoe*, as Scott boasts in his 1830 preface to the novel, procured him "freedom from the Rules," since thenceforth he was free to write of "England, as well as Scotland."[8]

Cooper's regret and Scott's self-satisfaction are not expressed in total earnestness. Among the sins that require "atonement," certainly writing a novel ranks quite low, and there is no real triumph for an author in breaking "Rules" he invented. Furthermore, Cooper proudly identified himself on the title page of *The Spy* and *The Pioneers* (1823) as "the author of Precaution," and he gave later editions of that novel the close attention he brought to revisions of his American fiction. It is arguable, too, that only because Scott set his first nine Waverley novels in Scotland was it strange for him to write about England. Nevertheless, Scott's and Cooper's retrospective assessments of their English novels reflect an investment in the relevance of an author's national identity to his or her literary authority, and because of this commonality we must not dismiss them. Scott, like Cooper, felt the need to justify his use of English material as if it were a dubious experiment. His "Dedicatory Epistle" to *Ivanhoe*—the longest preface he wrote for a first edition—developed an entire theory of genre to prepare "the English reader" for the idea that "his own ancestors" could be as "wild" as those "existing in the Highlands of Scotland," and in the 1830 preface to the novel, he explained that he changed national settings because of anxiety about repetition.[9] In the year of *The Sketch Book*, Scott and Cooper, so likely a pair, meet on unlikely ground: as outsiders whose widely diverging relation at the time to prestige, success, and England itself couldn't prevent them both from justifying their English novels.

This chapter puts Cooper and Scott in relation to each other by placing them in relation to London. In so doing, it revises our understanding of the ideological work of their fiction. Many readers of Cooper and Scott have argued that their historical fictions embody the needs of their expanding imperial societies: American expansionism in the age of manifest destiny, and rising, middle-class British nationalism in post-Napoleonic Europe.[10] I offer the Anglophone literary field as an equally appropriate arena for these ostensibly nationalist writers and argue that their representational modes embody, instead, an aesthetics of provinciality that incorporates national difference into a literary exchange wishfully distanced from nationalism itself. The cross-cultural address made compulsory by the London book trade produces the fantasy of a literary sphere defined by its own rules. Taking Cooper's *The Pioneers* (1823) and Scott's *The Heart of Mid-Lothian* (1818) as exemplary texts, I account for this purified notion of aesthetic production through tying literary form to the transnational movement of texts. As with my previous discussions of Edgeworth, Owenson, and Irving, I argue that Cooper and Scott helped define Romantic-era conceptions of literature's separateness from the social and political world. In the two novels that are my primary focus, that separateness is theorized in moments that self-reflexively gesture toward the meaning of aesthetic experience.

Notwithstanding their position in an Anglo-American world that privileged their class, race, gender, and religion, as provincials, Cooper and Scott were deeply influenced by their subordinate position in a literary field that privileged England.[11] In Scott's early Waverley novels, this is evident through the presence of English or Anglicized protagonists who guide his English readers on educational journeys north, as he "establishes the narrating persona of a Scot," as James Buzard has written, who presents "his culture . . . to the English."[12] In Cooper's *The Spy* and the early Leatherstocking Tales (1823–1827), the importance of England is less obvious but no less consequential. All authorized editions of Cooper's novels printed since the mid-nineteenth century incorporate substantive changes he made for new London editions, including thousands of textual revisions, long introductions, and dozens of new explanatory footnotes. As I have mentioned in previous chapters, these heavily revised editions were published for Colburn and Bentley's "Standard Novels" series and became the basis for Cooper's Author's Revised Edition and, following from this, for the authoritative scholarly editions of Cooper as well as the reprints now issued by the Library of America, Penguin, and Oxford. As with Irving's revisions to *The Sketch Book*, Cooper's transatlantic revisions have been entirely forgotten.[13]

Cooper's and Scott's common concern for England works differently in their fiction, and yet their strategies of address are marshaled for similar ends. The transatlantic textual history of *The Pioneers* shows that the pressures of the London book trade transformed that novel's marriage plot and its archetypical American hero into devices for Anglo-American cultural camaraderie. Amnesia about the novel's transformation—including a remarkable change to its famous last sentence—has buried its transatlantic address under its apparent national agenda, which blatantly drives the first American edition but from which Cooper distanced himself through revision. Scott's *The Heart of Mid-Lothian*, alternatively, wears an address to England on its sleeve: it allegorizes its relation to the marketplace through Jeanie Deans's pilgrimage from Edinburgh to London, precisely the journey that most copies of a Waverley novel took from Scott's Edinburgh printers to England for distribution. *The Heart of Mid-Lothian* climaxes as Jeanie Deans arrives in London and appeals to the sympathies of Queen Caroline, wife to King George II. In the dramatization of Jeanie's success, Scott encodes his self-consciousness as a provincial writer. No other scene in the fiction of the era more powerfully captures the aesthetics of provinciality than Jeanie's interview with her English Queen. *Mid-Lothian* provides a narrative allegory for what in *The Pioneers* remains relegated, more obscurely, to its textual history: shaped by a London-centered marketplace for books, these texts substitute for contentious political and national differences an exalted literary sphere defined by cross-cultural communion.

In this chapter's first section, I argue that the historical novel as a genre emerged just as much from Cooper's and Scott's engagement with distant English readers as it did from their engagement with the distant past. Following this, I investigate the effects of provinciality in *The Pioneers* and *Mid-Lothian* themselves.

The Provincial Aesthetics of the Historical Novel

Comparative study of American and Scottish culture predates by many decades the current interest in transatlantic literary relations.[14] In a brief but influential

1954 essay, John Clive and Bernard Bailyn foregrounded the importance of England and argued that a shared outsider position explained American and Scottish cultural affinity during the Enlightenment. Americans and Scots found themselves far from the center of empire; according to Clive and Bailyn, the eighteenth century's "highest achievements" stem from being caught between the "nativism" of a peripheral nation and the "cosmopolitan sophistication" associated with London and England.[15] This argument has been recently reinforced by literary scholars like Robert Crawford, Susan Manning, and others, who have expanded its reach into the mid-nineteenth century. Regardless of the political independence of the United States and the consolidation of British nationalism, they suggest, up through about 1850, there persisted in America and Scotland a relation to England we could describe as provincial. Despite such scholarship, we still have a limited understanding of how distance from England produced similar effects on American and Scottish literature. Like Clive and Bailyn's original essay, recent accounts remain fundamentally speculative about the effects of provinciality; they often invoke England only to pass it by, treating distance from the metropole as a point of departure for other topics, like religion or genre, rather than a subject for analysis in itself.[16] If we attend to the literary marketplace, however, as I have argued throughout this book, the importance of England can be assessed quite concretely. Chapters 1 and 2 demonstrated that the early nineteenth-century Scottish and American book trades developed unevenly in relationship to a powerful and dominant London book trade. In Scotland, this was reflected, broadly, through the dependence of Edinburgh publishers on London partnerships for capital investment and on those same partnerships to reach a proportionately huge English readership. Table 2 summarizes what scholars have been able to determine about the geographical distribution of the first editions of Scott's novels in his initial decade as the Author of Waverley. London booksellers handled on average two-thirds of a typical printing. *Rob Roy* (1817) is the exception that proves the rule; the high demand for the novel in Glasgow, where Scott set much of the narrative, led the publishers to keep most of its first edition in Scotland; even so, Owen Rees of Longman & Co. soon wrote from London that "we had only half sufficient to answer the demand."[17] In the United States, provinciality was reflected in the domestic book trade's dependence on the reprinting of British texts, widespread reverence for British culture, and on the fact that only success in London could firmly establish an author's reputation at home. Scott and Cooper emerged as novelists from deep within these conditions—both as readers and market-conscious professional authors.

Table 2. The London Distribution of the Waverley Novels, First Editions, 1814–1824

	% to London
Waverley (1814)	70
Guy Mannering (1815)	75
The Antiquary (1816)	50
Rob Roy (1817)	33
The Bride of Lammermoor (1819)	50
Ivanhoe (1819)	75
Kenilworth (1821)	71
The Fortunes of Nigel (1822)	70
St. Ronan's Well (1823)	71
Redgauntlet, (1824)	71
Average to London	63.6

Sources: On *Waverley*, see Garside, "*Waverley* and the National Fiction Revolution," 222; on *Rob Roy*, Garside, "The Rise of the Scottish Literary Market," 205; on *Guy Mannering*, *The Antiquary*, *The Bride of Lammermoor*, and *Ivanhoe*, the various "Notes on the Text" in relevant volumes of David Hewitt, ed., *Edinburgh Edition of the Waverley Novels* (1981–); on *Kenilworth*, *The Fortunes of Nigel*, *St. Ronan's Well*, and *Redgauntlet*, St. Clair, 638–639.

Throughout Scott's career, public discourse refracted his authorial image through the lens of the London marketplace, emphasizing the distance between his native land and his principal audience. Reviewers placed him within "the race of Scottish borderers," the "annual visitor from Edinburgh"—either to be congratulated for his "strong *nationality*" or criticized for "the neglect of Scottish feelings"; he's always beholden to what the *Quarterly* called "our southern readers" who, "ignorant [of] . . . the secret history of the literary world in the north," decide by a "sort of freemasonry" which parts of his work are "copied from nature" and which fail to seem "either probable or natural to an English reader."[18] One early parody, an anonymous burlesque of *The Lady of the Lake* (1810) rather ungenerously titled *The Ass on Parnassus* (1814), takes Scott's outsider status as its major theme. Published in London and soon thereafter in Philadelphia, the parody moves from Edinburgh to London and back with a donkey named "Neddy," the stand-in for Scott, on whose haunches Jeremiah Quiz rides along the way. Neddy travels south gathering antiquarian evidence ("proofs") for his lengthy footnotes: "For England *Neddy* stir'd his hoofs, / Nor stop'd to nibble grass, / Plodding the way to pick

up proofs, / To show he was no ASS" (19).[19] A song from *The Lady of the Lake*
(1810) transforms into a soliloquy for Neddy, who ties poetic inspiration to
travel:

> They bid me sleep and cease to bray,
>   They say my brain is warp'd and wrung;
> I cannot sleep on English brae,
>   I cannot cease to wag my tongue:
> But were I where Tweed gently glides,
> Free from poetic brawling tides,
> So sweetly would I sleep and bray,
> And not t' excite another fray.[20]

Neddy's compulsion to "wag [his] tongue" intensifies with his proximity to the
faraway market in England; if he stayed home, he would peacefully "sleep and
bray." In the parody's second part, *Marmion Feats!*, Neddy eventually arrives in
London, where a reader demands copies of *Lady of the Lake* "in each edition."
"Why did n't you bring some on your back?" the reader demands, and Neddy
answers, "No! no! not any!"—a failure that derives its comedy from linking a
bumbling and incompetent Walter Scott to the physical task of distributing
books in England.[21]

   Cooper's English audience mattered to him far more than is commonly
acknowledged. He took great care with transatlantic publication well before
he embarked on extensive textual revision for Bentley's "Standard Novels."
He sent proofs of *Precaution* to an agent in London in order to find a British
publisher, although we do not know if that agent's efforts resulted in Colburn's 1821 reprint.[22] Another transatlantic attempt with *The Spy* also failed
to prevent it from being pirated in London by W. B. Whittaker.[23] For *The
Pioneers*, Cooper tried again, employing Benjamin N. Coles, who approached
John Miller and then Whittaker himself, to see if an authorized edition was
possible. Miller told Coles that John Murray had seen *The Spy* but rejected it,
just as he had initially rejected Irving.[24] Cooper decided to try Murray anyway,
and Irving was there to help, just as Scott had stepped in for him.[25] When a
deal was finally proposed, Coles insisted that Cooper accept it: "The name of
Murray (tho' I don't like him altogether) is a host within itself and he poseses
[*sic*] a most powerful literary instrument in the Quarterly Review of which he
is the sole propriater [*sic*]."[26] In his own correspondence with Murray, Cooper

offered recommendations about how to redivide the two-volume American text of *The Pioneers* into the three-volume London format and also offered to write "a Preface more suited to the English Public."[27] With *The Prairie* (1827), Cooper turned to Colburn, who, along with his partner Richard Bentley, became Cooper's authorized London publishers.[28] "The Tale of the Prairie contains nothing to offend an English reader," Cooper assured Colburn while negotiating about the novel in 1826, proudly insisting that "these works . . . are so far known in England as to insure the sale of 1500 copies."[29] To highlight Cooper's interest in London is neither to deny his embeddedness within American political discourse of the Jacksonian era nor to forget that he considered it "a point of honour to continue rigidly as an American author," as he wrote to Colburn while working on the Standard Novels.[30] A focus on provinciality situates his novels within the uneven cultural dynamics that, despite appearances, statements of national allegiance reinforce.

Cooper's and Scott's provinciality relates to the double movement in their historical novels between the temporal journey they offer to all of their nineteenth-century readers and the geographical journey they offer specifically to English ones. I want to linger on the question of genre in order to suggest that highlighting such double movement modifies the way we understand the emergence of the historical novel. In a novel like *Waverley*, as the thick description that accompanies the hero's northern travels acclimate English readers to Scottish scenes and society, Scott brings all his readers to the past, where they need as much guidance as they would in a foreign land. These two journeys reinforce each other, but they can be profitably linked to different aspects of his art: his descriptive tendency, on one hand, and his dramatic sense, on the other. Georg Lukács argues that the former is subordinate to the latter in Scott's mastery of historical characterization. Lukács praises Scott's "dramatic element," which enables the "derivation of the individuality of characters from the historical peculiarity of their age."[31] Scott emphasizes the internal struggle within a character that makes his experience unique to a particular era rather than assimilable to our own. His work realizes the "quality of inner life, the morality, the heroism, capacity for sacrifice" that defines an individual's struggle with competing political or ideological forces of a specific moment.[32]

For Lukács, Scott's illustration of clan loyalty epitomizes his historicizing method. At one point, Waverley saves a wounded English soldier in battle, and a group of Highlanders, initially outraged, come to honor him when they learn the soldier resides on his family's estate. Such an event prepares us for the display of absolute devotion during the trial of Fergus MacIvor, when

Evan Dhu offers his own life in exchange for his chief's release. It is crucial for Lukács that these two events are tied to important stages in the novel's action—Waverley's first Jacobite battle and the final scene of judgment—since only such formal orchestration results in a realism of "historical faithfulness."[33] Lukács dismisses a feature of Scott's novels that might, on the surface, more obviously signify the past: "'local color' of description," which he classifies as "one among many ancillary, artistic devices [that] could never on its own reawaken the spirit of an age."[34] Lukács might agree, for example, that Waverley's first impressions of Tully-Veolan, contained in what Scott himself calls "a chapter of still life," epitomize this characteristic method, overloaded as the scene is with details about the Scottish peasantry and the architectural ornaments of the manor house.[35] Description of this kind fails to produce the historicism that follows from narrative. The past is made real, Lukács argues, only through putting details into motion as part of the drama of individuality.

Lukács fails to see that in Scott's more descriptive moments, the present asserts itself through the implicit invocation of English readers. In the Tully-Veolan chapter, description is filtered through their perspective: the houses outside the manor house "seemed miserable in the extreme, especially to an eye accustomed to the smiling neatness of English cottages," "a mere Englishman . . . might have wished the clothes [of the peasants] less scanty," and the "great size" of a "pigeon-house . . . would have turned the brains of all the antiquaries in England."[36] Scott does not apply his painstaking historical realism to the impressions Waverley gathers here; there is no sense that the temporal distance between Scott's protagonist and his readers makes Waverley notice different things than nineteenth-century English readers would be likely to observe. Here Scott subordinates the specificity of the "inner life" of the past, since some of this is only for his contemporaries. When he describes the prevalence of "idle useless curs" who bark at the heels of unwelcome travelers, for example, he acknowledges that the detail "is only thrown out there for consideration of the collectors of Mr. Dent's dog-taxes," a much-satirized Parliamentary reform passed in 1796, half a century after the novel's historical action.[37] In this and in similar moments, the representational priority of *Waverley* rests on explaining Scotland—on how, for example, "poverty, and indolence" were "combining to depress the natural genius . . . of a hardy, intelligent, and reflecting peasantry"—not on dramatizing Scottish history.[38] Scott's own assertion, in the "General Preface" to the Waverley novels (1829), of the priority of cross-cultural address suggests its centrality. Inspired by what "Miss Edgeworth so fortunately achieved for Ireland," Scott writes, "I felt that something might be attempted for my own country" that would "introduce her natives to those of the sister kingdom in a more favorable light than they had been placed hitherto, and tend to procure sympathy for their virtues and indulgence for their foibles."[39] This introductory drive—which, it should be noted, says nothing about the past—shaped Scott's fiction, and a similar drive shaped Cooper's.

The available division of Scott's art into these two aspects—descriptive/present, narrative/history—has enabled a wide range of opinion about Scott's influence on the history of the novel. George Levine traces the realistic imagination of the high Victorian period to the anti-narrative texture of the Waverley novels; "narratives touched by the realistic impulse," he writes, "try to resist or circumvent the formal conventions of narrative."[40] Levine juxtaposes the detail-gathering methods of realism to the plot effects of romance and locates *Waverley* easily: "If Scott had been a true 'romancer,' he would have attended more to his plots."[41] Ian Duncan takes an opposed view and argues that it is precisely the success of Scott's narrative ability that produces the ascendancy of the novel in Britain. Mimesis doesn't matter so much as "an over-determination of plot," which Duncan associates with romance revival.[42] He argues that Scott's plots produce the fantasy of a national present constituted as private and free from the traumas of history, an ideology that Dickens, Scott's successor as a national novelist, wholly absorbed. Scott's importance as a provincial, rather than national, novelist lies, however, in the combination of description and narrative, a fusion born from the market-driven centripetal directionality of his early novels. Recent critics attuned to the internal divisions within the British Isles have been able to reconcile the tension between description and drama through focusing more on Scott's role as a mediator between his culture and English readers.[43] Triangulating Scott and Cooper together in relation to such readers suggests that it was Scott's mediating role that most resonated in the United States—a role that American readers would have already associated with Scott's Irish antecedents.[44]

In an important *North American Review* piece on Catherine Maria Sedgwick's *Redwood* (1825), William Cullen Bryant defines the novel as a genre through its capacity for introduction. He brings home the lessons of Scott's and Edgeworth's success as he describes their methods for addressing audiences across a national divide. His description resembles Levine's take on *Waverley*. "Miss Edgeworth," Scott, and Sedgwick all abandon verisimilitude in their "catastrophes."[45] "[T]he plot of a novel," Bryant writes, "is little more than a contrivance to introduce interesting situations and incidents, well

drawn characters and fine sketches from life and nature."[46] He congratulates
Sedgwick for using native materials in a novel that "shall interest and delight
the world" and measures success according to how well it is "delightful and
captivating to a foreigner."[47] Indeed, Bryant's theory of fiction works best if
an author's implied audience resides elsewhere. But it is clear that the foreign
audience he has in mind nevertheless claims close kinship. This is what Bryant
thinks novels accomplish:

> [T]hey create a sort of illusion, which places ["the foreigner"] in the
> midst of the country where the action of the piece is going on. He
> beholds the scenery of a distant land, hears its inhabitants convers-
> ing about their own concerns in their own dialect, finds himself in
> the bosom of its families, is made the depository of their secrets,
> and the observer of their fortunes, and becomes an inmate of their
> firesides without stirring from his own. Thus it is that American
> novels are eagerly read in Great Britain, and novels descriptive of
> English and Scottish manners as eagerly read in America.[48]

Novels benefit from the interplay between distance and intimacy that defines
their appeal. The exoticism Bryant invokes with language like "foreigner" and
"distant land" evaporates in this passage's final sentence where, like Irving
in *The Sketch Book*, he circumscribes his readership to include only Anglo-
Americans. The strikingly bourgeois image of novel consumption as providing domestic hospitality and reading private letters requires a lot of common
ground for the "illusion" of disclosure and fireside exchange to function. This
depends, moreover, on the special authority Bryant grants to a writer who fic-
tionalizes his or her own surroundings; "It is a native writer that must or can
do this," he writes, "only on his native soil."[49] This restriction—the premise at
the heart of cultural nationalism—means nothing without the constant presence of non-"native" readers. American literature works "to exalt our national
reputation abroad, and to improve our national character at home."[50] These
goals are not separate; together they foster an ideal vision of intimate cross-
cultural exchange. The internal division that defines Scott's address to England
becomes the transatlantic division that Bryant describes, of American novels
being "eagerly read in Great Britain."

The profound interdependence of introductory realism and plot that, as I
have suggested, defines the historical novel, derives from—and is heightened
by—the cultural divisions Cooper and Scott navigated as they vaulted their

fiction toward England over tense cultural boundaries. The remainder of this chapter examines the effects of such vaulting, treating Cooper and Scott dialectically and as their contrasting strategies demand. An intertwined approach avoids claims about literary influence while it argues that their provincial aesthetics projects a striking vision of literature's retreat from politics. I begin with revisions Cooper made to *The Pioneers* that relate to his authorial persona and the novel's marriage plot. I then turn to Jeanie Deans's journey to London in *The Heart of Mid-Lothian*, an allegory that, in its turn, brings me back to *The Pioneers* and the transatlantic transformation of Natty Bumppo.

Transatlantic Revision in *The Pioneers*

As I discussed in the previous chapter, nineteenth-century copyright laws provided the opportunity for transatlantic revision. Copyright in the United States was limited to American citizens or residents, so a foreign author could not easily control the sale or integrity of his or her books there. In contrast, a well-connected American author could secure British copyright by supervising transatlantic publication in a timely manner. Once an author sold a novel to a London firm, that firm could claim, by law or custom, the right to sell the book throughout Britain. Cooper treated authorized London republication as an occasion for both major and minor modifications to his novels, and he privileged these revised texts when he issued later American editions of his work. Originally published in 1823 by Charles Wiley in New York and by John Murray in London, *The Pioneers* was republished in 1832 as No. 14 in Colburn and Bentley's Standard Novels series, which also included works by William Godwin, Charles Brockden Brown, Jane Austen, Harriet Beecher Stowe, and many others. The series—eventually associated exclusively with Bentley—included 127 volumes up through 1854, with Cooper's twenty-one titles making him the most frequently reprinted author. Like most other works, *The Pioneers* was reissued in "revised, corrected" form in order to secure a new copyright. This series drew on the huge success of Scott's Magnum Opus, which it emulated in price and physical appearance.[51] For the Standard Novels, Cooper modified his earliest published works, including *The Spy*, *The Pioneers*, and *The Last of the Mohicans* (1826). While the textual history of these novels involved many stages, including trivial modifications in the first London reprints, some revisions for second and third American editions, and late revisions for the Author's Revised Edition, the changes Cooper made for

Bentley were by far the most extensive. All revisions to *The Pioneers* I consider here, a mere fraction of the more than 2,300 substantive changes, were made for that edition; for the sake of clarity, I will refer to the original text as the Wiley text and the 1832 London edition as the Bentley text.[52]

In adapting anew for English readers, the Bentley text of *The Pioneers* promotes the union of two cultures of uneven stature. Cooper accomplishes this partly through revisions that change the terms of his affiliation with American culture while packaging it for a foreign audience. For the Bentley text, Cooper cut words and phrases of strong national feeling to erect a subtle but significant barrier between his voice and the Wiley text's original emphasis on national identification. Instead, the Bentley text's new introduction and footnotes highlight an authorial connection with locality made to seem personal, necessary, and natural. The suppression of overt politicized nationalism is accompanied by revisions that transform the marital union between Oliver Effingham, the grandson of a British army officer, and Elizabeth Temple, a quintessentially American heroine, into a harbinger of Anglo-American cultural communion. These changes leave Natty Bumppo farther outside a social world defined by national ambition, thus making his character a figure for the autonomous literary sphere that Cooper's novel comes, through transatlantic revision, to embody.

While the new Bentley text retains a significant amount of national feeling, the earlier Wiley text overflows. This difference is reflected most clearly in deletions. In the Bentley text, "the State of New York," for example, is no longer "great," as it was described in the Wiley text; the Susquehanna is no longer "mighty"; the United States no longer "boast[s]" of its rivers; and the forest's wild growth is no longer described as "unrestrained."[53] Many other grandiose descriptors do not appear in the Bentley text, including the "powerful number" of New York residents (*W*, 1:3; *B*, 3) and the "great variety" of furniture in Judge Temple's home (*W*, 1:66; *B*, 51). Specimens of the natural landscape are no longer described as "mighty" (*W*, 1:36; *B*, 28), "prodigious" (*W*, 1:117; *B*, 91), "virgin" (*W*, 2:9; *B*, 215), "proud" (*W*, 1:241; *B*, 185) (*W*, 2:39; *B*, 237), "majestic" (*W*, 2:39; *B*, 238), "momentous" (*W*, 2:47; *B*, 244), "rich" (*W*, 2: 97; *B*, 281), or "deep" (*W*, 2:191; *B*, 355). In some instances, characters lose what Cooper clearly considered particularly American traits, such as their "distinct and independent" role in society (*W*, 1:2; *B*, 2) or their knowledge of the legislative process, which one character describes "with the readiness of an American on the subject" (*W*, 2:247; *B*, 397). These deletions and others like them significantly alter the mood of Cooper's novel as they distance it from a

THE

PIONEERS,

OR THE

SOURCES OF THE SUSQUEHANNA;

A DESCRIPTIVE TALE.

BY THE AUTHOR OF "PRECAUTION."

"Extremes of habits, manners, time and space,
Brought close together, here stood face to face,
And gave at once a contrast to the view,
That other lands and ages never knew."
Paulding.

IN TWO VOLUMES.

VOL. I.

NEW-YORK:
PUBLISHED BY CHARLES WILEY.
E. B. Clayton, Printer.

1823.

Figure 3. James Fenimore Cooper, *The Pioneers*, 1st American ed. (New York: Wiley, 1823), title page.

Courtesy of the Huntington Library, San Marino, California.

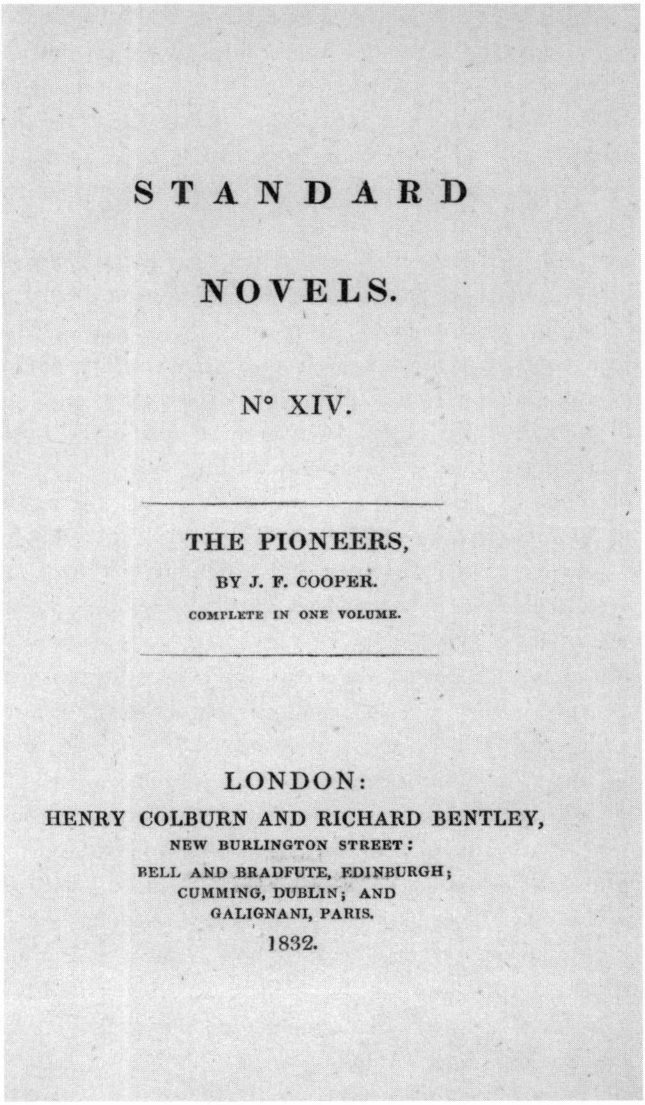

STANDARD

NOVELS.

N° XIV.

THE PIONEERS,

BY J. F. COOPER.

COMPLETE IN ONE VOLUME.

LONDON:

HENRY COLBURN AND RICHARD BENTLEY,

NEW BURLINGTON STREET:

BELL AND BRADFUTE, EDINBURGH;
CUMMING, DUBLIN; AND
GALIGNANI, PARIS.

1832.

Figure 4. James Fenimore Cooper, *The Pioneers* (London: Colburn and Bentley, 1832), half-title page for Standard Novels, No. 14.

Courtesy of the Huntington Library, San Marino, California.

hyperbolic nationalism. In one suggestive instance, the Wiley text lingers on the description of a cannon used to hunt a flock of pigeons; on the Fourth of July, Cooper writes, "It would be heard, with its echoes ringing among the hills, and telling forth its sounds, for thirteen times, with all the dignity of a two-and-thirty pounder" (*W*, 2:43). In the Bentley text, the description of the cannon merely notes that on the Fourth, "it would be heard ringing among the hills" (*B*, 240).

The authorial persona in the Bentley text suggests a new investment in how local identification privileges an essentialized relation to an author's native land rather than political membership in a nation-state. The Bentley text offers an earnest argument for the novel's authenticity as it reframes Cooper's realistic method as an outgrowth of the writer's biography. "The Author was brought an infant into this valley," Cooper writes in the new introduction, "and all his first impressions were here obtained . . . he thinks he can answer for the faithfulness of the picture he has drawn" (*B*, ix). The Bentley introduction indicates that because of this early experience, "there was a constant temptation" while writing "to delineate that which he had known, rather than that which he might have imagined" (*B*, v). One new footnote announces that certain comments "have reference to the facts" (*B*, 227), another justifies the story of a forest fire because "the writer" himself "witnessed [one] . . . in another part of New York" (*B*, 462), and yet another tersely insists that "all this was literally true" (*B*, 229). These interjections resonate with Bryant's definition of a native writer's authority. They appeal to the evidence of personal experience, connect the author more intimately to the world of *The Pioneers*, and shore up his authority to represent that world to foreign readers.

New explanatory passages work similarly to distance Cooper from national identification while they bring him closer to his fictional world as an expert. While the Wiley text takes for granted an American reader's knowledge, a new discourse of explication fills the Bentley text. This is not limited to its obvious use in added footnotes that define terms like "sleigh" (*B*, 3), "Santa-claus" (*B*, 41), "patent" (*B*, 42), "Yankee" (*B*, 44), "jobber" (*B*, 64), "dissenter" (*B*, 125), and "Susquehanna" (*B*, 133). For example, while the main text in the Wiley edition tells us that Elizabeth Temple was sent from home to "enjoy the advantages, which the city could afford to her education" (*W*, 1:6), the Bentley text guides its readers with a heavier hand, explaining that she "enjoy[ed] the advantages of education, which the city of New York could offer at that period" (*B*, 5). Similar additions exoticize American landscapes and inhabitants, as when Cooper uses racialized discourse in his depiction of Judge Temple's

African slave, Aggy, whose eyes tear up because of the cold. The Bentley text offers a new and direct explanation for these tears, "a tribute to its power, that the keen frosts of those regions always extracted from one of his African origin" (*W*, 1:4; *B*, 4). This not only objectifies the character that enables Cooper to display such knowledge; its construction of Aggy's physical response as typical and representative trades on the exclusive knowledge an American writer could derive from his or her proximity to the institution of slavery.

Some textual additions belong to both explication and storytelling. Cooper wrote a new passage justifying Judge Temple's laughter after a dangerous sleigh accident; in the Bentley text, it appears as a footnote but lacks the superscript asterisk in the main text that would draw a reader to the bottom of the page: "The spectators, from immemorial usage, have a right to laugh at the casualties of a sleigh-ride; and the Judge was no sooner certain that no harm was done, than he made full use of the privilege" (*B*, 39). Modern editors of the novel have assumed the Bentley edition erred in making this a footnote, and they print it as part of the main text despite Cooper's retention of it as a footnote in further authorized editions.[54] The confusion about its placement points to one new feature of Cooper's fictional project as it modulates to accommodate the transatlantic marketplace. His revisions repeatedly and almost imperceptibly demonstrate the intimate authority he claims in the introduction. The Bentley text suggests an approach to English readers that depends on belief and confidence in the author's sincerity about his personal history. Paradoxically, then, *The Pioneers* offers a more intimate reading experience as it is refashioned to address a more distant audience.

Changes in the representation of the marriage plot mirror this author-reader intimacy by transforming it into a vehicle for cross-cultural communion. In both versions of the novel, Cooper enlists a domestic plot inhabited by royalist and patriot families and directed toward conciliatory ends. Oliver Effingham marries the heiress of the family primarily responsible for his ancestors' ruin, since Judge Temple's estate is made of confiscated Effingham property purchased from the American government after the end of the Revolutionary War. *The Pioneers* displaces the injustice of Indian removal onto the far less remarkable plight of English loyalists who lost their colonized lands; "the more pressing burden" for Cooper, as Jared Gardner writes, is "the dispossession of the British."[55] When we learn at the novel's dénouement that Oliver's anger and resentment stems not from his presumed Indian heritage but from this more immediate cause, the Judge's good will enables the reconstitution of the Effingham-Temple alliance that the Revolutionary War had torn asunder. As Richard Slotkin has argued, this reconciliation of white families is meant to symbolize the future of the American nation.[56] Cooper's revisions for English readers, however, overlay this national allegory with a new kind of participation in the cause of Anglo-American camaraderie.

The Bentley text gives this new meaning force through changes that reduce the apparent antagonism between Oliver and Elizabeth, replacing what had been haughtiness and rivalry with sympathetic regard. In the London edition, Oliver's "passion" about his disinheritance becomes in two instances mere "anxiety" or "feeling" (W, 1:32; B, 25) (W, 2:158; B, 328); in one case, his "scornful smile" is deleted (W, 1:33; B, 25), and elsewhere his smile is no longer "equivocal" (W, 2:13; B, 218), "lurking" (W, 2:30; B, 231), or "bitter" (W, 2:306; B, 442). His disposition no longer "border[s] on ferocity" (W, 2:12; B, 217), and Elizabeth no longer regards a manner described as "proud, but forced" (W, 1:249; B, 192). Oliver's statements cease to be "impetuous" (W, 2:119; B, 298), "agitated" (W, 2:177; B, 343), or conveyed with "a little pique in his manner" (W, 2:92; B, 277). For her part, Elizabeth becomes more humble and ordinary, no longer described so often as "proud" (W, 1:34; B, 26) (W, 1:233; B, 180) (W, 1:269; B, 206), "stately" (W, 1:221; B, 170), "insinuating" (W, 1:250; B, 193), or "scornful" (W, 2:157; B, 327) and no longer having the same "grandeur" (W, 1:170; B, 55), "impetuosity" (W, 2:13; B, 218), or "archness" (W, 2:90; B, 276). The Bentley text deemphasizes the contentiousness of the Temple-Effingham conflict by changing the Wiley text's referral to Elizabeth as "the heiress" at least a dozen times, using instead neutral terms like her proper name, pronouns, or "companion."[57]

The choice to strip frequent reference to the system of inheritance that dominates the novel's proprietary struggle is reflected as well in changes that tone down the marriage trajectory's chivalrous tone. The Bentley text deletes references to Elizabeth as a "maiden," thus bringing her character down to a more realistic register.[58] The revised text also suggests Elizabeth's intuition about Oliver's race, the revelation of which removes the last impediment to their union. In the Wiley text, she and other characters are convinced of Oliver's rumored Indian racial heritage; in the Bentley text, Cooper assures us that Elizabeth "evidently put little faith in his aboriginal descent" (B, 277). This new evidence about her capacity for recognition allies the couple before they marry. Moreover, one modification in Elizabeth's upbringing makes her a more plausible bride for a young man with a genteel English education. Whereas in the Wiley text, Elizabeth asks the shopkeeper Le Quois to translate a letter she receives from Paris, in the Bentley text, the translation is unnecessary: Elizabeth is newly fluent in French (W, 2:246–247; B, 397).[59]

These changes anticipate the novel's resolution and make the marriage more plausible by removing a good deal of the antagonism and melodrama present in the Wiley text. To be sure, in the original text, the union was never a surprise; for the revised edition, Cooper deleted an early remark that links the two "in an association that was to endure for so long" (*W*, 1:34; *B*, 26). It is the new tone of their association, not the fact of it, that nudges the two familial representatives nearer to each other and makes their inevitable union the confirmation of a preexisting affinity rather than the collusion of opposites. The Bentley text reinforces this through the parallel move of pacifying the original tension between Judge Temple and Colonel Effingham. It splits responsibility for the destructive relationship between the two men, whereas the Wiley text makes the judge more culpable, leaving their business arrangement "entirely to the dictates of [Temple's] own judgment," an explanation that does not appear in the Bentley text (*W*, 1:26; *B*, 20). Further, when Temple describes his history with Effingham at the novel's end, Cooper substitutes a loaded verb for describing the Revolution with a more neutral one. In the Wiley text, the Judge says, "We *divided* in politics," whereas in the Bentley text, they merely "*differed*" (*W*, 2:306; *B*, 442; emphasis added). The new London edition of *The Pioneers* invests reconciliation with cross-cultural communion and makes them both a foregone conclusion.

Nowhere does this new meaning make itself felt more significantly than in the way the Bentley text of *The Pioneers* recasts Natty Bumppo. While the Wiley text's emphasis on national feeling and political reconciliation suggests that Natty's role in the marriage plot parallels his role in nation formation, the changes I have already discussed, as well as some additional revisions that relate specifically to Natty himself, work to bury this political reading under the guise of literary achievement. This new meaning depends on the significance certain moments acquire because of the Bentley text's palpable distance from an American audience and, following this, from the Wiley text's patriotism. An allegorical reading of *The Heart of Mid-Lothian* provides a compelling vocabulary for understanding Natty's transformation into a figure for transatlantic literary exchange, since Scott renders Jeanie Deans's London pilgrimage in the terms of the marketplace.

Jeanie Deans Goes to London

As I mentioned earlier, Scott accommodates his vast English audience by rout-
ing its readerly experience through the northern geographical journey of a
character like Edward Waverley. Writing of this plot device, Franco Moretti
adds that "[Waverley's] movement in space is also, and in fact above all, the
movement in *time*. . . . He travels backwards through the various stages of
social development described by the Scottish Enlightenment."[60] What is Scott
doing, we might ask, when he sends a protagonist in the opposite direction,
straight into London? Scott uses the centripetal plot of *The Heart of Mid-
Lothian* to encode the nineteenth-century project of sending stories to England.[61] The novel is set in the 1730s amid a tense political situation following
the death of Captain John Porteous at the hands of an Edinburgh crowd incensed that he had been pardoned for murder by King George II. It relates
the journey of Jeanie Deans from Edinburgh to London in the weeks after
the Porteous riots, where she pleads with Queen Caroline to help procure a
pardon for her sister, Effie, who's been wrongly convicted of infanticide and
sentenced to death. The novel reaches its climax at the end of Jeanie's journey,
when she entirely wins over the Queen, who, impressed with her "eloquence,"
convinces the King to pardon Effie.[62] Scott links the Porteous plot to Jeanie's
through the common central action of a monarchical pardon. And yet the
scene between Jeanie and the Queen by far exceeds the text's historical context.
By the time Scott wrote *Mid-Lothian*, his sixth full-length Scottish fiction, "he
had become highly self-conscious about his ongoing dialogue with the reader
of the Waverley Novels."[63] Such self-consciousness leads Scott to take as the
novel's major dramatic catalyst the uneven literary market in Britain.

The allegorical meaning of Jeanie Deans's journey depends on her relation
to her sister Effie, the Duke of Argyle, the interview with Queen Caroline,
and the novel's narrative voice, all of which make that journey impossible
to isolate or to relegate entirely to the past. As with *Waverley*, *Mid-Lothian*
uses England as a reference point for its descriptive passages. The narrator
seeks on occasion to "apprize the Southern reader" (*M*, 204) of certain details
about Scottish jurisprudence and deploys national comparison as shorthand
for some details: "England had her Tyburn" (*M*, 21) he writes, referring to
Edinburgh's site for public executions, and elsewhere he notes that a Scottish court custom has "something of the same effect which in England is
obtained" by other means (*M*, 216). Such moments invoke the presence of

Scott's contemporary reader and fold in the novel's eighteenth-century action with its moment of publication. This is accomplished as well through an immediate association of physical travel with the travel of literature. In the prologue to the novel, Peter Pattieson, the invented editor of the manuscript we are purportedly reading, eagerly expects a "periodical publication" to arrive (*M*, 8). As an approaching coach crashes, his hopes are dashed: instead of receiving the expected "intelligence from the mart of news" (*M*, 8), Pattieson meets lawyers who deliver the story of Jeanie Deans. The novel thus arrives as it passes by, on the very kind of road that will be the stage for its mythic action. Peter Pattieson's original hopes may have been for literary news, but the result is in fact the novel; like an English reader of Scott, Pattieson's appetite has been satisfied by a traveling story.

Scott strongly suggests that Jeanie's storytelling triumph in England parallels his own. As she prepares to leave Scotland, Jeanie hopes the King and Queen will have the dispositions of emotionally engaged novel readers; they are "but mortal man and woman," Jeanie tells her lover Reuben Butler, and "their hearts maun be made o' flesh and blood," ready to "melt" upon hearing "Effie's story" (*M*, 245). Like the hybrid linguistic makeup of a Waverley novel—Scotch dialect within English narration—Jeanie acquires a southern appearance after she enters England, "wearing shoes and stockings for the whole day" and "a large straw bonnet, like those worn by the English maidens" (*M*, 249), all the while retaining her "tidy, nice Scotch body" within (*M*, 250). Jeanie first tells her story in a room especially made for one: the "handsome library" of George Staunton's father (*M*, 291), where, "notwithstanding her northern accent and tone" (*M*, 295), Mr. Staunton absorbs her "account of herself" like one of the books on his commodious shelves (*M*, 291). She also meets the Duke of Argyle in his "splendid library" (*M*, 319), where he encourages her to speak a "plain tale" (*M*, 320). Like Scott's tales of Scotland, Jeanie needs the help of an editor, and she finds it in the Duke, a carefully constructed surrogate for the author. The Duke is a "true Scotsman and a real friend to the country" (*M*, 220) and the "benevolent enchanter" of his protégés, the Deanses, in the novel's fourth volume (*M*, 380). He's popular at the London court, though removed from it—just like Scott—and he acknowledges that "popularity . . . has its inconveniences" (*M*, 319). Significantly, the Duke edits her story twice: first as he reads the statement of Effie's innocence and marks the "most important" passages with the speed of a prolific novelist, "in a shorter time than can be supposed by men of ordinary talents" (*M*, 323), and second during the interview with the Queen, as he uses hand signals to manage Jeanie's speech and translates the Scotch term *bittock* for Queen Caroline, who, like an English reader, is in desperate need of a glossary (*M*, 339).

The interview itself solidifies the analogy between Jeanie's purpose and Scott's aims. The novel arrives, as it does for Peter Pattieson, by coach: the Duke sweeps Jeanie away on a "large turnpike road" (*M*, 328), and they arrive as "traveling companion[s]" (*M*, 330), ready to "speak plainly and boldly" to their audience (*M*, 329). When Jeanie does speak, her plea encapsulates the essence of the novel, for her tale comes out by way of careful association, in response to a question about the Porteous riots in Edinburgh. "Heark you, young woman," the Queen asks, "had you any friends engaged in the Porteous mob?" (*M*, 340). Soon after answering, Jeanie follows up with a narrative balancing act, typical in Scott's novels, between public and private concerns. Porteous and Effie are analogous criminals, having been judged by analogous juries (the court and the public); they are subject to the same absolute royal authority and worthy of the same moral sympathy:

> I would hae gaen to the end of the earth to save the life of John Porteous . . . but he is dead and gane to his place, and they that have slain him must answer for their ain act. But my sister—my puir sister Effie, still lives, though her days and hours are numbered!— She still lives, and a word of the King's mouth might restore her. . . . [W]hen the hour of trouble comes . . . it isna what we hae dune for oursells, but what we hae dune for others, that we think on maist pleasantly. And the thoughts that ye hae intervened to spare the puir thing's life will be sweeter in that hour, come when it may, than if a word of your mouth could hang the haill Porteous mob at the tail of ae tow. (*M*, 340–341)

Jeanie comes to Effie by association with Porteous, an issue that bookends her appeal; the intimate concern of her sister's life is framed within the context of larger political issues. Here Jeanie collapses the ethics of both situations, which makes her speech the climax in the novel's action and not only because it leads to her sister's pardon. Jeanie's reticence on the matter of the Porteous mob is crucial, since this prevents her from naming George Staunton, Effie's lover, as the guilty leader of the riots in Edinburgh. Her silence guarantees Staunton's freedom and thus clears the ground for the novel's final volume—for Effie's extravagant life with Staunton in London and the relocation of Jeanie, Butler, and David Deans to the Duke's estate in the west of Scotland. Jeanie's story, her plea, can be seen as a microcosm of Scott's narrative. After she has finished, the reviews come in: the narrator declares that she's spoken "with a pathos which was at once simple and solemn," and the Queen declares, "This is eloquence," before telling Jeanie she'll pursue her cause (*M*, 341). Like a successful Waverley novel, Jeanie has combated prejudice against the Scottish, who only moments earlier the Queen had called "barbarous" (*M*, 338). A London acquaintance of Jeanie's becomes impressed with the "notice and approbation" she has acquired and considers her in "a light . . . much more favorable" than she did before (*M*, 354).

Mid-Lothian's allegory of transcultural sympathy plays out in contemporary reviews, which suggest that, like Jeanie herself, the book signified to the general public as a Scotch product dressed up for sale in England. London's *Monthly Review* declared, for example, that *Mid-Lothian* "transport[s] us to other regions, where we are mere sojourners, and in which we find everything attractive because it is new and strange to our perception."[64] For other reviews, it is a novel "got up for bookselling purposes," as one London journal wrote, assisted by "the medium of Mr. James Ballantyne, Printer, and Archibald Constable and Company, Booksellers and Publishers, in the good city of Edinburgh."[65] The novel was rarely treated as a document about the past. "All his novels are Scotch," writes the *Monthly Review*,

> even to the back-bone; the vices and virtues of his countrymen are coloured in them with such warmth of feeling and such glow of imagination, as could only arise from an entire conviction of their existence, acquired by a long abode in their habitations and by a frequent and varied intercourse with every class of society among them. . . . It is to this charm of nationality, and to the more than dramatic representations of the thoughts, words, manners, and actions of his countrymen, which always attend his exemplification of it, that the success which his narratives have obtained is principally owing.[66]

In a few notable cases, Jeanie's interview with the Queen provides the logic and language for a review's praise of the novel as a whole, making Scott's allegory a self-fulfilling prophecy. Jeanie's speech marks a turning point in two reviews that criticize the novel until they comment on the interview scene. The *London Literary Gazette* begins by declaring the novel "inferior" but then changes its tone after quoting the speech as a reprinted excerpt: "We need scarcely to add, that we retract every censure upon *The Heart of Mid-Lothian.*"[67] *The British Critic* reacts similarly; it initially dismisses the novel as "careless[]" but eventually "agree[s] with Queen Caroline" that Jeanie's speech "is indeed eloquence."[68] These reviews have fallen into the system of sympathy Scott encodes in this episode made especially, it seems, for the periodicals— easily excerpted and easy to mimic.

Three notable illustrations highlight the relationship between Jeanie and her audience. An early illustration, first published in volume 10 of the pocket-sized 1823 edition of the series *Novels and Tales* and reprinted separately in *The Waverley Album*, places Jeanie on the border between the thick forest that envelops the Queen and the open sky that suggests her outsider status. Jeanie's pleading eye, her clasped hands, and the folds of her scarf bring the viewer in from the open air toward Queen Caroline, whose gaze seems difficult for Jeanie to attract. This exchange is a one-way transaction, not an "interview," as the caption reads, and the Duke, cut partly from the frame of the picture on the left, plays merely a supporting role. The Queen, despite her absent look, clearly dominates the picture, with her gleaming dress, gloves, and hair. Her authority, foregrounded by such emphasis, is symbolized by the tall, thick tree in the background that anchors the left portion of the image. Two late Victorian illustrations (1893), including one that derives from this 1823 image, amplify these dynamics. In the first image, Jeanie has just set off from Edinburgh, briefly in company with the Laird of Dumbiedikes. The hillsides of Scotland are bare and the sky is open, like Jeanie's portion of the picture in the 1823 illustration; she is barefoot and forlorn, an unlikely traveler. In the scene with the Queen, Jeanie has abandoned her scruffy guide for the courtly Duke who, in this rendering, holds equal representational space with the two women. The Duke's profile has replaced Jeanie's, so present in the former illustration, as she turns away from us to face an older and even more intimidating English Queen. The plumes of the Queen's headdress extend, like the branches of the oak behind her, far past the horizontal line that connects her gaze with Jeanie's. As in the earlier illustration, the Queen is part of the forest; Jeanie, coming from a barren Scotland, is in this rendering entirely enveloped by the thick English woods. These images depict the moment of Jeanie's plea, thus intensifying readerly interest and sympathy. Jeanie travels all the way from the open sky of Scotland to the deep forests of England—from outside in—not only to procure a pardon but to pursue storytelling itself. This is suggested especially by the 1823 illustration, in which Jeanie's body skirts the border between the sky and the forest, the dark shade of her dress a continuation of the

THE HEART OF MID-LOTHIAN.

THE INTERVIEW OF JEANIE DEANS WITH THE QUEEN.

Figure 5. "The Interview of Jeanie Deans with the Queen." *The Waverley Album*
(London: Charles Heath, c. 1823).

Courtesy of the Boston Athenaeum.

Figure 6. "Jeanie and the Laird of Dumbiedykes." *The Heart of Mid-Lothian*
(Boston: Estes and Lauriat, 1893–1894).

Figure 7. "Jeanie and Queen Caroline." *The Heart of Mid-Lothian*
(Boston: Estes and Lauriat, 1893–1894).

Courtesy of Widener Library, Harvard University.

line the trees make to the ground. The image asks the Queen if she will accept Jeanie into the comfort of the shade.

The story of Jeanie Deans going to London became one of Scott's most memorable narratives. John Galt's sketch "A Jeanie Deans in Love," printed in *Blackwood's*, takes for granted that Jeanie's journey to London defines her character. The Scottish servant girl in Galt's tale goes to London unheroically to seek a promotion for her lover, and her interview with English nobility provides the occasion to parody the market allegory in Scott's novel. The servant girl reports on the Duke she met in London: his "ceeveleezed and kind manner" shows that he "would be a patron to mony a . . . Edinburgh writer."[69] In a spoof where "in Love" means "in London," Galt suggests that Jeanie Deans's trip inevitably points to the English consumption of Scottish books. In the theater, Jeanie's London journey captured the imagination of English audiences more than other aspects of *Mid-Lothian*'s plot. Thomas Dibdin's adaptation *The Heart of Mid-Lothian: Or, the Lily of St. Leonard's* featured Jeanie's pilgrimage as its principal narrative; the play's final act climaxes with Jeanie's successful interview with the Queen—"This is eloquence!"—and then concludes with Jeanie's delivery of the pardon to Effie back in Edinburgh, entirely ignoring the novel's fourth volume.[70]

It was perhaps the easy portability of Scott's allegory that led Nassau Senior, in an 1821 retrospective on the Waverley novels, to dismiss the Queen's response. "Had [Jeanie's speech] *been* eloquence," he writes, "it must necessarily have been unperceived by the Queen."[71] After the novelty of Jeanie's story has worn off, Senior suggests that in this scene, Scott has revealed his overt literary game. The Queen's approving response reads like an artificial aesthetic judgment made with reference only to itself. Whereas Jeanie's speech interweaves the story of Effie with the story of Porteous, the Queen ignores them both to make a comment on style. The Queen's perception of Jeanie's "eloquence"—her ratification of it as "eloquence"—gestures away from politics out toward a realm of culture as separate from the King's court as the forested park at Richmond, where the interview takes place. In the moment when the Queen recognizes Jeanie's "eloquence," it hardly matters what she's talking about. What matters is only the Queen's authority to judge Jeanie's performance. Before Jeanie Deans leaves for London, Scott's narrator wonders if "these Tales" will "ever [find] their way across the Border" (*M*, 204), and Jeanie's successful audience with the Queen suggests what can happen if they do. Scott's allegory in *Mid-Lothian* stages a highly self-conscious acknowledgment of the provincial author's need to be judged by the authority of metropolitan readers. The Queen's sympathetic reaction remains disconnected from the historical struggle the novel otherwise narrates and projects literary exchange onto a sphere all its own.

The New Natty Bumppo

As *The Pioneers*—like Jeanie Deans—travels to its London audience, textual changes isolate Natty Bumppo from a growing American community he could never truly join. Such changes suggest that his independence, originally related to the nation, becomes a figure for the literary itself. Revisions for the Bentley edition thus contribute to the myth of Natty's innocence, which R. W. B. Lewis describes as a function of his outsider position. Writing of Cooper's use of the Adamic hero, Lewis notes that he sends the Leatherstocking, uncomfortable with society and its laws, far away "from the town and community of Templeton for the freer country of the west."[72] The London republication of *The Pioneers* works to associate Natty's isolation—itself dependent on an elision of the violence that makes the west "free"—with the ideology that literary exchange, like Natty himself and the interview between Jeanie and the Queen, rejects the contentiousness of a messy political world.

The Bentley text's new concern with cross-cultural communion changes the symbolic meaning of Natty's performances as a hunter and spokesperson for nature. For Cooper's new English audience, such performances consolidate his authority as a writer of fiction. They tie Cooper to his mythic hero despite the obvious void that separates Natty's voice from the ethnographic and informative voice in the narrative and the paratexts. Cooper produces the parallel between himself and the Leatherstocking similarly to the way Scott produces the parallel between Jeanie Deans and his authorial ambition. Natty Bumppo is more like this simple but well-spoken Lowland female character than he is like Scott's Highlanders, to whom George Dekker has compared him.[73] In the Bentley text, Natty is slightly more sympathetic than he is in the Wiley text; he is no longer "disdainful" (*W*, 1:10; *B*, 9) or "mutter[ing]" (*W*, 1:15; *B*, 12) while addressing Judge Temple, and he brings a new "earnestness" to his behavior at the trial scene (*W*, 2:213; *B*, 371). Natty's appeal for sympathy in court indeed parallels Jeanie's testimony in her audience with Queen Caroline: both scenes feature the powerful expression of unmediated emotion by a figure constructed as the innocent victim of the legal authority his or her interlocutor symbolizes.

In *The Pioneers*, Cooper stages the equivalent of the Queen's approving response to Jeanie Deans in moments where characters applaud Natty's intimate relation to nature. Because Cooper has downplayed the novel's nationalism in the Bentley text, such approving responses now register on a more purely aesthetic level. For example, Chingachgook twice hails Natty's slaying of wild game with the value judgment, "Good" (*W*, 2:77; *B*, 266) (*W*, 2.118; *B*, 297). Further, the small flame that guides Natty and Chingachgook as they fish on Lake Otsego contrasts drastically with the messy conflagration that Richard and the townspeople ignite at exactly the same time. The imagery Cooper uses to describe it is heavily aestheticized:

> Such an object, lighted as it were by magic, under the brow of the mountain, and in that retired and unfrequented place, gave double interest to the beauty and singularity of its appearance. It did not at all resemble the large and unsteady light of [Richard's] fire, being much more clear and bright, and retaining its size and shape with perfect uniformity. . . . A brilliant, though waving flame was now plainly visible, gracefully gliding over the lake, and throwing its light on the water, in such a manner as to tinge it slightly; though, in the air, so strong was the contrast, the darkness seemed to have the distinctness of material substances, as if the fire were embedded in a setting of ebony. (*W*, 2:68; *B*, 259) (*W*, 2:70; *B*, 261)

Cooper frames Natty's engagement with nature in language that amounts to a still-life portrait. Elizabeth models the reader's response to this image: "It is beautiful," she exclaims (*W*, 2:70; *B*, 261). In the Bentley text, a moment like this highlights literary achievement through infusing a common event with lofty significance.[74]

The Pioneers guides its reader's response more directly in a crucial moment when Cooper dramatizes Natty's insight into his natural surroundings. While traveling in the woods, Natty brings Oliver to a quiet brook and marvels at a drop of water's journey down the valley and eventually "under the bottom of a vessel . . . tossing in the salt sea" (*W*, 2:110; *B*, 291). Oliver's response to this speech is worthy of Queen Caroline, and his comment changes slightly during transatlantic revision:

> "Why, you are eloquent, Leatherstocking!" (*W*, 2:111)
> "You are eloquent, Leatherstocking!" (*B*, 292)

As the novel changes for new English readers, Oliver seems less surprised at his companion's power with words. While Natty does not literally travel to London, Cooper promotes his own literary authority as the novel itself travels there, using innumerable small modifications like the deletion of "Why." After transatlantic revision, Cooper hopes, one will no longer be shocked by the eloquence of *The Pioneers*. This reflects what D. H. Lawrence identified as Cooper's major theme: "Wish-Fulfillment!"[75] Natty comes to enact Cooper's literary ambition and to be a spokesperson for it, a role supported by the novel's subordination of the Wiley text's nationalism and the removal of antagonism from its marriage plot.

One stunning change isolates Natty through its suppression of the production of national feeling. It occurs in the book's final sentence, Cooper's most famous lines about manifest destiny. Here is the Wiley text:

He had gone far towards the setting sun,—the foremost in that
band of Pioneers, who are opening the way for the march of *our na-*
tion across the continent. (*W*, 2:329, emphasis added)

In the only use of the word "pioneers" since the novel's opening pages, Cooper constructs Natty as both the future and the past of a nation comprised of novel readers. The use of the first-person plural in the phrase "our nation" draws Cooper's implicitly American audience into the project of "opening the way." The reader watches Natty over the shoulders of Oliver and Elizabeth, who symbolize a national community that coheres through exclusion; for only if you can claim ownership of "our nation" can you join the silent chorus cheering Natty's western march. The passage makes such readers beholden to the "Pioneer" who ironically secures the future of their nation even as he rejects it by leaving town. This is our nation, Cooper suggests, and Natty Bumppo is our Pioneer.

Here is the Bentley text:

He had gone far towards the setting sun,—the foremost in that
band of Pioneers, who are opening the way for the march of *the na-*
tion across the continent. (*B*, 460, emphasis added)

For whom, now, does Natty clear the way? The substitution of a definite article for a possessive pronoun makes the "nation" something to observe, not something we own. In this sense, the American reader's involvement vanishes;

the reader is a witness, not a participant. Indeed, Cooper's new English readers are not involved directly in the national project that Natty and *The Pioneers* forward, so calling it "the nation" seems more appropriate than making it "our[s]." The substitution modifies the effects that calling the nation "our[s]" originally throws back on the married couple who look west with the reader. It opens them up for nonnational signification; they watch Natty from a greater distance—now, indeed, from across the Atlantic. The substitution of "the nation" for "our nation" pushes Natty farther away from Templeton than he has already run. This change divorces his mythic role from Cooper's American audience and cuts the last remaining thread tying him to the Olivers and Elizabeths reading the novel. For the novel's new English readers, Natty's destiny is merely a story. Not "our nation" but rather "the nation": the final lines of the revised edition of *The Pioneers* transform the Leatherstocking into material for aesthetic judgment. He is no longer one of us.

*   *   *

The separation of Natty Bumppo from a direct identification with a nationalized reading public epitomizes the effects that distance from England had on the provincial writer. Such distance is inscribed on the final page of the "Standard Novels" edition of *The Pioneers*, pictured in Figure 8, with its revised final sentence and the printer's colophon: "London: Printed by A. and R. Spottiswoode, New-Street-Square." I have been arguing that such effects produce in Cooper and Scott a willful idealization of literary exchange, despite the political concerns otherwise evident in their historical novels. Such projection attempts to lessen the liability of distance through numerous strategies for addressing readers. Scott's review of Jane Austen's *Emma* (1815) throws into relief the relevance of distance through a consideration of its absence in Austen's work. Scott describes what happens when a novel's scenes and subjects overlap with the experiences of its principle audience—precisely the advantage that eludes a provincial writer. He points to the mutual constitution of mimesis and recognition evidenced in a novel like *Emma*, which relies on "the art of copying from nature as she really exists in the common walks of life, and presenting to the reader, instead of the splendid scenes of an imaginary world, a correct and striking representation of that which is daily taking place around him."[76] The characters in Austen's fiction "conduct themselves," Scott writes, "upon the motives and principles which the readers may recognize as ruling their own and that of most of their acquaintances."[77] There is no room for distance or even difference between subject and audience in such a novel. In highlighting this seamlessness, Scott implicitly reflects on his own inability, as a romancer of Scotland, to achieve it. The contrast is also germane to Cooper, whose first novel was disguised as the kind of English domestic novel that, including Austen's, was available in America as a reprint or imported book. Austen's novels do not thematize as explicitly as Cooper's and Scott's a relation to readers in the language of national culture. This is because of the assumption, which Scott identifies in *Emma*, that they treat easily recognizable "motives and principles," representations of "daily" life for which no heavy-handed introductions are needed.

Most early nineteenth-century Scottish novels entered the marketplace by way of the kind of uneven London-Edinburgh publishing partnerships that defined Scott's career; many of them register such unevenness in their texts. Susan Ferrier's *Marriage* (1818), for example, follows its Scottish heroine Mary Douglas to London in a journey structurally similar to Jeanie Deans's in *Mid-Lothian*. "My heart's in the Highlands," Mary sings as she travels, only to show there's enough room in it for sympathy with the blind Mrs. Lennox, proprietor of an estate that was "perfectly English."[78] Mary eventually marries Mrs. Lennox's son but only after she has seen "Highland society," as Juliet Shields has argued, "through the eyes of those living in metropolitan England."[79] In *Peter's Letters to his Kinsfolk* (1819), which originally appeared in *Blackwood's*, John Gibson Lockhart makes a joke of provinciality by writing for its book publication a heavily ironized preface to "Mr. Davies, Bookseller, In the Strand, London."[80] *Peter's Letters*, which Ian Duncan has placed at the center of the "doctrinal emergence of a modern aesthetic conception of national culture," epitomizes as much as *Mid-Lothian* the literary idealizations at the heart of the aesthetics of provinciality.[81] So, too, does Christian Isobel Johnstone's *Clan-Albin* (1815), which dramatizes a tension between the preservation of a celebrated and distinctive Highland culture, even in the face of emigration, and the domestication and diffusion of its virtues throughout the British Empire.[82] The opening paragraph of James Hogg's *Confessions of a Justified Sinner* (1824) critiques the introductory discourse that English readers had come to expect from Scottish novels. "In recording the hideous events which follow," the fictional editor claims, "I am only relating to the greater part of the inhabitants of at least four counties of Scotland, matters of which they were before perfectly well informed."[83] The blatant ironies of the words "only" and "perfectly" undermine any claim to facticity, just as "the supernatural" element of *Confessions*, as Penny Fielding argues of Hogg's other

ing, looking back for a moment, on the verge of the wood. As he caught their glances, he drew his hard hand hastily across his eyes again, waved it on high for an adieu, and, uttering a forced cry to his dogs, who were crouching at his feet, he entered the forest.

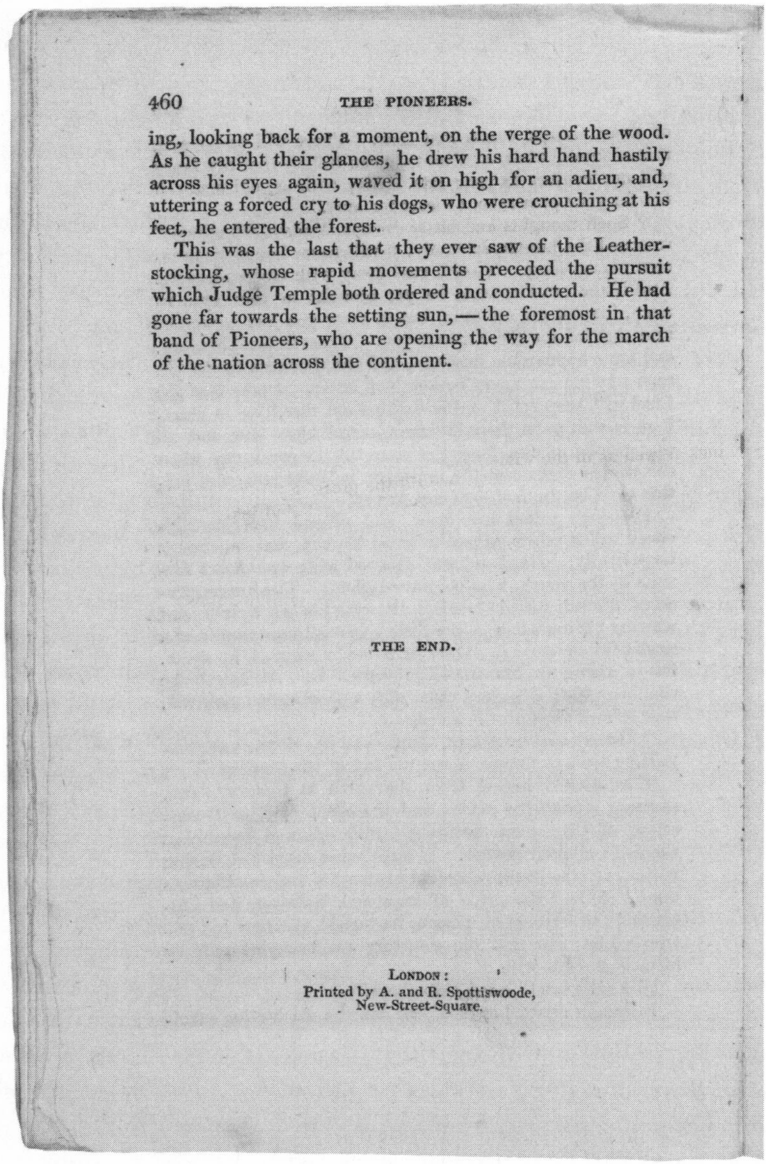

This was the last that they ever saw of the Leather-stocking, whose rapid movements preceded the pursuit which Judge Temple both ordered and conducted. He had gone far towards the setting sun,—the foremost in that band of Pioneers, who are opening the way for the march of the nation across the continent.

THE END.

LONDON :
Printed by A. and R. Spottiswoode,
New-Street-Square.

Figure 8. James Fenimore Cooper, *The Pioneers* (London: Colburn and Bentley, 1832), final page.

Courtesy of the Huntington Library, San Marino, California.

works, soon enough "undercuts apprehension of the local."[84] Hogg defines the ignorance of his English audience as a foil to the local knowledge his Scottish readers always possess—something Scott did with only slightly less irony in the opening to *The Antiquary* (1815), which introduced "the Queensferry" as "well known to all of my northern readers."[85] In Romantic-era Scotland, provinciality was a productive state of mind for novelists, not one to be lamented in the name of an indigenous national tradition. They played around with the idea of the London book trade as much as they played with the idea of history, the idea of a distinctive national culture, and the idea that literature transcends nationalized definitions of culture.

The same is true for American novels from the 1820s that stage the union of an English or Anglicized figure with an Americanized one. Such novels reconcile not only the residual loyalist-patriot tensions within the United States but also Anglo-American tensions that straddled the Atlantic Ocean. In *A New-England Tale*, for example, Sedgwick unites the orphaned, Puritan American girl Jane Elton with the Quaker Mr. Lloyd, a native Englishman brought to America as a young boy who "see[s] no reason to depart" from the traditions of "his ancestors."[86] This marriage embodies a universalized moral code—framed, for Sedgwick, in the language of religious tolerance—available only to proper and elite Anglo-American subjects.[87] Consider, too, the union between Anglican Charles Brown and the Puritan Mary Conant in Lydia Maria Child's *Hobomok* (1824), a couple who, Child suggests, would have been perfectly happy settling "in England or America."[88] Cooper's *The Spy* tackles these dynamics through the split narrative trajectory of the Wharton family, which projects an Anglo-American union that counters the novel's ostensible patriotism. The posterity of the Whartons depends on a remarkable coincidence that links the American marriage of Frances and Major Dunwoodie with the escape of Frances's brother Henry, a soldier in the British army for whom the American forces have a death warrant. Frances executes an elaborate plan to marry Dunwoodie at a certain hour in order to prevent him from pursuing her fugitive brother; the plan of detaining Dunwoodie for his nuptials ensures that Henry will have had time enough to reach safety in the Royalist camp.[89] Her relieved heart remains ever connected with a brother who returns to the United States only to fight *against* it during the War of 1812. Harvey Birch's love of country is thus overshadowed by the powerful image of his hillside dwelling, where "British and American uniforms hung peaceably by the side of each other."[90]

It is the explicit nature of its reckoning with English readers that assigns to provincial literature an important role in the consolidation of Romantic idealizations of the literary. American and Scottish fiction writers, and especially Cooper and Irving and Scott, made such idealizations a major theme in works that conquered the London marketplace and spread throughout the English-speaking world. While their success—and the success of Irish writers like Maria Edgeworth and Sydney Owenson—has been attributed to their immersion in any number of politically saturated circumstances, including ascendant nationalisms on both sides of the Atlantic, the marketplace for books led such authors to imagine a literary exchange that escapes political contentiousness altogether. The unique essence of national culture, in such an exchange, intensifies the literary experience as much as it structures the cross-cultural sympathies that define it.

Chapter 6

Rivalry with England in the
Age of Nationalism

The previous three chapters have analyzed the fiction of ambitious Irish, Scottish, and American authors who published and distributed their wares in London. The effects of provinciality, I have argued, produced wide-ranging ideas about literature's relationship to the nation within an idealized cross-cultural exchange, one that helped define the distinctively modern idea that literature inhabits its own sphere in society. In the aesthetics of provinciality, the fierce political tones of national rivalry are pacified and modulated to fit within the genteel literary arena. This chapter provides a contrasting view of the early nineteenth century through delving into the readerly expressions of Irish, Scottish, and American provincials who embraced national rivalry and national difference, throwing such gentility to the wind. It testifies to the power of provinciality in producing defensiveness, rage, envy, and pride. England, here, is a provocative adversary: the ancient enemy, the colonial power, the imperial aggressor, the denier of liberties, the dissolver of parliaments, the taxer without representation, the arrogant and self-confident cultural authority. This conception of "England" comes straight out of the contentious and divisive political world from which elite provincial authors so willfully retreated. It is marshalled in the realm of popular culture in the service of what I will be calling *provincial nationalism*: an ideology with a provocative aesthetics of its own.

Anti-English, provincial nationalism is evident within a diversity of sources untreated in current scholarship, including travel narratives, newspapers, periodicals, marginalia, and ephemeral printed matter. My goal, in turning to them, is to offer a dialectical counterpoint to the representational modes of provincial literature; three case studies suggest that trans-provincial resonances linking Irish, Scottish, and American culture were just as important to a vehemently politicized nationalism as they were to Romantic aesthetic ideologies. I begin with reactions to the volatile archive of metropolitan travel writing, a genre written by English authors who journeyed to Ireland, Scotland, and the United States and published their accounts back in London. These narratives, by Samuel Johnson, Joseph Mawman, John Carr, Thomas Ashe, Isaac Weld, Isaac Candler, and others, infuriated provincial readers, many of whom responded in print and in the margins of books to produce a complex and defensive rhetoric of national difference. Following this, the chapter turns to Ireland, where nationalists harnessed the memory of America's struggle for independence to define an Irish nationalism that rejected England. In literary magazines, radical serials like Walter Cox's *Irish Magazine* (1807–1815) and forgotten novels like Sarah Isdell's *The Vale of Louisiana* (1805)—one of the only fictional works of its time published in Dublin—Irish provincials demonstrated their continuing fascination with America and its ideologies. And finally, it considers the untold story of the American affection for Walter Scott's poetry during the War of 1812, when U.S. nationalists appropriated the anti-English rhetoric of Scott's poems of medieval Scotland to fuel their own defiance of England. It was during this war that Americans adopted a song of Walter Scott's, "Hail to the Chief," as the official anthem of the U.S. president—one of Scott's most lasting and hidden legacies in American culture.

Provincial nationalism developed in relation to the London-dominated transatlantic print networks explored throughout this book. The importance of London is clear from frustration expressed about the easy dissemination of metropolitan discourse compared to the difficulty of airing any objection to it. Provincial nationalism also developed in relation to the bloody conflicts that defined a period of rebellion and war, from the failed 1798 nationalist rebellion in Ireland to the War of 1812 between Great Britain and the United States. Such conflicts were more urgent in Ireland and the United States than in Scotland, England's partner in war and empire; provincial nationalism was accordingly a less potent phenomenon in "North Briton," where British nationalism reigned even while Scottish culture retained its distinctiveness. In assigning to *print* and to *war* important roles in the development of nationalism, the chapter follows well-established historiographical precedents, from Benedict Anderson to Linda Colley, which point to communication networks and violent conflict as the ideology's preconditions and stimuli.[1] In tracing the unexpected ways provincials engaged with the transatlantic circulation of print, the chapter also joins recent scholarship that acknowledges the transnational currents that inform and shape nationalism itself.[2] Provincial nationalism emerged from within transnational networks of circulation, not despite them.

Irish, Scottish, and American rivalries with England were interconnected phenomena: discourses and practices that were mutually reinforcing, cross-pollinating, and fueled by powerful and surprising analogies across time and space. Individuals made free and easy use of the rhetoric and histories of culturally allied provincial nations in order to articulate their own difference from and defiance of England. As the case of Scott's "Hail to the Chief" suggests, the authors that have featured so prominently in this book as accommodating figures in the literary field play a different role in this chapter as inspirations for anti-English rhetorical stances. Readers take center stage as anonymous participants in transatlantic print culture who left traces in multiple national archives—in texts they published, in marginalia they scribbled, and in actions and reactions others recorded. In a passionate discussion of "autonomy in the act of reading," Roger Chartier has argued that authors and texts cannot exert ultimate control over a reader's experience. "Reading is not simply submission to textual machinery," Chartier writes. "Whatever it may be, reading is a creative practice, which invents singular meanings and significations that are not reducible to the intentions of authors of texts or producers of books."[3] The sources in this chapter confirm this in ways that expand the conventional definition of reading out to the uses of print in acts of readerly expression. Reading was, indeed, a "creative practice" for provincials embroiled in the contentious political climate of the early nineteenth century.

Metropolitan Travel Narratives and the "Vortex of London"

Travel writing was a popular genre in late eighteenth- and early nineteenth-century England, much of it treating continental Europe, the "Orient," and the South Seas. Between 1770 and 1830, at least one hundred narratives were published in London about nations closer to home: the "sister kingdoms" of Scotland and Ireland as well as one former member of the British imperial family, the new United States. Many were reprinted multiple times in London and abroad.[4] In the late eighteenth century, persistent questions about the meaning of "Britain" fueled continuing metropolitan interest in Scotland as a hyper-aestheticized landscape and an important partner in a global empire

continually at war with France.[5] Events leading up to and following the 1801
Act of Union between Great Britain and Ireland sent English travelers to Ireland to help understand the problem of redefining the "United Kingdom."[6]
Rampant curiosity following the American Revolution and after the War of
1812 sent English travelers across the Atlantic to scrutinize the United States
and assess the viability of immigration.[7] Metropolitan narratives vary widely in
tone, purpose, and narrative form; they satisfy a basic desire for information,
trade in the worst kinds of stereotypes and prejudices, provide the loose impressions of wandering minds, and offer thoughtful meditations on national
difference, political economy, and aesthetic experience. Many travel narratives
to Scotland, Ireland, and the United States mulled over the limits of cultural
kinship with England, revealing the ambiguous nature of relationships that
each nation's political status failed in any way to clarify. Scotland had been
bound to England since the 1707 Union; Ireland, newly bound in 1801; and
the United States, unbound since 1783. Yet for travelers, Scotland remained as
"little known" as ever, Ireland "as little described as if the Atlantic had flowed
between us," and the United States, despite independence (and the Atlantic), just as culturally bound as before—as one traveler wrote, "The poetry
of Scott, Byron, and Southey is as familiar to the Americans as to us."[8] Such
narratives raise more questions than they could ever answer; indeed, scholars
working in each discrete national context have noticed a remarkable amount
of epistemological instability.[9] Metropolitans wanted to read about provincial
nations—to learn and, scornfully, to laugh. Responses were as varied as the
narratives themselves, but many were launched in a frustrated language of national defense. Offended provincials directed the majority of their ire toward
the authority of metropolitan discourse, which many critiqued as the shallow
product of a market-driven publishing industry particularly effective at pur-
veying bad opinions. Much of this frustrated commentary invokes London as
the blameworthy manufacturing center of prejudice.

Reactions to early Scottish travel narratives couched disappointment
within a critique of the marketplace, a strategy that would continue in responses to Irish and American narratives of the early nineteenth century. One
angry reader of Samuel Johnson's *Journey to the Western Islands of Scotland*
(1775), for example, expressed his disappointment that Johnson failed to overcome his prejudice against "this poor kingdom":

> The vortex of London . . . disgorges annually a certain number of
> South Britons, who, along with some birds of passage, make a tour

to Scotland every summer. . . . You came to this country, no doubt,
that you might write a tour: but you wrote a tour to gain an opportunity of making some reparation to injured Caledonia, whose fair
form you had heretofore disfigured with the stigma of contempt,
and bespattered with the ordure of calumny . . . I must remark, that
all the compliments you pay us are frigid and awkward. Indeed,
from this Tour, as well as from all your other works, it is evident,
that to you invective is more natural than eulogy.[10]

The personification of Scotland as "Caledonia" makes Johnson's failure particularly offensive and also very national as this complaint lumps the eminent
man of letters into an indistinguishable mass of "South Britons" whom London routinely vomits north. The writer's disappointment makes him expose
Johnson's principal motive—"no doubt, that you might write a tour." The *Edinburgh Review*'s account of Joseph Mawman's *An Excursion to the Highlands
of Scotland* (1805) began with a blunt opening salvo: "This is past all enduring." That Mawman was himself a bookseller was infuriating. "Here is a tour,
travelled, written, published, sold, and, for anything we know, *reviewed,* by one
and the same individual! We cannot submit patently to this monstrous mo-
nopoly." Objections about the book's unnatural path to publication modulate
into sarcastic dismissals of its content, particularly Mawman's clichéd response
to the Highlands, which "seized" him with "that fever of the spirits which is so
apt to attack all tourists who travel with a view to publication." Despite such
ecstasy, however, "Mr Mawman is not very partial to Scotland," which the reviewer illustrates through quoting his preference for the landscape of England
instead of Scotland's "wild and sterile sublimity." "We cannot submit tamely
to this trait of English nationality," the reviewer writes, proudly countering,
"we boldly challenge all England to produce anything like our Highlands."
The review ends by sending Mawman back from whence he came, with an
account of "his entry into London" and the image of him admiring "the grandeur of Finsbury Square."[11]

Reactions in Ireland to English travelers were just as severe. Novels provided a powerful arena for airing objections; a countervailing current in the
work of Maria Edgeworth and Sydney Owenson resists the accommodating
literary strategies I discussed in Chapter 3. Their London-published novels countered English prejudice on its own ground. In Edgeworth's *Ennui*
(1809), Lord Craiglethorpe, a much ridiculed "English lord travelling through
Ireland," intends to write "a book, a great book" upon the subject, as his

kinswoman Lady Geraldine sarcastically announces.[12] Lady Geraldine then elaborates a general complaint about the genre:

> [A]fter posting from Dublin to Cork, and from the Giants' Causeway to Killarney; after travelling east, west, north, and south, my wise cousin Craiglethorpe will know just as much of the lower Irish as the cockney who has never been out of London, and who will never, *in all his born days*, see an Irishman but on the English stage. . . . Yes, yes, write on, my good cousin . . . fill the little note-book, which will soon turn to a ponderous quarto. I shall have a copy, bound in morocco, no doubt, *from the author*, if I behave prettily.[13]

This travel writer is demeaned through the analogy with a London "cockney" who can never escape a theatrical culture flooded with the worst nationalized stereotypes. The passage exposes the pretentiousness and falsity of the genre through unmasking the morocco-bound "quarto" as the product of an emasculated "little note-book" (not such a "great book" after all). Edgeworth probably had in mind John Carr's *Stranger in Ireland* (1806), which she and her father, Richard Lovell Edgeworth, had reviewed in the *Edinburgh*. "[M]iserably disappointed," the Edgeworths write, "[w]e found Mr Carr's quarto, a book of stale jests, and fulsome compliments. All the old stories of bulls and blunders . . . are here collected for the edification of the public. . . . [T]o save himself the trouble of thought or arrangement, he has emptied and overwhelmed us with his common-place book."[14] The opening article of the *Dublin and London Magazine*—published, as its title suggests, in both cities—lambasted English travelers as it announced its priority to vindicate Ireland:

> Ireland and Irishman have been described by foreigners and natives. . . . The former, with very few exceptions, have been Englishmen; and, if we omit the names of Young and Wakefield, the remainder form a host of as imperious and ignorant calumniators as ever made observations on any country or people. No wonder, then, that a large portion of the public imbibed notions at variance with truth, and inimical to Ireland. To compare the population of that country with their own flattered their national vanity.[15]

The qualifying statements about good travelers only emphasizes this harangue's indignant characterization of the most offensive parties, the English:

"imperious and ignorant calumniators" who write about Ireland merely to bolster their own self-satisfied national pride.

Local publications with little chance of a London readership issued their own objections, including Dublin's *Irish Magazine*, which extended the critique of travel writing to English historiography. "The dignity and character of historical composition was never so degraded as by English writers when Irish affairs are the subject. They describe us to Europe as a nation of barbarians, a people who should be deprived of education, property, and life to promote their civilization; the most shocking atrocities are justified in the invader."[16] Special anger was reserved for a recent publication, William Belsham's *History of Great Britain* (1806), which dismissed the nationalist rebellion of 1798. The *Irish Magazine* drives its anger at the metropolitan representation of this charged episode in Ireland's recent history. "So far is [Belsham] hurried into the vortex of English prejudice," the article argues, "that his judgment is suspended while he wreaks his impotent vengeance."[17] In arguing that his view derives from "English prejudice" rather than a political aversion to radicalism, the article makes Belsham's rejection of the rebellion equivalent to a specific kind of English rejection of Ireland.

Other local publications were more ambivalent, such as the short-lived *Hibernia Magazine; and Dublin Monthly Panorama*, which was drawn to the very discourse it wished to critique. The preface to one series, "Letters on Ireland, by an Englishman," includes a distancing gesture notable for its fraught relation to the narrative that follows:

> To the sentiments contained in the following letters the conductors of The Panorama do not, by any means, pledge either themselves or the character of their Miscellany. They are written by an Englishman—the stile is epistolary and familiar, and the doctrines such as may sometimes hurt our pride. But they are invaluable, at least, as exhibiting the situation of the country, in the language of a man who has only studied her from books, and as it should appear, from a very superficial observation. The writer, we have reason, to conclude, is still in Ireland, and no doubt, has by this time rectified the erroneous impressions which are too palpably apparent at the commencement of his Letters.[18]

The editors clearly believed their readers had low expectations for a narrative "written by an Englishman," a fact that stood as its own condemnation.

Indeed, the preface strains to justify the dissemination of "superficial observations" that would hurt national "pride"; perhaps readers of the Panorama
enjoyed the spectacle of English arrogance and the bad feeling it inspired.
Far from offending the reader's "pride," the "erroneous impressions" of these
letters may in fact have bolstered it, with or without the kind of reformation
promised at the preface's conclusion.

Commentators in the United States found English visitors provoking well
before Francis Trollope's *Domestic Manners of the Americans* (1832) and Charles
Dickens's *American Notes* (1842). Many objected in terms strikingly similar to
the defensive discourse that circulated in Ireland. "[I]t has been the peculiar
lot of our country, to be visited by the worst kind of English travellers," writes
Washington Irving in "English Writers on America" (1819), an essay from *The
Sketch Book* that laments the "undue interest" such writings inspire among
his "countrymen." Irving directs his frustration at the marketplace for books.
"[T]he London press has teemed with volumes of travels through the republic;
but they seem intended to diffuse error rather than knowledge," he writes,
while "[o]ur retorts are never republished in England."[19] Philadelphia's *Port-
Folio*, reviewing Thomas Ashe's *Travels in America* (1808), expressed its "entire
contempt for both himself and his book" and in another article referred to
Ashe and other travelers as "unblushing miscreants."[20] The *North American
Review* wrote in its inaugural issue of a "disgraceful paper" in the *Quarterly
Review* that used many British travel narratives as evidence for its opinions.
"Of thousands who will have read this libel, by far the greater part will never
see any refutation of it." They despaired that the publication "should be made
use of, to carry into every library in England a collected mass of calumny and
falsehood against a whole nation."[21] A decade after this attack, the American
printers of the *Quarterly* took the drastic step of censoring their edition of that
London journal because of its objectionable review of William Faux's *Memorable Days in America* (1823). Advised that the review might be libelous, the
editors excised it at the last minute and took the occasion to complain bitterly
about the *Quarterly*'s previous offenses:

> The Publishers of the American edition of the Quarterly Review
> have hitherto reprinted the whole in exact conformity with the
> original. Some articles they would gladly have omitted or curtailed,
> as disgracing the high literary character of the Journal by abuse
> and misrepresentations of the United States. These articles have
> generally been written in a style of great vulgarity, and by persons

who are either entirely ignorant of the country, or who studiously misrepresent or falsify. Such paragraphs excite only contempt, mingled however with regret, that a journal abounding in valuable and able papers, should reduce itself to a level with the wretched scribblers, whose prejudices and falsehoods it condescends to copy and circulate.

With regard to this article the case is different. . . . It goes further.[22]

This publication—its very existence powerful evidence of the importance of metropolitan discourse in the United States—ironically registers its fierce rejection of "prejudices and falsehoods" through the very medium that has hitherto been their faithful repository.

Some Americans recorded their objections directly in the margins of offending books. One surviving copy of Isaac Weld's *Travels Through the States of North America* (1799) is covered with angry comments refuting its observations. Housed at the Library Company of Philadelphia, this copy of the fourth London edition of Weld's *Travels* has been handled by many readers, some clearly before it was listed in the Library Company's 1835 catalogue as one of two copies available for circulation. Worn down by frequent use and missing pages, the book contains marginalia written in the 1810s or 1820s.[23] Much of it demonstrates the incendiary nature of Weld's text. Considering "the generality of Americans," Weld writes at one point that "the sight of a wheat field or a cabbage garden would convey pleasure far greater than that of the most romantic woodland views. They have an unconquerable aversion to trees." In the margin, one reader angrily wrote, "The author is a liar" (*W*, 43). Later, Weld slanders American produce: "The peaches in their best state are but indifferent, being small and dry." "Lie! another, added to the number!" wrote one reader, "The American peaches are infinitely superior to the English" (*W*, 91). Much of the marginalia swings back and forth between objections expressed in national terms and those of a more local scale (often, given the location of the Library Company, regarding Philadelphia itself). A few readers responded angrily to Weld's charge that milk and fish cannot keep fresh in the heat of Philadelphia.[24] Another invoked local knowledge to refute an insult to the national landscape. "[T]he girth of trees in the woods of America is but very small in proportion to their height," Weld writes, "and trifling in comparison to that of the forest trees in Great Britain. The thickest tree I ever saw in the country was a sycamore . . . no more than about four feet four inches in diameter."

An empirically minded reader disagreed, writing "There are Chestnut Trees growing within ten miles of Philadelphia whose circumference measures 21 feet" (*W*, 202). The refutations continue throughout the book, but none more nationally suggestive than one following Weld's claim about the "anniversary of 'American Independence,'" which some "more properly call it, 'American Repentance.'" In the margin, this is called "a pack of lies" (*W*, 197). Much of the commentary betrays a simultaneous desire to read prejudicial discourse and to reject it. Unlike the more abstract and impersonal public addressed by refutations in newspapers and periodicals, the marginalia in these books hail an intimate public comprising fellow subscribers to the Library Company.

Comments that respond to previously written comments indicate that they were heard loud and clear. Much of what we might call second-degree marginalia was written years after the book's publication and contextualizes Weld's opinions without hostility or aversion.[25] Some readers refuted earlier objections, as in the case of American peaches. "English peaches, apricots + melons," wrote a second reader, agreeing with Weld, "are finer flavoured" (*W*, 91) (see figure 9). Some agreed with earlier comments but provide calm rationales for Weld's prejudices, as in one response to a reader who had rejected Weld's accusation that Americans act with "self-interest" (*W*, 305). "Mr. Weld sees with a jaundiced eye," the second reader explained, "as he judges of others by himself" (*W*, 306). Other second-degree marginalia treat the narrative as a commodity rather than a purveyor of information and expose Weld's opinions as mercenary products of the marketplace. Describing his journey through Pennsylvania, Weld wrote that "the taverns in this part of the country are kept by farmers, and they are all very indifferent." An exasperated early reader declared, "Lying! lying! Lying!!!" but a second reader suggested the origins of such slander, using a common personification of England: "Weld writes to please John Bull" (*W*, 92). Another comment invoked Weld's blatant appeal to the market near a complaint about the inquisitiveness of Virginians: "Remember, gentle reader, Weld is a <u>Book Maker</u>" (*W*, 172). While the earlier comments defensively rejected Weld's misrepresentations because of the currency they have as metropolitan discourse, the later comments—written at an emotional and temporal remove from the book's initial reception—called attention to the conditions that made such discourse seem authoritative.

The Library Company was a subscription institution that served an elite group of members and patrons not representative of the U.S. population as a whole.[26] But the marginalia a few visitors felt at liberty to scribble deserve our attention for the rare view they provide of readers' actual responses to

cultivate them. In the cultivated parts of Pennfylvania the farms rarely exceed three hundred acres;
towards the north, however, where the fettlements
are but few, large tracts of land are in the hands of
individuals, who are fpeculators and land jobbers.
Adjoining to the houfes there is generally a peach or
apple orchard. With the fruit they make cyder and
brandy; the people have a method alfo of drying the
peaches and apples, after having fliced them, in the
fun, and thus cured they laft all the year round.
They are ufed for pies and puddings, but they have
a very acrid tafte, and fcarcely any of the original fla-
vour of the fruit. The peaches in their beft ftate are
but indifferent, being fmall and dry; I never eat any
that were good, excepting fuch as were raifed with
care in gardens. It is faid that the climate is fo
much altered that they will not grow now as they
formerly did. In April and May nightly frofts are
very common, which were totally unknown formerly,
and frequently the peaches are entirely blighted.
Gardens are very rare in the country parts of Pennfylvania, for the farmers think the labour which they
require does not afford fufficient profit; in the neigh-
bourhood of towns, however, they are common, and
the culinary vegetables raifed in them are equal to
any of their refpective kinds in the world, *potatoes* ex-
cepted, which generally have an earthy unpleafant
tafte.

Though the fouth-eaft part of the ftate of Pennfylvania is better cultivated than any other part of
America, yet the ftyle of farming is on the whole very
flovenly. I venture, indeed, to affert, that the farmers do not raife more on their two hundred acres
than a fkilful farmer in Norfolk, Suffolk, or Effex, or
any well cultivated part of England, would do on
fifty acres of good land there. The farmer alfo, who
rents fifty acres of arable land in England, lives far
more comfortably in every refpect than the farmer in
Pennfylvania, or in any other of the middle ftates,
who

Figure 9. Isaac Weld, *Travels Through the States of North America, and the Provinces of Upper and Lower Canada, During the Years 1795, 1796, and 1797,* 4th ed. (London, 1800), 91, with marginalia. Accession #3808.O.

books they read with great emotional attention. In addition to Weld, consider the Library Company's copy of Isaac Candler's *A Summary View of America* (1824).[27] The comments in Candler's *A Summary View* are more difficult to date than those in Weld's *Travels*, but their vehemence implies they may have been roughly contemporaneous. In response to a report that "[t]he Americans have a current saying, that they are the most enlightened people on earth, and Congress actually passed a resolution to that effect many years ago," one reader wrote, in the margin, "A Lie Ahh!!!!" and another added a superscript "X" to this comment and then, on bottom of page, with a corresponding X, wrote, "A Confounding Lie" (*C*, 102). Some visceral reactions are nationalistic, such as those provoked by Candler's claim that "the defeat of the English troops at New Orleans was as much unknown to me, to my shame be it spoken, as if it had never occurred. Since my return, I have found scholars and politicians as ignorant as myself." One reader indignantly responded, "This confession of ignorance of a battle in which some of the most prominent of English officers were slain, is most ridiculous affectation," and a second reader echoes this: "I don't believe it!" (*C*, 480). Candler, faced with explaining a British military defeat, had resorted to the advantage the English could still claim: control over the dissemination of knowledge. The reader's pride was hurt by Candler's denial that America's reputation traveled; ignorance about America's triumphs was as hurtful as criticism of its faults.

Candler's graphic and critical depictions of slavery provoked widely divergent responses from readers; some defended the institution. Candler's depiction of the sexual practices of the slave system caused particular offense:

> If a master himself desires the company of a negress, be she married or single, she has no alternative but compliance: for resistance would be resented and force used, and no where could she obtain redress. Such is the unhappy condition of these miserable beings! It generally happens, that they become victims at a very early age, to the lust of either the master, his sons, or the overseer. So little regard is paid to decency and the common feelings of mankind, that incest is a crime of by no means rare occurrence. (*C*, 266–267)

"These sentiments are the conceptions of a wicked imagination!" one reader exclaimed and then assigned to that "imagination" a specifically national valence: "In almost every page of this Book the truth is disdainfully trodden upon and the print of the cloven foot of the Britain is deeply impressed therein"

(*C*, 267). A second reader, struck by the intensity of this response, sarcastically turned the tables: "Good American you feel the spirit of a sovereign & like other sovereigns you wish to scruff flattery" (*C*, 267). Candler's discussion of the interstate slave trade produced further controversy in the margins. "The African slave trade was condemned in Congress as iniquitous," Candler reminds his readers. "Its outrages on humanity were forcibly depicted . . . is the American slave trade fit for men?" In the margin, one reader wrote "ba!" And another reader, apparently fed up with such defensiveness, responded, "Whoever has written these interjections is a fool and devoid of the first principles of humanity & common sense" (*C*, 275). In a rare moment of self-identification, one reader answered Candler's rhetorical question, "[W]hat is to be said for that law of Virginia which imposes a tax on a black man who is nominally free, merely because he is black?" (*C*, 289–290). "I aver that there is no such law in Virginia," the appended comment insists, with the signature, "A Virginian" (*C*, 290). And finally, in the chapter of Candler's book on "Government," one reader erupted with racist indignation at the observation that "[t]he meanest citizens in America are the free blacks, for the slaves, as a matter of course, are not entitled to the appellation of citizens." In the margin, the reader replied, "d—n the blacks" (*C*, 396). These comments provide an extraordinary record of readers' visceral reactions to negative depictions of slavery and indicate the dissention they created among a self-conscious community of readers. Written from a variety of perspectives, including those of a Virginian reading a London-printed book owned by a Philadelphia library, they display a powerful collision between virulent racism and defensive nationalism even as some comments evince an aversion to that distasteful combination of reactions. One reader endorsed Candler's antislavery discussion through writing, simply, "This chapter should be stampt in letters of gold" (*C*, 272). National pride notwithstanding, the perspective of a traveling Englishman was welcomed by this reader because it produced a just view on an unjust institution.

* * *

On the whole, metropolitan travel writing inspired national thinking in authors, critics, and readers around the Anglophone Atlantic, especially in Ireland and the United States. One final comment written in Candler's book epitomizes more than any other the irony at the heart of the provincial's eager consumption of metropolitan books filled with prejudice. On the narrative's last page, a reader declares, "This book is not worth reading. A real old John

Bull" (*C*, 503). Written just above "THE END" and clearly after he or she finished reading every word, this dismissal could hardly have been effective at deterring future readers. The blithe confidence of traveling John Bulls offended provincials who knew their defenses would be lost in a marketplace flooded with books from London, which, like a "vortex," enveloped the public in a whirlwind of prejudice, lies, and bookmaking.

Some commentators sympathized with the sufferings of their fellow provincials. The Edgeworths' critique of Carr's *Stranger in Ireland* was published anonymously in the *Edinburgh Review* in the nationally inflected voice of that periodical, thus issuing an Irish defense of Ireland in the rhetorical guise of "our Scottish notions."[28] The *Belfast Monthly Magazine* issued a front-page attack on the same *Quarterly Review* article that so enraged the editors of the *North American Review*, declaring that it gave voice to "all the partial and splenetic hints of all real and fictitious travellers to America."[29] Washington Irving's *Salmagundi Papers* drew a humorous connection between English travelers to Ireland and to the United States in a satire modeled directly on Carr, "Stranger in New-Jersey; or, Cockney travelling."[30] Mathew Carey, who as an Irish émigré in Philadelphia was perhaps ideally situated to notice such trans-provincial analogies, invoked American travel narratives in *Vindiciae Hibernicae: or, Ireland Vindicated*, which he published himself in Philadelphia in 1819. In his strident attempt to expose the falsity of English accounts of Ireland, Carey writes,

> [T]he Irish were generally represented as incurably barbarous,
> savage, intolerant of law and order, and only to be ruled with a
> rod of iron. . . . The characters of nations are rarely drawn cor-
> rectly by their neighbours, or by interested, absurd, or prejudiced
> travellers. . . . Who, for instance, can recognise a single feature
> of the American character from the miserable productions of
> Ash, Fearon, Parkinson, Howlett, or the other numerous English
> travellers who have visited this country, apparently with a view of
> exposing our citizens, their manners and customs, to ridicule and
> contempt?[31]

The American case helps Carey build a general argument against the persistence of English prejudices when they "draw" the "character" of their "neighbors." As with so many rebuttals, however, this provincial found it difficult to make his voice heard. As he writes in his autobiography, "I confidently expected that the work would be reprinted in England and Ireland, or at all events in the latter—but I have been greatly disappointed."[32]

The American Origins of Irish Nationalism

Historians have made much of the importance of Irish immigrants like Carey, who as a group left an indelible mark on American culture. In the forty years after the Revolution, more than half of all immigrants to the United States were Irish, most of them Protestant (unlike Carey, who was Catholic).[33] In those years, the Irish played an important role in the political rivalries of the early national period; embraced by Jeffersonian-Republicans and virulently attacked by Federalists, they were the explicit targets of John Adams's Alien and Sedition Acts and helped bring Jefferson to power in 1800.[34] Many Irish immigrants fought for their adopted country during the War of 1812, a conflict that allowed for a replaying of the animosities of 1790s Ireland in North America.[35] The story of Irish America is well-trodden ground, but few scholars have addressed the persistent importance of the United States and the idea of "America" back in Ireland. America was a volatile subject for an Irish public radically divided by religion and politics, but for nationalists, it remained an important touchstone long after excitement over the American Revolution modulated into enthusiasm about the French Revolution. Indeed, France— the great Catholic nation, the fount of Jacobinism, and Britain's major enemy on the European stage—has been the major focus of historians interested in tracing the transnational currents within Irish nationalism.[36] But the example of America was equally important because it could claim priority as a precedent for Ireland in ways that France never could. The United States, after all, had been part of the British Empire, and, as the War of 1812 proved, it was willing to defend itself from continuing imperial insults. America fueled Irish nationalism because of the close analogy made possible by empire and through a specific rejection of England: its aristocracy, its taxes, its parliament, its imperial arrogance. This continued through the early decades of the nineteenth century, persisting beyond what Kevin Whelan has called the "retreat of radicalism" after the Act of Union marked the close of the 1790s.[37] While France provided Irish nationalists with the example of a cosmopolitan allegiance to the principles of republicanism, America supplied a specific language of constitutional rights and liberties that solidified a close analogy between the two sometimes British colonies.

The American valence of post-Union Irish nationalism is most evident in the pro-emigration pages of *The Irish Magazine, and Monthly Asylum for Neglected Biography*, edited from 1807 to 1815 by Walter "Watty" Cox, a radical Dublin journalist persecuted for waging ideological war against the ruling parties in England.[38] A consideration of this magazine in the context of Irish periodical culture suggests that Irish nationalism cannot be understood without accounting for a particularly American kind of rivalry with England. It is a rivalry that pro-British writers in Ireland found revealingly distasteful, as a brief consideration of Sarah Isdell's anti-emigration novel *The Vale of Louisiana* (1805) suggests. Isdell's adventure tale of the American Revolution suggests that there were many in Ireland who did not consider America a land of promise, including those who tapped it for romance.

For Irish nationalists, the meaning of America was forged in its successful struggle for independence. That struggle was remembered partly through the legacy of Irish leaders who supported the rights of the colonists, including Edmund Burke and Henry Grattan. By the early nineteenth century, Burke's defense of America in Parliament in the 1770s had become legendary. "His memorable speeches on the taxation of America," wrote *Walker's Hibernian Magazine* in 1810, "made his name resound through the universe, as the friend of mankind, wielding the thunder of heaven, and directing against the oppressors of his species."[39] Grattan invoked the lessons of the American Revolution in a bitter 1797 speech to the Irish Parliament denouncing an English general's suppressions of liberties in Ulster, including the right to own guns. "Will you sit by with folded arms, and suffer the deputy of an English minister to disarm the Irish?" Grattan dramatically asked.[40] "Remember America—remember America!" he exhorted. "Are these proceedings and laws more mild or more constitutional with regard to Ireland, than the proceedings committed, or acts passed against America?" The "ministers of England," he reminded his audience, "rebelled against the rights of America and were conquered."[41] Grattan's cautionary analogy depended on the resonance of invoking a colony's objections to Parliamentary rule. In the 1790s, more radical voices than Burke and Grattan openly wished for the success of an American experiment in Ireland, celebrating the first anniversary of the fall of the Bastille by carrying busts of Benjamin Franklin and images of the New World throwing a "blaze of light" upon the old.[42] Many periodicals published panegyrics of George Washington after he resigned from the presidency in 1796, including an original poem celebrating he "who freed his country from a galling yoke, / And the foul chains which bound her freedom broke."[43] Invocations of American freedom usually carried an implicit commentary on the "galling" situation in Ireland, just as the idea of Irish independence was commonly entangled with an American analogy. Robert Emmet invoked America in his last speech before being executed for treason. In a moving passage about his attempts at enlisting France as an ally for his failed 1803 nationalist rebellion, Emmet declared, "I wished to procure for my country the guarantee which Washington procured for America."[44]

Early nineteenth-century Irish periodicals kept their readers informed about the politics, economy, and culture of the United States—whether they had specifically nationalist agendas or not.[45] The case of America hit close to home because many in Ireland saw it as a possible future home. Their special attention to the United States, though, was often framed as a matter of the transatlantic circulation of print. In 1816, the pro-British *Ulster Register* reprinted selections from William Cobbett's *Register of New York* and bragged, "We believe we are the *only press* in Ireland that has been able to serve up this feast to the political epicure."[46] Many others highlighted the materiality of reprinted articles that originated from American publications. "Having lately had an opportunity of seeing a parcel of American newspapers, I was struck with some statements . . . [that] may be of use in your pages," wrote a correspondent to the radical *Belfast Monthly Magazine*, which later defended America from the *Quarterly*.[47] The *Rushlight*, also from Belfast, reprinted many excerpts from Washington Irving, including *The Sketch Book*, *The History of New York*, and *Tales of a Traveller*.[48] *Walker's Hibernian Magazine* "embellished" one of its issues with a likeness of the "newly-elected" Thomas Jefferson taken "from a highly approved Portrait, lately published by M. Carey, of Philadelphia."[49] When the *Dublin Magazine* reviewed "a pamphlet lately published in North America," they noted its origin by copying, verbatim, information from its title page: "Philadelphia, by Robert Smith, jun. No. 50, North Front-street, 1812."[50] In handling the affairs of the United States, these periodicals emphasized, too, that they were handling its material texts.

Watty Cox's *Irish Magazine* was more nationalistic and more preoccupied with America than most publications, featuring reprinted articles in almost every issue and publishing letters from American correspondents.[51] The magazine's American focus derived partly from Cox's own fascinating transatlantic life. Born in Ireland in 1770, Cox edited a radical Dublin newspaper in the 1790s and fled to America in 1804 to evade British authorities. After returning to Dublin in 1807, he founded the *Irish Magazine*, the seditious tone of which landed him many times in jail.[52] As editor, Cox promoted his anti-English,

pro-Catholic, and vehemently nationalistic views. In support of "the cause
of the poor Irish,"[53] the magazine was devoted to the memory of the 1798
Rebellion, to lamenting the Act of Union, to France (through celebrating Napoleon), and to America—which it presented as a beacon of liberty and a
refuge for oppressed Irish subjects. Cox justified the magazine's commitment
to America by idealizing its freedoms and arguing that it guaranteed Ireland's
future:

> We scarcely deem it necessary to apologize to our Irish Readers, for
> devoting so many of our columns to American subjects, as we know
> the Irish mind will be highly gratified at the rapid progress, which
> free America exhibits in arts, manufacturers and commerce. If
> America is not the land of our unfortunate ancestors it may truly be
> said to be the land of our children, as it is on its free and extensive
> bosom, they are to repose, whenever civil or religious persecution,
> renders their soil intolerable, or when commercial monopoly, would
> impose the restraints which pride and avarice, prepare to suffocate
> Irish industry.[54]

Cox addresses the fact of immigration, since some of his readers' children may
have already left home for a more nurturing "bosom" across the Atlantic. His
conception of the future of the Irish people is shot through with a vision of
America he promotes in order to bewail the situation at home. The complex
temporality of Cox's politics is defined by a contrast between the present states
of Ireland and the United States and by the extension of that contrast to an
anxious future filled with disappointment and hope. This contrast is present as
well in Cox's discussion of Joel Barlow's patriotic epic *The Columbiad* (1808),
lengthy passages of which he reprinted soon after its publication in New York.
Cox introduced the poem with wistful praise invoking Ireland's oppressed
state. "This elegant production breathes the inspiration of real genius," he
writes, "and the enthusiasm of the purest ideas of rational freedom, cherished
in the only soil that unfortunate man can say is his own, 'remote from slaves
and kings.'"[55] Contrasts between Ireland and the United States often involved
observations of a constitutional nature, as Cox emphasized in an essay lam-
basting British economic policy. "It was [*sic*] a British legislature to-day that
commands our trade and dictates our existence," he writes, and implies that
revolution might be Ireland's only recourse. "It was the tyranny of a British
parliament which interdicted the growing industry of young America, and

imposed taxation without representation, that made the name of England odious, and her government intolerable to Americans."[56]

This rhetoric of juxtaposition was widespread. Throughout Irish periodical culture, "oppressed Ireland" and "free America" churned around each other as two mutually reinforcing ideas. "[In] the present state and future prospects of America," writes the *Dublin Examiner* in 1816, "we can contemplate a scene that weakens in some measure, the effect of the disgusting picture which the old world has lately presented to us."[57] In impassioned language introducing a speech by James Madison, this magazine expressed a deep wish that transatlantic commerce and communication might encourage the spread of freedom:

> [I]s it not of the most incalculable advantage to the world, that the
> *citizens* of the United states, should hold the closest communion
> possible, with the *subjects* of other nations? What more effectual
> means could be taken, for the dissemination of proper principles of
> liberty, than, that those who possess them, and are benefited by the
> blessing, should be in constant communication with their less fortu-
> nate brethren of other countries?[58]

The link between citizenship and subjection, emphasized typographically through the use of italics, is especially powerful because of the insistence that the inequalities dividing the human family (the "brethren of other countries") are arbitrary and preventable. Who will save the Irish nation? The *Dublin Examiner* included a pleading postscript after Madison's speech:

> Oh! Washington! Oh! Franklin! May the memory of your achieve-
> ments and your wisdom, be for ever cherished by the adorers of
> freedom and worth! May your patriotism, and your conduct, be
> a bright example for the imitation of kindred spirits; and may the
> time be short, until those nations of the globe which are sunk in
> slavery, can boast of such an adamantine basis of liberty, of prosper-
> ity, of peace, of happiness, and of everlasting Glory, as you and your
> associates have established amidst the wilds of America![59]

The magazine's naïve and wholesale adoption of the American ideology—that nation's most cherished myths about itself—does not prevent there from being something wrenching about this improbable wish that the memory of American patriots might serve the cause of Irish liberty. The passage's shrill calls for "liberty" and "happiness" are overwhelmed by the alliterative statement at its center: that Ireland remains "sunk in slavery." Invocations of America's past and its present come with some pathos in a period, after the Union, when the prospect of Irish independence was dimmer than ever.

Another journal, the *Dublin Monthly Magazine*, reprinted a dramatic passage from Jonah Barrington's 1809 history of the Union that wistfully describes the lost promise of the age of Revolution. Barrington credits America's valiant struggle for inspiring the push for Irish Parliamentary autonomy, which had briefly been achieved from 1782 until the Union. Years later, Barrington chose a new title for this book: *The Rise and Fall of the Irish Nation* (1833).[60] The reprinted passage refers to the late 1770s, a time Barrington associates with unbounded possibility:

> Ireland began to feel herself affected by the struggles of America; the spirit of independence had crossed the Atlantic, and the Irish people, awakened from a trance, beheld with anxiety the contest, in which they now began to feel an interest. . . . Ireland became every day a more anxious spectator of the arduous conflict—every incident in America began to communicate a sympathetic impulse to the Irish people. The comment was critical—the nation became enlightened—a patriotic ardor took possession of her whole frame, and, before she had well considered the object of her solicitude, the spark of constitutional liberty had found its way into her bosom. . . . The disposition of Ireland to avail herself of the circumstances of those times, so favourable to the attainment of her rights, without departing from the principles of her loyalty, now openly avowed itself. Her determination to reclaim her constitution from the British government became unequivocal, and she began to assume the attitude and language of a nation "entitled to independence."[61]

The "spirit" of America, undaunted by the expanse of the ocean, wakes Ireland from a "trance" through the passage of electric impulses and "sparks," thus taking "possession" of her, animating her, and molding her "whole frame" into the "attitude" of a free nation. Ireland is Dr. Frankenstein's monster, and the American Revolution is the genius who created her. Barrington endorses this in a kinetic image that casts the movement of ideology in the discourse of sympathy and communication. Ireland's embrace of constitutional rights is a remarkably performative posture of entitlement defined through expression rather than action. This proleptically emphasizes the "fall" of the Irish nation after the Union, an understandable move given that Barrington was writing at a time when the memory of the radical 1790s had become dear.

Meanwhile, Irish nationalists longingly watched the American experiment forge ahead. In the *Irish Magazine*, reports about the contemporary emigrant experience bolstered Cox's idealization of America and fueled the transatlantic rhetoric of liberty. A particularly lyrical instance of this is a poem reprinted from "an American Paper" called "The Irish Orphan."[62] A verse dialogue between an "Irish Girl" and "a citizen of New York," the poem asserts America's commitment to saving the Irish from the evils of British subjection. The orphan arrives from her "native isle" after a life and journey filed with peril and death. While in sight of "freedom's shore," "under freedom's banner sailing," a British ship overtakes theirs and forces the men into military service. These "smiling pirates" thus leave the girl "unprotected" as she arrives in America: "A parent, and a brother, / With me from oppression run; / Death deprived me of my mother— / Cruel Britons *press'd* her son!" The "citizen," moved to condemn the "curst aggression" of Britain, comforts her by offering a place in the American family: "Here I swear to be thy brother / See a sister in my wife / Find a parent in my mother— / I'll protect thee with my life." The poem promises that emigration will reconstitute the familial bonds British imperial aggression has torn apart.

Other representations of life in America were less maudlin and melodramatic. In July 1808, Cox reprinted a boisterous notice of a St. Patrick's Day celebration held by the "Juvenile Sons of Erin" in New York.[63] The raucous event reportedly included eating, drinking, singing, bagpipe playing, and more than two dozen toasts and salutes—a party that lasted "until they hailed the morning." The notice reveals the values of a community Cox may have been a part of while he lived briefly in the city. Right away, the toasts highlight the contrast between the desolate state of Ireland and the freedoms of America. "*Ireland*," they cried, "may she like the 'shivering tenants of the frigid zone,' enjoy a *day* proportioned to the dreary darkness of her long and gloomy night." Immediately following this, they saluted "*America*—The resting place of liberty, the asylum of persecuted humanity—May she ever keep clear of such miserable systems as has [*sic*] prevailed in the old world under the name of government." Throughout the night, Irish and American patriots were toasted in equal proportion, the former for their "shining virtues and devotion to liberty" and the latter—particularly Washington and Jefferson—for their "bright example[s]" as "the hero and the statesman." One toast quoted Jefferson directly, and another voiced Robert Emmet's famous conclusion to his execution speech: "When my country takes her place among the nations of the earth, then, let my epitaph be written." With rousing musicality, the Sons of Erin alternated between Irish songs and American songs, from "St. Patrick's Day," "The Last Irish Harper," and "Paddy O'Rafferty" to "Hail Columbia," "Yankee Doodle," and "Jefferson['s] March." A dual allegiance was thoroughly on display—not Irish-American so much as Irish *and* American. The celebrants expressed Irish national pride by honoring Irish authors for their achievements, including Maria and Richard Lovell Edgeworth; they sang Sydney Owenson's ballads and praised "her laudable example in raising her country to a respectable rank in the scale of nations." Scorning "national prejudice," they also toasted an English writer for a book about Ireland that might "awake the compassion of some of his countrymen to the miseries of a people who deserve a better fate." Meanwhile, they also paid homage to the Jeffersonian party that welcomed them into the American political system as allies, thanking "Republican Editors" for "protect[ing] our national character" against "federal opponents." As new American citizens, too, they toasted "*The American Eagle*—Fostered under thy wings we live, we die in thy defense."

The publication of this notice in Dublin indicates not only that readers wanted information about life in America but also that the experiences of the Irish in America—and the ideologies editors like Cox associated with those experiences—affected the changing nature of Irish nationalism. Being an Irish nationalist increasingly involved a feeling of loss at not being American. This is dramatically (if obscurely) suggested in Cox's decision to cut the most incendiary toast recorded in the American paper. Cox evidently thought one comment went too far: "*Irish Slavery*—May the children of coercion, the chords of enslavement which are already stretched to their utmost extent, be by the energetic efforts of our countrymen rent asunder like cobwebs, and may they enjoy their portion of liberty and happiness after such a long—long absence."[64] The necessity of censoring this passage confirms the urgency of the general wish it contains. The discourse of "Irish slavery" referred specifically to Catholic Emancipation, a cause the magazine vehemently supported, but this toast advocated it in a language perhaps too closely tied to treason.[65]

There was of course a strong anti-nationalist and anti-republican party in Ireland, and for them, editors like Cox were scoundrels and affection for America ridiculous. Issac Weld, author of the travel narrative that angered American readers at the Library Company, was in fact Irish, and his London-printed book was written partly to discourage the "inhabitants" of his "native country" from seeking "refuge" in the United States (*W*, iii). Very little is known about the Irish author Sarah Isdell, but evidence internal to *The Vale of Louisiana: An American Tale* suggests that she, too, would have rejected the pro-emigration stance of the *Irish Magazine*. The story of an English family who lives unhappily in America during the Revolution and eventually returns home, this novel, addressed explicitly to "female" readers, rejects the New World as a refuge.[66] The novel's ambivalence about the politics of the Revolution suggests, too, that interest in the United States easily coexisted with skepticism about the tenets of the American ideology.

A historical romance almost entirely lost to history,[67] *The Vale of Louisiana* narrates the perilous adventures of the Wilmot family and their relatives, primarily George Wilmot and his wife, Anne; their two children, Oliver and Ellen; and two young family friends whom Oliver and Ellen eventually marry, Charlotte and Henry Plagel. George and Anne Wilmot elope in England without parental consent; immigrate to Charleston, South Carolina, sometime during the 1750s; and raise their children in relative peace until the Revolution throws their life into chaos. While George Wilmot and his family remain "neutral" during the war (*VI*, 83), Henry Plagel enlists in the Continental Army, marches into Boston with George Washington, crosses the Delaware, witnesses the death of Major André, and, because of the treachery of a French officer, is taken captive by Indians. Back in South Carolina, the Wilmots flee Charleston during battle, Anne Wilmot dies, and George Wilmot unwittingly kills Anne's brother, one of a band of British soldiers who come to harass them. After the war, George Washington himself offers the family an estate near New Orleans, the "Vale of Louisiana," which only sets the stage for more trouble, as a seductive French gentleman, St. Pierre, gains the family's confidence, tortures George Wilmot's conscience, abducts Ellen, and takes her to Cuba as his prisoner. The novel employs all the plot hijinks of an adventure romance to allow Henry Plagel, Ellen's lover, to rescue her from St. Pierre. Henry, having promised a dying soldier he will find his daughter in the West Indies, escapes from Indian captivity and travels to St. Domingo (i.e., Haiti), where the daughter is living with her mother, who is now the mistress of a rich planter. The mother dies, Henry adopts the girl, and—in the midst of a slave insurrection—they leave St. Domingo for Louisiana by way of Havana, where Henry heroically saves Ellen. Upon reuniting, the Wilmot/Plagel clan returns to "Old England," now reconciled to their families and inheritances, happily leaving the dangers of America behind (*V II*, 241).

This extraordinary novel, with its transatlantic, trans-Caribbean plot, deserves much more extended treatment than is possible here, for both its own sake and for its fascinating engagement with transatlantic literary culture—including wholesale borrowings from Charles Brockden Brown's *Wieland* (1798).[68] In the context of the present discussion, however, the novel's significance lies in the fraught way it memorializes the Revolution. George Washington, the hero of Irish nationalists, appears in this novel only for his "private virtues," the narrator insists, as benefactor of the Wilmots (*V*I, 2). In cordoning off his public role in the Revolution, Isdell brackets the question of the conflict's legitimacy—even as she allows herself to portray Washington positively: after the war, for example, Washington restores "order and regularity" to Charleston (*V*I, 135), and Henry, the novel's romantic hero, earns the reader's respect for fighting under his command. Both sides of the Revolutionary struggle, which Isdell calls a "civil war" (*V*I, 90), are treated sympathetically; while the loyalist George Wilmot vows to obey the "laws of my king" (*V*I, 81), his friend, Henry's father, supports "liberty" and "independence" (*V*I, 83). The war is still a catastrophe, but merely because it is a war, not because of any ideology behind it. The English soldiers who harass the Wilmots are just as bad as other characters who threaten the family, including the Indians, Portuguese assassins, Frenchified villains, and the rich and lascivious planter in St. Domingo. Scenes of domestic turmoil back in England suggest, too, that Isdell's tale of danger and woe knows no national boundaries.[69] The worst character in the novel is the deceitful French gentleman St. Pierre, who, under a different name (it turns out), is the French officer who betrays Henry to the Indians. Isdell does not endorse the American political experiment, but neither does she blame it alone for the unstable lives of her characters. *The Vale of Louisiana*, then, dismisses immigration and rejects independence from Britain as a viable option for Ireland, but it remains agnostic on the question of the American Revolution.

The early nineteenth century was not only a time for war's remembrance, of course; it was also a time of actual war. When the pan-European Napoleonic conflict drew the United States into war with Great Britain in 1812, nationalists in Ireland embraced the cause of their American brethren. Publications like Cox's *Irish Magazine* stoked tensions between Britain and the United States, between "John Bull" and "Brother Jonathan." In the years leading up to the war, Jeffersonian-Republicans pushed for a conflict most of the Irish living in the United States supported. A final toast from the St. Patrick's Day celebration in New York that Cox printed in the *Irish Magazine* in 1808 illustrates the binding power of a sharing a common adversary: "*War*—If peace cannot be maintained with national honor, then let us have war—Paddy is *always* ready and *willing* to lend Jonathan a hand to give the enemies of his country a sound drubbing."[70]

During the war itself, Cox trumpeted what he saw as the American cause, and when it ended, he—like many partisans of the conflict—considered the stalemate a resounding victory. In an 1815 letter to "my dear countrymen," Cox gloated about American martial achievements for which Irishmen and people of Irish descent were responsible. Britain, Cox writes,

> mistook the character of America; she imagined what was only parsimony, to be cowardice; she thought that a people, who had no objection to a just war, but the expense, were stupified by the appearance of her veterans; but the delusion was soon manifest. . . . The British navy, on Lake Champlain, saw itself stripped of a name, earned in twenty-two years of victory, by a new hero, the gallant McDonough [sic].[71]

Accompanying this letter was an engraving of Thomas Macdonough, an officer whose family emigrated from Ireland in the 1730s and whose father fought with renown in the Revolution.[72] Cox's celebration of the U.S. military in the pages of the *Irish Magazine* transformed the drama of a distant American battlefield into material for Irish national pride.

Hail to the Chief: The Americanization of Walter Scott During the War of 1812

Material for American national pride was also found in unlikely sources; during the War of 1812, the United States turned to the work of a distant Scottish poet. As in Ireland, this trans-provincial affinity was inspired by rivalry with England. A decade before *Waverley* (1814), Americans fell in love with Walter Scott's poetry, the genre that first made him famous, and their affection seemed only to increase during war. It was during the War of 1812 that Scott's song "Hail to the Chief" became indelibly embedded within American nationalism. Originally the war anthem of Highland chief Roderick Dhu in Scott's *The Lady of the Lake* (1810), the song's now-familiar melody was composed by John Sanderson for a London theatrical adaptation of Scott's poem, and its sheet music was printed throughout the United States. The song's melody was first played in honor of an American president during a celebration of the peace in Boston in 1815, although an apocryphal story has it that Dolley Madison ordered White House musicians to play "Hail to the Chief" for the president throughout the war itself.[73] It was during John Tyler's administration in the 1840s that the song "became a regular tribute to the U.S. president," a practice that, of course, persists today.[74] American affection for British culture also bequeathed to posterity "The Star-Spangled Banner," the famous poem Francis Scott Key wrote in 1814 to the tune of a British song, "To Anacreon in Heaven." The transatlantic adoption of Scott's "Hail to the Chief" is a virtually unknown episode in U.S. history and was part of a fascinating series of Americanizations Scott's poetry inspired.

Scott's poems, like his novels, tell stories about the past—in particular, about Scottish defiance of the English during times of civil war. Americans seized upon the Scottish-English rivalry that defines this historical world, blatantly ignoring Scott's Tory politics and refashioning his romantic Scottish nationalism as a powerful call to and expression of national feeling. This contrasts to the lesson William Cullen Bryant and James Fenimore Cooper learned from Scott's generous bridging of the English-Scottish divide in his Waverley novels, as I discussed in Chapter 5. It also contrasts to Washington Irving's reaction to the War of 1812 in the *Analectic Magazine*, which, as I argued in Chapter 4, precipitated a retreat from politics into a purified literary realm. During the War of 1812, many Americans drew an analogy between their present struggle with Britain and Scotland's historical struggles with England. This analogy, forged within the local arenas of newspapers, broadsides, theatrical performances, and celebrations, has given Scott one of his most enduring legacies in the United States.

The War of 1812 was a bitter conflict that divided public opinion in the United States. Hostilities originated from the impressment of American sailors, which the British navy pursued to increase their ranks while fighting Napoleon. The Jeffersonian-Republicans justified war to protect American sailors, while the Federalists opposed war because it would threaten commerce. Jefferson and his allies were motivated also by the acquisition of land. They wanted to wipe out the British presence in the Great Lakes region and the Ohio River Valley so the United States could expand west toward the Mississippi and north into Canada. Jefferson was optimistic: "The acquisition of Canada this year, as far as the neighborhood of Quebec, will be a mere matter of marching, and will give us experience for the attack of Halifax the next, and the final expulsion of England from the American continent."[75] The Jeffersonian agenda also extended to Native American lands. Tecumseh, the Shawnee chief, had at this time organized a confederacy of Indian nations to defend lands that included present-day Ohio, Indiana, and Illinois. In the decades leading to war, British, American, and Indian populations lived and traded together in this region in a delicate balance of power that the war interrupted.[76] The war itself lasted from June 1812 to January 1815 and was a disaster by almost any account. The United States failed to annex Canada, although fighting spread along the St. Lawrence River and Great Lakes, all the way from Montreal to Detroit. In one botched attempt at invasion, American soldiers burned the town of York, Ontario—the future site of the city of Toronto. In retaliation, British soldiers invaded and burned Washington. In New England, Federalists who hated the war held a convention at Hartford and threatened to secede from the union. In January 1815, General Andrew Jackson led American soldiers to victory at New Orleans, but the battle did not make any difference. Two weeks earlier, on Christmas Day, 1814, the peace treaty had already been signed at Ghent in Belgium. As far as Britain and the United States were concerned, the war was a draw. For Native Americans, however, it had a clear and devastating effect. Tecumseh was killed in battle in 1813 and with him died all hope for a powerful Indian Confederacy. At the treaty negotiations, the British abandoned their Indian allies and allowed the United States to expand unchecked into western territory.

In the years leading up to war, Scott's three major narrative poems established his prominence in the Anglophone Atlantic: *The Lay of the Last Minstrel* (1805), *Marmion* (1808), and *The Lady of the Lake*. Before "Hail to the Chief" was performed at the peace celebration in 1815, these poems appeared in the United States in at least thirty-three reprinted editions; forty-two theatrical performances; sixty-four derivative editions, including playscripts, parodies, and sheet music; and hundreds of times as excerpted, cited, referenced, or advertised texts in periodicals and newspapers.[77] The most widely circulated lines from Scott's first poem, *The Lay of the Last Minstrel*, establish the specifically Scottish valence of his nationalism. The poem dramatizes a sixteenth-century conflict on the English-Scottish border, a tale Scott presents in the voice of an aging minstrel who relates it hundreds of years later. Americans were drawn to lines from the minstrel's frame narrative that exhibit Scott's own self-consciousness about his role as a preserver of national tradition:

Breathes there the man, with soul so dead,
Who never to himself hath said,
    This is my own, my native land! [. . .]
If such there breathe, go mark him well;
For him no minstrel raptures swell; [. . .]
The wretch, concerted all in self,

Living, shall forfeit fair renown,
And doubly, dying, shall go down
To the vile dust, from whence he sprung,
Unwept, unhonored, and unsung.[78]

The bitterness of this passage carries overtones of the rivalry the poem as a whole focalizes through the figure of the minstrel, a vessel of the Scottish folklore tradition threatened with the passing of time and imperial English rule. The minstrel presents a national pride imbued with defensiveness and rage. The repetitiveness of his proprietary claim—"my own, my native land"— barely grasps at the moral value it seeks to express. There is a vulnerability to the patriot's stance matched only by the vulnerability of the traitor who, in denying his native land, will be lost to history altogether. In the passage, as Carrie Hyde has suggested, love of country is entirely defined through the negative example of the soulless "wretch" who will never become the subject of national memory.[79] During a time of war, Americans may have been drawn to the passage because of the deep anxiety and rivalry it lodges within the heart of national feeling. In the United States, this passage, especially its first three lines, was printed in newspapers under the headings "Love of Country," "The Patriot," and "Home"; cited in periodicals and pamphlets discussing Scott and the virtues of a national literature; included in poetry anthologies; and chosen as the epigraph to printed letters and essays encouraging patriotism, especially once the war began. Toward the end of the war, phrases from the passage— often "my own, my native land"—were wielded by statesmen, including John Randolph, to rail against the idea of New England secession.[80] In the ensuing decades, Cooper used them as the epigraph to *The Spy* (1821), and the lines or a portion of them were also quoted by authors like Lydia Maria Child and Sarah Hale, as well as politicians and members of Congress.

In late 1813, an American adaptation of *Marmion* was staged in Philadelphia.[81] This adaptation was by James Nelson Barker, an officer in the American army and eventually the mayor of Philadelphia. Barker's *Marmion* shows particularly well how rivalry with England could be appropriated by Americans, this despite the fact that in the original *Marmion*, Scott highlighted the *defeat* of the Scottish at the Battle of Flodden Field as the major dramatic event. While all the admirable characters in this poem are indeed Scottish, Marmion himself, though unattractive, is English, and readers in Scotland criticized Scott for focusing on an English victory.[82] In Barker's 1816 preface to his adaptation, he too chides Scott, writing that "the case of Scotland, 'His own, his native land,' had [in *Marmion*] found less support in the fine poetry of her gifted son."[83] In adapting the poem for the American stage, Barker corrected these faults by writing a new and defiant speech for the Scottish ruler, King James IV. The speech was calculated to resonate with a local audience:

> Let England know, the charter of our freedom
> In glorious fields our noble fathers won . . .
> How shall a free and gallant nation act?
> Still lay its sovereignty at England's feet—
> Still basely ask a boon from England's bounty—
> Still vainly hope redress from England's justice?
> No! by our martyred fathers' memories,
> The land may sink—but, like a glorious wreck,
> 'Twill keep its colors flying to the last.[84]

In his preface, Barker bragged that theatergoers reacted to this speech with standing ovations.[85] One well-remembered incident occurred in Philadelphia in December 1813, as Barker's father attended the performance. After these lines were delivered, "Old Mr. Barker" stood up and exclaimed, "No, sir! No! We'll nail them to the mast, and sink with the stars and stripes before we yield," a comment that received "shouts and applause" for "ten minutes."[86] This speech of King James and reactions to it demonstrate the portability of the spirit, if not the letter, of Scott's work, especially for those enthusiastic about the war itself.

In *The Lady of the Lake*, Scott presents romantic Scottish nationalism through the defiant but ultimately doomed passions of Roderick Dhu, a Highland chief and ally to the exiled Scottish peer Douglas, the poem's hero (and, famously, the namesake of Frederick Douglass). In this story, the English-Scottish rivalry is mapped onto divisions within Scotland itself, as Roderick's Highland clan battles with the Lowland King James V outside Edinburgh. King James is described in both the poem and its theatrical adaptations as of "Saxon" (i.e., English) extraction.[87] The poem figures the patriotism of Roderick and his clan as organic, fueled by war, and defiantly anti-English. The central drama occurs when Roderick activates feudal clan loyalties to fight the Saxon king. Such loyalty is exemplified by the patriotic anthem Roderick's men sing as they transport him across the lake to meet Douglas and his daughter, Ellen, the titular Lady of the Lake:

Hail to the Chief who in triumph advances!
    Honour'd and bless'd be the evergreen Pine!
Long may the tree in his banner that glances,
    Flourish, the shelter and grace of our line!
        Heav'n send it happy dew,
        Earth lend it sap anew,
    Gaily to bourgeon and broadly to grow;
        While ev're Highland glen,
        Sends our shout back again,
"Roderigh Vich Alpine Dhu, ho, iero!"[88]

The emblem of Roderick is the Pine tree—the last line translates to "Black Roderick, the descendant of Alpine"—a figure that emphasizes the natural dependence of vassals on their lord through the image of branches flowing from a sturdy trunk. Roderick's ferocity ultimately proves too brittle to prevail, and the poem rewards instead the more accommodating Douglas, who reconciles with King James while Roderick dies from battle wounds in prison. But during the contentious period of the War of 1812, Americans were drawn to Roderick's extreme and futile case.

John Sanderson originally wrote the melody of "Hail to the Chief" for Thomas Dibdin's adaptation of *Lady of the Lake*, which premiered in London in 1810. American theaters preferred Edmund John Eyre's *Lady of the Lake*, which was originally produced in Edinburgh in 1811, but Sanderson's "Hail to the Chief" was popular enough to be incorporated often into Eyre's version.[89] Between the play's premiere in Philadelphia in January 1812 and the middle of 1815, it received at least ten different productions, each with multinight engagements, in New York, Philadelphia, Baltimore, and Washington. During this time, sheet music of Sanderson's "Hail to the Chief" received eight printings in Boston, New York, Philadelphia, and Baltimore.[90] In the theatrical adaptation most popular in America, the actors playing Roderick's men entered the stage on a boat singing the now-familiar melody. The image of Roderick on the boat became iconic, and his character rivaled the "lady" herself as the proprietor of the lake in the story. In this sense, the lake became militarized in America; not so much offering a romance with Ellen Douglas at its center, the adaptations highlighted Roderick's fierce and doomed martial ambitions. The special American affection for this song during wartime is reflected in its bibliographical history. While seven of the twelve British printings of "Hail to the Chief" appeared before 1812, thirteen of the fifteen American printings appeared after 1812, once the war began.[91]

Figure 10. Walter Scott and John Sanderson, "Hail to the Chief," c. 1813.

The militarization of this poem might explain the interesting fact that in 1813, the U.S. navy named a warship they built on Lake Ontario *The Lady of the Lake*—the only American vessel named for a contemporary literary reference.[92] Newspapers all over the country affectionately tracked this boat's movements against the British as one of Commodore Isaac Chauncey's valued vessels—a "beautiful pilot-boat," as the schooner was described. A small ship carrying two or sometimes three guns, *The Lady of the Lake* was launched on April 8, 1813, and throughout that summer led munitions raids, offensive maneuvers, and reconnaissance missions.[93] The public prints recognized the playful irony of borrowing the name of a warship from Britain's most prized author, and it is clear Americans enjoyed the little theft from their rivals.[94] During the fall of 1813, for example, newspapers carried reports of a chase in early September between Commodore Chauncey and the British naval commander Sir James Yeo. According to these reports, Chauncey exchanged fire with Yeo in a brief encounter near Niagara, after which Yeo's ships fled into port near Kingston. Reports seized on the apparent cowardice of the British commander and ridiculed his status as a baronet. "Chauncey has chased Yeo all around the Lake, and has got him penned up," one dispatch reported, "The knight refused to come to action. The Lady of the Lake has this moment arrived with the information."[95] The chase inspired a poem that took advantage of the incident's literary potential. It was first printed in Baltimore the same week a new production of *The Lady of the Lake* was being staged.[96] The poem then reached a remarkably diverse range of readers as it was reprinted in dozens of papers, from South Carolina to New Hampshire. The playful ballad confirms and exploits widespread affection for Scott:

"The Courteous Knight; or, the Flying Gallant"

For a nautical knight, a lady—heigho!
    Felt her heart and her heart-strings to ache;
To view his dear person she look'd to and fro,
The name of the knight was sir James Lucas Yeo;
    And the *Lady*—'twas she *of the Lake*. [. . .]

From Ontario's margin the lady set sail,
    Expecting the knight on that sea;
She dreamt not that he in his promise would fail;
And from a fair lady, unmanlike turn tail;
    Yet he tarried—What could the cause be?[97]

The poem's first line—"For a nautical knight, a lady—heigho!" echoes the refrain from "Hail to the Chief" that ends each stanza: "Roderick Vich Alpine Dhu, ho! iero!" thus further solidifying the connection between the boat song made famous by the poem and the actual ship made famous by the war.

In the end, though, it was the antiwar region of New England that adopted the melody "Hail to the Chief" as a way of paying tribute to the president. The February 1815 peace celebration in Boston coincided with the anniversary of the birth of George Washington and included religious services, hymns, processions, gun salutes, patriotic toasts, a ball in honor of Washington, and the illumination of buildings all over town.[98] It also included the performance of a new "Ode on the Peace," entitled "Wreathes for the Chieftain," which offered new lyrics for "Hail to the Chief." The "Chieftain" is now Washington himself, who, in winning the Revolution, had "planted the Olive of peace in the soil that he gained." In the ode, peace is figured as a tree with "secure . . . branches"—perhaps in allusion to the sturdy pine tree of Roderick Dhu—and while the recent war had "scattered" and "shattered" it, the return of peace means that "Nee'r [sic] may the sacred tree, / Shorn of its verdure be."[99] The new lyrics were printed on a small press and "distributed among the crowd."[100] In one surviving copy of the sheet music to "Hail to the Chief," someone has pasted the new lyrics on the upper left corner of the first page, for easy reference (see figure 11).[101]

The Americanization of this Scottish song participates in the notorious practice of appropriating Native American signifiers as totems of American military might. The president is not only a Highland chief but also an Indian chieftain. During the War of 1812, the defeat of Tecumseh and the Native Americans remained the most important U.S. victory, and so the nation appropriated the martial dignity of its greatest enemy as their own. Scottish Highland chiefs and Indian chiefs were closely associated figures in the Anglo-American imagination.[102] They were both stereotyped as the valiant and intransigent defenders of tribes at the margins of the modern world—leaders, so the insidious stories go, of vanishing races. This analogy helped complete the Americanization of the song "Hail to the Chief," which rests on the adoption of figures drawn from the present and the past to help imagine the nation's continuing and future glory.

In the postwar period, sheet music to "Hail to the Chief" continued to be printed all over the nation as "Wreathes for the Chieftain" received its own editions in Boston and Philadelphia.[103] The melody was first played to honor

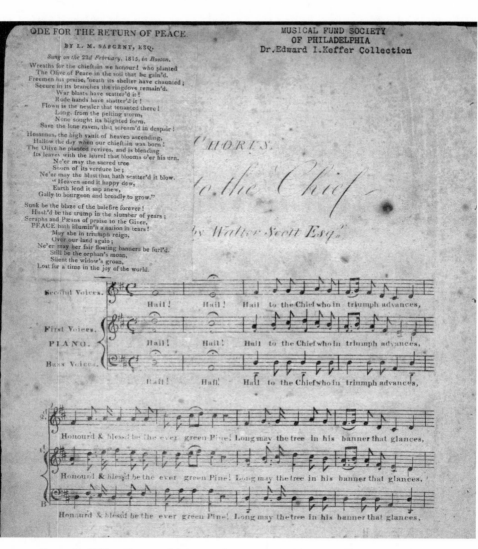

Figure 11. Walter Scott and John Sanderson, "Hail to the Chief," with new lyrics
from L. M. Sargent, "Ode for the Return of Peace," 1815 (detail).

a sitting president at a dinner honoring Andrew Jackson's legendary victory in New Orleans. Throughout the 1820s and 1830s, the continued printing of this sheet music, the performance of *Lady of the Lake*, and the use of "Hail to the Chief" on commemorative occasions made it unsurprising that John Tyler chose it as the official song for the U.S. commander in chief. The transformation of "Hail to the Chief" into "Wreathes for the Chieftain" and eventually into the martial anthem of the president—like the transformation of *Marmion* into a battle cry—emphasizes that the Americanization of Scott was animated by a deeply felt analogy between the world of Scott's poetry and the American situation during the War of 1812. This analogy depends on the specifically anti-English rivalry then showcased in Scott's work. Even though during the Napoleonic era, Scottish subjects—including Scott himself—were among the most vehement supporters of British imperial rule, Americans routed the spirit of their defiance through the romantic precedent of Scottish resistance.

* * *

Walter Scott's reputation has suffered from widespread shame that Americans loved such an aristocratic British author. In one of the most dramatic accusations in literary history, Mark Twain blamed Scott's novels and poems for the Civil War. According to Twain, Scott's depiction of knights and ladies, aristocratic codes of honor, and outmoded social hierarchies inspired Southern attachment to a feudalistic lifestyle. That lifestyle rejected the modern world, and only slavery could sustain it. According to Twain, Scott

> set the world in love with dreams and phantoms, with the silliness and emptiness, sham grandeurs, sham gauds, and sham chivalries of a brainless and worthless long-vanished society. He did measureless harm; more real and lasting harm, perhaps, than any other individual that ever wrote. But for the Sir Walter disease, the character of the Southerner would be wholly modern. For it was he that created rank and caste down there, and pride and pleasure in them. Sir Walter had so large a hand in making Southern character, as it existed before the war, that he is in great measure responsible for the war.[104]

Twain's outrageous assessment is actually quite helpful because the intensity of his disdain matches in degree, if not in kind, the intensity of Scott's influence in America. It is an influence of which Twain betrays not a little envy with the vehemence of his superlative condemnation. Twain was indeed correct to locate Scott's influence in the context of war; he just picked the wrong war. In 1812, Americans may have fought and endured a controversial war with Great Britain, but they did so with Walter Scott in their hearts.

Epilogue

The Scarlet Letter and the Decline of London

A teenage Nathaniel Hawthorne was busy reading after the War of 1812, especially in the years when Walter Scott's and Maria Edgeworth's popularity peaked and when Washington Irving and James Fenimore Cooper achieved transatlantic literary fame. Young Nathaniel was also busy bragging to his sisters. "I have read all most all the Books which have been published for the last hundred years," he wrote in a letter that mentions some of them directly, including *The Mysteries of Udolpho*, *Roderick Random*, *Tom Jones*, *Caleb Williams*, the tales of Monk Lewis, and the *Memoirs of R. L. Edgeworth*. One particular group stands out in Hawthorne's explicit references: "I shall read The Abbot by the Author of Waverley as soon as I can hire it," he wrote in 1820, just weeks after that novel was published; "I have read all Scott's novels except that. I wish I had not, that I might have the pleasure of reading them again."[1] His adolescent reading habits are notable for the absence of American books and for his punctual consumption of the latest British ones, demonstrated by his charming preference for Scott and—as we might infer from his interest in her father's *Memoirs*—the works of Maria Edgeworth. Like most American readers, Hawthorne fed his imagination with British literature. It was at this time of heavy transatlantic reading that he first betrayed interest in becoming a writer, a profession that he knew was governed by tastes and prejudices abroad. "What do you think of my becoming an Author," he wrote to his mother early in 1821. "How proud would you feel to see my works praised by the reviewers, as equal to the proudest productions of the scribbling sons of John Bull?"[2] The same uneven dynamics that determined Hawthorne's earliest reading lists led him to frame the profession of authorship as intrinsically

related to the Anglophile taste of reviewers. Hawthorne first expressed his
ambition to write while he was getting the most pleasure from the author who
was getting the most praise from the arbiters of culture he knew most authors
had to please. For the young Hawthorne, to be an "author" was to be like the
Author of Waverley.

While Scott's importance to Hawthorne is, in some ways, old news, the
provincial literary formation this book has described remains an unexplored
background for *The Scarlet Letter* (1850). That novel is a profound homage to
the aesthetics of provinciality, one that reflects changes in the English-language
publishing industry that originally produced it.[3] By the mid-nineteenth century, as I suggested at the end of Chapter 1, the growth and nationalization of
American publishing and the emergence of a truly British publishing industry
split between Edinburgh and London began to erase the unevenness that once
made similarities among writers from Ireland, Scotland, and the United States
so apparent. *The Scarlet Letter* registers the decline of London's dominance
through deriving Hester Prynne's artistic taste from her native England and
investing her willful, permanent settlement in Boston with aesthetic significance. That novel's famous ambiguity, as well as the rich interconnectedness
between "The Custom House" and the romance that follows, reflects a newly
organized literary field that no longer had a clearly authoritative audience to
which American writers could turn for recognition. As the genius of a specifically New England literary culture, Hawthorne of course remained a provincial within the United States.[4] But London had ceased to matter in the way
it once did.[5]

Hawthorne's earliest fiction deploys the literary strategies that Edgeworth,
Owenson, Scott, Irving, and Cooper used in the 1810s and 1820s, suggesting
that their wide influence installed the effects of provinciality within writings
with only a tenuous possibility of reaching London. Hawthorne's frequent use
of the discourse of introduction—including footnotes, historical asides, and
ethnographic description—in stories like "The Gentle Boy" (1830), "Roger
Malvin's Burial" (1832), and "My Kinsman, Major Molineaux" (1831) bears
the trace of a provincial aesthetics that depends for its effect on a reader's presumed outsider relationship to the knowledge it reveals. In *Fanshawe* (1828),
Hawthorne's awareness of such outsiderness is clear through his juxtaposition
of provincial and metropolitan perspectives in his description of the traveling
musician and poet Hugh Crombie. "His productions were upon subjects of
local and temporary interest," Hawthorne writes, "and would consequently
require a bulk of explanatory notes, to render them interesting or intelligible

to the world at large."[6] Also, in "The Gray Champion" (1835), Hawthorne derives "New England's hereditary spirit" from the triumph of Britain's Glorious Revolution in a way that resonates with the Anglo-American cultural camaraderie found in Irving and Cooper, especially because it depends on the vehement rejection of the Catholic and Gallicized Stuarts in favor of the genteel Protestant William of Orange.[7] The young Hawthorne also claimed literary authority based on his nationality, as evidenced in his first projected fictional work, *Seven Tales of My Native Land*—a title that resonates with Scott's famous line from *Lay of the Last Minstrel* (1805), "my own, my native land," discussed in the previous chapter.[8] This insistence on nativity, common throughout Hawthorne's early tales, implicitly invokes a foreign reader whose ignorance contrasts to the author's own expertise; the author's personal connection to the setting becomes a necessary condition for the authenticity of the texts that follow.[9] When Hawthorne revised "The Gentle Boy" (1832) for republication in *Twice Told Tales* (1837), he distanced himself from such rhetoric by deleting its final sentence. "My heart is glad of this triumph of our better nature," Hawthorne originally wrote, referring to the Puritans' increasing tolerance of Quakers; "it gives me a kindlier feeling for the fathers of my native land; and with it I will close the tale."[10] By cutting this sentence, Hawthorne demurs from the kind of authority that other texts invoke with considerable irony, such as the published version of "Alice Doane's Appeal" (1835), which was originally intended for *Seven Tales of My Native Land*. "Before us lay our native town," the narrator of that story declares, before Hawthorne complicates the relationship between nativity and knowledge through the false opposition between "truth" and "fiction" that foregrounds the climax of the story's ghostly conclusion.[11]

In *The Scarlett Letter*, Hawthorne deploys such language with marked self-consciousness, now that London was no longer the obvious point of reference for the American writer. The long acknowledged parallel between Hester's artistic talent and Hawthorne's skill as a novelist allegorizes this reshaping of the Anglophone literary field through an explicit reckoning with the aesthetics of provinciality and the obsolescence of its representational modes. This allegory is available through a comparative analysis of Hawthorne's relation, in "The Custom House," to "the natal soil" of Salem and Hester's to "her native village" in England— two claims of nativity the novel as a whole puts in dynamic tension.[12] The complex nature of this allegory suggests that *The Scarlet Letter* rejects cross-cultural communion as a value that defines literary exchange. Emerging from a U.S. literary field that newly questioned the importance of London, *The Scarlet Letter* ultimately forwards the notion that literary exchange is not governed at all by an author-reader relationship. It is, instead, useless: which is to say, fully autonomous. As we shall see, a key scene in *The Scarlet Letter* endorses this radical view of literary autonomy in the same breath as it exposes its ideological nature. This novel's most distinguishing feature is its remarkable negative capability; its simultaneous embrace and rejection of the autonomy of the literary is the irresolvable antinomy I consider as this book concludes.[13]

*   *   *

The beginning and the end of *The Scarlet Letter* invoke heraldry to draw a connection between the novel and the books of Hawthorne's boyhood, including *Waverley*. In "The Custom House," this occurs when Hawthorne accepts Surveyor Pue's ghost's request to make his manuscript public. To effect his commitment to the story of "old Mistress Prynne," Hawthorne recounts an exchange Donald Pease has called an act of "symbolic investiture."[14] Surveyor Pue declares, "I charge you . . . give to your predecessor's memory the credit which will be rightfully its due!" and Hawthorne replies, "I will!" (*SL*, 26). This dialogue repeats the structure of the story of General James F. Miller, a hero from the War of 1812, who was the collector at Salem's Custom House during Hawthorne's tenure. Hawthorne's sketch of General Miller, related earlier in the preface, connects his authorial assent with General Miller's patriotism. The General was elderly, elegant, benevolent, kind, and prone to reveries; "he lived a more real life within his thoughts" (*SL*, 18). Imagining the content of these reveries makes Hawthorne describe the late 1810s: "The evolutions of the parade; the tumult of the battle; the flourish of old, heroic music, heard thirty years before;—such scenes and sounds, perhaps, were all alive before his intellectual sense" (*SL*, 18). This short description, and particularly its evocation of "heroic music," strongly evokes the era when Scott's novels and poetry—including patriotic songs like "Hail to the Chief"—were mobilized as rallying points for American nationalism.

Hawthorne's account of General Miller's most famous words invites a closer connection between Scott and the General as well as between the General and Hawthorne:

> There was one thing that much aided me in renewing and recreat-
> ing the stalwart soldier of the Niagara frontier, —the man of true

and simple energy. It was the recollection of those memorable words
of his,—"I'll try, Sir!"—spoken on the very verge of a desperate and
heroic enterprise [the Battle of Niagara], and breathing the soul
and spirit of New England hardihood, comprehending all perils,
and encountering all. If, in our country, valor were rewarded by
heraldic honor, this phrase—which it seems so easy to speak, but
which only he, which such a task of danger and glory before him,
has ever spoken—would be the best and fittest of all mottoes for the
General's shield of arms. (*SL*, 19)

The General's exclamation, "I'll try, sir," prepares us for Hawthorne's declaration a few pages later, "I will!" as he commits to the less bloody task of writing
The Scarlet Letter. The parallel infuses Hawthorne's admittedly more confident
"I will!" with the nostalgia of "thirty years before" that comes with his effort,
here, of "renewing and recreating the stalwart soldier of the Niagara frontier."
If Hawthorne imagines the declaration of an intention to write as the echo of
this war hero's battle cry, then the "old, heroic music" of the 1810s Hawthorne
also describes must be remembered, too, as we read the story of "Mistress
Prynne" in a genre that Scott made famous.[15]
    The connection between General Miller and Hawthorne makes Scott
even more central to the novel when we consider the motto that marks Hester's and Dimmesdale's tombstone. Apparently, it was not always the case that
"our country" failed to "reward[]" with heraldry. The "herald's wording" on
the tombstone—"ON A FIELD, SABLE, THE LETTER A, GULES" (*SL*, 178)—is
nothing like the hardy words "I'll try!"; even so, General Miller may have
remembered another instance when the colors "sable" and "gules" were put to
use as the moral of a romance. Hawthorne's epitaph is a brilliant revision of
the following passage from the "Introductory" chapter of *Waverley*:

Upon th[e] passions it is no doubt true that the state of manners
and laws casts a necessary colouring; but the bearings, to use the
language of heraldry, remain the same, though the tincture may be
not only different, but opposed in strong contradistinction. The
wrath of our ancestors, for example, was coloured *gules*; it broke
forth in acts of open and sanguinary violence against the objects
of its fury: our malignant feelings, which must seek gratification
through more indirect channels, and undermine the obstacles which
they cannot openly bear down, may be rather said to be tinctured

sable. But the deep ruling impulse is the same in both cases; and the proud peer, who can now only ruin his neighbor according to law, by protracted suits, is the genuine descendent of the baron who wrapped the castle of his competitor in flames, and knocked him on the head as he endeavoured to escape from the conflagration.[16]

Scott colors the emotions of the past *gules*, scarlet, because the state did not regulate the passionate expression of wrath. In contrast, the passions of the present are mediated through the lawful channels of modern bureaucracy and are accordingly colored *sable*, or black. *Waverley* itself encapsulates the progression Scott narrates from scarlet to black, represented in the transition from the passionate expressions of Jacobite outlaws to the regulated emotions Edward Waverley eventually embraces in his new, lawful lowland life. In Hawthorne's epitaph, scarlet of course does not indicate wrath, but it still points to passion expressed without law, insofar as the "A" signifies Hester's antinomianism (e.g., "What we did had a consecration of its own" [*SL*, 133]). The color black signifies Puritan attempts to contain that passion within the mechanism of the law, to surround it like the background color of this heraldic shield. In both *Waverley* and *The Scarlet Letter*, then, a contrast between *gules* and *sable* marks the contrast between lawless passion and lawfulness. Hawthorne's epitaph reverses the colors' positions on Scott's temporal map: while *Waverley* buries passion in the past, *The Scarlet Letter* highlights passion by relegating the "sombre" nature of Puritan law to a dark background "relieved only by one ever-glowing point of light gloomier than the shadow" (*SL*, 178). That point of light—Hester's romantic antinomianism, thrown into relief on the shield as the scarlet A—escapes the historical contingency of strict Puritan law. Indeed, the apparent anachronism of Hester's passion has led many readers to agree with Leslie Fiedler's extreme view that *The Scarlet Letter* is "not at all the historical novel it has been often called."[17] Hawthorne's reversal of the progressive moral offered in *Waverley*—as well as other moments, such as when he invokes "Irving's Headless Horseman" (*SL*, 33)—suggests that this novel represents a rather complicated reckoning with Scott's work and the constellation of provincial literature that surrounded it.

While Hawthorne's fabricated story about Surveyor Pue's manuscript is passed off as a kind of literary ruse in which Scott might have indulged, "The Custom House" contains a companion authenticating strategy that is not a joke at all. In "The Custom House," Hawthorne's description of his family's roots in Salem accrues to him the authority to write about New England. The tale about the surveyor's manuscript and all its conventions displaces this very real authenticating procedure. The story of the manuscript, "of a kind always recognized in literature" (*SL*, 5), tries to make the issue of authenticity a game. But its playfulness is belied by the construction of a natural intimacy between Hawthorne and his subject matter, an intimacy that his first critics accepted entirely and that proved central to the novel's enduring reputation. Both the ruse and the reality derive from the strategies developed by Scott and his contemporaries. What signals *The Scarlet Letter*'s departure from those important precedents is the afterlife of these strategies in the romance itself, where they are evoked to explain Hester's artistic talent.

We hear often enough that Salem is Hawthorne's birthplace. It is "my native town," "my native place," "my native town," "the natal earth," "the natal spot," "my native town," "the natal soil," and "my old native town" (*SL*, 5, 8, 10, 11, 24, 34). In an important passage, he frames his nativity as deeply rooted, inevitable, and unique for an American:

> [T]hough invariably happiest elsewhere, there is within me a feeling
> for old Salem, which, in lack of a better phrase, I must be content
> to call affection. The sentiment is probably assignable to the deep
> and aged roots which my family has struck into the soil. It is now
> nearly two centuries and a quarter since the original Briton, the
> earliest emigrant of my name, made his appearance in the wild and
> forest-bordered settlement, which has since become a city. And
> here his descendants have been born and died, and have mingled
> their earthly substance with the soil; until no small portion of it
> must necessarily be akin to the mortal frame wherewith, for a little
> while, I walk the streets. In part, therefore, the attachment which I
> speak of is the mere sensuous sympathy of dust for dust. Few of my
> countrymen can know what it is; nor, as frequent transplantation is
> perhaps better for the stock, need they consider it desirable to know.
> (*SL*, 8)

Upon his return to Salem as a customs officer, Hawthorne does not let memory do its usual work of coloring a homecoming with scenes from early youth. Instead, time and organic matter, "dust for dust," make Hawthorne's home his own, no matter how undesirable that fact may be. It is crucial that this occurs despite his wishes. Hawthorne later refuses to call this "sensuous sympathy" anything like "love"; it is, rather, "instinct" (*SL*, 10). His historical relation to Salem is fundamentally impersonal; his "homefeeling with the past" has little to do with his own life (*SL*, 9). Writing in a nation where few can claim more than personal experience or willful affection as a resource for citizenship, Hawthorne taps the more organic resources of death and family history.

Two key moments link this organic connection to Salem with Hawthorne's relationship to the story of "Mistress Prynne." They transform his very particular connection with Salem into "proof" of his more general authority about the culture of New England. Indeed, he vigorously defends exclusive rights to local identity; not even a third-generation inhabitant can "claim to be called a Salemite" (*SL*, 10). Hawthorne generalizes and expands his authority when he refers to Surveyor Pue, who is not from Salem, as "my *official* ancestor" (*SL*, 26; emphasis mine) and when he describes his relation to the material this "ancestor" has left behind. Hawthorne echoes his own language about Salem when he describes his interest in the mysterious package as propelled by an "instinctive curiosity" (*SL*, 23), which he is as powerless to control as his affection for home (*SL*, 23). The "old scarlet letter" memorably exerts its power over his senses, much like the soil of Salem: "some deep meaning . . . streamed forth from the mystic symbol, subtly communicating itself to my sensibilities, but evading the analysis of my mind" (*SL*, 25). Like his connection with Salem, a "spell" that is no less puzzling or irrational ("it would be quite as reasonable to form a sentimental attachment to a disarranged checkerboard"), his connection to the scarlet letter derives from a "sensuous sympathy" that seems equally beyond his control: "I happened to place it on my breast . . . and involuntarily let it fall upon the floor" (*SL*, 10, 8, 25).

These echoes naturalize Hawthorne's relationship to the ensuing romance and train his readers to assent to the authenticity of *The Scarlet Letter*—a text we are made to believe was drawn organically from the dust of *its* native land. Hawthorne's mobility helps him here; indeed, he is now "a citizen of somewhere else" (*SL*, 34). No longer in Salem, Hawthorne, like *The Scarlet Letter*, we come to believe, finally, is 100 percent *New England*. The invention of this essential New Englandness is amplified in Hawthorne's importation of the possessive grammar of ancestral ties into the romance, where the repeated invocation of the first person plural conjures an insider community of New Englanders; he writes of "our wild forest land," "our elder towns," "our early annals," "our grave forefathers," "our forefathers," and "our sobre-hued community" (*SL*, 48, 71, 74, 75, 112, 177). Hawthorne has learned from authors like Scott how to make his identity matter, to have readers believe in the special knowledge only available to one involuntarily called by his ancestry to the task of writing. In his literary biography of Hawthorne, Henry James recounts the initial reception of *The Scarlet Letter* thirty years after its publication; its first readers recognized that "the thing was absolutely American; it belonged to the soil, to the air; it came out of the very heart of New England."[18] James's words could have been borrowed from "The Custom House," an authenticating preface that—in its attempt to portray *The Scarlet Letter* as having sprung organically from Hawthorne's ancestral "instincts"—seems to have succeeded.

Hester Prynne is more fond of her "native village" than Hawthorne is of Salem. *The Scarlet Letter* spends a significant amount of time fleshing out Hester's feelings about England and tying her artistic authority to her experience there, much like "The Custom House" does for Hawthorne and Salem. This sets up an important analogy between Hawthorne and Hester that is crucial to the way the novel negotiates the Anglophone literary field. Michael Gilmore has provided the most compelling account of Hawthorne's use of Hester and other characters as expressions of his own authorial identity. Gilmore's analysis focuses on Hawthorne's internal conflict as he struggles with his entry into the marketplace. While Dimmesdale represents the inauthentic author who dissembles to please popular taste, Hester represents the isolated truth teller who will not compromise her principles: "She is the first full-length representation in America of the alienated modern artist."[19] With the death of this pair, Gilmore argues, Hawthorne reflects the impossibility of inhabiting both contradictory roles at once. However, Hawthorne's rich description of Hester's relationship to England invests her artistic talent with a provenance that complicates Gilmore's analysis, which depends on a strictly national understanding of the marketplace. What does it mean that Hawthorne projects his own authorial identity onto two characters born and bred in England? The parallel between Hawthorne's and Hester's natively derived artistic authority acknowledges the scope of an Anglophone literary field that was beginning to change. Like any ambitious writer of the period, Hawthorne knew that publishing a novel meant entering into a marketplace that was ineluctably transatlantic. One way this novel reflects England's decreasing cultural power is through its derivation of the origins of Hester's talent using the same logic of Hawthorne's own locally derived literary authority. This gives Hester's English taste an American origin.

Hawthorne's focus on his ancestry in "The Custom House" trains us to trace Hester's talent for needlework back to England. Such a genealogy is possible through tracking the relations among passages that describe her art and her childhood. Her "delicate and imaginative skill" (*SL*, 57) is governed, we are twice told, by the "taste of the age" (*SL*, 39, 57), which Hawthorne explicitly contrasts to the somber "Puritanic mode of dress" (*SL*, 57). This anti-Puritanical taste appeals to her fellow colonists, who are of course "native Englishmen," too (*SL*, 155). Hester produces apparel and ornamental accessories for those who let themselves "follow[] their hereditary taste" and satisfy a desire for "gorgeously embroidered" things (*SL*, 156, 58). Hawthorne insists that Hester's artistic expression naturally represents the style her community loves: "She had in her *nature* . . . a taste for the gorgeously beautiful" (*SL*, 59; emphasis mine). His descriptions of Pearl's clothes and the scarlet letter, both products of Hester's needle, fitfully parallel each other; the former are "distinguished by a . . . fantastic ingenuity" and the latter by "fantastic flourishes" "fantastically embroidered with gold thread" (*SL*, 58, 39, 43). Hester's productions are "fantastic" because they are "modelled much after her own fancy"—another word derived from the root "fantasy" (*SL*, 39). Insofar as her "fancy" operates according to the taste of the age, we come to think it was a faculty formed in England.

In the forest scene, Hester implicitly connects that faculty with her original home. When Pearl first approaches Hester and Dimmesdale from across the brook, her mother describes the flowers this "fantastic little elf" has gathered for a crown, ornaments that augment her already "fantastic" dress (*SL*, 140). "'[H]ow strangely beautiful she looks, with those wild flowers in her hair!'" Hester says, "'It is as if one of the fairies, whom we left in our dear old England, had decked her out to meet us'" (*SL*, 140). Hester endows Pearl's flower-collecting instincts with an Englishness that reverberates back on her own instincts as the seamstress who dresses Pearl in a way that "heighten[s her] airy charm" (*SL*, 58). Another of Hawthorne's parallels between Pearl and the "A" reinforces this suggested Englishness; the brook reflects both "the brilliant picturesqueness of [Pearl's] beauty" and "the gold embroidery" of the letter itself (*SL*, 141, 143). This watery medium suggests Hester's needlework exudes the same playfulness and mystery invoked in her comment about Pearl's flowers. Her artistic instincts come from that magical place across the Atlantic that earlier Hester calls "our native land" (*SL*, 134).

Hawthorne frames Hester's essential Englishness as organic and inevitable, just like his own attachment to Salem. Pearl gets her "airy charm" from at least two sources: she inherits it from Hester as her natural child, and she embodies it by wearing her mother's "fantastic" clothes. Hawthorne's insistence that Hester's style originates in "her nature" and "own fancy" makes it difficult to see whether it is biology or art that makes Pearl's Englishness seem more organic. Indeed, Hester can't help herself: her child, the beautiful "A," the many ornaments "of which the dames of a court might gladly have availed themselves" (*SL*, 57) are as foreign as the English recreations and rituals that the next generation of New Englanders, who "wore the blackest shade of Puritanism" (*SL*, 157), would eventually banish. Furthermore, it is not long after we meet Hester that we follow her memories back to "her happy infancy" (*SL*, 42). On the scaffold with her infant, the crowd before her falls from view as Hester's memory floods her consciousness: "she saw again her native village, in Old England, and her paternal home. . . . She saw her own face, glowing with girlish beauty, and illuminating all the interior of the dusky mirror in which she had been wont to gaze at it" (*SL*, 42–43). Like the "tarnished mirror" of Hawthorne's imagination, described in "The Custom House" (*SL*, 27), the image of young Hester gazing at herself gives a striking element of depth to this scene. Hester's "preternaturally active" memory seems beyond her control, just like her artistic talent, as more and more images "came swarming back upon her" (*SL*, 42). Hester's comforting reminiscences, like Hawthorne's less pleasant sympathy for Salem, emerge of their own accord. As Hawthorne writes of himself, "instinct" is what "creates a kindred between the human being and the locality" (*SL*, 10). Similarly, "it was an instinctive device of her spirit" that catalyzes Hester's memory, which provides temporary relief from "the cruel weight" of her present circumstance (*SL*, 42). That the comfort she later takes in the exercise of her needle, which gives her "a part to perform in the world" (*SL*, 59), resembles the refuge she takes in the memory of home suggests how difficult it is for her to direct her affections toward Boston.

Hester's memory and art take her mind away from New England. And yet Hawthorne's keep his there. This strong parallel between Hester and Hawthorne—whose affections send them in opposite directions—indicates the decline of England's cultural authority for nineteenth-century Americans. On the most basic level, the essentializing of Hawthorne's attachment to home, like Hester's to England, signals the appropriateness of an American writer's focus on native themes and subjects. But Hawthorne's focus on American subjects is different than it is, for example, in a writer like Cooper. Insofar as the art-home link of Hester's character follows the pattern set in "The Custom House," the formal structure of *The Scarlet Letter* as a whole privileges Hawthorne's New England as setting the precedent and the ground for the logic of artistic development. Hawthorne insists that Hester's English taste follows in his footsteps: the afterlife of the art-home link in the romance transforms what in "The Custom House" had seemed to be a debt to Scott's claim to native authority into a theory of artistic expression—borne out in Hester's life—with an American provenance. At the same time, to the extent that Hawthorne uses Hester to project his own authorial identity, he constructs a bridge between English aesthetic achievement and this very American story. In this way, Hawthorne claims Elizabethan-era "taste" as his rightful heritage. In putting to work for American culture the "gorgeous," the "fantastic," the "fairy charm" of an English taste that Hester's needlework embodies, Hawthorne bypasses recent British literary history and claims a direct line of descent from the age of Shakespeare to himself. This also has the effect of bypassing the authority of the nineteenth-century London marketplace.

Hester's new and permanent attachment to Boston indicates the new importance of an American market for literature through the derivation of art from sin. Hester's experiences in Boston have led to a "new birth" that makes "the forest-land . . . her life-long home" (*SL*, 56). It is a new affiliation of her own making: "Her sin, her ignominy, were the roots which she had struck in to the soil" (*SL*, 56). The importance of her own agency in this matter contrasts with Hawthorne's claim that others forged the native identification he now endures because of "the deep and aged roots which my family [i.e., not I] has struck into the soil" (*SL*, 8). At the end of the novel, when Hester returns to New England and takes up the symbol of the scarlet letter, she amplifies her original role as the agent of her new rootedness; she resumes the letter entirely "of her own free will" (*SL*, 177). This is Hawthorne's ironic way of registering the increasing self-confidence of the American literary field, though it's figured here as "penitence" (*SL*, 177). Sacvan Bercovitch has argued that Hester's decision to return enacts the idea that the United States is a society that coheres despite internal divisions. She resumes the letter "in the spirit of integration" as she acknowledges that her radical individualism is merely a "point of view" that can after all be reconciled with her community.[20] Her return also suggests that community's new ability to attract the attention and ambition of an American writer who has left thoughts of London behind.

The Scarlet Letter makes it abundantly clear that Hester could have chosen a life back in England, both at the beginning and at the end of the novel. She stays to signal the legitimacy of a newly nationalized market that can accommodate ambitious fiction writers. The firm establishment of Hester's new "roots," though forged in sin, also signals the installation of her "fantastic ingenuity," which comes to express itself fully as Hawthorne's romance. The women who consult Hester on the margins of the town, who seek sympathy with her, and who absorb her wisdom are the nineteenth-century readers that can support a native writer. It hardly matters now where Hester has been or to what transatlantic location she sends her new productions, made still with "a lavish richness of golden fancy" (*SL*, 177). Had Hawthorne placed Pearl firmly back in England, perhaps on the land she inherited from Roger Chillingworth (*SL*, 176), *The Scarlet Letter* may have promoted the Anglo-American affinity that propels earlier provincial literature drawn to London. Indeed, the only thing we know about "that unknown region where Pearl had found a home" (*SL*, 177) is that it's *not* England; letters Hester receives (presumably from Pearl) are marked by a heraldic seal "unknown to English heraldry" (*SL*, 176). If Hester's willed return to Boston signals the new importance of an American audience, the specificity of this negative statement about Pearl signals the un-importance of an English one.

Unconcerned with metropolitan readers, *The Scarlet Letter* fails to embody the aesthetics of provinciality. While "The Custom House" borrows from the conventions of such an aesthetics, the radical separation of that preface from the romance itself, as well as the effects of their interconnectedness, translates debt into transcendence; the performance as a whole emerges from its generic origins in order to surpass them. Nowhere is this more apparent than in *The Scarlet Letter*'s self-reflexive treatment of the literary transaction that Edgeworth, Owenson, Scott, Irving, and Cooper all pursued in order to promote cross-cultural communion. This novel, in contrast, insists openly and symbolically on literature's uselessness. An author's achievements are "recognized," he writes in "The Custom House," only by the special few; "a man who has dreamed of literary fame" is bound "to find how utterly devoid of significance, beyond that circle, is all that he achieves" (*SL*, 21). Hawthorne "might as well have been a fiddler," as his imagined ancestors remark (*SL*, 10). In the romance itself, Hawthorne figures the isolation of a "circle" intelligible only to itself in his protagonists' inhabitation of a world apart. Hester is enclosed "in a sphere by herself," she "inhabited another sphere," and her cottage is "out of the sphere" of society (*SL*, 40, 59, 57); at one moment, "there was an absolute circle of radiance around" Pearl, who is "entirely out of the sphere of sympathy or human contact" (*SL*, 63, 92), and only in the forest can Hester and Dimmesdale "fe[el] themselves, at least, inhabitants of the same sphere" (*SL*, 129). The useless beauty of Hester's art is the product of this isolation, and her taste for the "gorgeously beautiful" is in total excess of its practical effect of providing "food for her thriving infant and herself" (*SL*, 59, 57). Hawthorne embraces literary autonomy in its purest ideological sense.

Few readers would deny that Hawthorne frames the beauty of Hester's embroidery, and therefore the aesthetics of his novel, as without an external purpose. Like the butterfly in "The Artist of the Beautiful" (1844), such things exist only for themselves. The fantasy of literary exchange *London and the Making of Provincial Literature* has considered involves the promotion of cultural camaraderie: recall the Smithian sympathies of Colambre in *The Absentee* (1812), the marriage of Horatio and Glorvina in *The Wild Irish Girl* (1806), the companionship Geoffrey Crayon imagines with his English readers in *The Sketch Book* (1819–1820), the way William Cullen Bryant casts Britons and Americans as fireside intimates, the relationship between Jeanie Deans and Queen Caroline in *The Heart of Mid-Lothian* (1818), and the Anglo-American alliance that *The Pioneers* (1823) projects into the future. The American book trade's nationalization and its increased production led Hawthorne to pursue a different goal in *The Scarlet Letter*, which was to divorce the literary exchange from this cross-cultural purpose.

Hawthorne may be more aware than his predecessors of the ideological nature of constructing an autonomous literary sphere—purposive or not. The scene in *The Scarlet Letter* that most powerfully addresses the purpose of art also exposes as a lie any claim for its uselessness:

> "What does the letter mean, mother?—and why dost thou wear it?—and why does the minister keep his hand over his heart?
>
> "What shall I say?" thought Hester to herself.—"No! If this be the price of the child's sympathy, I cannot pay it!"
>
> Then she spoke aloud.
>
> "Silly Pearl," said she, "what questions are these? There are many things in this world that a child must not ask about. What know I of the minister's heart? And as for the scarlet letter, I wear it for the sake of its gold thread!" (*SL*, 123)

Hawthorne never comes closer to voicing the idea that art exists for its own sake, and it's the biggest lie Hester ever told. At this moment, "some new evil had crept" into "her heart" and for the first time made her "false to the symbol on her bosom" (*SL*, 123). The letter, as we have seen, is a "specimen" of her artistic talent and obviously a symbol of *The Scarlet Letter*. In this moment, Hawthorne proposes the irreconcilable notions that art exists only to be beautiful and that such a claim is a damnable falsity. The novel ultimately sustains the pressure of these opposing ideas, which fuse together in this exchange to encapsulate the ideological thrust and deep self-consciousness of Hawthorne's most compelling tale.

Appendix

The London Republication of
American Fiction, 1797–1832

Author	Title	First American Edition	London Edition (with New Title, if Applicable)	Authorized?
Tyler, Royall	The Algerine Captive; or, The Life and Adventures of Doctor Updike Underhill: Six years a Prisoner among the Algerines	1797	1802	
Brown, Charles Brockden	Wieland; or The Transformation. An American Tale	1798	1811	
Rowson, Susanna	Reuben and Rachel; or, Tales of Old Times	1798	1799	A
Brown, Charles Brockden	Ormond; or The Secret Witness	1799	1800	A
Brown, Charles Brockden	Arthur Mervyn; or, Memoirs of the Year 1793	1799	1803, Arthur Mervyn. A Tale	A
Brown, Charles Brockden	Edgar Huntly; or, Memoirs of a Sleep-walker	1799	1803	
Anon.	St. Hubert; or, Mistaken Friendship	1800	1825, St. Hubert; or, the Trials of Angelina	
Wood, Sally	Julia and the Illuminated Baron	1800	1800	
Brown, Charles Brockden	Jane Talbot	1801	1804	
Brown, Charles Brockden	Clara Howard: in a Series of Letters	1801	1807, Philip Stanley; or, the Enthusiasm of Love	
Thayer, Caroline Matilda	The Gamesters; or, Ruins of Innocence: an Original Novel, Founded in Truth	1805	1806, Conrade; or, the Gamesters. A novel, Founded on Facts	

Author	Title	Date	Republication	A*
Anon.	Margaretta, or, The Intricacies of the Heart	1807	1807	
Irving, Washington	Salmagundi; or, the Whim-whams and Opinions of Launcelot Langstaff, Esq., and others	1807–1808	1811, Salmagundi . . . with an introductory essay and explanatory notes by John Lambert	
Sansay, Leonora	Secret History; or, The Horrors of St. Domingo	1808	1820, Zelica, The Creole; A Novel, by an American[a]	
Irving, Washington	A History of New York, from the Beginning of the World to the End of the Dutch Dynasty	1809	1820, A Humourous History of New York, from the Beginning of the World, to the End of the Dutch Dynasty	A*
Paulding, James Kirke	The Diverting History of John Bull and Brother Jonathan	1812	1813	
Irving, Washington	The Sketch Book of Geoffrey Crayon	1819–1820	1820	A*
Cooper, James Fenimore	Precaution	1820	1821	A*
			1839	A*
Irving, Peter	Giovanni Sbogarro; a Venetian Tale	1820	1820	
Cooper, James Fenimore	The Spy, a Tale of the Neutral Ground	1821	1822, The Spy: A Tale of the Neutral Ground, Referring to Some Particular Occurrences During the American War; Also Pourtraying American Scenery and Manners	
			1831, The Spy, a Tale of the Neutral Ground	A*
Anon.	Edmund and Margaret: or, Sobriety and Faithfulness rewarded.	1822	1828	A*

Author	Title	First American Edition	London Edition (with New Title, if Applicable)	Authorized?
Irving, Washington	Bracebridge Hall; or, the Humourists	1822	1822	A*
Neal, John	Logan, A Family History	1822	1823	
Paulding, James Kirke	A Sketch of Old England, by a New-England Man	1822	1822	
Sedgwick, Catharine Maria	A New-England Tale: Or, Sketches of New-England Character and Manners	1822	1822, A New-England Tale. From the Second American Edition	A
Cooper, James Fenimore	The Pioneers, or the Sources of the Susquehanna, A Descriptive Tale	1823	1823 / 1832	A / A*
Cooper, James Fenimore	The Pilot; A Tale of the Sea	1823	1824 / 1831	A / A
De Witt, Susan Linn	Justina; or, The Will: A Domestic Story	1823	1823, Justina; or, Religion Pure and Undefiled. A Moral Tale	
MacHenry, James	The Wilderness; or Braddock's Times. A Tale of the West	1823	1823, The Wilderness; or the Youthful Days of Washington. A Tale of the West.	
MacHenry, James	The Spectre of the Forest; or, Annals of the Housatonic. A New-England Romance.	1823	1824	
Neal, John	Seventy-Six	1823	1823	
Paulding, James Kirke	Koningsmarke, The Long Finne, A Story of the New World	1823	1823	

Author	Title			
Cheney, Harriet	A Peep at the Pilgrims in Sixteen Hundred and Thirty-Six: a Tale of Olden Times	1824	1825	
Cooper, James Fenimore	Lionel Lincoln; or, The Leaguer of Boston	1824	1825 1832	A A*
Irving, Washington	Tales of a Traveller, by Geoffrey Crayon	1824	1824	A*
MacHenry, James	O'Halloran; or, the Insurgent Chief; an Irish Historical Tale of 1798	1824	1824, The Insurgent Chief: Or, O'Halloran, An Irish Historical Tale of 1798	A
Sedgwick, Catharine Maria	Redwood	1824	1824	A
Smith, Margaret	A Winter in Washington; or, Memoirs of the Seymour Family	1824	1824	
Tucker, George	The Valley of the Shenandoah; or, Memoirs of the Graysons	1824	1825	
Ware, Henry	The Recollections of Jotham Anderson	1824	1829	
Hale, Sarah	Stranger of the Valley or, Louisa and Adelaide; an American Tale	1825	1826	
Jones, James Athearn	The Refugee. A Romance	1825	1825	A
MacHenry, James	The Hearts of Steel, An Irish Historical Tale of the Last Century	1825	1825	
Paulding, James Kirke	John Bull in America, or, The New Munchausen	1825	1825	

Author	Title	First American Edition	London Edition (with New Title, if Applicable)	Authorized?
Sedgwick, Catherine Maria	The Travellers: a Tale, Designed for Young People	1825	1825	
Cooper, James Fenimore	The Last of the Mohicans; a Narrative of 1757	1826	1826 1831	A A*
Flint, Timothy	Francis Berrian; or, the Mexican Patriot	1826	1834	
Cooper, James Fenimore	The Prairie	1827	1827 1832	A A*
Cooper, James Fenimore	The Red Rover	1827	1827 1834	A A*
Hale, Sarah	Northwood; A Tale of New England	1827	1827, Sidney Romelee, A Tale of New England	
Sedgwick, Catharine Maria	Hope Leslie; or, Early Times in the Massachusetts	1827	1828	A
Barnum, H. L.	The Spy Unmasked; or, Memoirs of Enoch Crosby, alias Harvey Birch, the Hero of the 'Spy, a Tale of the Neutral Ground'	1828	1829	
Cooper, James Fenimore	The Wept of the Wish-ton-Wish	1829	1829, The Borderers; or, the Wept of the Wish-ton-Wish 1833	A A*

Flint, Timothy	George Mason, the Young Backwoodsman; or, 'Don't Give up the Ship'	1829	1833, Don't Give up the Ship	
Irving, Washington	A Chronicle of the Conquest of Granada; by Fray Antonio Agapida	1829	1829, A Chronicle of the Conquest of Granada; from the Mss. of Fray Antonio Agapida by Washington Irving	A
Sealsfield, Charles	Tokeah; or, the White Rose	1829	1829, The Indian Chief; or, Tokeah and the White Rose. A Tale of the Indians and the Whites	A
Cooper, James Fenimore	The Water Witch; or, the Skimmer of the Seas	1830	1830	A
McClung, John	Camden: A Tale of the South	1830	1830	A
Sedgwick, Catharine Maria	Clarence; or, a Tale of our own Times	1830	1830	A
Cooper, James Fenimore	The Bravo; a Tale	1831	1831 The Bravo; a Venetian Tale	A
Jones, James Atheam	Haverill; or, Memoirs of an Officer in the Army of Wolfe	1831	1831	A
Paulding, James Kirke	The Dutchman's Fireside	1831	1831	
Bryant, William Cullen	Tales of Glauber-Spa	1832	1833	
Child, Lydia Maria	The Coronal; A Collection of Miscellaneous Pieces	1832	1833, The Mother's Story Book; or, Western Coronal. A Collection of Miscellaneous Pieces	A
Cooper, James Fenimore	The Heidenmauer; or, The Benedictines	1832	1832	A

Author	Title	First American Edition	London Edition (with New Title, if Applicable)	Authorized?
Irving, Washington	*The Alhambra: a Series of Tales and Sketches of the Moors and Spaniards*	1832	1832 *The Alhambra; by Geoffrey Crayon*	
Kennedy, John Pendleton	*Swallow Barn; or, A Sojourn in the Old Dominion*	1832	1832, *Swallow Barn; or, A Sojourn in Virginia. An American tale*	
Paulding, James Kirke	*Westward Ho!*	1832	1833, *The Banks of the Ohio; or, Westward Ho!*	

Note: Texts are organized chronologically according to initial American publication. First American and first London editions are listed, and I have provided the new London title if applicable. Entries marked (A) were authorized either by the author herself or the publisher, and those marked (A*) were authorized and revised substantially by the author. If a later London edition was revised, as in the case of Cooper's texts, I have listed that edition as well. I have compiled this table from the following sources: the standard editions of Charles Brockden Brown (Kent State University Press, 1977–), Washington Irving (Twayne, 1978–), and James Fenimore Cooper (SUNY Press, 1980–); William B. Cairns, "British Republication of American Writings, 1783–1833," *PMLA* 43.1 (1928): 303–310; Clarence Gohdes, *American Literature in Nineteenth Century England* (Carbondale: Southern Illinois University Press, 1944); Melissa Homestead and Camryn Hansen, "Susanna Rowson's Transatlantic Career," *Early American Literature* 45:3 (2010): 619–654; Melissa Homestead, "American Novelist Catharine Sedgwick Negotiates British Copyright, 1822–1857," *Yearbook of English Studies* 45 (forthcoming); and the online bibliographical database edited by P. D. Garside, J. E. Belanger, and S. A. Ragaz, *British Fiction, 1800–1829: A Database of Production, Circulation & Reception* (Designer A. A. Mandal [http://www.british-fiction.cf.ac.uk]). I have also cross-referenced all entries for 1797–1832 in Lyle H. Wright, *American Fiction: 1774–1850*, 2nd ed. (San Marino, CA: Huntington Library, 1969), with Garside et al., WorldCat, and the online database of the British Library.

a The authority of this much revised London edition of *Secret History* is disputed. Garside and other bibliographies attribute it to Sansay herself, but Michael Drexler believes it cannot be attributed to her. *Secret History; or, The Horrors of St. Domingo*, ed. Michael J. Drexler (Peterborough, Ontario: Broadview, 2007), 36.

Notes

INTRODUCTION

1. Richard Sher, *The Enlightenment and the Book* (Chicago: University of Chicago Press, 2006), 381.

2. Maria Edgeworth, *Castle Rackrent and Ennui*, ed. Marilyn Butler (New York: Penguin, 1992), 63.

3. Ibid., 123.

4. R. F. Foster, *Words Alone: Yeats and His Inheritances* (Oxford: Oxford University Press, 2011), 4; Katie Trumpener, *Bardic Nationalism: The Romantic Novel and the British Empire* (Princeton, NJ: Princeton University Press, 1997), 131.

5. Asa Briggs, "The Longmans and the Book Trade, c1730–1830," in *The Cambridge History of the Book in Britain*, vol. 5: *1695–1830*, ed. Michael F. Suarez and Michael L. Turner (Cambridge: Cambridge University Press, 2010), 407.

6. Peter Garside, "*Waverley* and the National Fiction Revolution," in *The Edinburgh History of the Book in Scotland*, vol. 3: *Ambition and Industry, 1800–1880*, ed. Bill Bell (Edinburgh: Edinburgh University Press, 2007), 222.

7. Walter Scott, *Waverley*, ed. P. D. Garside (New York: Penguin, 2011), 364; "General Preface" (1829), in *Waverley*, ed. Claire Lamont (Oxford: Clarendon Press, 1981), 352.

8. Georg Lukács, *The Historical Novel*, trans. Hannah and Stanley Mitchell (Lincoln: University of Nebraska Press, 1962; rept. 1983), 35, 36.

9. The epithet was in common circulation. See, for example, the *Monthly Review* (October 1823), 210.

10. Washington Irving, "Preface to the Revised Edition" (1848), in *History, Tales, and Sketches*, ed. James W. Tuttleton (New York: Library of America, 1983), 737–742; Edwin T. Bowden, *Washington Irving Bibliography* (Boston: Twayne, 1989), 122–126; Haskel Springer, "Introduction," in *The Sketch Book of Geoffrey Crayon* (Boston: Twayne, 1978), xi–xxxii.

11. This well-known comment of William Makepeace Thackeray is from the *Cornhill Magazine* and was republished in, and is quoted here from, *The Roundabout Papers* (London, 1869), 224.

12. Pierre Bourdieu, *The Field of Cultural Production*, ed. Randal Johnson (New York:

Columbia University Press, 1993), and *The Rules of Art: Genesis and Structure of the Literary Field*, trans. Susan Emanuel (Stanford, CA: Stanford University Press, 1992).

13. Pascale Casanova, *The World Republic of Letters*, trans. M. B. DeBevoise (Cambridge, MA: Harvard University Press, 2004).

14. Eric Hobsbawm, "Introduction: Inventing Traditions," in *The Invention of Tradition*, ed. Eric Hobsbawm and Terence Ranger (Cambridge: Cambridge University Press, 1983), 14.

15. Thanks to James Uden for discussing this etymology with me.

16. James Boswell, *Life of Johnson*, ed. Pat Rogers (Oxford: Oxford University Press, 1980), 469.

17. Qtd. in John O. Hayden, ed., *Scott: The Critical Heritage* (New York: Barnes & Noble, 1970), 79.

18. James Fenimore Cooper, *The Last of the Mohicans* (London: Colburn and Bentley, 1831), 72.

19. *Provincial* is relative term that can be useful in multiple contexts. It was also commonly used to describe English country towns and also booksellers in England who depended on the London trade. Provincial novels set in England flourished in the mid-Victorian period. Ian Duncan has argued that Irish and Scottish fiction of the early nineteenth century are more properly described as "regional" rather than "provincial." "The region," he writes, using Edgeworth and Scott as examples, "is a place in itself, the source of its own terms of meaning and identity, while the province is a typical setting defined by its difference from London." "The Provincial and Regional Novel," *A Companion to the Victorian Novel*, ed. Patrick Brantlinger and William B. Thesing (Oxford: Blackwell, 2002), 323. My account of Irish and Scottish fiction emphasizes the importance of London and, accordingly, follows the logic of Duncan's definition while disagreeing on terminology. This, of course, does not preclude the relevance of the term *provincial novel* for later English novels whose settings also depend much on London as a point of reference.

20. John Clive and Bernard Bailyn, "England's Cultural Provinces," *William and Mary Quarterly* 11 (1954): 200–213. I address comparative scholarship on Scotland and America more extensively in Chapter 5. See 116–117 and 235n14.

21. Thomas Bender, *A Nation Among Nations: America's Place in World History* (New York: Hill & Wang, 2006), 7. Throughout this book, I draw from recent transatlantic scholarship. An early encounter with Elisa Tamarkin's work first inspired me to ask, of London's importance to the provincial author, whether "cultural independence really mattered that much." *Anglophilia: Deference, Devotion, and Antebellum America* (Chicago: University of Chicago Press, 2008), 2. A number of state-of-the-field essays were also influential at an early stage, including David Armitage, "Three Concepts of Atlantic History," in *The British Atlantic World, 1500–1800*, ed. David Armitage and Michael J. Braddick (New York: Palgrave, 2002): 11–27; Laura Stevens, "Transatlanticism Now," *ALH* 16.1 (2004): 93–102; and Amanda Claybaugh, "Toward a New Transatlanticism: Dickens in the United States," *Victorian Studies* 48.3 (2006): 439–460, reprinted in *The Novel of Purpose: Literature and Social Reform in the Anglo-American World* (Ithaca, NY: Cornell University Press, 2006). I have added my own perspective on this methodological debate with "What We Need

from Transatlantic Studies" *ALH* 26.4 (Winter 2014). Studies that view American literary history from a transatlantic perspective include Lawrence Buell, "American Literary Emergence as a Postcolonial Phenomenon" *ALH* 4.3 (Fall 1992): 411–442; Leslie Eckel, *Atlantic Citizens: Nineteenth-Century American Writers at Work in the World* (Edinburgh: Edinburgh University Press, 2013); Christopher Hanlon, *America's England: Antebellum Literature and Atlantic Sectionalism* (Oxford: Oxford University Press, 2013); Meredith McGill, *American Literature and the Culture of Reprinting, 1834–1853* (Philadelphia: University of Pennsylvania Press, 2003); Tamarkin, *Anglophilia*; Leonard Tennenhouse, *The Importance of Feeling English: American Literature and the British Diaspora, 1750–1850* (Princeton, NJ: Princeton University Press, 2007); and Robert Weisbuch, *Atlantic Double-Cross: American Literature and British Influence in the Age of Emerson* (Chicago: University of Chicago Press, 1986). Important studies of British literature with transatlantic focus include James Chandler, *England in 1819: The Politics of Literary Culture and the Case of Romantic Historicism* (Chicago: University of Chicago Press, 1998), especially 441–480; Kate Flint, *The Transatlantic Indian, 1776–1930* (Princeton, NJ: Princeton University Press, 2008); Christopher Flynn, *Americans in British Literature, 1770–1832: A Breed Apart* (Aldershot, Hans, England: Ashgate, 2008); and Timothy Fulford, *Romantic Indians: Native Americans, British Literature, and Transatlantic Culture 1756–1830* (Oxford: Oxford University Press, 2006). For comparative studies of literature in Britain and the United States, see Claybaugh, *The Novel of Purpose*; W. M. Verhoeven, ed., *Revolutionary Histories: Transatlantic Cultural Nationalism, 1775–1815* (London: Palgrave, 2002); Laura Doyle, *Freedom's Empire: Race and the Rise of the Novel in Atlantic Modernity, 1640–1940* (Durham, NC: Duke University Press, 2008); Paul Giles, *Transatlantic Insurrections: British Culture and the Formation of American Literature, 1730–1860* (Philadelphia: University of Pennsylvania Press, 2001); and Eric Simpson, *Mercenaries in British and American Literature, 1790–1830: Writing, Fighting, and Marrying for Money* (Edinburgh: Edinburgh University Press, 2010). Work inspired by Paul Gilroy, *The Black Atlantic: Modernity and Double Consciousness* (Cambridge, MA: Harvard University Press, 1993), and Joseph Roach, *Cities of the Dead: Circum-Atlantic Performance* (New York: Columbia University Press, 1996), do not fit into easy nationalized categories. I address the historiography of transatlantic book history in Chapter 1.

22. Walter Scott, qtd. in William B. Todd and Ann Bowden, *Sir Walter Scott: A Bibliographical History, 1796–1832* (New Castle, DE: Oak Knoll Press, 1998), 998; Washington Irving, *History, Tales, and Sketches*, ed. James W. Tuttleton (New York: Library of America, 1983), 223; *Quarterly Review* (April 1821): 67.

23. To Mr. and Mrs. Ticknor, November 1, 1838, in *The Life and Letters of Maria Edgeworth*, vol. 2, ed. Augustus Hare (London, 1894), 275.

24. Maria Edgeworth to Mrs. William Griffith, dated April 20, 1826, Princeton University Libraries, Leonard L. Milberg Collection of Irish Prose.

25. Gallatin copied this comment in a letter he wrote to Cooper on March 9, 1827; qtd. in James Fenimore Cooper, *Letters and Journals*, vol. 1, ed. James Franklin Beard (Cambridge, MA: Harvard University Press, 1960), 189n3.

26. George Dekker, in *The American Historical Romance* (Cambridge: Cambridge University Press, 1987), provides to date the most comprehensive account of Walter Scott's

importance for American fiction and also includes an important discussion of Edgeworth. While Dekker traces the legacy of the "Waverley-model" in historical fiction, which emphasizes the historicism of the Scottish Enlightenment, this book traces the legacy and influence of Scott's and Edgeworth's concern with London in a messy and contentious literary field.

27. McGill, *American Literature and the Culture of Reprinting*, and Michael Warner, *Letters of the Republic: Publication and the Public Sphere in Eighteenth-Century America* (Cambridge, MA: Harvard University Press, 1990).

28. Ian Duncan, *Modern Romance and Transformations of the Novel: The Gothic, Scott, Dickens* (Cambridge: Cambridge University Press, 1992), and *Scott's Shadow: The Novel in Romantic Edinburgh* (Princeton, NJ: Princeton University Press, 2007); Trumpener, *Bardic Nationalism*; Leith Davis, Ian Duncan, and Janet Sorensen, eds., *Scotland and the Borders of Romanticism* (Cambridge: Cambridge University Press, 2004); Ina Ferris, *The Achievement of Literary Authority: Gender, History, and the Waverley Novels* (Ithaca, NY: Cornell University Press, 1991), and *The Romantic National Tale and the Question of Ireland* (Cambridge: Cambridge University Press, 2002); and Murray Pittock, *Scottish and Irish Romanticism* (Oxford: Oxford University Press, 2008).

29. Clarence Gohdes, *American Literature in Nineteenth Century England* (Carbondale: Southern Illinois University Press, 1944), 15; William B. Cairns, "British Republication of American Writings, 1783–1833," *PMLA* 43.1 (1928): 303–310; and William S. Ward, "American Authors and British Reviewers 1798–1826: A Bibliography," *American Literature* 49.1 (1977): 1–12.

30. McGill, *Culture of Reprinting*; Claybaugh, *The Novel of Purpose*; Leah Price, *The Anthology and the Rise of the Novel: From Richardson to George Eliot* (Cambridge: Cambridge University Press, 2000); David Brewer, *The Afterlife of Character: 1726–1825* (Philadelphia: University of Pennsylvania Press, 2005); Lara Langer Cohen, *The Fabrication of American Literature: Fraudulence and Antebellum Print Culture* (Philadelphia: University of Pennsylvania Press, 2012); and Patricia Crain, *The Story of A: The Alphabetization of America from* The New England Primer *to* The Scarlet Letter (Stanford, CA: Stanford University Press, 2000).

31. The common alliterative pairing Peter Shillingsburg uses in his title, *From Gutenberg to Google: Electronic Representations of Literary Texts* (Cambridge: Cambridge University Press, 2006), neatly encapsulates the feeling we are experiencing an epoch-defining moment, and the recently completed, multivolume histories of the book in America, Britain, Scotland, and Ireland testify to the establishment of book history as an interdisciplinary field in the humanities. See John Barnard, David McKitterick, and I. R. Willison, eds., *The Cambridge History of the Book in Britain*, 6 vols. (Cambridge: Cambridge University Press, 1999–2009); Bill Bell, ed., *The Edinburgh History of the Book in Scotland*, 4 vols. (Edinburgh: University of Edinburgh Press, 2007–2014); Robert Welch and Brian Walker, eds., *The Oxford History of the Irish Book*, 5 vols. (Oxford: Oxford University Press, 2006–2012); David Hall, ed., *A History of the Book in America*, 5 vols. (Chapel Hill: University of North Carolina Press, 2000–2010).

32. Jonathan Loesberg, *A Return to Aesthetics: Autonomy, Indifference, and Postmodernism*

(Stanford, CA: Stanford University Press, 2005). For recent overviews of the aesthetic turn in literary studies, see Marjorie Levinson, "What Is New Formalism?" *PMLA* 122.2 (2007): 558–569, and Cindy Weinstein and Christopher Looby, "Introduction," in *American Literature's Aesthetic Dimensions*, ed. Weinstein and Looby (New York: Columbia University Press, 2012): 1–19. Jacques Rancière conceives of aesthetic experience according to what he calls the "distribution of the sensible." Aesthetics, for Ranciere, "is a delimitation of spaces and times, of the visible and the invisible, of speech and noise, that simultaneously determines the place and the stakes of politics as a form of experience." "The Distribution of the Sensible: Politics and Aesthetics," in *The Politics of Aesthetics*, trans. Gabriel Rockhill (London: Continuum, 2004), 13.

33. The minute historicizing tools of book history—descriptive bibliography, publication history, the economic data of the book trade, the history of reading, the reprinting, modification, and dissemination of texts—are for the most part anathema to scholars interested in aesthetics. Meanwhile, Leon Jackson's important book-historical study of authorship explicitly rejects the specificity of aesthetic experience. He argues that books were almost indistinguishable from other objects, like "brooms and baskets," through which gift economies created "social bonds" in the antebellum United States: "I cannot say with confidence that the affective freight of literature was unique," Jackson writes, "indeed, I conjecture that the difference with brooms and baskets was more likely a matter of degree than kind." *The Business of Letters: Authorial Economies in Antebellum America* (Stanford, CA: Stanford, University Press, 2008), 5–6.

34. The grammar of this formulation is inspired by the opening sentences of Christopher Looby, *Voicing America: Language, Literary Form, and the Origins of the United States* (Chicago: University of Chicago Press, 1996): "Nations are not born, but made. And they are made, ineluctably, in language"(2).

35. *Edinburgh Review* (January 1820): 79.

36. Washington Irving to Charles Leslie, October 31, 1820, qtd. in Ben McClary, *Washington Irving and the House of Murray* (Knoxville: University of Tennessee Press, 1969), 32n19.

37. Duncan, *Scott's Shadow*, xiii.

38. Bourdieu, *The Field of Cultural Production*, 37.

39. Michael Hechter, *Internal Colonialism: The Celtic Fringe in British National Development, 1536–1966* (Berkeley: University of California Press, 1975).

40. James N. Green, "The Rise of Book Publishing," in *A History of the Book in America*, vol. 2, ed. Gross and Kelley.

41. Ferris, *The Romantic National Tale*.

42. John Cannon, *The Oxford Companion to British History* (Oxford: Oxford University Press, 1997), 763.

43. William St. Clair, *The Reading Nation in the Romantic Period* (Cambridge: Cambridge University Press, 2004), 453–454; Michael Winship, "The Transatlantic Book Trade and Anglo-American Literary Culture in the Nineteenth Century," in *Reciprocal Influences: Literary Production, Distribution, and Consumption in America*, ed. Steven Fink and Susan S. Williams (Columbus: Ohio University Press, 1999), 119.

44. Duncan, *Scott's Shadow*, xi.

45. Jane Millgate, "Archibald Constable and the Problem of London: 'Quite the Connection We Have Been Looking For,'" *Library* 18 (1996): 110–123.

46. Simon Eliot, "Appendix B: Statistical Evidence for the 1825–6 Crisis," in *The Edinburgh History of the Book in Scotland*, vol. 3, ed. Bell, 492.

47. Casanova, 82–125.

48. Ibid., 12.

49. Ibid., 24.

50. For Casanova, too, other center/periphery structures exist on smaller scales and with significant variations in discrete linguistic or national literary fields ruled by cultural capitals of their own. By insisting on the noncoincidence of literary and political power, Casanova's model of world literature differs from Franco Moretti's, which applies Wallerstein's world systems school of economic history to define the kind of inequality found in the world literary system. "Conjectures on World Literature," *New Left Review* 1 (2000): 54–68. Moretti later admitted that the inequality of the world literary system does not exactly coincide with economic inequality. "More Conjectures" [2003] reprinted in *Distant Reading* (London: Verso, 2013), 107–119. James English summarizes what some have called the "Gallicized exaggeration" of Casanova's theory in "Cultural Capital and the Revolutions of Literary Modernity, from Bourdieu to Casanova," in *A Handbook of Modernism Studies*, ed. Jean-Michel Rabaté (Somerset, NJ: John Wiley, 2013), 373.

51. James Buzard, *Disorienting Fiction: The Autoethnographic Work of Nineteenth-Century British Novels* (Princeton, NJ: Princeton University Press, 2005), 70. Buzard's account of the origins of ethnography in the work of Scott, Owenson, and Edgeworth suggests that the term *culture* accurately describes the entity that provincial writers represented as they fashioned their fiction for the metropolis. Nancy Ruttenburg's characterization of Cooper's use of "seemingly ethnographic objectivity" suggests the applicability of Buzard's account in the early nineteenth-century United States. *Democratic Personality: Popular Voice and the Trial of American Authorship* (Stanford, CA: Stanford University Press, 1998), 314. While Brad Evans and Nancy Bentley argue for a much later genealogy for the emergence of "the ethnographic imagination" in the United States, the transatlantic circulation of texts and the powerful analogies among Irish, Scottish, and American fiction suggest its relevance in this earlier period. See Brad Evans, *Before Cultures: The Ethnographic Imagination in American Literature, 1865–1920* (Chicago: University of Chicago Press, 2005), and Nancy Bentley, *The Ethnography of Manners: Hawthorne, James, Wharton* (Cambridge: Cambridge University Press, 1995).

52. See Franco Moretti, "Conjectures on World Literature," *New Left Review* 1 (2000): 54.

53. Richard Poirier, *A World Elsewhere: The Place of Style in American Literature* (New York: Oxford University Press, 1966), 16.

54. Jerome McGann, *The Romantic Ideology: A Critical Investigation* (Chicago: University of Chicago Press, 1983); Terry Eagleton, *The Ideology of the Aesthetic* (Cambridge, MA: Blackwell, 1990); Raymond Williams, *Culture and Society, 1780–1950* (London: Penguin, 1958).

55. David Hume, "Of the Standard of Taste," in *Essays: Moral, Political, and Literary*, ed. Eugene F. Miller (Indianapolis, IN: Liberty Fund, 1985), 244–245.

56. Timothy M. Costelloe has recently demonstrated the centrality of resemblance and recognition in the writings of Joseph Addison, Francis Hutcheson, Edmund Burke, Joshua Reynolds, and Archibald Allison. Timothy Costelloe, *The British Aesthetic Tradition: From Shaftesbury to Wittgenstein* (Cambridge: Cambridge University Press, 2013), 11–131.

57. Qtd. in Costelloe, 44.

58. Edmund Burke, "Introduction on Taste," added to the 1759 edition of *A Philosophical Enquiry into the Sublime and the Beautiful*, ed. David Womersley (New York: Penguin, 1998), 69.

59. John Hutchinson, *The Dynamics of Cultural Nationalism: The Gaelic Revival and the Creation of the Irish Nation State* (London: Allen & Unwin, 1987), 13.

60. *Germany; by the Baroness Staël Holstein, Translated from the French*, vol. 1 (New York, 1814), 181–182. On Staël's importance in the period, see John Claiborne Isbell, *The Birth of European Romanticism: Truth and Propaganda in Staël's 'De l'Allemagne', 1810–1813* (Cambridge: Cambridge University Press, 1994). Ina Ferris, in *The Romantic National Tale*, emphasizes the importance of Staël to Irish fiction, especially Sydney Owenson.

61. Madame de Staël, *Corinne, or Italy* [1807] (New York: Oxford University Press, 2008), 13.

62. Staël, *Germany*, 166.

63. Preface to *Lyrical Ballads* (1802), in *William Wordsworth: A Critical Edition of the Major Works*, ed. Stephen Gill (Oxford: Oxford University Press, 1984), 597, 605.

64. Hume, 239.

65. Shaftesbury and Addison were the first to identify the disinterestedness of the observer as a value. See M. H. Abrams, "Art-as-Such: The Sociology of Modern Aesthetics," in *Doing Things with Texts: Essays in Criticism and Critical Theory*, ed. Michael Fischer (New York: Norton, 1989), and Edward Cahill, *Liberty of the Imagination: Aesthetic Theory, Literary Form, and Politics in the Early United States* (Philadelphia: University of Pennsylvania Press, 2012), 153.

66. Adam Smith, *The Theory of Moral Sentiments*, ed. Ryan Patrick Hanley (New York: Penguin, 2009), 31.

67. Eric Slauter, in *The State as a Work of Art: The Cultural Origins of the Constitution* (Chicago: University of Chicago Press, 2009), points out that most aesthetic theorists of the mid-eighteenth century were not English. "Why was the midcentury discourse of taste dominated by provincials?" "One clue," he surmises, "comes in the frequent appeal by some of these writers to the notion of the arts as a space for agreement and for the elimination of social and cultural difference" (106).

68. John Guillory, *Cultural Capital: The Problem of Literary Canon Formation* (Chicago: University of Chicago Press, 1993); Clifford Siskin, *The Work of Writing: Literature and Social Change in Britain, 1700–1830* (Baltimore: Johns Hopkins University Press, 1998).

69. Siskin, 10.

70. Immanuel Kant, *Critique of the Power of Judgment*, ed. Paul Guyer (Cambridge University Press, 2000), 176.

71. Ibid., 176–177.

72. Eagleton, *The Ideology of the Aesthetic*, 76.

73. Scott, *Waverley*, 361.

74. Saree Makdisi, for example, argues that the portrait "reifies the past and ossifies history." *Romantic Imperialism: Universal Empire and the Culture of Modernity* (Cambridge: Cambridge University Press, 1998), 97. See also George Levine, *The Realistic Imagination: English Fiction from Frankenstein to Lady Chatterley* (Chicago: University of Chicago Press, 1981), 104; James Buzard, *Disorienting Fiction*, 89; and Michael Gamer, "Waverley and the Object of (Literary) History," *MLQ* 70.4 (2009): 524. A recent essay discusses the anachronistic invocation of Henry Raeburn, a painter who was Scott's contemporary, not Waverley's; Emma Rosalind Peacocke, "Facing History: Galleries and Portraits in Waverley's Historiography," *European Romantic Review* 22.2 (2011): 187–208.

75. Raymond Williams, xvi.

76. Scott, *Waverley*, 361.

77. The poetry of Walter Scott, his compatriot Thomas Campbell, the Irish poet Thomas Moore, and the American William Cullen Bryant were all published in London and partake in some of the representational modes of the aesthetics of provinciality as I describe them. A full consideration of poetry, however, is beyond the scope of this project. Many apologies, especially, to Robert Burns.

78. Joseph Rezek, "The Orations on the Abolition of the Slave Trade and the Uses of Print in the Early Black Atlantic," *Early American Literature* 45.3 (Fall 2010): 655–682, and "The Print Atlantic: Phillis Wheatley, Ignatius Sancho, and the Cultural Significance of the Book," in *Early African American Print Culture*, ed. Jordan A. Stein and Lara Cohen (Philadelphia: University of Pennsylvania Press, 2012), 19–39.

79. Ignatius Sancho, *The Letters of the Late Ignatius Sancho*, ed. Vincent Caretta (New York: Penguin, 1998), 112.

80. The word *provincial* (to etymologize again) was first used to refer to the administrator of a province, an association with governance that captures the membership of this book's major authors in the ruling classes of their societies and their rise to prominence within them.

81. Gilroy, 37, 2, 14.

82. Some analogies proved more powerful than others. Highlanders and Indians were often compared to one another, for example, while Irish Catholic peasants were often compared to African slaves.

83. Washington Irving, *The Analectic Magazine* (March 1815): 246. I discuss this passage at length in Chapter 4.

84. Frederic Jameson, *The Political Unconscious: Narrative as a Socially Symbolic Act* (Ithaca, NY: Cornell University Press, 1981), 291.

85. Recently literary critics have expressed much impatience with ideology critique and symptomatic reading, the classic tools of historicism that have dominated the field since Jameson's famous dictum, "Always historicize!" (*The Political Unconscious*, 9). Stephen Best and Sharon Marcus, for example, have proposed "surface reading," a methodology that eschews a hermeneutics of suspicion in favor of attending to "what is evident, perceptible, apprehensible in texts; what is neither hidden nor hiding; what, in the geometric sense, has length and breadth but no thickness, and therefore covers no depth." "Surface Reading: An Introduction," *Representations* 108.1 (Fall 2009): 9. The historicizing method I use both

plumbs depths and grazes surfaces, suggesting that we are better served by combining such methods than choosing between them.

CHAPTER I

1. See John Barnard, David McKitterick, and I. R. Willison, eds., *The Cambridge History of the Book in Britain*, 6 vols. (Cambridge: Cambridge University Press, 1999–2009); Bill Bell, ed., *The Edinburgh History of the Book in Scotland*, 4 vols. (Edinburgh: University of Edinburgh Press, 2007–2014); Robert Welch and Brian Walker, eds., *The Oxford History of the Irish Book*, 5 vols. (Oxford: Oxford University Press, 2006–2012); David Hall, ed., *A History of the Book in America*, 5 vols. (Chapel Hill: University of North Carolina Press, 2000–2010); William St. Clair, *The Reading Nation in the Romantic Period* (New York: Cambridge University Press, 2004); Meredith McGill, *American Literature and the Culture of Reprinting, 1834–1853* (Philadelphia: University of Pennsylvania Press, 2003); James Raven, *The Business of Books: Booksellers and the English Book Trade* (New Haven, CT: Yale University Press, 2007); Richard Sher, *The Enlightenment and the Book* (Chicago: University of Chicago Press, 2006).

2 While many scholars have explored the importation and reprinting of British literature in the early United States (see especially McGill, *Culture of Reprinting*, and James N. Green, "The Rise of Book Publishing," in *A History of the Book in America*, vol. 2: *An Extensive Republic: Print, Culture and Society in the New Nation, 1790–1840*, ed. Robert Gross and Mary Kelley [Chapel Hill: University of North Carolina Press, 2010], 75–127), there is ample evidence that the British were mightily interested in American literature, especially in the 1820s, as my Chapter 4 and the Appendix show. See also William B. Cairns, "British Republication of American Writings, 1783–1833," *PMLA* 43.1 (1928): 303–310, and William S. Ward, "American Authors and British Reviewers 1798–1826: A Bibliography," *American Literature* 49.1 (1977): 1–12.

3. David Armitage, "Three Concepts of Atlantic History," in *The British Atlantic World, 1500–1800*, ed. David Armatige and Michael J. Braddick (New York: Palgrave, 2002), 21.

4. Ibid., 11.

5. Niall Ó. Ciosáin, "Oral Culture, Literacy, and Reading, 1800–50," in *The Oxford History of the Irish Book*, vol. 4, ed. Murphy, 173. For demographics, see John Cannon, *The Oxford Companion to British History* (Oxford: Oxford University Press, 1997), 763. On literacy in Scotland, see Bill Bell, "Introduction," in *The Edinburgh History of the Book in Scotland*, vol. 3, ed. Bell, 7.

6. Raven, *Business of Books*, 149; John Crawford, "Libraries," in *The Edinburgh History of the Book in Scotland*, vol. 3, ed. Bell, 189.

7. St. Clair, *The Reading Nation*. Mark Rose writes, "The *Donaldson* decision meant that booksellers had a new interest in investing in current literary productions to replace a continuously expiring stock" ("Copyright, Authors, and Censorship," in *The Cambridge History of the Book in Britain*, vol. 5, ed. Suarez and Turner, 124).

8. James Raven, "The Book as a Commodity," in *The Cambridge History of the Book in Britain*, vol. 5, ed. Suarez and Turner, 85–117.

9. Michael Suarez, "Introduction," *The Cambridge History of the Book in Britain*, vol. 5, ed. Suarez and Turner, 35.

10. Sher, 265.

11. *A Catalogue of Books, Ancient and Modern; Containing the Works of the Principal Authors, and the Best Editions . . . at the Shop of William Creech, at the Cross, Edinburgh* (Edinburgh, 1793).

12. *The Scots Magazine* (September 1778): 496–506.

13. Qtd. in Sher, 317.

14. This calculation is drawn from Sher, 270.

15. Iain Beavan and Warren McDougall, "The Scottish Book Trade," in *The Cambridge History of the Book in Britain*, vol. 5, ed. Suarez and Turner.

16. Mary Pollard, *The Dublin Trade in Books, 1550–1800* (Oxford: Oxford University Press, 1989), 116; Sher, 443–502.

17. Charles Benson, "The Dublin Book Trade," in *The Oxford History of the Irish Book*, vol. 4: *The Irish Book in English, 1800–1891*, ed. James H, Murphy (Oxford: Oxford University Press, 2011).

18. Charles Benson, "The Irish Trade," in *The Cambridge History of the Book in Britain*, vol. 5, ed. Suarez and Turner, 370.

19. Pollard, 161.

20. Benson, "The Irish Trade," 372.

21. Qtd. in James N. Green, "English Books and Printing in the Age of Franklin," in *A History of the Book in America*, vol. 1: *The Colonial Book in the Atlantic World*, ed. David Hall (Chapel Hill: University of North Carolina Press, 2000), 282.

22. Hugh Amory, "Reinventing the Colonial Book," *A History of the Book in America*, vol. 1, ed. Hall, 52.

23. The catalogue of books Jefferson donated to the Library of Congress in 1815 lists such titles in abundance, many from the last two decades of the eighteenth century. For Jefferson's preference for Dublin editions, see Kevin J. Hayes, *The Road to Monticello: The Life and Mind of Thomas Jefferson* (Oxford: Oxford University Press, 2008), 193–194.

24. Rosalind Remer, *Printers and Men of Capital: Philadelphia Book Publishers in the New Republic* (Philadelphia: University of Pennsylvania Press, 1996), 24–38, and Green, "The Rise of Book Publishing."

25. "Most publishers of the 1790s," writes James N. Green, "got their start by importing books" ("The Rise of Book Publishing," 79).

26. *Gentleman's Magazine* (November 1796): 915.

27. Letter to James Brown, dated April 1800, in William Dunlap, *The Life of Charles Brockden Brown*, vol. 2 (Philadelphia, 1815), 100.

28. Beavan and McDougall, "The Scottish Book Trade."

29. Meredith McGill, "Copyright," in *A History of the Book in America*, vol. 2, ed. Gross and Kelley, 199. In three overlapping essays, Charles Benson establishes the importance of the Act of Union for the Irish case: "The Dublin Book Trade," "The Irish Trade," and "Printers and Booksellers in Dublin, 1800–1850," in *Spreading the Word*, ed. Robin Myers and Michael Harris (Winchester, England: St. Paul's Bibliographies, 1990), 47–59.

30. William Wakeman in 1821, qtd. in Benson, "Printers and Booksellers," 47.

31. Qtd. in Benson, "Irish Trade," 379–380.

32. William Carleton, *Traits and Stories of the Irish Peasantry*, qtd. in Benson "Printers and Booksellers," 47.

33. "I have ordered from London a complete set of Tales & Editions," Constable wrote to Edgeworth on August 19, 1823 (National Library of Scotland, MS. 671, fol. 114v). Of Edgeworth's major novels, only *Castle Rackrent* has a significant Dublin publishing history, probably because it was published in London before the 1801 Copyright Act.

34. Claire Connolly, "The National Tale, 1800–1829," in *The Oxford History of the Irish Book*, vol. 4, ed. Murphy, 400.

35. Benson, "Printers and Booksellers," 52; Connolly, "The National Tale, 1800–1829," 409.

36. Ina Ferris, *The Romantic National Tale and the Question of Ireland* (Cambridge: Cambridge University Press, 2002), 6.

37. *The Cyclopaedian Magazine and Dublin Monthly Register* (March 1807): 130.

38. Preface to vol. 1 of *Dublin and London Magazine* (November 1825): ii.

39. Connolly, "The National Tale, 1800–1829," 399; Ferris, 131.

40. Qtd. in Benson, "Printers and Booksellers," 47.

41. Maria Edgeworth, "To-Morrow," in *Popular Tales* (Boston: Samuel Parker, 1823), 363.

42. Ibid., 394.

43. Ibid., 397.

44. List of subscribers printed in *Practical Education*, vol. 2 (New York, 1801), n.p.

45. Remer, 38; for a list of imprints, see WorldCat.

46. Frank Ferguson, "The Industrialization of Irish Book Production, 1790–1900," in *The Oxford History of the Irish Book*, vol. 4, ed. Murphy, 10.

47. Remer, 69.

48. Green, "The Rise of Book Publishing"; McGill, *Culture of Reprinting*.

49. *Catalogue of Novels and Romances Being Part of an Extensive Collection for Sale by M. Carey and Son* (c.1818). Photocopy at the Library Company of Philadelphia. Jane Austen and Walter Scott are listed anonymously.

50. Green, "The Rise of Book Publishing," 75.

51. William Charvat, *Literary Publishing in America, 1790–1830* (Philadelphia: University of Pennsylvania Press, 1959), 18.

52. Michael Winship, "The Transatlantic Book Trade and Anglo-American literary Culture in the Nineteenth Century," in *Reciprocal Influences: Literary Production, Distribution, and Consumption in America*, ed. Steven Fink and Susan S. Williams (Columbus: Ohio University Press, 1999), 119.

53. McGill, *Culture of Reprinting*; see also Trish Loughran, *The Republic in Print: Print Culture in the Age of U.S. Nation Building, 1770–1870* (New York: Columbia University Press, 2007), and *A History of the Book in America*, vol. 2, ed. Gross and Kelley.

54. In 1800, England's population was 8.6 million, compared to 5.2 million in the United States, while in 1830, England's was 13.2 million compared to 12.9 million in the

United States (figures summarized in St. Clair, 453–454). Lee Sotlow and Edward Stevens remark about the United States that "a 25 percent illiteracy rate at the opening of the nineteenth century is quite likely," an estimate much higher than England's even half a century later. *The Rise of Literacy and the Common School in the United States: A Socioeconomic Analysis to 1870* (Chicago: University of Chicago Press, 1981), 39.

55. Joel Porte, *The Romance in America: Studies in Cooper, Poe, Hawthorne, Melville, and James* (Middletown, CT: Wesleyan University Press, 1969), 6.

56. Mathew Carey, *Autobiography*, in *The New England Magazine* (February 1834): 101.

57. St. Clair, 632.

58. Ian Duncan, *Scott's Shadow: The Novel in Romantic Edinburgh* (Princeton, NJ: Princeton University Press, 2007), xi.

59. Richard Altick, *The English Common Reader: A Social History of the Mass Reading Public, 1800–1900* (Chicago: University of Chicago Press, 1957), 267–269.

60. Jane Millgate, "Archibald Constable and the Problem of London: 'Quite the Connection We Have Been Looking For,'" *Library* 18 (1996): 112.

61. Ross Alloway, "Agencies and Joint Ventures," in *The Edinburgh History of the Book in Scotland*, vol. 3, ed. Bell, 10; Simon Eliot, "Appendix B: Statistical Evidence for the 1825–6 Crisis," in *The Edinburgh History of the Book in Scotland*, vol. 3, ed. Bell, 492.

62. See Alloway, "Agencies and Joint Ventures."

63. Millgate, "Archibald Constable and the Problem of London," 112.

64. Letter from William Blackwood to Thomas Cadell, March 5, 1822, National Library of Scotland, MS 30301, p. 275 (copy); cited in "Publishing Papers" for John Gibson Lockhart, *Some Passages in the Life of Mr Adam Blair Minister of the Gospel at Cross-Meikle* (1822); P. D. Garside, J. E. Belanger, and S. A. Ragaz, *British Fiction, 1800–1829: A Database of Production, Circulation & Reception*, designer A. A. Mandal (http://www.british-fiction. cf.ac.uk [accessed July 6, 2013]), 1822A054. Hereafter cited as *DBF*.

65. *Analectic Magazine* (October 1813): 350.

66. St. Clair, 195.

67. Longman published Mary Brunton, James Hogg, Christian Johnstone, Charles Maturin, Thomas Moore, Sydney Owenson, Jane Porter, and Scott; John Murray published Brunton, Cooper, Irving, and Scott; Henry Colburn published Cooper, Owenson, Maturin, and John Galt; Thomas Cadell (or with his partner Davies) published Galt, Johnstone, Elizabeth Hamilton, Susan Ferrier, and John Gibson Lockhart; Richard Phillips published Galt and Owenson; Simpkin and Marshall published Banim and Scott; and Joseph Johnson and his successors published Edgeworth (list culled from various author records in *DBF* [accessed July 5, 2013]).

68. Given in "Publishing Papers" for Sydney Owenson's *O'Donnel* (1814) and *The O'Briens and the O'Flahertys* (1827), *DBF* (accessed July 6, 2013), 1814A045, 1827A056.

69. Butler, *Maria Edgeworth: A Literary Biography* (Oxford: Clarendon Press, 1972), 492.

70. Ben McClary, *Washington Irving and the House of Murray* (Knoxville: University of Tennessee Press, 1969), 215.

71. On Murray splitting the profits for *The Pioneers*, see James Franklin Beard,

"Historical Introduction" to *The Pioneers* (Albany: State University of New York Press, 1980), xxxix–xl; Colburn paid Cooper £200 for *The Prairie* and £300 for *Red Rover*, both in 1827; given in "Publishing Papers" for *The Prairie* and *Red Rover*, respectively, *DBF* (accessed July 6, 2013]), 1827A025, 1827A026. On the 1830 deal for *The Bravo* and *The Heidenmauer*, see James Franklin Beard, *James Fenimore Cooper: Letters and Journals*, vol. 2 (Cambridge, MA: Harvard University Press, 1960), 47, 52–53. Regarding payment for his revised editions, see Chapter 5, this volume.

72. Given in "Publishing Papers" for Susan Ferrier's *The Inheritance* (1824) and John Gibson Lockhart's *Renigald Dalton* (1823), *DBF* (accessed July 6, 2013), 1824A033, 1823A055.

73. Given in "Publishing Papers" for *Rob Roy, Tales of My Landlord, Second Series*, and *Ivanhoe*, *DBF* (accessed November 24, 2014), 1818A055, 1818A056, 1820A061; Jane Millgate, "Making It New: Scott, Constable, Ballantyne, and the Publication of *Ivanhoe*," *Studies in English Literature* 34.4 (1994): 807.

74. In endpapers to the first volume of *St. Alban's Abbey*, in *The Poetical Works of Anne Radcliffe* (London: Henry Colburn, 1834), n.p. See also Connolly, "The National Tale, 1800–1829," 404.

75. "Prospectus of an Uniform Edition of Maria Edgeworth," endpapers dated "January, 1832," in the back pages of the *Edinburgh Review* (December 1831).

76. On the relationship between Scott's *Magnum Opus* and the Standard Novels, see Jane Millgate, *Scott's Last Edition: A Study in Publishing History* (Edinburgh: University of Edinburgh Press, 1987).

77. *The Spectator* (March 29, 1834): 308.

78. Scott E. Casper, "Introduction" to *The Industrial Book: 1840–1880*, ed. Casper et al., vol. 3 of *A History of the Book in America*, 5 vols. (Chapel Hill: University of North Carolina Press, 2007), 4. See also Michael Winship, "The National Book Trade System: Part I, Distribution and the Trade," in *The Industrial Book: 1840–1880*, ed. Casper, 117–130; McGill, *Culture of Reprinting*; Loughran, *The Republic in Print*; and Lara Langer Cohen, *The Fabrication of American Literature: Fraudulence and Antebellum Print Culture* (Philadelphia: University of Pennsylvania Press, 2012), 10–13.

79. Eric Lupfer, "Periodicals and Serial Publications: Part 2, The Business of American Magazines," *The Industrial Book: 1840–1880*, ed. Casper et al., 248–258.

80. Altick, 384.

81. Henry James, *Hawthorne* (London: Macmillan, 1879), 111.

82. Bill Bell, "Introduction," in *Ambition and Industry: 1800–1880*, ed. Bill Bell (Edinburgh: Edinburgh University Press, 2007), *The Edinburgh History of the Book in Scotland*, vol. 3, 11.

83. Ibid.

84. David Finkelstein, *The House of Blackwood: Author-Publisher Relations in the Victorian Era* (University Park: Pennsylvania State University Press, 2002), 11.

85. Connolly, "The National Tale, 1800–1829," 402.

86. Many thanks to Kate Marshall for discussing digital media with me.

CHAPTER 2

1. On London and Constable, see Jane Millgate, "Archibald Constable and the Problem of London: 'Quite the Connection We Have Been Looking For,'" *Library* 18 (1996): 110–123; on the Careys and London, see David Kaser, *Messrs. Carey & Lea of Philadelphia: A Study in the History of the Book Trade* (Philadelphia: University of Pennsylvania Press, 1957).

2. On Scott's effect on U.S. publishers, see James N. Green, "The Rise of Book Publishing," in *A History of the Book in America*, vol. 2: *An Extensive Republic: Print, Culture and Society in the New Nation, 1790–1840*, ed. Robert Gross and Mary Kelley (Chapel Hill: University of North Carolina Press, 2010), 107–109.

3. J. O. Robinson to Constable, June 1, 1825, National Library of Scotland, MS 326, fol. 433 (hereafter cited as NLS).

4. This case study has depended on new archival research and a synthesis of the work of book historians and bibliographers who, working in discrete national traditions, have established some of the facts but have not aggregated them or accounted for their full significance. Jane Millgate, "Archibald Constable and the Problem of London" and "Making It New: Scott, Constable, Ballantyne, and the Publication of *Ivanhoe*," *Studies in English Literature* 34.4 (1994): 795–811; David Kaser, *Messrs. Carey & Lea*, esp. 91–116, and "Waverley in America," *Papers of the Bibliographical Society of America* 51 (1957): 163–167; William B. Todd and Ann Bowden, *Sir Walter Scott: A Bibliographical History* (New Castle, DE: Oak Knoll Press, 1998); James N. Green, "Ivanhoe in America," *Annual Report of the Library Company of Philadelphia for the Year 1994* (1995): 8–14; David Randall, "Waverley in America," *Colophon* 1.1 (1935): 39–55; and Earl Bradsher, *Mathew Carey: Editor, Author and Publisher: A Study in American Literary Development* (New York: Columbia University Press, 1912).

5. Michael Everton, *The Grand Chorus of Complaint: Authors and the Business Ethics of American Publishing* (New York: Oxford University Press, 2011).

6. Everton, *Grand Chorus of Complaint*; Robert Spoo, *Without Copyrights: Piracy, Publishing, and the Public Domain* (New York: Oxford University Press, 2013); Melissa J. Homestead and Camryn Hansen, "Susanna Rowson's Transatlantic Career," *Early American Literature* 45.3 (2010): 619–654.

7. Scott to James Ballantyne, qtd. in Millgate, "Making It New," 807.

8. Information in this paragraph has been drawn from Millgate, "Making It New" and "Problem of London."

9. Carey & Son to Longman & Co., April 5, 1817, qtd. in Bradsher, 79.

10. Constable to Scott, May 31, 1822, qtd. in Todd and Bowden, 561. Information in this paragraph has been drawn from Kaser, *Messrs. Carey & Lea*, 91–116.

11. Constable to Robinson & Co., October 8, 1818, qtd. in Millgate, "Problem of London," 118.

12. Information in this paragraph has been drawn from Millgate, "Problem of London," and Kaser, *Messrs. Carey & Lea*.

13. Constable & Co. to Hurst, Robinson, February 23, 1819, NLS MS 790, p. 377.

14. Constable & Co. to Hurst, Robinson, March 31, 1819, NLS, MS 790, p. 430.

15. Qtd. in Todd and Bowden, 495.

16. Robert Cadell to Archibald Constable, December 10, 1819, NLS MS 323, fol. 116r: "The American Copy [of *Ivanhoe*] went to Liverpool this evening." Constable also used the term when writing to Hurst, Robinson: "The American copy of the 3rd Tales of my Land-lord" (September 1, 1819, NLS, MS 23618, fol. 134r–v).

17. Kaser, *Messrs. Carey & Lea*; Green, "Ivanhoe in America"; Todd and Bowden, *Sir Walter Scott.*

18. Cadell to Constable, April 22, 1822, NLS, MS 323, fol. 233. Earlier, Cadell had writ-ten, "There cannot be doubt of the benefit we will derive from the sale of the Supp[lement to the *Encyclopedia Brittanica*] for the American Market" (Cadell to Constable, December 15, 1817, NLS, MS 322, fol. 230), and, a week later, of other books, "there is a chance of selling a large number of both in America" (Cadell to Constable, December 22, 1817, NLS, MS 322, fol. 246v).

19. Kaser, working with sources at the Historical Society of Pennsylvania, understand-ably misidentified the Edinburgh correspondent as Archibald Constable, whose name ap-pears as the signatory on the letter. My consultation with the Constable archives at the National Library of Scotland demonstrates that Robert Cadell was writing on behalf of Constable and the firm. The handwriting is clearly Cadell's, not Constable's; at the time the letter was written and dated from Edinburgh, Constable was in England, where he had gone for his health, and Cadell wrote repeatedly to Constable about his correspondence with America—a series of exchanges, as we will also see, to which Constable himself re-mained somewhat oblivious. On July 11, 1822, Constable wrote to Walter Scott, "I have now been a year in England" (NLS, MS 677, fol. 72r). Kaser discusses the exchange between Carey's and Constable's firms in "Waverley in America" and *Messrs. Carey & Lea*, 102–104.

20. Robert Cadell, writing for Constable & Co., to Messrs. Carey & Son, April 27, 1822, archived under Archibald Constable, Lea & Febiger Collection [0227B], Historical Society of Pennsylvania (hereinafter cited as HSP).

21. Ibid.

22. Ibid.

23. H. C. Carey & I. Lea to Archibald Constable, June 8, 1822, *Letter Books*, vol. 1, Lea & Febiger Collection [0227B], HSP. The original of this letter does not survive in the Constable archives at the National Library of Scotland.

24. Everton, 32.

25. H. C. Carey & I. Lea to Archibald Constable, June 8, 1822, *Letter Books*, vol. 1, Lea & Febiger Collection [0227B], HSP.

26. Ibid.

27. Cadell to Constable, April 18, 1822, NLS, MS 323, fol. 244r.

28. Constable to Cadell, April 20, 1822, NLS, MS 319, fol. 322v–323r.

29. Constable & Co. to Hurst, Robinson, February 2, 1820, NLS, MS 23619, fol. 1–2. A similar note is included with the advance sheets of *Rob Roy*, which, as Cadell assured Constable, were sent to London "sealed up and marked not to be opened in England" (Cadell to Constable, December 19, 1817, NLS, MS 322, fol. 238r). This comment about the *Monastery* demonstrates that Hurst, Robinson was granted the American copies even when they did not act as publishers (cf. Todd and Bowden, 518, who speculate otherwise).

30. See Kaser, *Messrs. Carey & Lea*, 95–102, for a discussion of the errors in these two novels.

31. *Boston Daily Advertiser*, July 23, 1822; emphases in original.

32. *National Gazette and Literary Register*, July 31, 1822.

33. Ibid.

34. Robert Cadell, writing for Constable & Co., to Carey & Sons, July 24, 1822, archived under Archibald Constable, Lea & Febiger Collection [0227B], HSP.

35. Ibid.

36. Constable to Cadell, July 2, 1822, NLS, MS 320, 46v.

37. Kaser, "Waverley in America."

38. On July 3, 1822, Cadell wrote to W. B. Gilley, of New York, politely refusing an offer for advance sheets ("we have arrangements with your shores for early copies of the Works of the Author of Waverley published by us"), and on July 24, 1822, Cadell wrote to Isaiah Dobson with a similar message (NLS, MS 791, 576–77; NLS, MS 791, 591). These refusals survive as transcriptions in Constable letterbooks, but unfortunately, the original offers from Gilley and Dobson do not.

39. John Miller to Carey & Son, September 24, 1822; qtd. in Bradsher, 129.

40. Carey & Son to John Miller, January 31, 1823; qtd. in Bradsher, 129–130.

41. For Carey's preference of Liverpool over London, see Carey & Son to John Miller, June 17, 1823; qtd. in Bradsher, 85. *Quentin Durward* (1823) was sent through Miller in London, as this chapter shows. Correspondence at the National Library of Scotland indicates that a number of Scott's later works, including *Chronicles of the Cannongate* (1827), *Tales of a Grandfather* (1828), and *Anne of Geierstien* (1829), were also sent through Miller in London.

42. *National Gazette and Literary Register*, July 28, 1823.

43. Constable to Cadell, May 8, 1823, NLS, MS 320, fol. 103r.

44. J. O. Robinson to Constable, May 3, 1823, NLS, MS 326, fol. 319v–320r; emphases in original.

45. Ibid., fol. 319r; emphasis in original.

46. Cadell to Constable, May 8, 1823, NLS, MS 323, fol. 394r, v.

47. Cadell to Constable, May 12, 1823, NLS, MS 323, fol. 395r, v, 396r, v; emphases in original.

48. Constable to Cadell, May 15, 1823, NLS. MS 320, fol. 105.

49. Walter Scott to Archibald Constable, May 15, 1823, in *The Letters of Sir Walter Scott*, ed. H. J. C. Grierson, 12 vols. (London: Constable, 1932–1937), 7:389; Scott's second comment quoted here was related in Cadell to Constable, May 19, 1823, NLS, MS 323, fol. 399. After the mid-1820s, things went more smoothly, and once Scott avowed authorship of the Waverley novels in 1826, the Careys' firm dealt with him directly, agreeing to pay £295 for an advance copy of his nine-volume *Life of Napoleon* (1827). Kaser, *Messrs. Carey & Lea*, 42.

50. Todd and Bowden, 720.

51. Qtd. in John C. Francis, comp., *John Francis, Publisher of the Athenaeum: A Literary Chronicle of Half a Century*, vol. 1 (London: Bentley, 1888), 492.

52. Walter Scott, *Tales of My Landlord, Fourth Series* (Edinburgh: Cadell, 1832), xxxvii–xi. Further citations are given parenthetically in the text.

CHAPTER 3

1. Jane Austen, *Pride and Prejudice*, ed. Tony Tanner (New York: Penguin, 1972), 190; hereafter abbreviated *P* and cited parenthetically.

2. Franco Moretti, *Atlas of the European Novel, 1800–1900* (New York: Verso, 1998), 14.

3. This phrase is from *Northanger Abbey* (1818), ed. Marilyn Butler (New York: Penguin, 1995), 174.

4. While some scholars have proposed a more heterogeneous audience for Edgeworth's fiction than an exclusively English one, including "other Anglo-Irish landlords" (Robert Tracy, "Maria Edgeworth and Lady Morgan: Legality Versus Legitimacy," *Nineteenth-Century Fiction* 40.1 [1985]: 1), a broader British audience, or a cosmopolitan audience situated in Britain and the cities of Europe (Marilyn Butler, "General Introduction," *Castle Rackrent, Irish Bulls, Ennui*, ed. Jane Desmarais, Tim McLoughlin, and Marilyn Butler [London: Pickering and Chatto, 1999], lxv), I follow the common assumption that Edgeworth's primary addressee was indeed English, as her novels' publication history and narrative structures suggest. The power of an English audience for Sydney Owenson, especially for *The Wild Irish Girl*, remains less disputed. Writing principally of Owenson, Ina Ferris takes "the national tale's address to an English reader" entirely for granted (*The Romantic National Tale and the Question of Ireland* [Cambridge: Cambridge University Press, 2002], 12).

5. Edgeworth fares worse in this tradition than Owenson. For Edgeworth as a conservative member of the Anglo-Irish gentry, see S. B. Egenolf, "Maria Edgeworth in Blackface: Castle Rackrent and the Irish Rebellion of 1798," *ELH* 72.4 (2005): 845–869; Thomas Flanagan, *The Irish Novelists, 1800–1850* (New York: Columbia University Press, 1959); W. J. McCormack, *Ascendancy and Tradition in Anglo-Irish Literary History from 1789 to 1939* (Oxford: Clarendon Press, 1985); and Seamus Deane, *Strange Country: Modernity and Nationhood in Irish Writing Since 1790* (Oxford: Clarendon Press, 1997). For Owenson's more radical politics, see Katie Trumpener, *Bardic Nationalism: The Romantic Novel and the British Empire* (Princeton, NJ: Princeton University Press, 1997); Mary Jean Corbett, *Allegories of Union in Irish and English Writing, 1790–1870* (Cambridge: Cambridge University Press, 2000); and Julia Anne Miller, "Acts of Union: Family Violence and National Courtship in Maria Edgeworth's *The Absentee* and Sydney Owenson's *The Wild Irish Girl*," in *Border Crossings: Irish Women Writers and National Identities*, ed. Kathryn Kirkpatrick (Tuscaloosa: University of Alabama Press, 2000), 13–37. Kevin Whelan summarizes the contrast when he argues that Edgeworth denies modernity to Ireland while Owenson "advances an antiimperial project, narrating the Irish nation as one which had regressed rather than advanced under colonialism" ("Writing Ireland, Reading England," in *The Wild Irish Girl: A National Tale*, ed. Claire Connolly and Stephen Copley [London: Pickering and Chatto, 2000], xx). For a more complicated view of Edgeworth as having conflicted, resistant, or at times cosmopolitan allegiances, see Marilyn Butler, *Maria Edgeworth: A Literary Biography* (Oxford: Oxford University Press, 1972), and "Edgeworth's Ireland: History, Popular Culture, and Secret Codes," *NOVEL: A Forum on Fiction* 34.2 (2001): 267–292; as well as a series of articles by Mitzy Myers: "'Completing the Union': Critical Ennui, the Politics of

Narrative, and the Reformation of Irish Cultural Identity," *Prose Studies* 18 (1995): 41–77; "'Goring John Bull': Maria Edgeworth's Hibernian High Jinks Versus the Imperial Imaginary," in *Cutting Edges: Postmodern Critical Edges in Eighteenth-Century Satire*, ed. James E. Gill (Knoxville: University of Tennessee Press, 1995), 367–394; and "'War Correspondence: Maria Edgeworth and the En-Gendering of Revolution, Rebellion, and Union," *Eighteenth-Century Life* 22.3 (1998): 74–91.

6. *Essay on Irish Bulls*, rev. ed. (London, 1808), 2. Originally published in 1802, the book was cowritten with her father, Richard Lovell Edgeworth.

7. In addition to many of the scholars listed in note 5 above, see also Terry Eagleton, *Heathcliff and the Great Hunger: Studies in Irish Culture* (New York: Verso, 1995); Brian Hollingworth, *Maria Edgeworth's Irish Writing: Language, History, Politics* (New York: St. Martin's, 1999); and James Buzard, *Disorienting Fiction: The Autoethnographic Work of Nineteenth-Century British Novels* (Princeton, NJ: Princeton University Press, 2005).

8. Ina Ferris, *The Romantic National Tale*, and Mary Corbett exemplify the near-universal critical practice of taking the Act of Union as a critical point of departure; see also Tracy; Trumpener; and Myers, "Completing the Union."

9. Her study was the culmination of a revival of interest in the 1990s, a decade in which, as Marilyn Butler has written, "more critical work has appeared on the Anglo-Irish 'national novel' than in any decade since 1800–1810, when, by common consent, the subgenre first appeared" (Butler, "Edgeworth's Ireland," 267).

10. Ferris, *The Romantic National Tale and the Question of Ireland*, 3.

11. Ibid., 1, 154. Ferris focuses more on Owenson than Edgeworth, given the latter's prominence in previous criticism. She traces the genre's evolution from the immediate period after the Union, when Irish writers responded to English-authored travel writing with fictions of encounter, to the more volatile 1820s, as the push for Catholic Emancipation under the leadership of Daniel O'Connell brought a new urgency to Irish fiction (as proscriptive rather than reactive), revitalized debates about the 1798 rebellion, and paradoxically brought the genre of the national tale to the brink of dissolution. Claire Connolly's recent book, *A Cultural History of the Irish Novel, 1790–1829* (Cambridge: Cambridge University Press, 2012), extends Ferris's project of a careful historicist readings of the period's fiction.

12. Scott elaborated upon his debt to Edgeworth in the 1829 "General Preface" to the Waverley novels. The connection between Irish and Scottish literature was obvious in the early nineteenth century. Ina Ferris's *The Achievement of Literary Authority* (Ithaca, NY: Cornell University Press, 1992) powerfully argued for the importance of Edgeworth to Scott, and Peter Garside's seminal essay, "Popular Fiction and National Tale: Hidden Origins of Scott's Waverley," *Nineteenth-Century Literature* 4.1 (1991): 30–53, established the importance of Owenson. Katie Trumpener's subsequent *Bardic Nationalism* made a broad case for the powerful connections between Irish and Scottish fiction of the Romantic period, a topic that Murray Pittock has revisited in *Scottish and Irish Romanticism* (Oxford: Oxford University Press, 2008). See also R. F. Foster's *Words Alone: Yeats and His Inheritances* (Oxford: Oxford University Press, 2011), which contains an illuminating chapter on Irish-Scottish connections in the early nineteenth century. While Americanists have long, if

reluctantly, acknowledged the importance of Scott in the United States, there exists almost no work on the importance of Edgeworth and Owenson, even though they were both extremely popular and widely read.

13. Maria Edgeworth, *Castle Rackrent and Ennui*, ed. Marilyn Butler (New York: Penguin, 1992), 63; hereafter abbreviated *C* and cited parenthetically. In subsequent editions, the "Glossary" appeared more appropriately after the main text.

14. A number of scholars have recently examined Smith's influence on Edgeworth. See especially Pittock; and Connolly, *A Cultural History of the Irish Novel*. James Chandler briefly discusses Edgeworth in *An Archeology of Sympathy: The Sentimental Mode in Literature and Cinema* (Chicago: University of Chicago Press, 2013). Conversations with Chandler subsequent to a seminar at the "Scottish Romanticism and World Literature" conference in Berkeley in 2006 (called "Edgeworth between Smith and Scott") have been formative to my thinking on this topic.

15. Butler, "General Introduction," vii, xiii.

16. Maria Edgeworth, *The Absentee*, ed. W. J. McCormack (New York: Penguin, 2001), 79; hereafter abbreviated *A* and cited parenthetically.

17. Adam Smith, *The Theory of Moral Sentiments*, ed. Ryan Patrick Hanley (New York: Penguin, 2009), 91; see also 24 and 236; hereafter abbreviated *T* and cited parenthetically. Adam Smith makes a prominent appearance in *Ennui* as the author of *The Wealth of Nations*, a book that one of Glenthorn's Scottish advisors invokes as he tries to teach him about estate management (*Castle Rackrent and Ennui*, ed. Butler, 191).

18. On the limits of Smithian sympathy in Edgeworth's novels, see Pittock, 166–186, and Connolly, *A Cultural History of the Irish Novel*, 100–101. Juliet Shields turns to Smith to discuss the goals of Scottish writers of the late eighteenth and early nineteenth centuries as they addressed England in a way strikingly similar to Edgeworth. "Only by cultivating the self-control necessary to regulate their sensibility could Scots become Britons and transform an unequal union of interests into a harmonious union of sympathies." *Sentimental Literature and Anglo-Scottish Identity, 1745–1820* (Cambridge: Cambridge University Press, 2010), 11–12.

19. Colambre takes the name Evans and describes himself as an "Englishman" (*A*, 131) a term Mr. Burke adopts (*A*, 134). The assumed character Evans, though, lives in Wales, a fact that confuses his driver, Larry Brady (and which confuses some literary scholars): "I heard you're a Welshman, but, whether or no, I am sure you are a jantleman" (*A*, 139). The Welsh residence of Evans/Colambre is apparently calculated to suggest to the Clonbrony tenants that he would not be in regular contact with the landowning class in England: When Mrs. Burke mentions that he might someday "hear this business talked of," Mr. Burke objects: "Mr. Evans lives in Wales, my dear" (*A*, 138).

20. Chandler, *An Archeology of Sympathy*, 169.

21. As many critics have noted, this heroine's name derives from the Irish ballad "Gracey Nugent." Edgeworth's decision to strip her of this resonant name has been the subject of fierce debate; for example, see Butler, "Edgeworth's Ireland," 284–286.

22. Walter Scott, "General Preface," in *Waverley*, ed. Claire Lamont (Oxford: Clarendon Press, 1981), 353.

23. *Monthly Review* (July 1813): 320.

24. For Edgeworth's trip to London, see Butler, *Maria Edgeworth*; Augustus Hare, ed., *The Life and Letters of Maria Edgeworth*, vol. 1 (London, 1894), and Christina Colvin, ed., *Maria Edgeworth: Letters from England, 1813–1844* (Oxford: Clarendon Press, 1971), 1–74.

25. To Mrs. Ruxton, June 1813 (qtd. in Colvin, 72).

26. *Edinburgh Review* (July 1812): 126.

27. While Edgeworth's English novel *Belinda* (1801) met with considerable success and was reprinted in Anna Barbauld's *British Novelists* series in 1810, *Patronage* was a critical failure. While the *Edinburgh* praised *Patronage*, others objected because of its setting outside Edgeworth's known realm of experience in Ireland and, as Ina Ferris has demonstrated, in settings of public life reserved typically for men (*The Achievement of Literary Authority*, 68). Even the *Edinburgh*, however, when reprinting excerpts from *Patronage*, "cannot resist" giving scenes "in which Miss Edgeworth's inimitable talent for pourtraying [*sic*] her poor countrymen is displayed." *Edinburgh Review* (January 1814): 422.

28. *Monthly Review* (July 1813): 320; *Critical Review* (August 1812): 122. The *Quarterly Review* wrote, "Other writers have caught nothing but the general feature" of the Irish; "to Miss Edgeworth's keen observation and vivid pencil, it was reserved to separate the genus into its species and individuals, and to exhibit the most accurate and yet the most diversified views that have ever been drawn of national character" (*Quarterly Review* [June 1812]: 336).

29. *Edinburgh Review* (July 1812): 126; emphasis in original.

30. Jane Austen to Anna Austen, September 28, 1814. *Jane Austen's Letters*, ed. Deirdre Le Faye (Oxford: Oxford University Press, 1995), 278. It is worth nothing that Austen made this comment in the same letter in which she disparaged Scott, just a few sentences earlier: "I do not like him, & do not mean to like Waverley if I can help it—but I fear I must."

31. For *Pride and Prejudice*, see Colvin, 46; for *Mansfield Park* and *Emma*, see Hare, 245, 249.

32. Hare, 239–244.

33. Maria Edgeworth, *Ormond* (New York: Penguin, 2000), 34, 45; hereafter abbreviated *O* and cited parenthetically.

34. Under his breath, Ormond calls White Connal an "Insufferable coxcomb" (131); Edgeworth emphasizes that Ormond's interaction with this character "was useful in forming our hero's character" (127).

35. Alexander Broadie, "Sympathy and the Impartial Spectator," in *The Cambridge Companion to Adam Smith*, ed. Knud Haakonssen (Cambridge: Cambridge University Press, 2006), 172–173.

36. Qtd. in Broadie, 173.

37. Maria Edgeworth, *Harrington*, ed. Susan Manly (Peterborough, Ontario: Broadview, 2004), 67. This preface introduces both *Harrington* and *Ormond*, which were published together.

38. Qtd. in Claire Connolly, "The Politics of Love in The Wild Irish Girl," in *The Wild Irish Girl: A National Tale*, ed. Claire Connolly and Stephen Copley (London: Pickering and Chatto, 2000), lviii.

39. Sydney Owenson, in *The Wild Irish Girl: A National Tale*, ed. Connolly and Copley, 7.

40. Ibid., 249; hereafter abbreviated *W* and cited parenthetically.

41. Robert Tracy influentially called this the "Glorvina solution" (10).

42. Even critics who are skeptical of the allegory agree that any resistance to the unionist allegory registers only on a political level. Ina Ferris notes that *The Wild Irish Girl* "is an imperial romance with a distinctly abrasive edge" (*Romantic National Tale*, 48), as does Julia Miller, who argues that Owenson's "feminism . . . overrides [her] liberal politics and provides an inadvertent critique of the Act of Union itself" (15).

43. Trumpener, 141.

44. On her public performances as Glorvina, see Mary Campbell, *Lady Morgan: The Life and Times of Sydney Owenson* (London: Pandora Press, 1988), and James Newcomer, *Lady Morgan the Novelist* (Lewisburg, PA: Bucknell University Press, 1990); on self-referentiality in Owenson's later fiction, see Ferris, *Romantic National Tale*, 74–101.

45. In the footnotes, we follow Owenson everywhere, from her conversation with a peasant in Westmeath in 1797 (*W*, 88), to a "rural festival" in Tipperary in 1802 (*W*, 139), to a cabin in Sligo that offered her rest in 1804 (*W*, 20), to a "little marine sketch" of Dublin bay in 1805 (*W*, 14), to a letter she received on "July 3d, 1805" regarding the "Bard of Magilligans" (*W*, 193), to a February 1806 offer from that Bard himself to sell her his harp (*W*, 196), and through undated adventures in Westmeath (*W*, 24), Munster (*W*, 60), a barrister's office in Dublin (*W*, 95), the principality of "*Sliabh-Ban*" (*W*, 114), and Connaught itself, where she "play[ed] the Spanish guitar in the hearing of some . . . peasants" (*W*, 68). Like Glorvina, the Owenson of the footnotes sometimes relies on her father for accounts of Irish culture (*W*, 28, 44, 88), and she seems as anxious as the Prince and his household about being taken seriously.

46. In an anecdotal footnote, Owenson describes how a lover of Carolan once interrupted him while composing on the harp; his posture, "alone . . . hung over his harp," directly alludes to Glorvina's own posture when Horatio once interrupts her "alone, and bending over her harp" (*W*, 87, 65).

47. Qtd. in Timothy Costelloe, *The British Aesthetic Tradition: From Shaftesbury to Wittgenstein* (Cambridge: Cambridge University Press, 2013), 86.

48. *Germany; by the Baroness Staël Holstein, Translated from the French*, vol. 1 (New York, 1814), 183.

CHAPTER 4

1. Emphasis added. Washington Irving, *The Sketch Book*, vol. 2 (London, 1820), 346; for the original sentence, see *The Sketch Book*, no. 6 (New York, 1820), 51–52. When quoting from *The Sketch Book*, I will refer to the first New York editions, published by Van Winkle, and the first London edition, published by John Murray and John Miller. The New York editions will be abbreviated thus: *SB* [#] (New York) and the London editions *SB* [#] (London).

2. Washington Irving to Henry Brevoort, May 13, 1820, in Pierre Irving, *The Life and Letters of Washington Irving*, vol. 1, 379.

3. Michael Gilmore provides a different account of *The Sketch Book*'s embrace of the "aesthetic as an autonomous sphere uncontaminated by practical concerns"; see "The Literature of the Revolutionary and Early National Periods," in *The Cambridge History of American Literature*, vol. 1, ed. Sacvan Bercovitch (New York: Cambridge University Press, 1994), 670.

4. Important studies of Irving's *The Sketch Book* and American culture include Michael Warner, "Irving's Posterity," *ELH* 67 (2000); Jeffrey Rubin-Dorsky, *Adrift in the Old World: The Psychological Pilgrimage of Washington Irving* (Chicago: University of Chicago Press, 1988); and William L. Hedges, *Washington Irving: An American Study, 1802–1832* (Baltimore: Johns Hopkins University Press, 1965).

5. Thomas Jefferson to Nathaniel Burwell, March 14, 1818; facsimile reproduced in Andrew Burstein, *Jefferson's Secrets: Death and Desire at Monticello* (New York: Basic Books, 2005), 95.

6. James Fenimore Cooper, review of J. G. Lockhart's *Memoirs of Sir Walter Scott* (1838), qtd. in George Dekker, *American Historical Romance* (New York: Cambridge University Press, 1987), 57. Sedgwick's dedication reads, "To Maria Edgeworth, as a slight expression of the writer's sense of her eminent services in the great cause of human virtue and improvement, this humble tale is respectfully dedicated." *A New-England Tale*, ed. Susan K. Harris (New York: Penguin, 2003), 2.

7. See Chapter 6, this volume.

8. *Blackwoods Edinburgh Magazine* (July 1820): 368–369. Emphasis in original.

9. See Sir Walter Greg, "The Rationale of Copy-text," *Studies in Bibliography* 3 (1950–1951): 19–36, and Fredson Bowers, *Bibliography and Textual Criticism* (Oxford: Clarendon Press, 1964). The Greg-Bowers theory of final intentions has been aggressively criticized by Jerome McGann, *A Critique of Modern Textual Criticism* (Chicago: University of Chicago Press, 1983). Most major American authors are still read in editions that follow the Greg-Bowers method, including Irving, James Fenimore Cooper, Ralph Waldo Emerson, Henry Thoreau, Nathaniel Hawthorne, Herman Melville, Mark Twain.

10. Meredith McGill, *American Literature and the Culture of Reprinting, 1834–1853* (Philadelphia: University of Pennsylvania Press, 2003), 39.

11. Besides McGill, other important works in American studies that emphasize materiality over authorship include Cathy Davidson, *The Revolution and the Word: The Rise of the Novel in America* (Oxford: Oxford University Press, 1986); Michael Warner, *The Letters of the Republic: Publication and the Public Sphere in Eighteenth-Century America* (Cambridge, MA: Harvard University Press, 1990); Patricia Crain, *The Story of A: The Alphabetization of America from* The New England Primer *to* The Scarlet Letter (Stanford, CA: Stanford University Press, 2000); Matthew Brown, *The Pilgrim and the Bee: Reading Rituals and Book Culture in Early New England* (Philadelphia: University of Pennsylvania Press, 2007); Trish Loughran, *The Republic in Print: Print Culture in the Age of U.S. National Building, 1770–1870* (New York: Columbia University Press, 2007); Leon Jackson, *The Business of Letters: Authorial Economies in Antebellum America* (Stanford, CA: Stanford University Press,

2008); and Lara Langer Cohen, *The Fabrication of American Literature: Fraudulence and Antebellum Print Culture* (Philadelphia: University of Pennsylvania Press, 2012). See also David Hall, ed., *A History of the Book in America*, 5 vols. (Chapel Hill: University of North Carolina Press, 2000–2010).

12. Pierre Bourdieu, *The Field of Cultural Production*, ed. Randal Johnson (New York: Columbia University Press, 1993), 30.

13. On residence requirements for copyright, see Clarence Gohdes, *American Literature in Nineteenth Century England* (Carbondale: Southern Illinois University Press, 1944), 16–17, and Meredith McGill, "Copyright," in *An Extensive Republic: Print, Culture and Society in the New Nation, 1790–1840*, ed. Robert Gross and Mary Kelley (Chapel Hill: University of North Carolina Press, 2010), 189–211. It wasn't until the mid-1850s that an American author's physical presence in England was required to secure copyright.

14. Gohdes, 15.

15. Letter to James Brown, dated April 1800, in William Dunlap, *The Life of Charles Brockden Brown*, vol. 2 (Philadelphia, 1815), 100, qtd. in S. W. Reid, "Textual Essay," in *Wieland; or, The Transformation: An American Tale* (Kent, OH: Kent State University Press, 1977), 350n1. Thanks to Melissa Homestead for alerting me to Brown's role in these London editions.

16. S. W. Reid, "Textual Essay," in *Ormond; Or, The Secret Witness* (Kent, OH: Kent State University Press, 1982), 344. *Wieland* was issued in 1811 by Henry Colburn. For more on Brown's transatlantic editions, see S. W. Reid, "Brockden Brown in England: Notes on Henry Colburn's 1822 Editions of His Novels," *Early American Literature* 9.2 (Fall 1974): 188–195.

17. I discuss Cooper's involvement with his London editions in Chapter 5, this volume. Cooper published his first novel, *Precaution*, in an authorized London edition in 1821, but that book met with little success; see Wayne Franklin, *James Fenimore Cooper: The Early Years* (New Haven, CT: Yale University Press, 2007), 240–269. His second novel, *The Spy*, was pirated in London and was very popular; all of Cooper novels after *The Spy* received authorized editions.

18. See Melissa Homestead, "American Novelist Catharine Sedgwick Negotiates British Copyright, 1822–1857," *Yearbook of English Studies* 45 (forthcoming), and "Introduction" to Catharine Maria Sedgwick, *Clarence* (Peterborough, Ontario: Broadview, 2011). On Neal, see Joshua Ratner, "John Neal, Novelist or Journal Editor," in "American Paratexts" (Ph.D. diss., University of Pennsylvania, 2010).

19. William B. Cairns, "British Republication of American Writings, 1783–1833," *PMLA* 43.1 (1928): 310.

20. Amanda Claybaugh, *The Novel of Purpose: Literature and Social Reform in the Anglo-American World* (Ithaca, NY: Cornell University Press, 2007), 3.

21. Gohdes, 14–46.

22. Camryn Hansen, "A Changing Tale of Truth: *Charlotte Temple*'s British Roots," in *Charlotte Temple*, ed. Marion L. Rust (New York: Norton, 2011), 183–189. See also Homestead and Hansen, "Susanna Rowson's Transatlantic Career," *Early American Literature* 45.3 (2010): 619–654.

23. See *Clotel: An Electronic Scholarly Edition* (Charlottesville: University of Virginia Press, 2010), http://rotunda.upress.virginia.edu/clotel/.

24. For a comprehensive account of the composition and textual history of *Moby-Dick*, see the Northwestern-Newberry edition of *Moby-Dick*, ed. Hershel Parker (Evanston and Chicago: Northwestern University Press and the Newberry Library, 1988), 581–808. John Bryant and Haskell Springer's recent Longman edition of *Moby-Dick* makes the novel's complicated textual history available to readers by reprinting the American text; highlighting places where it was revised for Bentley, including all substantive changes; and providing extended "revision narratives" to explain each site of textual difference. While this edition is invaluable for the way it provides access to both versions of the text, Bryant and Springer engage in a guessing game when in their "revision narratives," they attribute changes to Melville or the British publisher. We simply do not know what Melville did to the novel in the six weeks he had the American proofs. For further discussion of the textual histories of Melville's novels, including *Typee* and *Moby-Dick*, see John Bryant, *Melville Unfolding: Sexuality, Politics, and The Versions of* Typee, *A Fluid-Text Analysis, with an Edition of the* Typee *Manuscript* (Ann Arbor: University of Michigan Press, 2008), and "Rewriting *Moby-Dick*: Politics, Textual Identity, and the Revision Narrative," *PMLA* 125.4 (2010): 1043–1060.

25. See Rubin-Dorsky, *Adrift in the Old World*; Gilmore, "The Literature of the Revolutionary and Early National Periods"; Hedges, *Washington Irving*; Andrew Burstein, *The Original Knickerbocker: The Life of Washington Irving* (New York: Basic Books, 2007); Henry A. Pochmann, "Washington Irving: Amateur or Professional?" in *Critical Essays on Washington Irving*, ed. Ralph M. Aderman (Boston: G. K. Hall & Co., 1990); and Stanley T. Williams, *The Life of Washington Irving*, vol. 1 (New York: Oxford University Press, 1935).

26. Edward Cahill, *Liberty of the Imagination: Aesthetic Theory, Literary Form, and Politics in the Early United States* (Philadelphia: University of Pennsylvania Press, 2012), 202.

27. See *Analectic Magazine* (November 1814): 433–434. Further citations for the *Analectic* will appear parenthetically in the text. I have followed the Twayne edition in attributing individual *Analectic* articles to Irving; see *Miscellaneous Writings, 1803–1859*, ed. Wayne R. Kime (Boston: Twayne, 1981).

28. Stanley T. Williams, 141; Irving, qtd. in Williams, 416n70.

29. See Gilmore, "The Literature of the Revolutionary and Early National Periods," and Robert Spiller, *The American Literary Revolution, 1783–1837* (New York: Anchor Books, 1976). Benjamin Spencer marks 1815 as crucial to this shift in *The Quest for Nationality: An American Literary Campaign* (Syracuse, NY: Syracuse University Press, 1957). See also Robert E. Streeter, "Association Philosophy and Literary Nationalism in the *North American Review*, 1815–1825," *American Literature* 17 (1945): 243–254. Theo Davis complicates our understanding of associationist philosophy by arguing that it values not the particularity of national distinctiveness but instead how those distinctions are absorbed, aesthetically, as typical. "Literature of the early national period begins to examine ordinary experience with a new attention to ordinary lives and material details, yet it still aims to fashion widely available types out of such local currency." *Formalism, Experience, and the Making of American Literature* (Cambridge: Cambridge University Press, 2010), 48.

30. The *Analectic* has much in common with the "eclectic" magazines of the 1830s and 1840s that also comprised mostly unauthorized reprints from the British press (see McGill, *Culture of Reprinting*, 26ff.).

31. Gulian Verplank, "Fisher Ames" (April 1814, 328). For the other biographies, see January 1814, 54–61 (Aylwin); May 1814, 382–403 (Ellsworth); and March 1814, 231–241 (Adams).

32. Alison, *The Nature and Principles of Taste* (1790), qtd. in Spiller, 494. Reviews of Greenfield's *Essays on the Sources of the Pleasures Received from Literary Composition* appeared in the *Analectic* in May and August 1814.

33. The *British Review*'s piece on Genlis's *De l'influence des femmes sur la littérature française* appeared in the *Analectic* in February 1813.

34. Washington Irving, "A Biographical Sketch of Thomas Campbell," in *The Poetical Works of Thomas Campbell*, ed. Irving (New York, 1810), xxxvii–xxxviii.

35. See Edwin T. Bowden, *Washington Irving Bibliography* (Boston: Twayne, 1989), 122–126; Williams, *The Life of Washington Irving*, 168–191; Pierre Irving, ed., *The Life and Letters of Washington Irving*, vol. 1 (London, 1862), 273–371; Washington Irving, "Preface to the Revised Edition" (1848), in *History, Tales, and Sketches*, ed. James W. Tuttleton (New York: Library of America, 1983), 737–742. John Miller, who published the first volume of *The Sketch Book*, later printed authorized editions of James Fenimore Cooper and Catharine Maria Sedgwick. As Chapter 2 shows, Miller was as an agent for some American publishers who acquired British books for reprinting.

36. "Preface to the Revised Edition" (1848), in Irving, *History, Tales, and Sketches*, 742.

37. *The Sketch Book* 6 (New York), 5–8. Irving revised most of the first New York texts for second editions before he arranged for London republication. All revisions that I discuss here were introduced in the London texts. I have manually collated the first New York editions against photocopies of the first London editions. For a textual analysis of *The Sketch Book*, see *The Sketch Book*, ed. Haskell Springer (Boston: Twayne Publishers, 1978).

38. *SB* 2 (New York): 101.

39. Ben McClary, *Washington Irving and the House of Murray* (Knoxville: University of Tennessee Press, 1969), viii.

40. Washington Irving to Ebenezer Irving, August 15, 1820, in Pierre Irving, *Life and Letters*, 385.

41. The exceptions, of course, are Irving's modern editors. All of the first seven American numbers are available in digital format through Early American Imprints, Series II.

42. *SB* 2 (London), n.p.

43. All the sketches that appeared in the last American number, including "Westminster Abbey," "The Angler," "Stratford-on-Avon," and "Little Britain," may have been written after Scott convinced Murray to become Irving's publisher. The texts of these sketches, first published in London, were not subsequently revised for the New York text.

44. *SB* 2 (London): 3.

45. Ibid., 8.

46. Ibid., 9–10.

47. *SB* 6 (New York): 25; *SB* 2 (London): 295.

48. *SB* 6 (New York): 25; *SB* 2 (London): 295. Emphasis added.

49. *SB* 6 (New York): 26–27; *SB* 2 (London): 297.

50. *SB* 5 (New York): 426; *SB* 2 (London): 110.

51. *SB* 2 (London): 296–297.

52. As Lawrence Buell has suggested, the sketch as a whole "cast[s] the British rather than the American as the simpleton." See his "Nineteenth-Century Transatlantic (Mis) Understandings," in *Transatlantic Traffic and (Mis)Translations*, ed. Robin Peel and Daniel Maudlin (Lebanon: University of New Hampshire Press, 2013), 8.

53. *SB* 2 (London): 307.

54. Ibid., 45, 110.

55. Ibid., 110.

56. Ibid., 110–111, 115, 117–119, 131–133.

57. Ibid., 114, 115, 118, 130.

58. Ibid., 134.

59. Ibid., 306–307.

60. *SB* 5 (New York): 349.

61. In "The Pride of the Village," Irving also deletes a footnote from the New York text that cross-referenced an earlier number of *The Sketch Book* (*SB* 6 [New York]: 34).

62. *SB* 2 (London): 70, 88. In the New York text, Master Simon imitates unnamed "the opera dancers," and Irving leaves the reference to Markham's conduct book *Country of Contentments* unexplained (*SB* 5 [New York]: 386, 406–407).

63. *SB* 5 (New York): 355–356.

64. *SB* 2 (London): 318–319.

65. *SB* 6 (New York): 104; *SB* 2 (London): 398.

66. *SB* 2 (London): 359, 412.

67. *SB* 6 (New York): 114; *SB* (London): 407.

68. *SB* 6 (New York): 54; *SB* 2 (London): 348. Emphasis added.

69. *SB* 6 (New York): 56; *SB* 2 (London): 350.

70. Washington Irving to Henry Brevoort, May 13, 1820, in *Life and Letters*, 379.

71. *SB* 2 (New York): 114.

72. *SB* 2 (London): 225.

73. Ibid., 216.

74. Ibid., 234.

75. Ibid., 229.

76. Ibid., 255.

77. Ibid., 134, 234.

78. Ibid., 118.

79. Ibid., 415–418.

80. Leslie Fiedler, *Love and Death in the American Novel* (New York: Criterion, 1960), 26, 341.

81. Irving, *History, Tales, and Sketches*, 779. In this concluding section, I quote from the Library of America edition, which reprints the Twayne edition, because Irving did not revise any of the passages I discuss.

82. Ibid., 808. For the Edgeworth quotation, see *Essay on Irish Bulls*, rev. ed. (London, 1808), 2.

83. Irving, *History, Tales and Sketches*, 813, 810.

84. Ibid., 814.

85. Washington Irving to Henry Brevoort, August 15, 1820, in Pierre Irving, *Life and Letters*, 385.

86. John Murray to Washington Irving June 29, 1821, qtd. in McClary, 36. For the review itself, see *Quarterly Review* (April 1821): 50–67.

87. *Quarterly Review* (April 1821): 50, 51.

88. Ibid., 67.

89. Ibid., 53.

90. John Murray published Walter Scott's *Tales of My Landlord, First Series* in 1816, which contained the novel *Old Mortality*. Murray notoriously allowed Scott to write an anonymous review of his own Waverley novels in the *Quarterly* (January 1817).

91. Warner, "Irving's Posterity," 790.

CHAPTER 5

1. William Cullen Bryant, "Discourse on the Life, Genius, and Writings of James Fenimore Cooper," in *Precaution: A Novel*, new ed. (New York: Hurd and Houghton, 1871), 7. For the first English review of *Precaution*, see *Gentleman's Magazine*, April 1821, 345.

2. Bryant, 345.

3. James Fenimore Cooper, *The Spy: A Tale of Neutral Ground*, ed. James P. Elliot (New York: AMS Press, 2002), 15.

4. Cooper, *The Spy*, 15; Cooper, *Precaution*, rev. ed. (London: Colburn & Bentley, 1839), v. For a detailed narrative of Cooper's involvement with the publication of *Precaution*, see Wayne Franklin, *James Fenimore Cooper: The Early Years* (New Haven, CT: Yale University Press, 2007), 240–269.

5. William B. Todd and Ann Bowden, *Sir Walter Scott: A Bibliographical History, 1796–1832* (New Castle, DE: Oak Knoll Press, 1998), 502–506. The theatrical adaptations included *Ivanhoe; or, The Jew's Daughter*, by Thomas Dibdin, which premiered on Drury Lane on January 20, 1820; *The Hebrew, A Drama*, which premiered on Drury Lane on March 2, 1820; and *Ivanhoe; or, The Knight Templar, A Musical Drama*, which premiered the same night at Covent Garden; see Henry A. White, *Sir Walter Scott's Novels on the Stage* (New Haven, CT: Yale University Press, 1927), 102–123.

6. James N. Green, "*Ivanhoe* in America," in *The Annual Report of the Library Company of Philadelphia for the Year 1994* (Philadelphia: Library Company of Philadelphia, 1995), 8–14; Todd and Bowden, *Sir Walter Scott*, 509–511.

7. Jane Millgate, *Walter Scott: The Making of a Novelist* (Edinburgh: Edinburgh University Press, 1984); Ina Ferris, *The Achievement of Literary Authority: Gender, History, and the Waverley Novels* (Ithaca, NY: Cornell University Press, 1991); Green, "*Ivanhoe* in America."

8. Walter Scott, "Introduction to *Ivanhoe*" [1830], in *Ivanhoe*, ed. Ian Duncan (Oxford: Oxford University Press, 1996), 12.

9. Scott, "Dedicatory Epistle," ibid., 16–17.

10. On Cooper, see Richard Slotkin, *The Fatal Environment: The Myth of the Frontier in The Age of Industrialization, 1800–1890* (Middletown, CT: Wesleyan University Press, 1986), and Philip Fisher, *Hard Facts: Setting and Form in the American Novel* (New York: Oxford University Press, 1985); and on Scott, see Georg Lukács, *The Historical Novel*, trans. Hannah Arendt and Stanley Mitchell (Lincoln: University of Nebraska Press, 1983), and Ian Duncan, *Modern Romance and Transformations of the Novel: The Gothic, Scott, Dickens* (Cambridge: Cambridge University Press, 1992).

11. Careful readers of Cooper and Scott have subordinated the importance of English readers to other concerns; James Buzard, *Disorienting Fiction: The Autoethnographic Work of Nineteenth-Century British Novels* (Princeton, NJ: Princeton University Press, 2005), is a notable exception to this. On Cooper's myths of American innocence, see R. W. B. Lewis, *The American Adam: Innocence, Tragedy, and Tradition in the Nineteenth Century* (Chicago: University of Chicago Press, 1955). On Cooper's problematic relation to the discourses of race, gender, and nation, see Paul Downes, *Democracy, Revolution, and Monarchism in Early American Literature* (New York: Cambridge University Press, 2002); Jared Gardner, *Master Plots: Race and the Founding of American Literature: 1787–1845* (Baltimore: Johns Hopkins University Press, 1998); Cynthia Jordan, *Second Stories: The Politics of Language, Form, and Gender in Early American Fictions* (Chapel Hill: University of North Carolina Press, 1989); Dana Nelson, *National Manhood: Capitalist Citizenship and the Imagined Fraternity of White Men* (Durham, NC: Duke University Press, 1998); Nancy Ruttenburg, *Democratic Personality: Popular Voice and the Trial of American Authorship* (Stanford, CA: Stanford University Press, 1998); and Ezra Tawil, *The Making of Racial Sentiment: Slavery and the Birth of the Frontier Romance* (Cambridge: Cambridge University Press, 2008). On Scott's role in Scottish literary history, see David Daiches, "Scott's Achievement as a Novelist," *Nineteenth Century Fiction* 6 (1951): 81–95, 153–173; Ian Duncan, *Scott's Shadow: The Novel in Romantic Edinburgh* (Princeton, NJ: Princeton University Press, 2007); and Millgate, *Walter Scott*. On Scott's role in the rise of the novel, historicism, nationalism, and empire in Britain, see James Chandler, *England in 1819: The Politics of Literary Culture and the Case of Romantic Historicism* (Chicago: University of Chicago Press, 1998); Duncan, *Modern Romance*; Ferris, *The Achievement of Literary Authority*; James Kerr, *Fiction Against History: Scott as Storyteller* (Cambridge: Cambridge University Press, 1989); George Levine, *The Realistic Imagination: English Fiction from* Frankenstein *to* Lady Chatterley (Chicago: University of Chicago Press, 1981); Saree Makdisi, *Romantic Imperialism: Universal Empire and the Culture of Modernity* (Cambridge: Cambridge University Press, 1998); Caroline McCraken-Flesher, *Possible Scotlands: Walter Scott and the Story of Tomorrow* (New York: Oxford University Press, 2005); Harry Shaw, *The Forms of Historical Fiction: Sir Walter Scott and his Successors* (Ithaca, NY: Cornell University Press, 1983); and Katie Trumpener, *Bardic Nationalism: The Romantic Novel and the British Empire* (Princeton, NJ: Princeton University Press, 1997).

12. Buzard, *Disorienting Fiction*, 67.

13. The editorial policy of the MLA-approved text of Cooper, *The Writings of James*

Fenimore Cooper, ed. James Franklin Beard (Albany: State University of New York Press, 1980–), privileges the author's final intentions and thus incorporates all of Cooper's later revisions. The text of the Author's Revised Edition (1849–1851), used for the illustrated F. O. Darley edition (1859–1861) was standard until the SUNY edition replaced it. All modern reprints I have seen bow to the authority of SUNY. For a general history of Cooper's texts, see Robert E. Spiller and Philip C. Blackburn, *A Descriptive Bibliography of the Writings of James Fenimore Cooper* (New York: R. R. Bowker, 1934).

14. Scholars of the long eighteenth century have considered the influence of Scottish philosophers on the American educational system and American political thought, Scottish reactions to the American Revolution and constitutional government, strong common roots in dissenting religion, and the importance of literary projects like romantic nationalism and the historical novel. See Robert Crawford, *Devolving English Literature* (Oxford: Clarendon Press, 1992); George Dekker, *The American Historical Romance* (New York: Cambridge University Press, 1987); Owen Dudly Edwards and George Shepperson, eds., *Scotland, Europe, and the American Revolution* (New York: St. Martin's, 1977); Dalphy I. Fagerstrom, "Scottish Opinion and the American Revolution," *William and Mary Quarterly* 11 (1954): 252–275; Andrew Hook, *Scotland and America: A Study of Cultural Relations, 1750–1835* (Glasgow: Blackie, 1975); Susan Manning, *The Puritan-Provincial Vision: Scottish and American Literature in the Nineteenth Century* (Cambridge: Cambridge University Press, 1990); Terrence Martin, *The Instructed Vision: Scottish Common Sense Philosophy and the Origins of American Fiction* (Bloomington: Indiana University Press, 1961); Richard B. Sher and Jeffrey R. Smitten, eds., *Scotland and America in the Age of the Enlightenment* (Princeton, NJ: Princeton University Press, 1990); and Gary Wills, *Inventing America: Jefferson's Declaration of Independence* (New York: Doubleday, 1978).

15. John Clive and Bernard Bailyn, "England's Cultural Provinces: Scotland and America," *William and Mary Quarterly* 11 (1954): 212–213.

16. For example, Ian Dennis invokes the "overpowering national example of England" in his discussion of Irish, Scottish, and American fiction, but his Girardian account fails to treat England as an historical reality. *Nationalism and Desire in Early Historical Fiction* (London: Macmillan, 1997), 1. In a more thorough study, Manning, in *Puritan-Provincial Vision*, subordinates the Scottish and American provincial's fraught psychology to an analysis of puritan struggles with Calvinist theology, while Crawford's comparative discussion considers a shared "aesthetic of eclecticism" (*Devolving English Literature*, 181).

17. Letter from Owen Rees to [John Ballantyne], January 12, 1818. Longman Archives, Longman I, 100, no. 206 (draft), cited in "Publishing Papers" for *Rob Roy* (1817); P. D. Garside, J. E. Belanger, and S. A. Ragaz, *British Fiction, 1800–1829: A Database of Production, Circulation & Reception*, designer A. A. Mandal, http://www.british-fiction.cf.ac.uk (accessed August 5, 2014), 1822A054.

18. John O. Hayden, *Scott: The Critical Heritage* (New York: Barnes & Noble, 1970), 26, 62, 157, 42, 99, 68, 114, 116. These quotations are from reviews published between 1805 and 1817; the last three are from Scott's own unsigned review of the Waverley novels in the *Quarterly* (January 1817).

19. Quotations from *The Ass on Parnassus* and its sequel, *Marmion Feats!*, are taken

from Mathew Carey's 1815 Philadelphia reprint edition. These Scott parodies were extremely popular in the United States, although they were apparently more popular in the mid-Atlantic region than in New England. Boston publishers Bradford and Read, upon receiving this parody from Carey, wrote, "One favor we request—Don't send us any more such books as we have this morning and two or three days since recd to wit—"Jeremiah Quiz"—and [illegible]—for we can do nothing with them, unless give them away—and that we can't well afford. We know that you Philadelphians are pretty quizical; but you ought not to quiz us poor <u>Yankees</u> too hard" (Bradford & Read to Mathew Carey, June 15, 1815, Lea & Febiger Collection [0227B], Historical Society of Pennsylvania).

20. *The Ass on Parnassus*, 24.

21. *Marmion Feats!*, 47–48.

22. Franklin, *James Fenimore Cooper*, 268–269.

23. Ibid., 353–354.

24. John Miller to Benjamin N. Coles, June 15, 1822, in Spiller and Blackburn, *Descriptive Bibliography*, 216. Coles did not tell Cooper that Murray had rejected *The Spy*; instead, he wrote, "I have not yet enquired of Murray or Longman and from what I learn of them it is almost useless to do so" (Benjamin N. Coles to James Fenimore Cooper, June 17, 1822; letter reprinted in Spiller and Blackburn, 217). Both Miller and Whittaker wanted *The Pioneers*, but Coles warned Cooper that "Messrs. Whittaker are men of property but the public prejudice is excited against any work appearing from their press having heretofore produced but few works of merit." Benjamin N. Coles to Cooper, June 17, 1822; letter reprinted in Spiller and Blackburn, 217.

25. On Irving's help with *The Pioneers*, see James Franklin Beard, "Historical Introduction" to *The Pioneers* (Albany: State University of New York Press, 1980), xxviii–xlii.

26. Benjamin N. Coles to Cooper, July 13, 1822, in Spiller and Blackburn, 220.

27. Such a preface did not, in the end, appear in Murray's edition. James Fenimore Cooper to John Murray II, November 29, 1822, in James Fenimore Cooper, *The Letters and Journals of James Fenimore Cooper*, 6 vols., ed. James Franklin Beard (Cambridge, MA: Harvard University Press, 1960), 1:85. John Miller published Cooper's next three novels, *The Pilot* (1824), *Lionel Lincoln* (1826), and *The Last of the Mohicans* (1826).

28. Spiller and Blackburn, 175.

29. James Fenimore Cooper to Henry Colburn, October 17, 1826, Spiller and Blackburn, 223.

30. James Fenimore Cooper to Henry Colburn, March 14, 1831, in *The Letters and Journals of James Fenimore Cooper*, 6 vols., ed. Beard, 2:61.

31. Lukács, 40, 19.

32. Ibid., 50.

33. Ibid., 59.

34. Ibid., 50.

35. Walter Scott, *Waverley*, ed. P. D. Garside (New York: Penguin, 2011), 38.

36. Ibid., 34, 35, 38.

37. Ibid., 35.

38. Ibid., 36

39. Walter Scott, "General Preface," in *Waverley*, ed. Claire Lamont (Oxford: Clarendon Press, 1981), 353.

40. Levine, 15.

41. Ibid., 96–97.

42. Duncan, *Modern Romance*, 5.

43. Buzard, *Disorienting Fiction*.

44. While George Dekker's seminal study of "the Waverley tradition in American fiction" focuses aptly on Scott's historicism and also on Edgeworth as an important precedent for Cooper, I am arguing that London's gravitational pull proved no less influential; Dekker, *American Historical Romance*, 5.

45. *NAR* (April 1825): 269.

46. Ibid., 269.

47. Ibid., 250.

48. Ibid., 250–251.

49. Ibid., 250.

50. Ibid., 272.

51. Millgate compares Bentley's Standard Novels to Scott's Magnum Opus (*Scott's Last Edition*, 99). On the Standard Novels and copyright, see William St. Clair, *The Reading Nation in the Romantic Period* (New York: Cambridge University Press, 2004), 361–365.

52. As discussed above, John Murray published the first London edition of *The Pioneers* in 1823, the year of its New York publication; this English edition varies from the New York edition on which it is based, and while the novel's modern editor assigns about two-thirds of these changes to Cooper, in the absence of external evidence, the origin of the changes remains anybody's guess. Cooper revised *The Pioneers* immediately for two further New York editions in 1823, which Carey, Lea, and Carey used for their stereotyped edition, first issued in 1827. I have manually collated the texts of *The Pioneers* using the first Wiley edition and the first printing of the Bentley edition, both held at the Huntington Library. None of the changes I discuss were introduced into either Murray's first English edition or the early revised American editions. For more information about the textual history of *The Pioneers*, see the textual apparatus in *The Pioneers*, ed. Beard.

53. Cooper, *The Pioneers*, vol. 1 (New York: Charles Wiley, 1823), 1, 36, and Cooper, *The Pioneers* (London: Bentley, 1831), 1, 28. Hereafter abbreviated *W* for the Wiley text and *B* for the Bentley text and cited parenthetically. When appropriate, I provide relevant page numbers for both texts.

54. See "Textual Notes" in Beard's edition (497).

55. Gardner, 90.

56. Slotkin, 85, 100.

57. Changes to the word "heiress" occur mostly in vol. 2 of the Wiley text; see (*W*, 2:13; *B*, 217) (*W*, 2:74; *B*, 264) (*W*, 2:84; *B*, 271) (*W*, 2:89; *B*, 275) (*W*, 2:92; *B*, 277) (*W*, 2:93; *B*, 278) (*W*, 2:124; *B*, 301) (*W*, 2:233; *B*, 387) (*W*, 2:250; *B*, 300) (*W*, 2:254; *B*, 402) (*W*, 2:256; *B*, 403) (*W*, 2:258; *B*, 425).

58. See the Wiley text's uses of the word "maiden" that got cut or changed (*W*, 1:34; *B*,

26) (*W,* 1:130; *B,* 101) (*W,* 1:234; *B,* 181) (*W,* 1:269; *B,* 207) (*W,* 2:13; *B,* 217) (*W,* 2:67; *B,* 259) (*W,* 2:100; *B,* 283) (*W,* 2:121; *B,* 299) (*W,* 2:131; *B,* 307) (*W,* 2:176; *B,* 342) (*W,* 2:270; *B,* 414).

59. In another instance, Le Quois originally addresses Elizabeth in Gallicized English; in the Bentley text, he addresses her completely in French (*W,* 1:10; *B,* 84).

60. Franco Moretti, *Atlas of the European Novel, 1800–1900* (London: Verso, 1998), 37–38.

61. I thus disagree with Shaw, who writes that "nothing is more important about Jeanie Deans than her status as historically other from Scott and from us" (*Forms of Historical Fiction,* 226).

62. Walter Scott, *The Heart of Mid-Lothian,* ed. David Hewitt and Alison Lumsden (Edinburgh: Edinburgh University Press, 2004), 341. Hereafter abbreviated *M* and cited parenthetically by page number.

63. Millgate, *Walter Scott,* 152–153.

64. *Monthly Review* (December 1818): 363.

65. *British Critic* (September 1818): 247; *Gentleman's Magazine* (November 1818): 426.

66. *Monthly Review* (December 1818): 362–363.

67. *London Literary Gazette* (August 8, 1818): 497–500.

68. *British Critic* (September 1818): 247, 260.

69. *Blackwoods Edinburgh Magazine* (August 1821): 6.

70. Thomas Dibdin, *The Heart of Mid-Lothian; Or, the Lily of St. Leonard's* (London, 1819), 57. Dibdin's play premiered on January 13, 1819. Two other famous episodes from the novel, the Porteous riots and Effie's trial, are not dramatized in this play but rather narrated. Dibdin's adaptation was "unanimously showered . . . with heart[y] praises" and ran with full houses for 179 performances in nine months, an unprecedented success for a melodrama in this period (White, 58). Daniel Terry's contemporaneous adaptation ran for only fifteen nights and was a comparative failure, a verdict attributable to its omission of the London narrative, a liberty that *Blackwood's Edinburgh Magazine,* reviewing Terry, declared was "unwarranted" (qtd. in White, 66). In Dibdin's drama, Jeanie's walk to London retains much of the language that makes the parallel between her journey and Scott's artistic project so striking. The Duke tells Jeanie in his library to "speak plainly and boldly"; in the interview with the Queen, he translates Jeanie's use of the term *bittock* before the Queen issues her approving response (Dibdin, 54–56). Dibdin's play also elevated the role of the Duke's personal manager, Archibald, who coordinates all of the Duke's appointments, including the one with the Queen, a direct allusion to Scott's Edinburgh publisher, Archibald Constable. Early theater reviews greatly admired the London episode in Dibdin's play; one review wrote that any objections to the "perpetual change of place" necessitated by following Jeanie from Edinburgh to London "sinks into nothing in the representation" (*Theatrical Inquisitor, and Monthly Mirror,* vol. xiv, 1819, 77). The preface to a reprint of the Dibdin playtext published after an 1828 revival noted that "the scene where [Jeanie] pleads for her sister's cause to Queen Caroline strikes direct to the heart, with all the fervour of affection, and the eloquence of truth." Anon., "Remarks" in *Cumberland's Minor Theatre* (London, n.d. [1828]), 6.

71. Qtd. in Hayden, 226.

72. Lewis, 100.

73. Dekker, *American Historical Romance,* 40.

74. Ruttenburg concurs that moments like this in *The Pioneers* express Cooper's "authorial practice" (*Democratic Personality*, 331).

75. D. H. Lawrence, *Studies in Classic American Literature* (1923; repr. New York: Viking Press, 1968), 47.

76. Scott, "Review of *Emma*" (1815), in *Jane Austen: The Critical Heritage*, ed. B. C. Southam (London: Routledge, 1968), 63.

77. Ibid., 64.

78. Susan Ferrier, *Marriage*, ed. Herbert Foltinek and Kathryn Kirkpatrick (Oxford: Oxford University Press, 2001), 264.

79. Juliet Shields, *Sentimental Literature and Anglo-Scottish Identity, 1745–1820* (Cambridge: Cambridge University Press, 20010), 132.

80. Lockhart writes, in the voice of Peter Morris, "The high terms in which you are pleased to express yourself concerning the specimens of my Letters from Scotland, which have fallen into your hands, are, I assure you, among the most valued testimonies of approbation which have ever come in my way. To receive applause from one's acquaintance is more delightful than to receive it from strangers." John Gibson Lockhart, *Peter's Letters to His Kinsfolk* (London, 1819), ix.

81. Duncan, *Scott's Shadow*, 47.

82. See Shields, 124ff.

83. James Hogg, *The Private Memoirs and Confessions of a Justified Sinner*, ed. John Carey (Oxford: Oxford University Press, 1999), 1.

84. Penny Fielding, *Scotland and the Fictions of Geography* (Cambridge: Cambridge University Press, 2008), 163; Fielding makes this claim in relation to Hogg's stories, not *Confessions*, but her assessment applies here.

85. Walter Scott, *The Antiquary*, ed. David Hewitt (New York: Penguin, 1998), 5.

86. Catherine Maria Sedgwick, *A New-England Tale*, ed. Susan K. Harris (New York: Penguin, 2003), 180–181.

87. The domestic union of Mr. Lloyd's exemplary deportment and Jane Elton's "consciousness of having acted right"—reminiscent of the values Maria Edgeworth propounds in *The Absentee*'s Anglo-Irish marriage—succeeds in the world of the novel only through the exclusion of outsiders, including a French dancing master who's excessively ridiculed and a group of North African Algerians, mentioned anecdotally, whose American hostage "procure[s] his freedom along with some English captives" (Sedgwick, 74, 169).

88. Lydia Maria Child, *Hobomok*, ed. Carolyn L. Karcher (New Brunswick, NJ: Rutgers University Press, 1999), 104.

89. "The clock stood directly before the eyes of Frances, and she turned many an anxious glance at the dial; but the solemn language of the priest soon caught her attention, and her mind became intent upon the vows she was uttering. The ceremony was quickly over, and as the clergyman closed the words of benediction, the clock told the hour of nine. This was the time that Harper had deemed so important, and Frances felt as if a mighty load was at once removed from her heart." James Fenimore Cooper, *The Spy: A Tale of Neutral Ground*, ed. James P. Elliot (New York: AMS Press, 2002), 369.

90. Ibid., 356.

CHAPTER 6

1. Benedict Anderson credits print with establishing a pervasive sense of "empty, homogeneous time" that allows millions of strangers to imagine themselves part of the same community. This sense of simultaneity, Anderson argues, is the precondition for nationalism, the ultimate proof of which lies in a soldier's willingness to "die for such limited imaginings." *Imagined Communities: Reflections on the Origins and Spread of Nationalism* (London: Verso, 1983), 24, 7. On the importance of communication networks more generally, see Karl W. Deutsch, *Nationalism and Social Communication* (Cambridge, MA: MIT Press, 1966). Historians of nationalism have long acknowledged the importance of war, including Linda Colley, *Britons: Forging the Nation* (New Haven, CT: Yale University Press, 1992), and Steven Watts, *The Republic Reborn: War and the Making of Liberal America, 1790–1820* (Baltimore: Johns Hopkins University Press, 1987).

2. See, for example, *The British Atlantic World, 1500–1800*, ed. David Armitage and Michael J. Braddick (New York: Palgrave, 2002); W. M. Verhoeven, ed., *Revolutionary Histories: Transatlantic Cultural Nationalism, 1775–1815* (New York: Palgrave, 2002); and Thomas Bender, *A Nation Among Nations: America's Place in World History* (New York: Hill & Wang, 2006).

3. Roger Chartier, "Texts, Printings, Readings," in *The New Cultural History*, ed. Lynn Hunt (Berkeley: University of California Press, 1989), 156.

4. Bibliographical information from 104 narratives published in London between 1770 and 1832 suggests shifts in public interest about Ireland, Scotland, and the United States. Counting first editions, narratives to Scotland were most frequent in the earliest decades of this period and declined after 1800; narratives to Ireland were infrequent before 1790, increased in the decade after the Union, and fell off sharply in the 1820s; while narratives about the United States increased at a modest rate in the two decades after independence but increased dramatically in the late 1810s and 1820s. The following travel narratives were most important. For Scotland: Samuel Johnson, *A Journey to the Western Islands of Scotland* (1775); John Knox, *A View of the British Empire, More Especially Scotland* (1784); James Boswell, *The Journal of Tour to the Hebrides* (1785); William Gilpin, *Observations Relative Chiefly to the Picturesque* (1789); John Lanne Buchanan, *Travels in the Western Hebrides* (1793); and James Hall, *Travels in Scotland by an Unusual Route* (1807). For Ireland: Thomas Campbell, *A Philosophical Survey of the South of Ireland* (1777); Arthur Young, *A Tour in Ireland* (1780); George Cooper, *Letters on the Irish Nation* (1800); John Carr, *A Stranger in Ireland* (1806); and Edward Wakefield, *An Account of Ireland* (1812). For North America and the United States: William Bartram, *Travels Through North and South Carolina* (1791); Isaac Weld, *Travels Through the States of North America* (1799); Thomas Ashe, *Travels in America Performed in 1806* (London, 1808); John Lambert, *Travels Through Lower Canada, and the United States of North America* (London, 1810); Henry Bradshaw Fearon, *Sketches of America* (1818); Isaac Candler, *A Summary View of America* (1824); Basil Hall, *Travels in North America* (1829); and Frances Trollope, *Domestic Manners of the Americans* (1832).

5. See Matthew Wickman, "Travel Writing and the Picturesque," in *The Edinburgh Companion to Scottish Romanticism*, ed. Murray Pittock (Edinburgh: Edinburgh University

Press, 2011), 61–71; Saree Makdisi, *Romanticism and Imperialism* (Cambridge: Cambridge University Press, 1998), 70–99; Colley, 101–145.

6. See Ina Ferris, *The Romantic National Tale and the Question of Ireland* (Cambridge: Cambridge University Press, 2002).

7. Jane Louise Mesick, *The English Traveller in America, 1785–1835* (New York: Columbia University Press, 1922).

8. Samuel Johnson, *The Journey to the Western Islands Scotland and The Journal of a Tour to the Hebrides*, ed. Peter Levi (New York: Penguin, 1984), 42; George Cooper, *Letters on the Irish Nation: Written during a Visit to that Kingdom, in the Autumn of the Year* 1799 (London, 1800), iv, qtd. in Ferris, *Romantic National Tale*, 27; Isaac Candler, *A Summary View of America* (London, 1824), 349.

9. Penny Fielding, *Scotland and the Fictions of Geography: North Britain, 1760–1830* (Cambridge: Cambridge University Press, 2008); Wickman, "Travel Writing and the Picturesque"; Ferris, *Romantic National Tale*; and Mesick, *The English Traveller in America*. These travel narratives are more akin to the touristic genre James Buzard locates at the center of nineteenth-century definitions of *culture* than the travel narratives of the "contact zone" Mary Louise Pratt critiques as instruments of "imperial meaning-making"—more a matter mild, elite rivalries and inequalities, that is, than of "highly asymmetrical relations of domination and subordination"; James Buzard, *The Beaten Track: European Tourism, Literature, and the Ways to Culture, 1800–1918* (Oxford: Clarendon Press, 1993); Mary Louise Pratt, *Imperial Eyes: Travel Writing and Transculturation* (New York: Routledge, 1992), 4.

10. *The Weekly Magazine, or, Edinburgh Amusement* (February 9, 1775): 204–206. This letter was originally printed in Edinburgh's *Caledonia Mercury*, a newspaper.

11. *Edinburgh Review* (July 1806): 284, 288, 290–291.

12. Maria Edgeworth, *Ennui*, in *Castle Rackrent and Ennui*, ed. Marilyn Butler (New York: Penguin, 1992), 210.

13. Ibid., 221.

14. *Edinburgh Review* (April 1807): 42–43.

15. *The Dublin and London Magazine* (March 1825): 1.

16. *The Irish Magazine* (January 1808): 36.

17. Ibid., 38. I discuss this magazine more fully below.

18. *Hibernia Magazine; and Dublin Monthly Panorama* (January 1810): 22.

19. Washington Irving, *The Sketch-Book of Geoffrey Crayon*, Part I (New York, 1819), 103, 107–108, 101; these quotations are from the first edition. Irving, of course, proved to be the exception to his rule that American "retorts" rarely get published in England.

20. *Port-Folio* (February 1809): 162; "An Oration in Defense of the American Character," reprinted in *Port-Folio* (July 1815): 19.

21. *North American Review* (May 1815): 61, 65.

22. *Quarterly Review*, Boston edition (July 1823): 338–339. An examination of the signatures of the Boston publication indicate that this notice—dated March 1, 1824—was printed on cancels after the original article was pulled from the edition. For the suppressed article, see the London edition of the *Quarterly* (July 1823): 338–370.

23. Isaac Weld, *Travels Through the States of North America, and the Provinces of*

Upper and Lower Canada, During the Years 1795, 1796, and 1797, 4th London edition, 1800. The Library Company's copy of this edition (#3808.O) is listed incorrectly as the third edition in *A Catalogue of the Books Belonging to the Library Company of Philadelphia*, vol. 2 (1835), 727. The marginalia, written in a number of hands, can be confidently dated because many comments were trimmed slightly when the book received a new binding sometime between 1807, when the library acquired the book, and the late 1820s (James N. Green, email correspondence, October 9, 2013). Hereafter abbreviated *W* and cited parenthetically.

24. In response to the comment about milk and fish, one indignant reader declares, "Lie upon Lie!" (*W*, 184), and another writes, with bitter sarcasm, "The heat was so intense one season that the pebble stones, with which the street was paved, were melted and flowed with great impetuosity into the delaware" (*W*, 184).

25. Most of the second-degree marginalia appears to have been inscribed after the new binding (see note 23, above).

26. In 1793, the cost of a share at the Library Company was $40 and annual dues were $2. Members of the general public, however, were "permitted to read in the library without charge." Edwin Wolf, *At the Instance of Benjamin Franklin: A Brief History of the Library Company of Philadelphia, 1731–1976* (Philadelphia: Library Company of Philadelphia, 1995), 23.

27. Isaac Candler, *A Summary View of America*, 1st ed. (1824), listed in Library Company of Philadelphia, *Catalogue*, vol. 2 (1835), 728 (#5899.O). Hereafter abbreviated *C* and cited parenthetically.

28. *Edinburgh Review* (April 1807): 47.

29. *The Belfast Monthly Magazine* (July 31, 1814): 1–4. The article in question was a review of Charles Ingersoll's *Inchiquin, The Jesuit's Letters* (1810), published in the *Quarterly Review* (January 1814): 494–539.

30. Washington Irving, *History, Tales, and Sketches*, ed. James W. Tuttleton (New York: Library of America, 1983), 94.

31. Mathew Carey, *Vindiciae Hibernicae: Or, Ireland Vindicated*, 2nd ed., rev. (Philadelphia, 1823), 165–166.

32. *The New England Magazine* (May 1834): 400.

33. From 1783 to 1820, the Irish comprised 199,300 of the estimated 366,500 total immigrants. Hans-Jürgen Grabbe, "European Immigration to the United States in the Early National Period, 1783–1820," *Proceedings of the American Philosophical Society* 133.2 (June 1989): 194; cited in Alan Taylor, *The Civil War of 1812* (New York: Knopf, 2010), 81, 477n24.

34. David Wilson, *United Irishmen, United States: Immigrant Radicals in the Early Republic* (Ithaca, NY: Cornell University Press, 1998).

35. Taylor, 75–100; see also Edward C. Carter, "A 'Wild Irishmen' Under Every Federalist's Bed: Naturalization in Philadelphia, 1789–1806," *Pennsylvania Magazine of History and Biography* 94 (July 1970): 331–346.

36. R. F. Foster, in *Modern Ireland: 1600–1972* (New York: Penguin, 1988), for example, emphasizes "the importance of the French connection" in his account of the 1790s (286).

37. Kevin Whelan, "The Green Atlantic: Radical Reciprocities Between Ireland and America in the Long Eighteenth Century," in *A New Imperial History: Culture, Identity, and*

Modernity in Britain and the Empire, 1660–1840, ed. Kathleen Wilson (Cambridge: Cambridge University Press, 2004), 230. Whelan's important essay downplays the persistence of transatlantic radical currents in Ireland and America after 1800.

38. Tom Clyde, in *Irish Literary Magazines: An Outline History and Descriptive Bibliography* (Dublin: Irish Academic Press, 2003), writes that Cox's *Irish Magazine* was a "Sectarian" publication and that Sir Robert Peel claimed its purpose was to "ferment a bitter hatred against England" (77).

39. *Walker's Hibernian Magazine* (August 1810): 345–346. See Burke's "Speech on American Taxation" (1774), "Speech on Conciliation with America" (1775), and "Letter to the Sheriffs of Bristol" (1777).

40. Henry Grattan, *The Speeches of the Right Hon. Henry Grattan*, vol. 3 (London, 1822), 302. General Gerard Lake was the instigator in this episode (see Foster, *Modern Ireland*, 276).

41. Grattan, 305–306.

42. Whelan, "The Green Atlantic," 223.

43. *Walker's Hibernian Magazine* (October 1800): 248.

44. Robert Emmet, "Speech from the Dock" (1803), in *Irish Writing: An Anthology of Irish Literature in English, 1789–1939*, ed. Stephan Regan (Oxford: Oxford University Press, 2008), 21, 23. Emmet's speech was printed and reprinted around the Atlantic world throughout the nineteenth century.

45. The *Belfast Monthly Magazine* (1808–1814), edited by the United Irishman William Drennan; *The Irish Magazine* (1807–1815), edited in Dublin by the seditious radical Walter Cox; the pro-British *Ulster Register* (1816–1818); the radical Belfast literary journal *The Rushlight* (1824–825); the politically ambivalent *Dublin Magazine; or, Monthly Memorialist* (1812–1813), *Dublin Examiner* (1816–1817), and *Dublin and London Magazine* (1825–1828); and many other journals of the period covered the American scene.

46. *The Ulster Register* (August 9, 1816).

47. *Belfast Monthly Magazine* (February 1811): 92.

48. See *The Rushlight* (December 10, 17, 24, 1824) for excerpts from these works.

49. *Walker's Hibernian Magazine* (April 1801): n.p.

50. *The Dublin Magazine; or Monthly Memorialist* (November 1812): 25.

51. The few scholars who have written about Cox and the *Irish Magazine* have ignored his interest in America, including a modern anthology that credits the magazine with an important role in Irish nationalism. Brendan Clifford, ed., *The Origins of Irish Catholic Nationalism* (Belfast: Athol Books, 1992). On the *Irish Magazine*, see also Elizabeth Tilley, "Periodicals," in *The Oxford History of the Irish Book*, vol. 4: *The Irish Book in English, 1800–1891*, ed. James H. Murphy (Oxford: Oxford University Press, 2011), 145–149.

52. In 1815, the government offered Cox a pension if he would shut down the *Irish Magazine* and move permanently to America; once in New York, he founded another magazine, *The Exile*, with an equally radically agenda. After *The Exile* failed, Cox became disillusioned with American politics and moved to France in 1820 and then eventually back to Ireland, where the authorities discovered him in 1835 and revoked his pension. Cox died in poverty in 1837. Nancy J. Curtin, "Walter Cox," in *Oxford Dictionary of National*

Biography (Oxford: Oxford University Press, 2004); online edition, January 2008, http://www.oxforddnb.com/view/article/6531 (accessed September 3, 2013).

53. *Irish Magazine* (January 1809): "Preface," 1.

54. *Irish Magazine* (November 1808): 527.

55. *Irish Magazine's* (January 1809): 41–43. In eliding the presence of actual "slaves" in America, Cox absorbs the dominant rhetoric of freedom in the period, which ignored the institution of slavery in its exultation of "freedom."

56. *Irish Magazine* (September 1815): 385.

57. *Dublin Examiner* (July 1816): 195.

58. *Dublin Examiner* (December 1816): 106.

59. Ibid., 114.

60. The book was originally called *Historic Anecdotes and Secret Memoirs of the Legislative Union between Great Britain and Ireland* (London, 1809).

61. *The Dublin Monthly Magazine* (February 1810): 73–74.

62. *Irish Magazine* (February 1815): 95; the original was published in *The Columbia Phoenix* (June 29, 1811).

63. *Irish Magazine* (July 1808): 351–353; for the original notice, see New York's *Public Advertiser* (March 19, 1808).

64. *The Public Advertiser* (New York), March 19, 1808. Side-by-side comparison of the *Public Advertiser* and the *Irish Magazine* indicates this passage was cut from the former, although my attribution of the censorship to Cox himself is (admittedly) speculative.

65. As his editorship continued, Cox printed other accounts of American St. Patrick's Day celebrations. In 1811, the "Hibernian society" of Charleston, South Carolina, saluted "the Memory of Washington," "the People of the United States—'Thy spirit, independence,'" and "the United States of America—the abode of liberty, and the persecuted patriot's asylum." This notice included reports as well from New York and Philadelphia; *Irish Magazine* (June 1811): 257–260.

66. Sarah Isdell, *The Vale of Louisiana*, vol. 2 (Dublin, 1805), 1. The full phrase in vol. 2 is "As in all human probability, my reader is a female." Hereafter cited *V* and cited parenthetically with volume and page number.

67. Claire Connolly is the only scholar I am aware of who has mentioned this novel, in *Cultural History of the Irish Novel, 1790–1829* (Cambridge: Cambridge University Press, 2012), 99–100. In its own time, *The Vale of Louisiana* may have suffered particularly because its publication only in Dublin limited its circulation (no periodicals reviewed it) and because an Irish author writing on an American subject does not fit neatly into a nationalized definition of culture. The book is not digitized and is available only in four libraries worldwide, including the Houghton Library. Isdell's second novel, *The Irish Recluse* (1809), was published in London, reviewed and advertised at the time, and has received modest scholarly attention, including more extended treatment from Connolly.

68. Parallels between Isdell's and Brown's novels suggest beyond a reasonable doubt that Isdell read and absorbed much of *Wieland* and used it as a model for her own gothic American tale. The villain St. Pierre, for example, wreaks havoc in the Vale with his unique ability to throw voices, the same skill that Carwin uses to torture the characters in Brown's

novel. In *The Vale of Louisiana*, St. Pierre uses this ability to drive a penitent George Wilmot to the attempted murder of his own daughter, Ellen, and he explains how he learned ventriloquism in a confessional letter similar to Carwin's in *Wieland*. In addition to this, the two novels share a subtitle, "An American Tale," and have similarly named characters: Wilmot/Wieland, Plagel/Pleyel. Isdell's use of Brown suggests that *Wieland* was available to Irish readers before that novel was reprinted in London by Henry Colburn in 1811.

69. The novel includes a shocking scene back in England in which a pack of dogs owned by Wilmot's brother attacks his own wife, who retaliates by throwing her shoe at him (*V*II, 74–75).

70. *Irish Magazine* (July 1808): 351. Reprinted from New York *Public Advertiser* (March 19, 1808).

71. *Irish Magazine* (January 1815): 1.

72. Rodney Macdonough, *The Life of Commodore Thomas Macdonough, U.S. Navy* (Boston, 1909), 11–19.

73. The anecdote about the Madisons has been told with authority, despite lack of evidence; see, for example, Gordon Wood, *Empire of Liberty: A History of the Early Republic, 1789–1815* (New York: Oxford University Press, 2009), 663.

74. Elsie K. Kirk, "'Hail to the Chief': The Origins and Legacies of an American Ceremonial Tune," *American Music* 15.2 (Summer 1997): 133.

75. Thomas Jefferson to William Duane, August 4, 1812, Library of Congress, Thomas Jefferson Papers, Series 1, General Correspondence, 1651–1827, http://hdl.loc.gov/loc.mss/mtj.mtjbib021175 (accessed October 20, 2013).

76. Taylor, *The Civil War of 1812*.

77. These data have been compiled from my own research and a number of printed and digital sources. For information about American imprints and derivative imprints of Scott's poems, see the relevant sections of William B. Todd and Ann Bowden, *Sir Walter Scott: A Bibliographical History, 1796–1832* (New Castle, DE: Oak Knoll Press, 1998). Information about performances of Scott's work has been compiled using contemporary newspaper advertisements and also the following references: William Dunlap, *History of the American Theatre* [1833] (rpt., New York: Burt Franklin, 1963); George Odell, *Annals of the New York Stage* (New York: Columbia University Press, 1927); and H. Philip Bolton, *Scott Dramatized* (London: Mansell Publishing, 1992). For bibliography of Scott's music in America, see Richard Wolfe, *Secular Music in America, 1801–1825: A Bibliography* (New York: New York Public Library, 1964).

78. Walter Scott, *Lay of the Last Minstrel* (Philadelphia, 1805), Canto VI, Stanza 1, pp. 125–126.

79. Carrie Hyde, "Outcast Patriotism: The Dilemma of Negative Instruction in 'The Man without a Country," *ELH* 77 (2010): 928–929.

80. The passage appears in its entirety in *The Polyanthos*, Boston (September 1806): 119; *The American Watchman*, Wilmington, DE (March 13, 1811); *The War*, New York (July 18, 1812); *Rhode-Island Republican*, Newport (April 27, 1814); *The Shamrock*, New York (July 2, 1814); *Hallowell Gazette*, Maine (November 2, 1814); and in the anthology *The Parnassian Garland; or, Beauties of Modern Poetry* (Philadelphia, 1814). As an epigraph, see *The Cabinet;*

A Repository of Polite Literature, Boston (February 9, 1811), 81, and *The Petersburg Daily Courier*, Virginia (December 22, 1814). For John Randolph's letter regarding New England secession, see *The Examiner*, New York (December 24, 1814): 174; *Nile's Weekly Register*, Baltimore (vol. 7, 1815): 261; and *The Vermont Mirror*, Middlebury (February 1, 1815). See also citations in *The Monthly Anthology, and Boston Review* (October 1806): 551; John Irving, *An Oration Delivered before the Tammany Society, or Columbian Order* (New York, 1810), 4; Charles Ingersoll, *Inchiquin, The Jesuit's Letters* (New York, 1810), 145; Lemuel Shaw, *A Discourse Delivered before the Officers and Members of the Humane Society of Massachusetts* (Boston, 1811), 17; and *The Port Folio*, Philadelphia (September 1815): 288.

81. Charles Durang, *History of the Philadelphia Stage* (1855), manuscript scrapbook at the Kislak Center for Special Collections, Rare Books and Manuscripts, University of Pennsylvania, 103. This copy of Durang was "Arranged and Illustrated" by Thompson Wescott in 1868. Barker's *Marmion* ran intermittently from January 1 to February 15, 1813; for notices of this production, see *Paulson's American Daily Advertiser*, Philadelphia (January 4 and February 15, 1812) and *The Democratic Press*, Philadelphia (January 16 and February 4, 1813).

82. See *Edinburgh Review* (April 1809): 1–35.

83. James Nelson Barker, *Marmion; or, the Battle of Flodden Field: A Drama* (Philadelphia, 1816), iii.

84. Ibid., 53–55.

85. Barker writes that "an audience of his countrymen" apprehended "the coincidence" he alludes to in these lines, which during the performance inspired "shouts and applause" (Barker, v). In the preface, too, he makes the analogy between James's comments and America explicit: "James imputes nothing to England which England's history does not record as her deed . . . [England] did enter the Scottish harbours, to burn and pillage, to enslave and murder. . . . [S]uch was England to Scotland in the sixteenth century; and such, precisely such, had she recently been to America" (v).

86. This is recorded in Durang in *History of the Philadelphia Stage* (Philadelphia, 1855). See also David Grimsted, *Melodrama Unveiled: American Theater and Culture, 1800–1850* (Chicago: University of Chicago Press, 1968), 60–61.

87. Walter Scott, *Lady of the Lake* (Philadelphia, 1810), Canto 4, Stanza 26, p. 136. See also Edmund John Eyre, *Lady of the Lake: A Melo-Dramatic Romance* (New York, 1811), Act 2, Scene 2, p. 35.

88. Quoted here from sheet music. See also Eyre's adaptation, *Lady of the Lake*, Act 1, Scene 3, p. 20. The lines in Eyre are a slightly truncated version of the original stanza in Scott, *Lady of the Lake*, Canto 2, Stanza 19–20, pp. 59–60.

89. Dibdin's play was not performed in America until the 1850s. See Kirk, "'Hail to the Chief.'"

90. See relevant entries in Wolfe, *Secular Music in America, 1801–1825*.

91. See Todd and Bowden, 193–227.

92. More typical titles were the Adams or the Neptune or the Constitution; see "A Complete List of the American Navy including The Vessels on the Lakes," *Norwich Courier*, Norwich, CT (September 1, 1813).

93. For "beautiful pilot boat," see *Poulson's Daily Advertiser*, Philadelphia (May 5, 1813)

and *The Evening Post*, New York (August 19, 1813). For the April 8 launch date, see *Democratic Press*, Philadelphia (April 18, 1813). In the late spring and early summer of 1813, references to the schooner can be found in about fifty different newspapers, from New England to Virginia.

94. "Whilst the British are carrying on a war of plunder and depredation on inoffensive villages, women and children, we have in this instance paid one of their poets the highest compliment. 'The Lady of the Lake' is truly an appropriate and poetical name. She sails remarkably, and can beat to the windward with such rapidity as to astonish the beholders." *The Long-Island Star*, Brooklyn, NY (May 12, 1813).

95. *New-Jersey Journal*, Elizabethtown, NJ, September 21, 1813. This report is typical of the dozens of notices that appeared in newspapers.

96. For the advertisement of the production of Eyre's *Lady of the Lake*, which began on October 8, see the *Baltimore Patriot* (October 7, 1813). In the summary of the play included in this advertisement, "Hail to the Chief" is mentioned as a highlight of the third scene.

97. *The Voice of the Nation*, Philadelphia (October 7, 1813). A headnote to the poem reads, "From the Baltimore Whig. . . . The public will hear with astonishment that a British knight, of high reputation, should have declined the advances of an American Lady, who has already made some noise in the world, and is likely soon to make more." For reprintings of the poem, see *The City Gazette*, Charleston, SC (October 9, 1813); *The Washington Reporter*, Washington, PA (October 18, 1813); *Essex Register*, Salem, MA (October 23, 1813); *New-Hampshire Sentinel*, Keene, NH (October 23, 1813); *Orange County Patriot; or, the Spirit of 'Seventy-Six*, Goshen, NY (November 2, 1813); *New-Hampshire Patriot* (November 2, 1813); and *The Reporter*, Brattleboro, VT (November 13, 1813).

98. Kirk, 131–133. For reports on the celebration, see the *Boston Daily Advertiser* (February 20, 22, 24, and 25, 1815).

99. See sheet music, "Wreathes for the Chieftain" (Boston, c1815).

100. *Boston Daily Advertiser* (February 24, 1815).

101. James Sanderson, "Hail to the Chief" (Philadelphia: G. E. Blake, c. 1812–1815). Keffer Collection of Sheet Music, in the Kislak Center for Special Collections, Rare Books and Manuscripts, University of Pennsylvania, fol. M1.A13 K4, Box 10, no. 21.

102. Kate Flint, *The Transatlantic Indian, 1776–1930* (Princeton, NJ: Princeton University Press, 2009), and Colin Calloway, *White People, Indians, and Highlanders: Tribal Peoples and Colonial Encounters in Scotland and America* (Oxford: Oxford University Press, 2008).

103. See relevant entries in Wolfe, *Secular Music*.

104. Mark Twain, *Life on the Mississippi* (New York: Library of America, 1982), 500–502.

EPILOGUE

1. Letter to Elizabeth M. Hathorne, October 31, 1820; to Louisa Hathorne, September 28, 1819; to Elizabeth Hathorne, ca. 1820–1821, in *The Centenary Edition of the Works of Nathaniel Hawthorne*, vol. 15: *The Letters*, ed. Thomas Woodson et al. (Columbus: Ohio State University Press, 1984–1985), 132, 114, 134.

2. Letter to Elizabeth C. Hathorne, March 13, 1821, in *The Letters*, ed. Woodson, 15:139.

3. Scholars have amply demonstrated Hawthorne's embeddedness within Puritan history and mid-nineteenth-century politics, but they have not provided a satisfactory account of his relationship to the fiction that dominated his boyhood and early career. Exceptions to this include George Dekker, *The American Historical Romance* (New York: Cambridge University Press, 1987), and Michael Davitt Bell, *Hawthorne and the Historical Romance of New England* (Princeton, NJ: Princeton University Press, 1971). For Hawthorne's relationship to Puritan history and nineteenth-century politics, see especially Michael Colacurcio, "Footsteps of Ann Hutchinson: The Context of *The Scarlet Letter*," *ELH* 39.3 (1972): 459–494, *Doctrine and Difference: Essays in the Literature of New England* (New York: Routledge, 1997), and *The Province of Piety: Moral History in Hawthorne's Early Tales* (Cambridge, MA: Harvard University Press, 1984); Sacvan Bercovitch, *The Office of the Scarlet Letter* (Baltimore: Johns Hopkins University Press, 1991); Lauren Berlant, *The Anatomy of National Fantasy: Hawthorne, Utopia, and Everyday Life* (Chicago: University of Chicago Press, 1991); and Jonathan Arac, "The Politics of *The Scarlet Letter*," in *Ideology and Classic American Literature*, ed. Sacvan Bercovitch and Myra Jehlen (New York: Cambridge University Press, 1986), 247–266.

4. Lawrence Buell, *New England Literary Culture: From Revolution Through Renaissance* (New York: Cambridge University Press, 1986).

5. This is a fundamentally different take on the mid nineteenth century from one concerned with the arrival of a uniquely "American" literature. While the effects of the newly important American reading public, including the disappearance of formal features produced by a concern with foreign readers, made some works of the 1850s available for scholars like F. O. Matthiessen to recognize them as part of America's "coming to its first maturity . . . in the whole expanse of art and culture," I am interested in exploring how Hawthorne's appeal to literary autonomy emerged from contingent conditions in the marketplace for books. F. O. Matthiessen, *American Renaissance: Art and Expression in the Age of Emerson and Whitman* (Oxford: Oxford University Press, 1941), vii.

6. Nathaniel Hawthorne, *The Centenary Edition of the Works of Nathaniel Hawthorne*, vol. 3: *The Blithedale Romance and Fanshawe*, ed. William Charvat et al. (Columbus: Ohio State University Press, 1964), 367.

7. Nathaniel Hawthorne, "The Gray Champion," in *Nathaniel Hawthorne's Tales*, ed. James McIntosh (New York: Norton, 1987), 65.

8. Nelson F. Adkins identifies this collection as an early work but does not mention Scott. "The Early Projected Works of Nathaniel Hawthorne," *Papers of the Bibliographical Society of America* 39 (1945): 121–122. See also Colacurcio, *Province of Piety*, 39–98.

9. As Lauren Berlant writes, the title enacts a "double articulation of subjectivity and landscape" (*The Anatomy of National Fantasy*, 35).

10. See the appendix to "The Gentle Boy," in *Nathaniel Hawthorne's Tales*, ed. McIntosh, 264.

11. "Alice Doane's Appeal," in *The Centenary Edition of the Works of Nathaniel Hawthorne*, vol. 11: *The Snow-Image and Uncollected Tales*, ed. William Charvat et al., 268.

12. Nathaniel Hawthorne, *The Scarlet Letter*, ed. Seymour Gross (New York: Norton, 1988), 24, 42. Hereafter abbreviated *SL* and cited parenthetically.

13. Laura Doyle has made the striking proposal that the scarlet "A" stands for "Atlantic"; she argues that Hawthorne's "elision" of transatlantic migration and the colonization process "performs a displacement of the violence against Indian Americans." *Freedom's Empire: Race and the Rise of the Novel in Atlantic Modernity, 1640–1940* (Durham, NC: Duke University Press, 2008), 310. My discussion might point to "A"-tlantic, too, though "A"-utonomous, "A"-nglophone, "A"-esthetic, and "A"-rt are contenders in the A-game as well.

14. Donald Pease, "Hawthorne in the Custom-House: The Metapolitics, Postpolitics, and Politics of *The Scarlet Letter*," *boundary 2* 32 (2005): 57.

15. Narratives of the story of General Miller that Hawthorne may have read and that include the "I'll try, sir!" moment include "The Battle of Lundy's Lane," a poem by Caleb Stark published in *The New Hampshire Book* (1844), which was edited by Charles James Fox; *Incidents in American History* (1847), by John Weber Barber; and *The Fredoniad, or, Independence Preserved* (1827), an epic poem by Richard Emmons. In the Emmons poem, General Miller's phrase occurs in close proximity to a line that directly echoes Scott's song, "Hail to the Chief." Emmons writes, "'*I'll try, Sir,*' were the words that Miller said, / So well the warrior scann'd the peril dread" (269); earlier he writes, of General Scott (not the poet), who observes another general at the battle, "Such feelings came to Scott, when he beheld / The chief advancing through the glimmering field" (253). This echoes the first line of Walter Scott's poem: "Hail to the chief who in triumph advances!" Emmons's poem thus suggests that the heroism on the battlefield of the War of 1812 was often expressed in language Scott popularized and that the spirit of veterans like Miller could easily have been associated with his patriotic poetry.

16. Walter Scott, *Waverley*, ed. P. D. Garside (New York: Penguin, 2011), 5–6. Patricia Crain finds another plausible source for the epitaph in Andrew Marvell's poem "The Unfortunate Lover." *The Story of A: The Alphabetization of America from* The New England Primer *to* The Scarlet Letter (Stanford, CA: Stanford University Press, 2000), 201–202.

17. Leslie Fiedler, *Love and Death in the American Novel* (New York: Criterion Books, 1960), 231.

18. Henry James, *Hawthorne* (London: Macmillan, 1879), 111.

19. Michael Gilmore, *American Romanticism and the Marketplace* (Chicago: University of Chicago Press, 1985), 85.

20. Bercovitch, 32, 92.

Bibliography

ARCHIVES CONSULTED

The American Antiquarian Society
America's Historical Newspapers
American Periodical Series Online
The Boston Athenaeum
British Periodicals Series Online
Early American Imprints, I and II
The Historical Society of Pennsylvania
The Houghton Library, Harvard University
The Huntington Library
The Kislak Center for Special Collections, Rare Books and Manuscripts, University of
    Pennsylvania
The Library Company of Philadelphia
The National Library of Ireland
The National Library of Scotland
The New York Public Library
Princeton University Libraries, Special Collections
Trinity College Library, Dublin
Widener Library, Harvard University

PERIODICALS

The Analectic Magazine
The Belfast Monthly Magazine
Blackwood's Edinburgh Magazine
The Boston Daily Advertiser
The British Critic
The British Review

The Columbia Phoenix
The Critical Review
The Cornhill Magazine
Cumberland's Minor Theatre
The Cyclopaedian Magazine and Dublin Monthly Register
The Dublin and London Magazine
The Dublin Examiner
The Dublin Magazine, and Monthly Memorialist
The Edinburgh Review
The Gentleman's Magazine
The Hibernia Magazine
The Irish Magazine (alt. title: *The Irish Catholic Magazine*)
The London Literary Gazette
The Monthly Review
The National Gazette and Literary Register
The New England Magazine
The North American Review
The Polyanthos
The Port-Folio
Poulson's Daily Advertiser
The Public Advertiser
The Quarterly Review
The Quarterly Review (Boston edition)
The Rushlight
The Scots Magazine
The Spectator
Theatrical Inquisitor, and Monthly Mirror
The Ulster Register
Walker's Hibernian Magazine
The Weekly Magazine; or, Edinburgh Amusement

PUBLISHED SOURCES

Abrams, M. H. "Art-as-Such: The Sociology of Modern Aesthetics." In *Doing Things with Texts: Essays in Criticism and Critical Theory*, ed. Michael Fischer. New York: Norton, 1989.

Aderman, Ralph M., ed. *Critical Essays on Washington Irving*. Boston: G. K. Hall, 1990.

Adkins, Nelson F. "The Early Projected Works of Nathaniel Hawthorne." *Papers of the Bibliographical Society of America* 39 (1945): 119–155.

Alloway, Ross. "Agencies and Joint Ventures." In *Ambition and Industry, 1800–80*, ed. Bill Bell. Vol. 3 of *The Edinburgh History of the Book in Scotland*. 4 vols. Edinburgh: Edinburgh University Press, 2007.

Altick, Richard D. *The English Common Reader: A Social History of the Mass Reading Public, 1800–1900*. Chicago: University of Chicago Press, 1957.

Amory, Hugh. "Reinventing the Colonial Book." In *A History of the Book in America*, vol. 1, ed. Hall.

Amory, Hugh, and David D. Hall, eds. *The Colonial Book in the Atlantic World*. Vol. 1 of *A History of the Book in America*. 5 vols. Chapel Hill: University of North Carolina Press, 2007.

Anderson, Benedict. *Imagined Communities: Reflections on the Origins and Spread of Nationalism*. London: Verso, 1983.

Arac, Jonathan. "Establishing National Narrative." In *The Cambridge History of American Literature: 1590–1820*, vol. 1, ed. Sacvan Bercovitch. New York: Cambridge University Press, 1994.

———. "The Politics of *The Scarlet Letter*." In *Ideology and Classic American Literature*, ed. Sacvan Bercovitch and Myra Jehlen. New York: Cambridge University Press, 1986.

Armitage, David. "Three Concepts of Atlantic History." In *The British Atlantic World, 1500–1800*, ed. Armitage and Braddick.

Armitage, David, and Michael J. Braddick, eds. *The British Atlantic World, 1500–1800*. New York: Palgrave, 2002.

The Ass on Parnassus and Marmion Feats! London, 1814. Rpt. Philadelphia, 1815.

Austen, Jane. *Jane Austen's Letters*. Ed. Deirdre Le Faye. Oxford: Oxford University Press, 1995.

———. *Persuasion*. 1818. Ed. R. W. Chapman. Oxford: Oxford University Press, 1988.

———. *Pride and Prejudice*. 1813. Ed. Tony Tanner. New York: Penguin, 1972.

———. *Northanger Abbey*. 1818. Ed. Marilyn Butler. New York: Penguin, 1995.

Barker, James Nelson. *Marmion; or, the Battle of Flodden Field: A Drama*. Philadelphia, 1816.

Barnard, John, David McKitterick, and I. R. Wilson, eds. *The Cambridge History of the Book in Britain*. 6 vols. Cambridge: Cambridge University Press, 1998–.

Beard, James Franklin. "Historical Introduction." In James Fenimore Cooper, *The Pioneers*, ed. Beard.

———. *James Fenimore Cooper: Letters and Journals*. Vol. 2. Cambridge, MA: Harvard University Press, 1960.

Beavan, Iain, and Warren McDougall. "The Scottish Book Trade." In *The Cambridge History of the Book in Britain: 1695–1830*, vol. 5, ed. Suarez and Turner.

Belanger, Jacqueline. "'Le Vrai N'est Pas Toujours Vraisemblable': The Evaluation of Realism in Edgeworth's Irish Tales." In *An Uncomfortable Authority: Maria Edgeworth and Her Contexts*, ed. Heidi Kaufman and Christopher J. Fauske. Newark: University of Delaware Press, 2004.

Bell, Bill, ed. *The Edinburgh History of the Book in Scotland*. 4 vols. Edinburgh: University of Edinburgh Press, 2007–2014.

———. "Introduction." In *Ambition and Industry: 1800–1880*, ed. Bill Bell. Vol. 3 of *The Edinburgh History of the Book in Scotland*. 4 vols. Edinburgh: Edinburgh University Press, 2007.

Bell, Michael Davitt. *Hawthorne and the Historical Romance of New England*. Princeton, NJ: Princeton University Press, 1971.

Bender, Thomas. *A Nation Among Nations: America's Place in World History*. New York: Hill and Wang, 2006.

Benson, Charles. "The Dublin Book Trade." In *The Oxford History of the Irish Book: The Irish Book in English, 1800–1891*, vol. 4, ed. James H. Murphy. Oxford: Oxford University Press, 2011.

———. "The Irish Trade." In *The Cambridge History of the Book in Britain: 1695–1830*, vol. 5, ed. Suarez and Turner.

———. "Printers and Booksellers in Dublin, 1800–1850." In *Spreading the Word*, ed. Robin Myers and Michael Harris. Winchester, England: St. Paul's Bibliographies, 1990.

Bentley, Nancy. *The Ethnography of Manners: Hawthorne, James, Wharton*. Cambridge: Cambridge University Press, 1995.

———. "Literary Forms and Mass Culture, 1870–1920." In *Cambridge History of American Literature: Prose Writing, 1860–1920*, ed. Sacvan Bercovitch. Cambridge: Cambridge University Press, 2005.

Bercovitch, Sacvan. *The Office of the Scarlet Letter*. Baltimore: Johns Hopkins University Press, 1991.

Berlant, Lauren. *The Anatomy of National Fantasy: Hawthorne, Utopia, and Everyday Life*. Chicago: University of Chicago Press, 1991.

Best, Stephen, and Sharon Marcus. "Surface Reading: An Introduction." *Representations* 108.1 (Fall 2009): 1–21.

Bolton, H. Philip. *Scott Dramatized*. London: Mansell Publishing, 1992.

Boswell, James. *Life of Johnson*. Ed. Pat Rogers. Oxford: Oxford University Press, 1980.

Bourdieu, Pierre. *The Field of Cultural Production*. Ed. Randal Johnson. New York: Columbia University Press, 1993.

———. *The Rules of Art: Genesis and Structure of the Literary Field*. Trans. Susan Emanuel. Stanford, CA: Stanford University Press, 1992.

Bowden, Edwin T, ed. *Washington Irving Bibliography*. Boston: Twayne, 1989.

Bowers, Fredson. *Bibliography and Textual Criticism*. Oxford: Clarendon Press, 1964.

Bradsher, Earl. *Mathew Carey: Editor, Author and Publisher: A Study in American Literary Development*. New York: Columbia University Press, 1912.

Brewer, David. *The Afterlife of Character: 1726–1825*. Philadelphia: University of Pennsylvania Press, 2005.

Briggs, Asa. "The Longmans and the Book Trade, c1730–1830." In *The Cambridge History of the Book in Britain: 1695–1830*, vol. 5, ed. Suarez and Turner.

Broadie, Alexander. "Sympathy and the Impartial Spectator." In *The Cambridge Companion to Adam Smith*, ed. Knud Haakonssen. Cambridge: Cambridge University Press, 2006.

Brown, David. *Walter Scott and the Historical Imagination*. London: Routledge, 1979.

Brown, Matthew. *The Pilgrim and the Bee: Reading Rituals and Book Culture in Early New England*. Philadelphia: University of Pennsylvania Press, 2007.

Brown, William Wells. *Clotel: An Electronic Scholarly Edition*. Charlottesville: University of Virginia Press, 2010.

Bryant, John. *Melville Unfolding: Sexuality, Politics, and the Versions of* Typee, *a Fluid-Text Analysis, with an Edition of the* Typee *Manuscript*. Ann Arbor: University of Michigan Press, 2008.

———. "Rewriting *Moby-Dick*: Politics, Textual Identity, and the Revision Narrative." *PMLA* 125.4 (2010): 1043–1060.

Bryant, William Cullen. "Discourse on the Life, Genius, and Writings of James Fenimore Cooper." In *Precaution: A Novel*. New ed. New York: Hurd and Houghton, 1871.

Buell, Lawrence. "American Literary Emergence as a Postcolonial Phenomenon." *ALH* 4.3 (Fall 1992): 411–442.

———. *New England Literary Culture: From Revolution Through Renaissance*. New York: Cambridge University Press, 1986.

———. "Nineteenth-Century Transatlantic (Mis)Understandings." In *Transatlantic Traffic and (Mis)Translations*, ed. Robin Peel and Daniel Maudlin. Lebanon: University of New Hampshire Press, 2013.

Burke, Edmund. *A Philosophical Enquiry into the Sublime and the Beautiful*. Ed. David Womersley. New York: Penguin, 1998.

Burstein, Andrew. *Jefferson's Secrets: Death and Desire at Monticello*. New York: Basic Books, 2005.

———. *The Original Knickerbocker: The Life of Washington Irving*. New York: Basic Books, 2007.

Butler, Marilyn. "Culture's Medium: The Role of the Review." In *The Cambridge Companion to British Romanticism*, ed. Stuart Curran. Cambridge: Cambridge University Press, 1993.

———. "Edgeworth's Ireland: History, Popular Culture, and Secret Codes." *NOVEL: A Forum on Fiction* 34.2 (2001): 267–292.

———. "General Introduction." In *Castle Rackrent, Irish Bulls, Ennui*, ed. Jane Desmarais, Tim McLoughlin, and Marilyn Butler. Vol. 1 of *The Novels and Selected Works of Maria Edgeworth*. 9 vols. London: Pickering and Chatto, 1999.

———. Introduction. *Castle Rackrent and Ennui*. Ed. Marilyn Butler. London: Penguin, 1992.

———. *Maria Edgeworth: A Literary Biography*. Oxford: Clarendon Press, 1972.

Butler, Marilyn, and Tim McLoughlin. "Introductory Note." In *Castle Rackrent, Irish Bulls, Ennui*, ed. Jane Desmarais, Tim McLoughlin, and Marilyn Butler. Vol. 1 of *The Novels and Selected Works of Maria Edgeworth*. 9 vols. London: Pickering and Chatto, 1999.

Buzard, James. *The Beaten Track: European Tourism, Literature, and the Ways to Culture, 1800–1918*. Oxford: Clarendon Press, 1993.

———. *Disorienting Fiction: The Autoethnographic Work of Nineteenth-Century British Novels*. Princeton, NJ: Princeton University Press, 2005.

Cahill, Edward. *Liberty of the Imagination: Aesthetic Theory, Literary Form, and Politics in the Early United States*. Philadelphia: University of Pennsylvania Press, 2012.

Cairns, William B. "British Republication of American Writings, 1783–1833." *PMLA* 43.1 (1928): 303–310.

Calloway, Colin. *White People, Indians, and Highlanders: Tribal Peoples and Colonial Encounters in Scotland and America.* Oxford: Oxford University Press, 2008.

Campbell, Mary. *Lady Morgan, the Life and Times of Sydney Owenson.* London: Pandora Press, 1988.

Candler, Isaac. *A Summary View of America.* London, 1824.

Cannon, John. *The Oxford Companion to British History.* Oxford: Oxford University Press, 1997.

Carey, Mathew. *Autobiography. The New England Magazine.* 1834–1835.

———. *Vindiciae Hibernicae: Or, Ireland Vindicated.* 2nd ed., rev. Philadelphia, 1823.

Carpenter, Kenneth E. "Sites of Reading: Part I, Libraries." In *The Industrial Book: 1840–1880*, ed. Scott E. Casper et al. Vol. 3 of *A History of the Book in America.* Chapel Hill: University of North Carolina Press, 2007.

Carter, Edward C. "A 'Wild Irishmen' Under Every Federalist's Bed: Naturalization in Philadelphia, 1789–1806." *Pennsylvania Magazine of History and Biography* 94 (July 1970): 331–346.

Casanova, Pascale. *The World Republic of Letters.* Cambridge, MA: Harvard University Press, 2004.

Casper, Scott E. "Introduction." In *The Industrial Book: 1840–1880*, ed. Scott E. Casper et al. Vol. 3 of *A History of the Book in America.* 5 vols. Chapel Hill: University of North Carolina Press, 2007.

A Catalogue of Books, Ancient and Modern; Containing the Works of the Principal Authors, and the Best Editions . . . at the Shop of William Creech, at the Cross, Edinburgh. Edinburgh, 1793.

Catalogue of Novels and Romances Being Part of an Extensive Collection for Sale by M. Carey and Son. Philadelphia, c. 1818.

A Catalogue of the Books Belonging to the Library Company of Philadelphia. Vol. 2. Philadelphia, 1835.

Chandler, James. *An Archeology of Sympathy: The Sentimental Mode in Literature and Cinema.* Chicago: University of Chicago Press, 2013.

———. *England in 1819: The Politics of Literary Culture and the Case of Romantic Historicism.* Chicago: University of Chicago Press, 1998.

Chartier, Roger. "Texts, Printings, Readings." In *The New Cultural History*, ed. Lynn Hunt. Berkeley: University of California Press, 1989.

Charvat, William. *Literary Publishing in America, 1790–1830.* Philadelphia: University of Pennsylvania Press, 1959.

Child, Lydia Maria. *Hobomok.* 1824. Ed. Carolyn L. Karcher. New Brunswick, NJ: Rutgers University Press, 1999.

Christensen, Jerome. *Romanticism at the End of History.* Baltimore: Johns Hopkins University Press, 2000.

Ciosáin, Niall Ó. "Oral Culture, Literacy, and Reading, 1800–50." In *The Oxford History of the Irish Book*, vol. 4, ed. Murphy.

Claybaugh, Amanda. *The Novel of Purpose: Literature and Social Reform in the Anglo-American World*. Ithaca, NY: Cornell University Press, 2007.

———. "Toward a New Transatlanticism: Dickens in the United States." *Victorian Studies* 48.3 (2006): 439–460.

Clifford, Brendan, ed. *The Origins of Irish Catholic Nationalism*. Belfast: Athol Books, 1992.

Clive, John. *Scotch Reviewers: The Edinburgh Review, 1802–1815*. London: Faber, 1957.

Clive, John, and Bernard Bailyn. "England's Cultural Provinces: Scotland and America." *William and Mary Quarterly* 11 (1954): 200–213.

Clyde, Tom. *Irish Literary Magazines: An Outline History and Descriptive Bibliography*. Dublin: Irish Academic Press, 2003.

Cohen, Lara Langer. *The Fabrication of American Literature: Fraudulence and Antebellum Print Culture*. Philadelphia: University of Pennsylvania Press, 2012.

Colacurcio, Michael. *Doctrine and Difference: Essays in the Literature of New England*. New York: Routledge, 1997.

———. "Footsteps of Ann Hutchinson: The Context of the Scarlet Letter." *ELH* 39.3 (1972): 459–494.

———. *The Province of Piety: Moral History in Hawthorne's Early Tales*. Cambridge, MA: Harvard University Press, 1984.

Colley, Linda. *Britons: Forging the Nation*. New Haven, CT: Yale University Press, 1992.

Colvin, Christina, ed. *Maria Edgeworth: Letters from England, 1813–1844*. Oxford: Clarendon Press, 1971.

Connolly, Claire. *A Cultural History of the Irish Novel, 1790–1829*. Cambridge: Cambridge University Press, 2012.

———. "The National Tale, 1800–1829." In *The Oxford History of the Irish Book*, vol. 4, ed. Murphy.

———. "The Politics of Love in *The Wild Irish Girl*." In *The Wild Irish Girl: A National Tale*, ed. Claire Connolly and Stephen Copley. London: Pickering and Chatto, 2000.

Cooper, James Fenimore. *Letters and Journals*. Vols. 1–2. Ed. James Franklin Beard. Cambridge, MA: Harvard University Press, 1960.

———. *The Last of the Mohicans*. London: Colburn and Bentley, 1831.

———. *The Pioneers, or The Sources of the Susquehanna; A Descriptive Tale*. London: Colburn and Bentley, 1832.

———. *The Pioneers, or The Sources of the Susquehanna; A Descriptive Tale*. New York: Wiley, 1823.

———. *The Pioneers, or The Sources of the Susquehanna; A Descriptive Tale*. 1823. In *The Writings of James Fenimore Cooper*, ed. James Franklin Beard. 20 vols. Albany, NY: SUNY Press, 1980.

———. *Precaution*. 1820. Rev. ed. London: Colburn & Bentley, 1839.

———. *The Spy: A Tale of Neutral Ground*. 1821. In *The Writings of James Fenimore Cooper*, ed. James P. Elliot. 20 vols. New York: AMS Press, 2002.

Corbett, Mary Jean. *Allegories of Union in Irish and English Writing, 1790–1870*. Cambridge: Cambridge University Press, 2000.

Costelloe, Timothy. *The British Aesthetic Tradition: From Shaftesbury to Wittgenstein*. Cambridge: Cambridge University Press, 2013.

Crain, Patricia. *The Story of A: The Alphabetization of America from* The New England Primer *to* The Scarlet Letter. Stanford, CA: Stanford University Press, 2000.

Crawford, John. "Libraries." In *The Edinburgh History of the Book in Scotland*, vol. 3, ed. Bell.

Crawford, Robert. *Devolving English Literature*. Oxford: Clarendon Press, 1992.

Curtin, Nancy J. "Walter Cox." In *Oxford Dictionary of National Biography*. Oxford University Press, 2004.

Daiches, David. "Scott's Achievement as a Novelist." *Nineteenth Century Fiction* 6 (1951): 81–95, 153–173.

Davidson, Cathy. *The Revolution and the Word: The Rise of the Novel in America*. Oxford: Oxford University Press, 1986.

Davis, Leith, Ian Duncan, and Janet Sorensen, eds. *Scotland and the Borders of Romanticism*. Cambridge: Cambridge University Press, 2004.

Davis, Theo. *Formalism, Experience, and the Making of American Literature*. Cambridge: Cambridge University Press, 2010.

Deane, Seamus. *Strange Country: Modernity and Nationhood in Irish Writing Since 1790*. Oxford: Clarendon Press, 1997.

———. "The Production of Cultural Space in Irish Writing." *boundary 2* 21 (1994): 117–144.

Dekker, George. *The American Historical Romance*. New York: Cambridge University Press, 1987.

———. *James Fenimore Cooper: The American Scott*. New York: Barnes & Noble, 1967.

Deleuze, Gilles, and Félix Guattari. *Kafka: Toward a Minor Literature*. Trans. Dana Polan. Minneapolis: University of Minnesota Press, 1986.

Dennis, Ian. *Nationalism and Desire in Early Historical Fiction*. London: Macmillan, 1997.

Deutsch, Karl W. *Nationalism and Social Communication*. Cambridge, MA: MIT Press, 1966.

Dibdin, Thomas. *The Heart of Mid-Lothian; Or, the Lily of St. Leonard's*. London, 1819.

Donoghue, Frank. *The Fame Machine: Book Reviewing and Eighteenth-Century Literary Careers*. Stanford, CA: Stanford University Press, 1996.

Downes, Paul. *Democracy, Revolution, and Monarchism in Early American Literature*. New York: Cambridge University Press, 2002.

Doyle, Laura. *Freedom's Empire: Race and the Rise of the Novel in Atlantic Modernity, 1640–1940*. Durham, NC: Duke University Press, 2008.

Drexler, Michael J. "A Note on the Text." In *Secret History: or, The Horrors of St. Domingo*, by Leonora Sansay. Ed. Michael J. Drexler. Peterborough, Ontario: Broadview, 2007.

Duncan, Ian. *Modern Romance and Transformations of the Novel: The Gothic, Scott, Dickens*. Cambridge: Cambridge University Press, 1992.

———. "The Provincial and Regional Novel." In *A Companion to the Victorian Novel*, ed. Patrick Brantlinger and William B. Thesing. Oxford: Blackwell, 2002.

———. *Scott's Shadow: The Novel in Romantic Edinburgh*. Princeton, NJ: Princeton University Press, 2007.

Dunlap, William. *History of the American Theatre*. 1833. Rpt. New York: Burt Franklin, 1963.

———. *The Life of Charles Brockden Brown*. Vol. 2. Philadelphia, 1815.

Dunne, Tom. *Maria Edgeworth and the Colonial Mind*. University College, Cork: 1984.

Durang, Charles. *History of the Philadelphia Stage*. Philadelphia, 1855.

Eagleton, Terry. *Heathcliff and the Great Hunger: Studies in Irish Culture*. New York: Verso, 1995.

———. *The Ideology of the Aesthetic*. Cambridge, MA: Blackwell, 1990.

Eckel, Leslie. *Atlantic Citizens: Nineteenth-Century American Writers at Work in the World*. Edinburgh: Edinburgh University Press, 2013.

Edgeworth, Maria. *The Absentee*. 1812. Ed. W. J. McCormack and Kim Walker. New York: Oxford University Press, 1988.

———. *Castle Rackrent and Ennui*. 1800 and 1809. Ed. Marilyn Butler. New York: Penguin, 1992.

———. *Essay on Irish Bulls*. Rev. ed. London, 1808.

———. *Harrington*. 1817. Ed. Susan Manly. Ontario, Canada: Broadview, 2004.

———. *Ormond*. 1817. Ed. Claire Connolly. New York: Penguin, 1999.

———. *Patronage*. London, 1814.

———. *Popular Tales*. 1805. Boston, 1823.

———. *Practical Education*. 1798. New York, 1801.

Edgeworth, Maria, and Rachel Mordecai Lazarus. *The Education of the Heart: The Correspondence of Rachel Mordecai Lazarus and Maria Edgeworth*. Ed. Edgar E. MacDonald. Chapel Hill: University of North Carolina Press, 1977.

Edwards, Owen Dudly, and George Shepperson, eds. *Scotland, Europe, and the American Revolution*. New York: St. Martin's Press, 1977.

Egenolf, S. B. "Maria Edgeworth in Blackface: Castle Rackrent and the Irish Rebellion of 1798." *ELH* 72.4 (2005): 845–869.

Eliot, Simon. "Appendix B: Statistical Evidence for the 1825–6 Crisis." In *Ambition and Industry, 1800–80*, ed. Bill Bell. Vol. 3 of *The Edinburgh History of the Book in Scotland*. 4 vols. Edinburgh: Edinburgh University Press, 2007.

Emmet, Robert. "Speech from the Dock." In *Irish Writing: An Anthology of Irish Literature in English, 1789–1939*, ed. Stephan Regan. Oxford: Oxford University Press, 2008.

Emmons, Richard. *The Fredoniad, or, Independence Preserved*. 1827. Boston, 1830.

English, James. "Cultural Capital and the Revolutions of Literary Modernity, from Bourdieu to Casanova." In *A Handbook of Modernism Studies*, ed. Jean-Michel Rabaté. Somerset, NJ: Wiley & Sons, 2013.

Evans, Brad. *Before Cultures: The Ethnographic Imagination in American Literature, 1865–1920*. Chicago: University of Chicago Press, 2005.

Everton, Michael. *The Grand Chorus of Complaint: Authors and the Business Ethics of American Publishing*. New York: Oxford University Press, 2011.

Eyre, Edmund John. *Lady of the Lake: A Melo-Dramatic Romance*. New York, 1811.

Fagerstrom, Dalphy I. "Scottish Opinion and the American Revolution." *William and Mary Quarterly* 11 (1954): 252–275.

Ferguson, Frank. "The Industrialization of Irish Book Production, 1790–1900." In *The Oxford History of the Irish Book*, vol. 4, ed. Murphy.

Ferrier, Susan. *Marriage*. Ed. Herbert Foltinek and Kathryn Kirkpatrick. Oxford: Oxford University Press, 2001.

Ferris, Ina. *The Achievement of Literary Authority: Gender, History, and the Waverley Novels*. Ithaca, NY: Cornell University Press, 1991.

———. *The Romantic National Tale and the Question of Ireland*. Cambridge, UK: Cambridge University Press, 2002.

Fiedler, Leslie. *Love and Death in the American Novel*. New York: Criterion Books, 1960.

Fielding, Penny. *Scotland and the Fictions of Geography: North Britain, 1760–1830*. Cambridge: Cambridge University Press, 2008.

Finkelstein, David. *The House of Blackwood: Author-Publisher Relations in the Victorian Era*. University Park: Pennsylvania State University Press, 2002.

Fisher, Philip. *Hard Facts: Setting and Form in the American Novel*. New York: Oxford University Press, 1985.

Flanagan, Thomas. *The Irish Novelists, 1800–1850*. New York: Columbia University Press, 1959.

Flint, Kate. *The Transatlantic Indian, 1776–1930*. Princeton, NJ: Princeton University Press, 2009.

Flynn, Christopher. *Americans in British Literature, 1770–1832: A Breed Apart*. Aldershot, England: Ashgate, 2008.

Fontana, Biancamaria. *Rethinking the Politics of Commercial Society: The Edinburgh Review, 1802–1832*. Cambridge: Cambridge University Press, 1985.

Foster, R. F. *Modern Ireland: 1600–1972*. New York: Penguin, 1988.

———. *Words Alone: Yeats and His Inheritances*. Oxford: Oxford University Press, 2011.

Francis, John C. *John Francis, Publisher of the Athenaeum: A Literary Chronicle of Half a Century*. 2 vols. London, 1888.

Franklin, Wayne. *James Fenimore Cooper: The Early Years*. New Haven, CT: Yale University Press, 2007.

Fulford, Timothy. *Romantic Indians: Native Americans, British Literature, and Transatlantic Culture 1756–1830*. Oxford: Oxford University Press, 2006.

Fulford, Timothy, and Peter J. Kitson, eds. *Romanticism and Colonialism: Writing and Empire 1780–1830*. Cambridge: Cambridge University Press, 1998.

Gallagher, Catherine. *Nobody's Story: The Vanishing Acts of Women Writers in the Marketplace, 1670–1820*. Oxford: Clarendon Press, 1994.

Gamer, Michael. "Waverley and the Object of (Literary) History." *MLQ* 70.4 (2009): 495–525.

Gardner, Jared. *Master Plots: Race and the Founding of American Literature: 1787–1845*. Baltimore: Johns Hopkins University Press, 1998.

Garside, P. D., J. E. Belanger, and S. A. Ragaz. *British Fiction, 1800–1829: A Database of Production, Circulation & Reception*. Designer A. A. Mandal. http://www.british-fiction. cf.ac.uk.

Garside, Peter. "Popular Fiction and National Tale: Hidden Origins of Scott's Waverley."
    Nineteenth-Century Literature 4.1 (1991): 30–53.

———. "The Rise of the Scottish Literary Market." In *Ambition and Industry, 1800–80*, ed.
    Bill Bell. Vol. 3 of *The Edinburgh History of the Book in Scotland.* 4 vols. Edinburgh:
    Edinburgh University Press, 2007.

———. "*Waverley* and the National Fiction Revolution." In *Ambition and Industry, 1800–
    80*, ed. Bill Bell. Vol. 3 of *The Edinburgh History of the Book in Scotland.* 4 vols. Edin-
    burgh: Edinburgh University Press, 2007.

Gellner, Ernest. *Nations and Nationalisms.* Oxford: Blackwell, 1983.

Giles, Paul. *Transatlantic Insurrections: British Culture and the Formation of American Litera-
    ture, 1730–1860.* Philadelphia: University of Pennsylvania Press, 2001.

Gilmore, Michael. *American Romanticism and the Marketplace.* Chicago: University of Chi-
    cago Press, 1985.

———. "The Literature of the Revolutionary and Early National Periods." In *The Cam-
    bridge History of American Literature: 1590–1820*, vol. 1, ed. Sacvan Bercovitch. New
    York: Cambridge University Press, 1994.

Gilroy, Paul. *The Black Atlantic: Modernity and Double Consciousness.* Cambridge, MA:
    Harvard University Press, 1993.

Gohdes, Clarence. *American Literature in Nineteenth Century England.* Carbondale: South-
    ern Illinois University Press, 1944.

Goodman, Nan. "A Clear Showing: The Problem of Fault in James Fenimore Cooper's *The
    Pioneers.*" *Arizona Quarterly* 49.2 (1993): 1–22.

Grattan, Henry. *The Speeches of the Right Hon. Henry Grattan.* London, 1822.

Green, James N. "English Books and Printing in the Age of Franklin." In *A History of the
    Book in America: The Colonial Book in the Atlantic World*, vol. 1, ed. David Hall. Cha-
    pel Hill: University of North Carolina Press, 2000.

———. "Ivanhoe in America." In *The Annual Report of the Library Company of Philadel-
    phia for the Year 1994.* Philadelphia: Library Company of Philadelphia, 1995.

———. "The Rise of Book Publishing." In *An Extensive Republic: Print, Culture and Soci-
    ety in the New Nation, 1790–1840*, ed. Robert Gross. Vol. 2 of *A History of the Book in
    America.* 5 vols. Chapel Hill: University of North Carolina Press, 2010.

Greg, Walter. "The Rationale of Copy-text." *Studies in Bibliography* 3 (1950–1951): 19–36.

Grimsted, David. *Melodrama Unveiled: American Theater and Culture, 1800–1850.* Chicago:
    University of Chicago Press, 1968.

Gross, Robert. "Introduction." In *A History of the Book in America*, vol. 2, ed. Gross and
    Kelley.

Gross, Robert, and Mary Kelley, eds. *An Extensive Republic: Print, Culture and Society in the
    New Nation, 1790–1840.* Vol. 2 of *A History of the Book in America.* 5 vols. Chapel Hill:
    University of North Carolina Press, 2010.

Groves, Jeffrey D. "The National Book Trade System: Part II, Trade Communication." In
    The Industrial Book: 1840–1880, ed. Scott E. Casper et al. Vol. 3 of *A History of the Book
    in America.* 5 vols. Chapel Hill: University of North Carolina Press, 2007.

Guillory, John. *Cultural Capital: The Problem of Literary Canon Formation*. Chicago: University of Chicago Press, 1993.

Habermas, Jürgen. *The Structural Transformation of the Public Sphere*. Trans. Thomas Burger. Cambridge, MA: MIT Press, 1991.

Hall, David, ed. *A History of the Book in America*. 5 vols. Chapel Hill: University of North Carolina Press, 2000–.

———. "The Uses of Literacy in New England, 1600–1850." In *Cultures of Print: Essays in the History of the Book*. Amherst: University of Massachusetts Press, 1996.

Hanlon, Christopher. *America's England: Antebellum Literature and Atlantic Sectionalism*. Oxford: Oxford University Press, 2013.

Hansen, Camryn. "A Changing Tale of Truth: *Charlotte Temple*'s British Roots." In *Charlotte Temple*, ed. Marion L. Rust. New York: Norton, 2011.

Hare, Agustus, ed. *The Life and Letters of Maria Edgeworth*. Vol. 1. Boston, 1895.

Hawthorne, Nathaniel. "Alice Doane's Appeal." 1831. In *The Snow-Image and Uncollected Tales*, ed. William Charvat et al. Vol. 11 of *The Centenary Edition of the Works of Nathaniel Hawthorne*. 23 vols. Columbus: Ohio State University Press, 1974.

———. *Fanshawe*. 1828. In *The Blithedale Romance and Fanshawe*, ed. William Charvat et al. Vol. 3 of *The Centenary Edition of the Works of Nathaniel Hawthorne*. 23 vols. Columbus: Ohio State University Press, 1964.

———. *The Letters*. 1813–1853. Ed. Thomas Woodson et al. Vols. 15 and 16 of *The Centenary Edition of the Works of Nathaniel Hawthorne*. 23 vols. Columbus: Ohio State University Press, 1984–1985.

———. *Nathaniel Hawthorne's Tales*. Ed. James McIntosh. New York: Norton, 1987.

———. *The Scarlet Letter*. 1850. Ed. Seymour Gross et al. 3rd ed. New York: Norton, 1988.

Hayden, John O. *Scott: The Critical Heritage*. New York: Barnes & Noble, 1970.

Hayes, Kevin J. *The Road to Monticello: The Life and Mind of Thomas Jefferson*. Oxford: Oxford University Press, 2008.

Hechter, Michael. *Internal Colonialism: The Celtic Fringe in British National Development, 1536–1966*. Berkeley: University of California Press, 1975.

Hedges, William L. *Washington Irving: An American Study, 1802–1832*. Baltimore: Johns Hopkins University Press, 1965.

Heineman, Helen. "Frances Trollope in the New World: Domestic Manners of the Americans." *American Quarterly* 21.3 (Autumn 1969): 544–559.

Hewitt, David, ed. *The Edinburgh Edition of the Waverley Novels*. 30 vols. Edinburgh: Edinburgh University Press, 1993–.

Hobsbawm, Eric. "Introduction: Inventing Traditions." In *The Invention of Tradition*, ed. Eric Hobsbawm and Terence Ranger. Cambridge: Cambridge University Press, 1983.

Hogg, James. *The Poetic Mirror; Or, the Living Bards of Britain*. London, 1816. Rpt. Philadelphia, 1817.

———. *The Private Memoirs and Confessions of a Justified Sinner*. Ed. John Carey. Oxford: Oxford University Press, 1999.

Hollingworth, Brian. *Maria Edgeworth's Irish Writing: Language, History, Politics*. New York: St. Martin's Press, 1999.

Homestead, Melissa J. "American Novelist Catharine Sedgwick Negotiates British Copyright, 1822–1857." *Yearbook of English Studies* 45 (2015 forthcoming).

———. "Introduction." In *Clarence*, by Catherine Maria Sedgwick. Ed. Melissa Homestead. Peterborough, Ontario: Broadview, 2011.

Homestead, Melissa J., and Camryn Hansen. "Susanna Rowson's Transatlantic Career." *Early American Literature* 45.3 (2010): 619–654.

Hook, Andrew. *Scotland and America: A Study of Cultural Relations, 1750–1835*. Glasgow: Blackie, 1975.

Hume, David. *Essays: Moral, Political, and Literary*. Ed. Eugene F. Miller. Indianapolis, IN: Liberty Fund, 1985.

Hutchinson, John. *The Dynamics of Cultural Nationalism*. London: Allen and Unwin, 1987.

Hyde, Carrie. "Outcast Patriotism: The Dilemma of Negative Instruction in 'The Man Without a Country.'" *ELH* 77 (2010): 915–939.

Ingersoll, Charles. *Inchiquin, The Jesuit's Letters*. New York, 1810.

Irving, Pierre, ed. *The Life and Letters of Washington Irving*. Vol. 1. London, 1862.

Irving, Washington. "A Biographical Sketch of Thomas Campbell." In *The Poetical Works of Thomas Campbell*. ed. Washington Irving. New York, 1810.

———. "A Biographical Sketch of Thomas Campbell." 1815. *Washington Irving: Miscellaneous Writings, 1803–1859*. Ed. Wayne R. Kime. In *Complete Works of Washington Irving*. 29 vols. Boston: Twayne, 1981.

———. *Bracebridge Hall, Tales of a Traveller, the Alhambra*. Ed. Andrew B. Myers. New York: Library of America, 1991.

———. *History, Tales, and Sketches*. Ed. James W. Tuttleton. New York: Library of America, 1983.

———. *Miscellaneous Writings, 1803–1859*. Ed. Wayne R. Kime. In *Complete Works of Washington Irving*. 29 vols. Boston: Twayne, 1981.

———. *The Sketch Book of Geoffrey Crayon*. Ed. Haskell Springer. Boston: Twayne, 1978.

———. *The Sketch Book of Geoffrey Crayon*. 2 vols. London: John Miller and John Murray, 1820.

———. *The Sketch Book of Geoffrey Crayon*. 7 parts. New York: Van Winkle, 1819–1820.

Isbell, John Claiborne. *The Birth of European Romanticism: Truth and Propaganda in Staël's "De l'Allemagne," 1810–1813*. Cambridge: Cambridge University Press, 1994.

Isdell, Sarah. *The Vale of Louisiana: An American Tale*. 2 vols. Dublin, 1805.

Iser, Wolfgang. *The Implied Reader: Patterns of Communication in Prose Fiction from Bunyan to Beckett*. Baltimore: Johns Hopkins University Press, 1974.

Jackson, Leon. *The Business of Letters: Authorial Economies in Antebellum America*. Stanford, CA: Stanford University Press, 2008.

James, Henry. *Hawthorne*. London: Macmillan, 1879.

Jameson, Frederic. *The Political Unconscious: Narrative as a Socially Symbolic Act*. Ithaca, NY: Cornell University Press, 1982.

Johnson, Samuel. *The Journey to the Western Islands Scotland*. Ed. Peter Levi. New York: Penguin, 1984.

Jordan, Cynthia. *Second Stories: The Politics of Language, Form, and Gender in Early American Fictions*. Chapel Hill: University of North Carolina Press, 1989.

Kant, Immanuel. *Critique of the Power of Judgment*. Ed. Paul Guyer. Cambridge: Cambridge University Press, 2000.

Kaser, David. *Messrs. Carey & Lea of Philadelphia: A Study in the History of the Booktrade*. Philadelphia: University of Pennsylvania Press, 1957.

———. "Waverley in America." *Papers of the Bibliographical Society of America* 51 (1957): 163–167.

Kerr, James. *Fiction Against History: Scott as Storyteller*. Cambridge: Cambridge University Press, 1989.

Kime, Wayne R. "Introduction." In *Washington Irving: Miscellaneous Writings, 1803–1859*, ed. Kime. In *Complete Works of Washington Irving*. 29 vols. 1976–.

———. "Textual Commentary." In *Washington Irving: Miscellaneous Writings, 1803–1859*, ed. Kime. In *Complete Works of Washington Irving*. 29 vols. 1976–.

Kirk, Elsie K. "'Hail to the Chief': The Origins and Legacies of an American Ceremonial Tune." *American Music* 15.2 (Summer 1997): 123–136.

Klancher, John. *The Making of English Reading Audiences, 1790–1832*. Madison: University of Wisconsin Press, 1987.

Lambert, John, ed. *Salmagundi*. London, 1811.

Lawrence, D. H. *Studies in Classic American Literature*. 1923. New York: Viking Press, 1968.

Leerssen, Joep. *Remembrance and Imagination: Patterns in the Historical and Literary Representation of Ireland in the Nineteenth Century*. Cork: Cork University Press in association with Field Day, 1996.

Levine, George. *The Realistic Imagination: English Fiction from Frankenstein to Lady Chatterley*. Chicago: University of Chicago Press, 1981.

Levinson, Marjorie. "What Is New Formalism?" *PMLA* 122.2 (2007): 558–569.

Lew, Joseph. "Sydney Owenson and the Fate of Empire." *Keats-Shelley Journal* 39 (1990): 39–65.

Lewis, R. W. B. *The American Adam: Innocence, Tragedy, and Tradition in the Nineteenth Century*. Chicago: University of Chicago Press, 1955.

Lloyd, David. *Nationalism and Minor Literature: James Clarence Mangan and the Emergence of Irish Cultural Nationalism*. Durham, NC: Duke University Press, 1987.

Lockhart, John Gibson. *Peter's Letters to His Kinsfolk*. London, 1819.

Loesberg, Jonathan. *A Return to Aesthetics: Autonomy, Indifference, and Postmodernism*. Stanford, CA: Stanford University Press, 2005.

Looby, Christopher. *Voicing America: Language, Literary Form, and the Origins of the United States*. Chicago: University of Chicago Press, 1996.

Loughran, Trish. *The Republic in Print: Print Culture in the Age of U.S. National Building, 1770–1870*. New York: Columbia University Press, 2007.

Lukács, Georg. *The Historical Novel.* Trans. Hannah and Stanley Mitchell. Lincoln: University of Nebraska Press, 1983.

Lupfer, Eric. "Periodicals and Serial Publications: Part 2, The Business of American Magazines." In *The Industrial Book: 1840–1880,* ed. Scott E. Casper et al. Vol. 3 of *A History of the Book in America.* 5 vols. Chapel Hill: University of North Carolina Press, 2007.

Macdonough, Rodney. *The Life of Commodore Thomas Macdonough, U.S. Navy.* Boston, 1909.

Makdisi, Saree. *Romantic Imperialism: Universal Empire and the Culture of Modernity.* Cambridge: Cambridge University Press, 1998.

Manning, Susan. *The Puritan-Provincial Vision: Scottish and American Literature in the Nineteenth Century.* Cambridge: Cambridge University Press, 1990.

Martin, Terrence. *The Instructed Vision: Scottish Common Sense Philosophy and the Origins of American Fiction.* Bloomington: Indiana University Press, 1961.

Matthiessen, F. O. *American Renaissance: Art and Expression in the Age of Emerson and Whitman.* Oxford: Oxford University Press, 1941.

McClary, Ben. *Washington Irving and the House of Murray.* Knoxville: University of Tennessee Press, 1969.

McCormack, W. J. *Ascendancy and Tradition in Anglo-Irish Literary History from 1789 to 1939.* Oxford: Clarendon Press, 1985.

McCormack, W. J., and Kim Walker. Introduction. In *The Absentee,* ed. W. J. McCormack and Kim Walker. Oxford: Oxford University Press, 1988.

McCraken-Flesher, Caroline. *Possible Scotlands: Walter Scott and the Story of Tomorrow.* New York: Oxford University Press, 2005.

McGann, Jerome. *A Critique of Modern Textual Criticism.* Chicago: University of Chicago Press, 1983.

———. *The Romantic Ideology: A Critical Investigation.* Chicago: University of Chicago Press, 1983.

McGill, Meredith. *American Literature and the Culture of Reprinting, 1834–1853.* Philadelphia: University of Pennsylvania Press, 2003.

———. "Copyright." In *A History of the Book in America,* vol. 2, ed. Gross and Kelly.

Mellor, Anne. *Romanticism and Gender.* New York: Routledge, 1993.

Melville, Herman. *Moby-Dick: A Longman Critical Edition.* Ed. John Bryant and Haskell Springer. London: Longman, 2009.

———. *Moby-Dick.* Ed. Hershel Parker. Evanston, IL: Northwestern University Press, 1988.

Mesick, Jane Louise. *The English Traveller in America, 1785–1835.* New York: Columbia University Press, 1922.

Miller, Julia Anne. "Acts of Union: Family Violence and National Courtship in Maria Edgeworth's *The Absentee* and Sydney Owenson's *The Wild Irish Girl.*" In *Border Crossings: Irish Women Writers and National Identities,* ed. Kathryn Kirkpatrick. Tuscaloosa: University of Alabama Press, 2000.

Millgate, Jane. "Archibald Constable and the Problem of London: 'Quite the Connection We Have Been Looking For.'" *Library* 18 (1996): 110–123.

———. "Making It New: Scott, Constable, Ballantyne, and the Publication of *Ivanhoe*." *Studies in English Literature* 34.4 (1994): 795–811.

———. *Scott's Last Edition: A Study in Publishing History*. Edinburgh: Edinburgh University Press, 1987.

———. *Walter Scott: The Making of a Novelist*. Edinburgh: Edinburgh University Press, 1984.

Moore, Thomas. "Odes and Epistles." 1806. In *The Poetical Works of Thomas Moore*, ed. Charles Kent. London: George Routledge and Sons, 1883.

Moretti, Franco. *Atlas of the European Novel, 1800–1900*. London: Verso, 1998.

———. "Conjectures on World Literature." *New Left Review* 1 (January–February 2000): 54–68.

———. *Distant Reading*. London: Verso, 2013.

Munday, Michael. "The Novel and Its Critics in the Early Nineteenth Century." *Studies in Philology* 79 (1982): 205–226.

Myers, Mitzi. "'Completing the Union': Critical Ennui, the Politics of Narrative, and the Reformation of Irish Cultural Identity." *Prose Studies* 18 (1995): 41–77.

———. "'Goring John Bull': Maria Edgeworth's Hibernian High Jinks Versus the Imperial Imaginary." In *Cutting Edges: Postmodern Critical Edges in Eighteenth-Century Satire*, ed. James E. Gill. Knoxville: University of Tennessee Press, 1995.

———. "War Correspondence: Maria Edgeworth and the En-Gendering of Revolution, Rebellion, and Union." *Eighteenth-Century Life* 22.3 (1998): 74–91.

Nelson, Dana D. *National Manhood: Capitalist Citizenship and the Imagined Fraternity of White Men*. Durham, NC: Duke University Press, 1998.

Nerone, John. "Periodicals and Serial Publications: Part I, Newspapers and the Public Sphere." In *The Industrial Book: 1840–1880*, ed. Scott E. Casper et al. Vol. 3 of *A History of the Book in America*. 5 vols. Chapel Hill: University of North Carolina Press, 2007.

Newcomer, James. *Lady Morgan the Novelist*. Lewisburg, PA: Bucknell University Press, 1990.

Odell, George. *Annals of the New York Stage*. New York: Columbia University Press, 1927.

Owenson, Sydney. "Prefatory Address to the 1846 Edition." In *The Wild Irish Girl: A National Tale*, ed. Claire Connolly and Stephen Copley. London: Pickering and Chatto, 2000.

———. *The Wild Irish Girl: A National Tale*. Ed. Claire Connolly and Stephen Copley. London: Pickering and Chatto, 2000.

The Parnassian Garland; or, Beauties of Modern Poetry. Philadelphia, 1814.

Peacocke, Emma Rosalind. "Facing History: Galleries and Portraits in Waverley's Historiography." *European Romantic Review* 22.2 (2011): 187–208.

Pease, Donald. "Hawthorne in the Custom-House: The Metapolitics, Postpolitics, and Politics of *The Scarlet Letter*." *boundary 2* 32 (2005): 53–70.

Pittock, Murray. *Scottish and Irish Romanticism*. Oxford: Oxford University Press, 2008.

Pochmann, Henry A. "Washington Irving: Amateur or Professional?" In *Critical Essays on Washington Irving*, ed. Ralph M. Aderman. Boston: G. K. Hall & Co., 1967.

Poirier, Richard. *A World Elsewhere: The Place of Style in American Literature*. New York: Oxford University Press, 1966.

Pollard, Mary. *The Dublin Trade in Books, 1550–1800*. Oxford: Oxford University Press, 1989.

Porte, Joel. *The Romance in America: Studies in Cooper, Poe, Hawthorne, Melville, and James*. Middletown, CT: Wesleyan University Press, 1969.

Pratt, Mary Louise. *Imperial Eyes: Travel Writing and Transculturation*. New York: Routledge, 1992.

Prendergast, Christopher, ed. *Debating World Literature*. London: Verso, 2004.

Price, Leah. *The Anthology and the Rise of the Novel: From Richardson to George Eliot*. Cambridge: Cambridge University Press, 2000.

Radcliffe, Anne. *The Poetical Works of Anne Radcliffe*. London: Henry Colburn, 1834.

Rancière, Jacques. *The Politics of Aesthetics*. Trans. Gabriel Rockhill. London: Continuum, 2004.

Randall, David. "Waverley in America." *Colophon* 1.1 (1935): 39–55.

Ratner, Joshua. "American Paratexts." Ph.D. diss., University of Pennsylvania, 2010.

Ratner, Lorman A. "American Nationalism Fifty Years After the Revolution." In *Washington Irving: A Tribute*, ed. Andrew B. Myers. Tarrytown, NY: Sleepy Hollow Restorations, 1972.

Raven, James. "The Book as Commodity." In *The Cambridge History of the Book in Britain*, vol. 5, ed. Suarez and Turner.

———. *The Business of Books: Booksellers and the English Book Trade*. New Haven, CT: Yale University Press, 2007.

Reid, Margaret. *Cultural Secrets as Narrative Form*. Columbus: Ohio University Press, 2004.

Reid, S. W. "Brockden Brown in England: Notes on Henry Colburn's 1822 Editions of His Novels." *Early American Literature* 9.2 (Fall 1974): 188–195.

———. "Textual Essay." In *Ormond; Or, The Secret Witness*. Kent, Ohio: Kent State University Press, 1982.

———. "Textual Essay." In *Wieland; or, The Transformation: An American Tale*. Kent, Ohio: Kent State University Press, 1977.

Reilly, Elizabeth Carroll, and David D. Hall. "Modalities of Reading." In *A History of the Book in America*, vol. 1, ed. Hall.

Remer, Rosalind. *Printers and Men of Capital: Philadelphia Book Publishers in the New Republic*. Philadelphia: University of Pennsylvania Press, 1996.

Rezek, Joseph. "The Orations on the Abolition of the Slave Trade and the Uses of Print in the Early Black Atlantic." *Early American Literature* 45.3 (Fall 2010): 655–682.

———. "The Print Atlantic: Phillis Wheatley, Ignatius Sancho, and the Cultural Significance of the Book." In *Early African American Print Culture*, ed. Jordan A. Stein and Lara Langer Cohen. Philadelphia: University of Pennsylvania Press, 2012.

———. "What We Need from Transatlantic Studies." *American Literary History* 26.4 (2014): 791–803.

Richardson, Alan, and Sonia Hofkosh. *Romanticism, Race, and Imperial Culture, 1780–1834*. Bloomington: Indiana University Press, 1996.

Roach, Joseph R. *Cities of the Dead: Circum-Atlantic Performance*. New York: Columbia University Press, 1996.

Rose, Mark. "Copyright, Authors, and Censorship." In *The Cambridge History of the Book in Britain*, vol. 5, ed. Suarez and Turner.

Rubin-Dorsky, Jeffrey. *Adrift in the Old World: The Psychological Pilgrimage of Washington Irving*. Chicago: University of Chicago Press, 1988.

Ruttenburg, Nancy. *Democratic Personality: Popular Voice and the Trial of American Authorship*. Stanford, CA: Stanford University Press, 1998.

Sancho, Ignatius. *The Letters of the Late Ignatius Sancho*. Ed. Vincent Caretta. New York: Penguin, 1998.

Sanderson, John. "Chorus: Hail to the Chief." London, 1810; New York, 1813.

Sargent, L. M. "Ode for the Return of Peace." Boston, 1815.

Scharf, J. Thomas and Thompson Westcott. *History of Philadelphia, 1609–1884*. Vol. 2. Philadelphia, 1884.

Scott, Walter. *The Antiquary*. Ed. David Hewitt. New York: Penguin, 1998.

———. "General Preface." 1829. In *Waverley*, ed. Claire Lamont. Oxford: Oxford University Press, 1981.

———. *The Heart of Mid-Lothian*. 1818. Ed. Tony Inglis. New York: Penguin, 1994.

———. "Introduction to Ivanhoe." 1830. In *Ivanhoe*, ed. Ian Duncan. Oxford: Oxford University Press, 1996.

———. *Lay of the Last Minstrel*. Philadelphia, 1805.

———. *The Letters of Sir Walter Scott*. Ed. H. J. C. Grierson. 12 vols. London: Constable, 1932–1937.

———. "Review of *Emma*." 1815. In *Jane Austen: The Critical Heritage*, ed. B. C. Southam. Vol. 1. London: Routledge, 1968.

———. *Tales of My Landlord, Fourth Series*. Edinburgh: Cadell, 1832.

———. *Waverley*. 1814. Ed. P. D. Garside. New York: Penguin, 2011.

Sedgwick, Catherine Maria. *A New-England Tale*. 1822. Ed. Susan K. Harris. New York: Penguin, 2003.

Shaw, Harry. *The Forms of Historical Fiction: Sir Walter Scott and His Successors*. Ithaca, NY: Cornell University Press, 1983.

Sher, Richard. *The Enlightenment and the Book: Scottish Authors and Their Publishers in Eighteenth-Century Britain, Ireland, and America*. Chicago: University of Chicago Press, 2006.

Sher, Richard, and Jeffrey R. Smitten, eds. *Scotland and America in the Age of the Enlightenment*. Princeton, NJ: Princeton University Press, 1990.

Shields, Juliet. *Sentimental Literature and Anglo-Scottish Identity, 1745–1820*. Cambridge: Cambridge University Press, 2010.

Shillingsburg, Peter. *From Gutenberg to Google: Electronic Representations of Literary Texts*. Cambridge: Cambridge University Press, 2006.

Simpson, Eric. *Mercenaries in British and American Literature, 1790–1830: Writing, Fighting, and Marrying for Money*. Edinburgh: Edinburgh University Press, 2010.

Siskin, Clifford. *The Work of Writing: Literature and Social Change in Britain, 1700–1830*. Baltimore: Johns Hopkins University Press, 1998.

Slauter, Eric. *The State as a Work of Art: The Cultural Origins of the Constitution*. Chicago: University of Chicago Press, 2009.

Slotkin, Richard. *The Fatal Environment: The Myth of the Frontier in the Age of Industrialization, 1800–1890*. Middletown, CT: Wesleyan University Press, 1986.

Smith, Adam. *The Theory of Moral Sentiments*. Ed. Ryan Patrick Hanley. New York: Penguin, 2009.

Sotlow, Lee, and Edward Stevens. *The Rise of Literacy and the Common School in the United States: A Socioeconomic Analysis to 1870*. Chicago: University of Chicago Press, 1981.

Spencer, Benjamin. *The Quest for Nationality: An American Literary Campaign*. Syracuse, NY: Syracuse University Press, 1957.

Spiller, Robert E., ed. *The American Literary Revolution, 1783–1837*. New York: Anchor Books, 1976.

Spiller, Robert E., and Philip C. Blackburn. *A Descriptive Bibliography of the Writings of James Fenimore Cooper*. New York: R. R. Bowker, 1934.

Spoo, Robert. *Without Copyrights: Piracy, Publishing, and the Public Domain*. New York: Oxford University Press, 2013.

St. Clair, William. *The Reading Nation in the Romantic Period*. New York: Cambridge University Press, 2004.

Staël, Germain de. *Corinne, or Italy*. 1807. Trans. and ed. Sylvia Raphael. New York: Oxford University Press, 2008.

———. *Germany; by the Baroness Staël Holstein, Translated from the French*. Vol. 1. New York, 1814.

Stevens, Laura. "Transatlanticism Now." *ALH* 16.1 (2004): 93–102.

Streeter, Robert E. "Association Psychology and Literary Nationalism in the North American Review, 1815–1825." *American Literature* 17 (1945): 243–254.

Suarez, Michael F. "Introduction." In *The Cambridge History of the Book in Britain: 1695–1830*, vol. 5, ed. Suarez and Turner.

Suarez, Michael F., and Michael L. Turner, eds. *The Cambridge History of the Book in Britain: 1695–1830*. Vol. 5. Cambridge: Cambridge University Press, 2009.

Sutherland, John. *The Life of Walter Scott: A Critical Biography*. Oxford: Blackwell, 1995.

———. *Victorian Novelists and Publishers*. Chicago: University of Chicago Press, 1976.

Tamarkin, Elisa. *Anglophilia: Deference, Devotion, and Antebellum America*. Chicago: University of Chicago Press, 2007.

Tawil, Ezra. *The Making of Racial Sentiment: Slavery and the Birth of the Frontier Romance*. Cambridge: Cambridge University Press, 2008.

Taylor, Alan. *The Civil War of 1812*. New York: Knopf, 2010.

Tennenhouse, Leonard. *The Importance of Feeling English: American Literature and the British Diaspora, 1750–1850*. Princeton, NJ: Princeton University Press, 2007.

Thackeray, William Makepeace. *The Roundabout Papers*. London, 1869.

Tilley, Elizabeth. "Periodicals." In *The Oxford History of the Irish Book*, vol. 4, ed. Murphy.

Todd, William B., and Ann Bowden. *Sir Walter Scott: A Bibliographical History, 1796–1832*. New Castle, DE: Oak Knoll Press, 1998.

Tracy, Robert. "Maria Edgeworth and Lady Morgan: Legality Versus Legitimacy." *Nineteenth-Century Fiction* 40.1 (1985): 1–22.

Traister, Bryce. "The Wandering Bachelor: Irving, Masculinity, and Authorship." *American Literature* 74.1 (2002): 111–137.

Trumpener, Katie. *Bardic Nationalism: The Romantic Novel and the British Empire.* Princeton, NJ: Princeton University Press, 1997.

Tulloch, Graham, ed. *Ivanhoe*, by Walter Scott. In *Edinburgh Edition of the Waverley Novels*, ed. David Hewitt. Edinburgh: Edinburgh University Press, 1998.

Twain, Mark. *Life on the Mississippi.* New York: Library of America, 1982.

Verhoeven, W. M., ed. *Revolutionary Histories: Transatlantic Cultural Nationalism, 1775–1815.* New York: Palgrave, 2002.

Wagenknecht, Edward. *Washington Irving: Moderation Displayed.* Oxford: Oxford University Press, 1962.

Ward, William S. "American Authors and British Reviewers 1798–1826: A Bibliography." *American Literature* 49.1 (1977): 1–12.

Warner, Michael. *The Letters of the Republic: Publication and the Public Sphere in Eighteenth-Century America.* Cambridge, MA: Harvard University Press, 1990.

———. "Irving's Posterity." *ELH* 67 (2000): 773–799.

Watts, Steven. *The Republic Reborn: War and the Making of Liberal America, 1790–1820.* Baltimore: Johns Hopkins University Press, 1987.

Weinstein, Cindy, and Christopher Looby, eds. *American Literature's Aesthetic Dimensions.* New York: Columbia University Press, 2012.

Weisbuch, Robert. *Atlantic Double-Cross: American Literature and British Influence in the Age of Emerson.* Chicago: University of Chicago Press, 1986.

Welch, Robert, and Brian Walker, eds. *The Oxford History of the Irish Book.* 5 vols. Oxford: Oxford University Press, 2006–2012.

Weld, Isaac. *Travels Through the States of North America.* 4th ed. London, 1800.

Welsh, Alexander. *The Hero of the Waverley Novels: With New Essays on Scott.* Exp. ed. Princeton, NJ: Princeton University Press, 1992.

Whelan, Kevin. "The Green Atlantic: Radical Reciprocities Between Ireland and America in the Long Eighteenth Century." In *A New Imperial History: Culture, Identity, and Modernity in Britain and the Empire, 1660–1840*, ed. Kathleen Wilson. Cambridge: Cambridge University Press, 2004.

———. "Writing Ireland, Reading England." In *The Wild Irish Girl: A National Tale*, ed. Claire Connolly and Stephen Copley. London: Pickering & Chatto, 2000.

White, Henry A. *Sir Walter Scott's Novels on the Stage.* New Haven, CT: Yale University Press, 1927.

Wickman, Matthew. "Travel Writing and the Picturesque." In *The Edinburgh Companion to Scottish Romanticism*, ed. Murray Pittock. Edinburgh: Edinburgh University Press, 2011.

Williams, Raymond. *Culture and Society, 1780–1950.* London: Penguin, 1958.

Williams, Stanley T. *The Life of Washington Irving.* 2 vols. New York: Oxford University Press, 1935.

Wills, Gary. *Inventing America: Jefferson's Declaration of Independence*. New York: Double-day, 1978.

Wilson, David. *United Irishmen, United States: Immigrant Radicals in the Early Republic* Ithaca, NY: Cornell University Press, 1998.

Winship, Michael. "The National Book Trade System: Part I, Distribution and the Trade." In *The Industrial Book: 1840–1880*, ed. Scott E. Casper et al. Vol. 3 of *A History of the Book in America*. Chapel Hill: University of North Carolina Press, 2007.

———. "The Transatlantic Book Trade and Anglo-American Literary Culture in the Nineteenth Century." In *Reciprocal Influences: Literary Production, Distribution, and Consumption in America*, ed. Steven Fink and Susan S. Williams. Columbus: Ohio University Press, 1999.

Wohlgemut, E. "Maria Edgeworth and the Question of National Identity." *Studies in English Literature, 1500–1900* 39.4 (1999): 645–658.

Wolf, Edwin. *At the Instance of Benjamin Franklin: A Brief History of the Library Company of Philadelphia, 1731–1976*. Philadelphia: Library Company of Philadelphia, 1995.

Wolfe, Richard. *Secular Music in America, 1801–1825; A Bibliography*. New York: New York Public Library, 1964.

Wood, Gordon. *Empire of Liberty: A History of the Early Republic, 1789–1815*. New York: Oxford University Press, 2009.

Wordsworth, William. *A Critical Edition of the Major Works*. Ed. Stephen Gill. Oxford: Oxford University Press, 1984.

Zboray, Ronald J. "The Transportation Revolution and Antebellum Book Distribution Reconsidered." *American Quarterly* 38.1 (1986): 53–71.

Index

Page numbers in italics indicate illustrations.

Acknowledgments

I am grateful to the many individuals who made the writing of this book possible in a number of cities, provincial and metropolitan. In Los Angeles, where it first took shape in the English department at UCLA: Nathan Brown, Frederick Burwick, Michael Colacurcio, Noah Comet, John Alba Cutler, Helen Deutsch, Joseph Dimuro, Jennifer Fleissner, Aaron Gorelik, Julian Knox, Allison Kuharski, Joyce Lee, Barbara Packer, Saree Makdisi, Meredith Neuman, Mark McGurl, Dawn Medina, Anne Mellor, Michael Meranze, Sianne Ngai, Felicity Nussbaum, Tom O'Donnell, Sam See, James Shultz, Eric Sundquist, Erin Suzuki, Dennis Tyler, and the Americanist Research Colloquium. In Philadelphia, at the Library Company of Philadelphia, the McNeil Center for Early American Studies, and the University of Pennsylvania's Workshop for the History of Material Texts: Benjamin Bankhurst, Nancy Bentley, George Boudreau, Max Cavitch, Roger Chartier, Irene Cheng, Brian Connolly, Paul Conrad, Stuart Curran, Caitlin Fitz, Michael Gamer, Cassandra Good, Michael Goode, Connie King, Zachary Lesser, Heather Love, Will Mackintosh, Whitney Martinko, Cathy Matson, Alyssa Mt. Pleasant, Daniel K. Richter, Dawn Peterson, John Pollack, Joshua Ratner, Elena Schneider, Peter Stallybrass, Daniel Traister, and (especially) James N. Green. In New York City: Rachel Adams, Andrew Delbanco, Chad Kia, Billy Kingsland, Greg Londe, Rachel Saltz, Jake Short, Jordan Alexander Stein, Ezra Tawil, and (especially) David Kurnick. In Boston, my current provincial home: Minou Arjomand, Anne Austin, Steve Biel, Mary Bilder, Samuel Bowen, Lawrence Buell, William Carroll, Amanda Claybaugh, Theo Davis, Elizabeth Maddock Dillon, Jonathan Foltz, Anna Henchman, William Hunting Howell, Gene Jarrett, Laura Korobkin, Maurice Lee, Christine Loken-Kim, John Matthews, Susan Mizruchi, Leland Monk, Patrick Mullen, Kevin Ohi, Magdalena Ostas, Carrie Preston, Anita Patterson, Christopher Ricks, Charles Rzepka, Nina Silber, Caitlin Steinberg, Keith Vincent, James Uden, and James A. Winn. Equal thanks are due to Henry Abelove, John Anderson, Johanna Archbold, Hester

Blum, Emily Burkes-Nossiter, Pascale Casanova, Christopher Castiglia, Hillary Chute, Lara Langer Cohen, Catriona Crowe, Ian Duncan, Melissa Homestead, Penny Fielding, Kate Flint, Wayne Franklin, Roy Foster, Mary Kelley, David McClay, Meredith McGill, Michael Seidel, Eric Slauter, Elisa Tamarkin, Fredrika Teute, and Colm Toíbín.

Fellowships from the McNeil Center and the Boston University Center for the Humanities provided much-appreciated support for writing this book at crucial stages of its development. Archival research was generously funded by the Bibliographical Society of America, the Huntington Library, the Keats-Shelley Association of America, the Library Company of Philadelphia, the Newberry Library, and UCLA. I am grateful for the knowledgeable staffs at these institutions as well as at the American Antiquarian Society; the Boston Athenaeum; the Historical Society of Pennsylvania; the Houghton Library; the Kislak Center for Special Collections, Rare Books and Manuscripts, at the University of Pennsylvania; the National Library of Ireland; the National Library of Scotland; the New York Public Library; the Trinity College Library, Dublin; and Widener Library.

Chapter 2 appeared originally as "Furious Booksellers: The 'American Copy' of the Waverley Novels and the Language of the Book Trade," *Early American Studies* (2013) and portions of the Introduction and Chapter 5 as "Cooper and Scott in the Anglophone Literary Field: *The Pioneers*, *The Heart of Mid-Lothian*, and the Effects of Provinciality," *ELH* (2011). They are reprinted here in revised form by permission of the University of Pennsylvania Press and Johns Hopkins University Press.

At the University of Pennsylvania Press, my highest thanks go to Jerry Singerman for his unfailing editorial support; to Peter Stallybrass for his early and sustained enthusiasm about the project; to Meredith McGill and Juliet Shields, who provided invaluable feedback on the manuscript; and to Hannah Blake and Erica Ginsburg, who expertly ushered the book through production.

I owe immeasurable debts to Christopher Looby, the ideal mentor; to Lana Finley, Carrie Hyde, Kate Marshall, and Ian Newman, essential friends and interlocutors; to Chris, Erica, and Samuel Rezek, my beloved local family; and to Geoff and Jackie Rezek, my first champions and the worthy dedicatees of this book. My deepest thanks go to Ash Anderson, my husband, who sustains and amazes me every day.